Nietzsche and the Politics of Difference

Nietzsche and the Politics of Difference

Edited by
Andrea Rehberg and Ashley Woodward

DE GRUYTER

ISBN 978-3-11-152067-4
e-ISBN (PDF) 978-3-11-068843-6
e-ISBN (EPUB) 978-3-11-068845-0

Library of Congress Control Number: 2022940874

Bibliographic information published by the Deutsche Nationalbibliothek
The Deutsche Nationalbibliothek lists this publication in the Deutsche Nationalbibliografie; detailed bibliographic data are available on the internet at http://dnb.dnb.de.

© 2024 Walter de Gruyter GmbH, Berlin/Boston
This volume is text- and page-identical with the hardback published in 2022.

www.degruyter.com

Table of Contents

Abbreviations —— IX

Andrea Rehberg and Ashley Woodward
Introduction —— 1

Part 1 **Politics and Difference**

Alan Watt
Nietzsche, Rancière and the Disputation of Politics —— 15

Tracy Colony
Composing Time: Stiegler on Nietzsche, Nihilism and a Possible Future —— 33

Part 2 **Politics and Identity**

Glen Baier
Nietzsche's Diagnosis of Socrates in *The Birth of Tragedy*: Voyeurism and the Denigration of Difference —— 55

William A. B. Parkhurst
***Ecce Homo* – Notes on Duplicates: The Great Politics of the Self —— 75**

Niklas Corall
Voluntary Submission and the 'Politics of Truth': Nietzsche and Foucault on the Danger of the Fully Normalised 'Last Human' —— 95

Andrea Rehberg
Towards Immanence – A Nietzschean Trajectory —— 121

Part 3 Nietzsche and Deleuze on a New Politics

Jonas Oßwald
Echoes of a New Politics: Deleuze's Nietzsche and the Political —— 145

Lilian Kroth
The Topology of Difference: Deleuze's Nietzsche in his Politics of Folded Spaces and Subjects —— 163

Gabriel Valladão Silva
Fake or Just Stupid? – Post-Truth Politics, Nihilism and the Politics of Difference in Light of Deleuze's *Nietzsche and Philosophy* —— 183

Julie Van der Wielen
The Idiot: Deleuze's Nietzsche for a Politics of Difference —— 203

Part 4 The Politics of the Agon

Pia Morar
Disparate Conceptions of the Agon: Nietzsche and Agonistic Democracy —— 227

Sven Gellens
Agonal Human Rights: A Re-evaluation of Democracy Through Nietzsche's Physio-Psychology of Will to Power —— 247

Part 5 Plurality, Affirmation, Immanence

Marinete Araujo da Silva Fobister
Nietzsche and a Politics of Difference: Realising the Forces in the Margins —— 269

George W. Shea, IV
Nietzsche, Foucault and the Politics of the Ascetic Ideal —— 289

Michael J. McNeal
The Quandary of Identity and the Prospective Appearance of Free Spirits in our Globalising Age —— 311

Notes on Contributors —— 337

Index —— 341

Abbreviations

Primary Nietzsche sources are cited in the chapters by abbreviation according to the standard conventions listed here, except where older or non-standard editions are being used. Nietzsche's works are typically cited by section number and, in the cases of *Ecce Homo*, *On the Genealogy of Morals* and *Twilight of the Idols*, an additional reference to the chapter title or essay number (see below). References to *Thus Spoke Zarathustra* include the part number and chapter title (often abbreviated), for example, Z I, Reading. Prefaces of works are referenced by a "Preface" after the abbreviated title, for example, TI Preface. All passages from Nietzsche's *Nachlass* are cited from KSA or KGW, as KSA/KGW, volume number, manuscript number, and then fragment number in brackets, for example, KSA 7, 5 [103]. In some cases, especially for notes running across several pages, the page number of KSA/KGW was added. Nietzsche's letters are cited according to the following scheme: Bf. to/from sender/recipient, date, KGB section/volume number, Bf. number and, for long letters, occasional page numbers, for example, Nietzsche to Franz Overbeck, 22/06/1880, KGB III/1, Bf. 33. The English translations of Nietzsche's works used in the chapters are listed in the respective bibliographies. At times, alternative translations are used, but these are always distinguished by different abbreviations, for example, GM for the Clark and Swensen translation, GoM for the Kaufmann and Hollingdale translation. Below, those of Nietzsche's texts cited in German are also included.

A	*The Antichrist*
ASC	*Birth of Tragedy*, Attempt at Self-Criticism
BAW	*Historisch-kritische Gesamtausgabe: Werke*
BGE	*Beyond Good and Evil*
BT	*The Birth of Tragedy*
BWN	*Basic Writings of Nietzsche*
COK	On the Concept of the Organic since Kant
CW	*The Case of Wagner*
D	*Daybreak*
DS	David Strauss, the Writer and the Confessor [UM I]
EH	*Ecce Homo* [EH Preface; Wise; Clever; Books: Z, CW; Destiny]
ENB	*Writings from the Early Notebooks*
FEI	On the Future of Our Educational Institutions
GM	*On the Genealogy of Morals* (cited by essay number followed by section number)
GS	*The Gay Science*
GSt	The Greek State
GT	*Die Geburt der Tragödie*
HC	Homer's Contest
HCP	Homer and Classical Philology
HH	*Human All Too Human*
HH II	*Human All Too Human II*
HkP	Homer und die klassische Philologie
HL	On the Uses and Disadvantages of History for Life [UM II]
JGB	*Jenseits von Gut und Böse*
KGB	*Nietzsche Briefwechsel: Kritische Gesamtausgabe*
KGW	*Nietzsche Werke: Kritische Gesamtausgabe*

KSA	*Sämtliche Werke: Kritische Studienausgabe*
LNB	*Writings from the Late Notebooks*
NCW	*Nietzsche contra Wagner*
PPP	*The Pre-Platonic Philosophers*
PTAG	*Philosophy in the Tragic Age of the Greeks*
SE	*Schopenhauer as Educator* [UM III]
SLN	*Selected Letters of Friedrich Nietzsche*
TI	*Twilight of the Idols* [TI Socrates, Reason, Fable, Skirmishes, Ancients]
TL	*On Truth and Lie in an Extra-Moral Sense*
UM	*Untimely Meditations*
UO	*Unfashionable Observations*
WP	*The Will to Power*
WS	*The Wanderer and His Shadow*
Z	*Thus Spoke Zarathustra* [Z, Prologue; Z I, Metamorphoses, Hinterworldly, Passions, War, Idol, Goals, Neighbour; Z II, Isles, Self-Overcoming, Poets, Redemption; Z III Virtue, Tables]

Andrea Rehberg and Ashley Woodward
Introduction

We live in a time when the suppression of difference seems to be the express aim of much political activity. Even where it is not the explicit aim, it is a not-undesired side-effect of a politics of equalisation, as has been observed across the globe, from the UK and the Trump-era US to parts of Eastern Europe, China, India, Russia and so on. Given that today we are faced with a host of political challenges of domination and resistance, the question raised in this volume is how Nietzsche helps us to think through and to address some of the problems with which we are faced today, but also how his writings complicate our desire for swift solutions to seemingly intractable problems: how to resist slavishness in thought and action, how to maintain hard-won civil liberties and rights in the face of encroaching hegemonic discourses, practices and forces, or how to counteract global environmental degradation; in short, how to oppose 'totalitarian' movements of homogenisation, universalisation and equalisation, and instead to affirm, both politically and ontologically, a culture of *difference*.

All too often difference is understood as that which merely pertains between given entities or identities but, starting with Nietzsche, the thought of an originary difference that is irreducible to identity and, importantly, constitutive of identity gains traction. At the same time, the affirmation of difference as plurality or multiplicity goes hand in hand with difference as an ontological issue. The Nietzschean thought of difference thus marks the intersection of the purely ontological and the political.

Many recent and contemporary political philosophers and theorists distinguish between 'the political' and 'politics', where the former encompasses aspects of a transcendental or ontological nature, whereas the latter concerns the empirical field in which the political articulates itself. The contributors to this collection variously cover aspects of both, either by concentrating solely on Nietzsche's thoughts relevant to these aspects or, just as often, by interpreting Nietzsche's works through the lens of one or more key figures in contemporary continental philosophy, such as Alain Badiou, Gilles Deleuze, Michel Foucault, Jacques Rancière or Bernard Stiegler. In fact, one of the outstanding features of the present collection is the sheer breadth of topics covered, from human rights, migrants, fake news and populism, to the monstrous, the idiot and the question of space, to name but a few.

Although, on the one hand, Nietzsche was often deeply critical of politics and politicians, on the other hand, he advocated a 'great politics' (*große Politik*) and frequently expressed his admiration for great statesmen such as Napoleon.

While he questioned the value and implications of democracy and the ideal of equality it involves, several commentators (such as William E. Connolly, Lawrence J. Hatab and Mark Warren) have extracted a Nietzschean sense of democracy from his writings. In fact, it has often been noted that Nietzsche's thought contains – or at least implies – a complete political ontology, and this has been teased out by a host of twentieth-century poststructuralist thinkers, such as Derrida, Deleuze, Foucault, Irigaray, Lyotard, Nancy and those who have come after them. They, and we, are grappling with thorny questions of the possible intersections between political theory and political engagement, such as how to envisage forms of resistance without agency, what ateleological action looks like, and how to maintain a sense of the political without relapsing into the intellectual coordinates provided by a substance-metaphysical framework and its purported grounds.

At the intersection of the ontological (the political) and the empirical (politics), Nietzsche's thinking beyond subject, substance, telos or ground, and in terms of differentials of forces and impersonal events and processes, induces us to examine our traditional ways of thinking and our cherished anthropocentric investments. Given these strictures, the question is, in what ways does Nietzsche's thought harbour the resources for a contemporary politics of difference and a thought of difference equal to it? These are some of the most intractable, yet at the same time most urgent, questions facing anyone aiming to think with Nietzsche today. This is not to suggest that these are completely new questions – they have been asked in a variety of texts for many decades – but they have taken on a new urgency, given the perilous state the world is in at the beginning of the third millennium. And since Nietzsche is arguably one of the most rigorously post-metaphysical thinkers, if we pay close attention to what he says, we might be able to reinvigorate our political thinking beyond modes supported by the established consensus.

There has been an explosion of interest in Nietzsche and politics/the political over the last decade or so, as evidenced by a spate of books on the topic. Let us briefly review some recent essay collections, in order to set the context for the current volume, and also to highlight its distinctiveness.[1] The stated

---

[1] There have also been some important recent monographs on Nietzsche and politics, of which we will mention two. Hugo Drochon's *Nietzsche's Great Politics* (2016) is very much a scholarly exegesis and seeks to understand Nietzsche's politics in its original context: Bismarck's Germany. The original claim of the book is that when Nietzsche became mad, he was only just beginning to move from the philosophical to a political phase of his work. The book then aims to reconstruct what this politics would have looked like: for Nietzsche, society has been through a period of being weakened by democracy but will become strengthened with the overcoming

aim of the monumental *Nietzsche, Power and Politics* (2008) is to take stock of the main currents in the controversies around Nietzsche and political thought at the beginning of the twenty-first century. It contains many well-established Nietzsche scholars and presents many well-known (as well as lesser-known) positions on a wide variety of topics. It contains some essays which engage with contemporary political issues, but it does not take this as a focus. The large volume aims, instead, at a very broad coverage. *Nietzsche and Political Thought* (2013) collects commissioned essays by recognised specialists on Nietzsche and the political. (Many of the authors also appear in other collections mentioned here.) The chapters make contributions to a wide variety of themes on Nietzsche and the political, without any more specific focus or overarching aim. Such themes include perfectionism, agonism, justice, the politics of the event, the multitude, democratic theory and Nietzsche's relation to a wide variety of thinkers, including Spinoza, Simondon, Laruelle and Badiou.

Nietzsche as Political Philosopher (2014) is another edited volume presenting a diverse range of topics and including a real mixture of well-established and newer scholars. The introduction gives a valuable overview of the many existing positions and issues in the debates around Nietzsche and politics (to which we refer the reader without such a background knowledge), and there is also a useful general bibliography. Sections are organised according to the various political positions argued: for example, there is a section which focuses on the democratic, or liberal, or egalitarian readings; one on aristocratic, anti-liberal, or non-egalitarian readings; and a section on moral and ethical thought. For the most part, the essays are exegetical, and seek to understand Nietzsche's own political thought – sometimes in relation to other thinkers, but generally not in relation to contemporary political problems and issues.

The recent interest in Nietzsche and the political indicated by these titles has predominantly been in the nature of scholarly exegesis, which aims to uncover what Nietzsche's political philosophy was. There is a lively debate in this area, involving such controversies as whether he was a political thinker at all, and if he was, then what kinds of political positions he held. Works such as the three edited volumes listed above gather a wide range of views on such topics, very often including the same well-established scholars.

---

of the state and the coming of 'good Europeans'. Dominic Losurdo's *Nietzsche: The Aristocratic Rebel* (first published in Italian in 2002 but appearing in English translation in 2020) also places Nietzsche's political thought in its historical context, drawing attention in original ways to his indebtedness to popular liberal and illiberal reactionary movements, and to contemporary debates around issues such as women's rights, the abolition of slavery, colonialism and race in the latter half of the nineteenth century.

The current volume evolved from papers given at the 24th Annual Conference of the Friedrich Nietzsche Society, held at and sponsored by Newcastle University, UK, as well as by the British Society for the History of Philosophy. It differs from the collections described above in two important respects. First, it presents novel perspectives on Nietzsche and the political by featuring the fresh voices of many early-career researchers (rather than the same established set of scholars). Second, and most importantly, it has a different and sharper focus: rather than scholarly exegesis alone, the ambition is to reflect on the usefulness of Nietzsche's ideas for the contemporary political situation. Unlike other collected volumes on Nietzsche and the political, it takes a specific thematic focus: the politics of difference. This theme recalls the creative ways in which Nietzsche's thought was appropriated by French philosophers of the 1960s and 1970s, often for ends significantly at a tangent to Nietzsche's own political views. In the same spirit, this volume collects contributions which interrogate Nietzsche's radical thought for the contemporary situation, both in general terms, and with respect to a variety of specific contemporary issues and problems, such as identity, refugees, marginalised members of society, neoliberalism and 'post-truth'. As such, it complements and extends, rather than repeats, the important volumes on Nietzsche and politics listed above.

Some of the questions addressed by the contributions to this volume are: Can contemporary political phenomena be interpreted in terms of Nietzsche's understanding of reactive and active forces? If so, how? What is the role of slave morality in the constitution and operations of recent political movements and trends? Are there any pockets of what Nietzsche calls nobility left in the political realm? If so, where? What is a thought of the political beyond substance metaphysics? Can the Nietzschean sense of agon serve as a viable model for contemporary political thought? Beyond utility and calculative rationality, can Nietzsche's thought mobilise a political activism?

Unsurprisingly, given the topic of this collection, a number of contributors engage with more or less specific aspects of contemporary culture, society and politics (e.g., Fobister, McNeal, Rehberg, Valladão Silva), while others stay on a more intra- or inter-textual level, charting connections between Nietzsche and his intellectual forebears and readers. Key themes that cut across many chapters concern the question of Nietzschean nihilism, interpretations of the will to power, the problematic of identity and alterity in Nietzsche's works, the difference between politics and the political in Nietzsche's thought, or the interplay between political and ontological difference; and several chapters touch upon the above-mentioned thorny issue of a Nietzschean democracy. Some chapters centrally or tangentially examine the relation between Nietzsche and other philosophers, above all Deleuze, Foucault, Rancière and Stiegler. Despite these broad continuities between chapters, what is notable – and heartening – is the sheer variety of topics and approaches to be found across these chapters, which attests to the seemingly inexhaustible richness and variety of Nietzsche's thought, as well as to its continuing relevance for the contemporary political context.

This volume is organised according to five thematic sections. The opening section, Politics and Difference, introduces ways in which notions of difference may be relevant to political issues. It does this through readings of two influential French philosophers whose connections with Nietzsche are vital but have so far been little appreciated. These approaches certainly do not exhaust all such possibilities, and each chapter in the volume presents its own perspective on this issue. However, we begin with these studies because they give some clear examples of how the political might be thought with notions of difference by recent philosophers, recalling and reworking Nietzsche's thought, in ways relevant to current contexts.

Alan Watt's paper, "Nietzsche, Rancière and the Disputation of Politics", aims to resolve the recurring question of whether Nietzsche is a political thinker, and so makes an appropriate opening to the volume by exploring an issue which is fundamental to all that follows. Rancière's novel answer to the question 'what is politics?' is seen as a new way of affirming Nietzsche's politicalness. Rancière's reframing of politics is discussed in some detail, and Nietzsche's accounts in the first essay of On the Genealogy of Morality are shown to harbour the resources for such a reframing. The chapter concludes that, despite certain tonal differences, Nietzsche's thinking has significant affinities with Rancière's understanding of politics, and that, in turn, Rancière's insistence on disputing the political provides valuable insights into what is at stake in Nietzsche's politics. In this chapter, political modalities of the notion of difference are expressed through the themes of disagreement, dissensus and disputation.

Tracy Colony's chapter, "Composing Time: Stiegler on Nietzsche, Nihilism and a Possible Future", argues that Nietzsche was one of Bernard Stiegler's key philosophical interlocutors. The basis for Stiegler's engagement with Nietzsche was his understanding of the German philosopher as a tragic thinker. Beyond the merely oppositional logics of metaphysics, Stiegler accorded Nietzsche a more originary insight into the necessary composition of apparently oppositional tendencies. This is a mode of thinking which employs a logic of difference beyond oppositionality. This was the basis for his understanding of Nietzsche as able to diagnose the reactive tendencies at work in society today, and also as a resource for thinking the possibility of a different future. As such, the differential notion of composition becomes essential to Stiegler's thinking of politics.

The next section of the book, Politics and Identity, focuses on the critical targets of Nietzsche's philosophy associated with a logic of identity. The first two chapters focus on Nietzsche's work itself, while the second two extend the import of his analyses to more current avatars of identity. Glen Baier's chapter, "Nietzsche's Diagnosis of Socrates in *The Birth of Tragedy:* Voyeurism and the Denigration of Difference", analyses Nietzsche's depiction of Socrates in *The Birth of Tragedy* in order to demonstrate that he sees Socrates as hostile to difference. This reading of the text focuses on Nietzsche's characterisation of Socrates' gaze. The chapter contends that Nietzsche treats Socrates as a philosophical voyeur, someone who relies on his gaze to monitor and direct the world. Baier claims that it is this voyeuristic, Socratic gaze that denigrates difference and imposes expectations of sameness on the world.

William A. B. Parkhurst's "*Ecce Homo* – Notes on Duplicates: The Great Politics of the Self" argues that every self-quotation in Nietzsche's *Ecce Homo* is an intentional self-misquotation. It offers examples of these misquotations and demonstrates that Nietzsche and others closely edited his texts, including the quotations. The chapter presents historical, contextual and genetic evidence for these misquotations being intentional. The chapter concludes that these intentional misquotations are an attempt at self-parody and that they are a form of great politics insofar as they undermine the unity of authorial identity and thereby the metaphysics of the self.

Niklas Corall's chapter, "Voluntary Submission and the 'Politics of Truth': Nietzsche and Foucault on the Danger of the Fully Normalised 'Last Human'", elaborates what is meant by 'true discourse' and what its normalising and subduing dimensions are. Corall examines Foucault's adoption of Nietzsche's concept of the 'will to truth', and the 'politics of truth' that Foucault postulates from it, which is deployed strategically as a means of normalising social relations and constituting normalised subjects. The chapter reads Nietzsche's narrative philosophical practice in *Thus Spoke Zarathustra* as a strategy to counteract the 'greatest danger' of humanity developing into the completely normalised 'Last Human'.

Andrea Rehberg's chapter, "Towards Immanence – A Nietzschean Trajectory", explores how Nietzsche's thought can help us to understand, but also to overcome, contemporary populism. It draws out the politically and philosophically significant features of populism, but then to goes beyond the phenomena of populism to a Nietzschean reading of reactivity in terms of nobility and slavishness, and of the ascetic ideal, as analysed in *On the Genealogy of Morality*. It next discusses the import of Nietzsche's physiological thinking for these phenomena. The chapter concludes with a brief foray into 'immanence', as conceived by Nietzsche and Deleuze, since it is arguably only on this terrain that the phenomena of reactivity, and specifically the phenomena of populism, can ultimately be overcome.

Following on from this, the section, Nietzsche and Deleuze on a New Politics, pays sustained attention to probably the most significant philosopher to have established and developed the theme of difference in Nietzsche's works, namely, Gilles Deleuze. In the first chapter in this section, "Echoes of a New Politics: Deleuze's Nietzsche and the Political", Jonas Osswald introduces the "new politics" which emerges through Deleuze's reading of Nietzsche, contrasting it with other, more problematic approaches to "anti-foundational" politics. Via Oliver Marchart's critique of the latter, it illustrates how post-foundationalism repeats the recoding of society criticised in Deleuze's essay on Nietzsche, "Nomadic Thought". It shows that these efforts of recoding are expressions of the obsession of a specific figure, which resembles the Nietzschean priest. It concludes with an outline of Nietzsche's new politics, developed from the idea of an inverted teleology, or the question of how to share a cause without sharing a telos.

Next, in "The Topology of Difference: The Politics of Space according to Nietzsche and Deleuze", Lilian Valerie Kroth develops a particular understanding of the political in Deleuze, drawing not only on his reading of Nietzsche, but of Foucault and of Leibniz, in order to demonstrate the links between thought, subjectivity, topology and politics. This is then extended to a debate within postcolonial theory, initiated by Gayatri Chakravorty Spivak, regarding how well the conceptual resources of Foucault and Deleuze can think what is at stake politically in the difference of 'the Other'.

The final two chapters in this section – Gabriel Valladão Silva's "Fake or Just Stupid?" and Julie Van der Wielen's "The Idiot: Deleuze's Nietzsche for a Politics of Difference" – complement each other by revealing two sides of a "new politics" that can be understood through Deleuze's reading of Nietzsche, both of which eschew identifiable positions and policies. On the one side, Valladão Silva shows how the recently emergent politics of post-truth can be understood as a form of reactive nihilism which cares only about maintaining power and is willing to sacrifice anything construed as different in order to maintain that power. On the other side, Van der Wielen's chapter uncovers the capacity for resistance, and an affirmation of difference, through Deleuze's conceptual persona of the Idiot, whose very idiocy is understood, via Nietzsche, as the unwillingness to accept given ideas and values. The figure of the Idiot functions to introduce and to affirm difference in a way which is political, but alien to what is usually considered to be politics. Both perspectives move what is at stake in politics away from concepts with a truth-value, towards judgements of the *will* that is manifest through such concepts, as well as through actions and institutions. A comparison of these chapters raises the question: would it be possible to conceive the latter (the affirmation of difference in the figure of the Idiot) as theorising an adequate resistance to the former (the reactive nihilism of post-truth)? Or are there more difficult issues at stake that need to be worked through? In any case, both chapters demonstrate very well how Nietzsche's concepts, via Deleuze's innovative and influential reading, can be mobilised in a way which is remarkably insightful with respect to recent trends in the current political landscape.

One way in which a politics of difference is clearly evident in a significant area of current Nietzsche research is the debate around "agonistic democracy", which is explored in the next section, The Politics of the Agon. Supporters of this view contend that, while Nietzsche himself frequently opposed democracy as a political philosophy, his philosophical thought provides resources for a particular conception of democracy which would overcome the difficulties of levelling and homogenisation he sees with it. Nietzsche's understanding of the ancient Greek concept of the agon is thought to provide the inspiration for a model of democracy based on friendly conflict and competition which both promotes the great achievements of outstanding individuals and preserves differences. Such a view is, of course, contested by those (such as Frederick Appel, Bruce Detwiler, Don Dombowsky and John Richardson) who insist that Nietzsche's views are incompatible with any form of democracy. The two chapters collected in the Politics of the Agon section of this volume weigh in on either side of this debate, though both in ways which are distinctly original and move the terms of the debate in new directions. In her chapter "Disparate Conceptions of the Agon: Nietzsche and Agonistic Democracy", Pia Morar notes that supporters of the agonistic democracy thesis rarely pay close attention to Nietzsche's understanding of the agon. Remedying this, she traces the influence of Jacob Burckhardt's work on Nietzsche's understanding and argues that both considered the agon to be essentially aristocratic, referring only to competition amongst the elite. While Morar concedes that there *are* conceptual resources for an agonistic conception of democracy in Nietzsche, she argues that they are relatively meagre in comparison with those of other thinkers.

In contrast to Morar's deflationary account, Sven Gellens' "Agonal Human Rights: A Re-evaluation of Democracy Through Nietzsche's Physio-Psychology of Will to Power" begins with the thesis of agonistic democracy and seeks to expand it by considering human rights from a Nietzschean perspective. He notes that contemporary theoretical oppositions to the idea of human rights object to the assumption of univeralisation based on a metaphysical conception of what it means to be human. Drawing on psychological research, he argues that a "formal" conception of human rights, based on a scientific determination of human needs, can replace such metaphysical conceptions. Such a view, he argues, is consistent with Nietzsche's works insofar as he sought a "physio-psychological" understanding of values, in which psychological features are seen as based in physiological facts. On this surer footing, Gellens argues, human rights can be re-interpreted as *conditions* for the flourishing of human beings, a flourishing which allows and promotes differences rather than reducing all human beings to a single, homogenous, metaphysical model.

In recent years, the far-right interpretation of Nietzsche's philosophy has resurfaced under the banner of the Alt Right, with the popular icon of the movement Richard Spencer citing Nietzsche as a formative influence.[2] These uptakes of Nietzsche's work are used by the Alt Right to construe their enemies – defenders of rights for political minorities, such as women, people of colour, and those of non-standard sexualities and genders – as the weak, the slavish, motivated by *ressentiment* to undermine the strong (i.e., those who have traditionally held the majority of political power, especially white men). Yet such a politics can easily be seen from the reverse perspective, in which it is motivated by the *ressentiment* of conservatives in the face of changing balances of power. Moreover, this politics typically bemoans the plurality of types of individuals and the diversity of multiculturalism. Against this latest entry in the unfortunate line of Nietzsche's questionable influences, the chapters in the fifth and final section of this volume, Plurality, Affirmation, Immanence, demonstrate how Nietzsche's philosophy affirms difference understood not simply as hierarchy and the 'pathos of distance', but as *plurality*.

Marinete Araujo da Silva Fobister's chapter, "Nietzsche and a Politics of Difference: Recognising the Forces in the Margins", argues that Nietzsche's ontology of forces can be used to better understand the experiences and potentials of migrants in the context of education. Drawing on research on 'the London effect' – the demonstrated capacity of migrant children to excel in schools in multicultural London – Fobister argues that this may be understood in terms of an 'excess of forces' released by the very migratory situation of these children. Such excesses are also to be found in the contemporary nihilistic West, in which forces of all kinds – physical, intellectual, cultural, creative – are no longer uniformly structured by institutions and anchored by traditional values. Fobister elaborates these potentials through the idea of geophilosophy, with which we might think of forces, modes of thought and ways of life as deterritorialised and reterritorialised in the migrant experience. Such movements create an excess of forces which

---

[2] Graeme Wood, "His Kampf", *The Atlantic*, June 2017, https://www.theatlantic.com/magazine/archive/2017/06/his-kampf/524505/. Accessed 6/6/2022.

have the potential to be discharged in either constructive and creative, or destructive and nihilistic, ways. Appreciating the 'forces in the margins' means recognising and affirming the potentials of social, cultural and individual plurality that exist in the contemporary confluence of nihilism and mass migration.

In his essay "Nietzsche, Foucault, and the Politics of the Ascetic Ideal", George W. Shea IV contends that a germinal politics of difference can be discerned in Nietzsche's critique of the ascetic ideal. On this basis, Shea further argues that Foucault's later work can be understood as a considered theorisation of the political implications of this critique. When read in this light, Shea concludes that Foucault, working from Nietzschean insights, offers a politics that neither negates nor replicates the ascetic ideal and the metaphysical valuation of truth but instead contends with it. This is ultimately a politics that resists the totalitarian, autocratic and homogenising temptation to subsume all divergences into one and instead affirms multiplicity and difference.

Michael J. McNeal's chapter, "The Quandary of Identity and the Prospective Appearance of Free Spirits in our Globalising Age", considers the prospects for the appearance of free spirits in our increasingly decadent times. Given neoliberal globalisation's disruption of identities and homogenisation of cultures, how might free spirits recognise and overcome its nihilism while becoming who they are? McNeal's chapter employs Nietzsche's interrelated analyses of culture and identity to assess globalisation's destruction of autochthonous values and the forms of life they sustained via its universalisation of Anglo-European decadence values. Against its banalisation of difference, the chapter considers potentials for radical life-affirmation and argues that prospective free spirits may adopt Nietzschean ironism to experiment agonically with, and to transmute, globalisation's dissipative values.

The editors hope that this volume will open up new perspectives on Nietzsche's work and its continued relevance for contemporary political problems and challenges, and also that it will be seen to demonstrate that – and how – philosophical approaches can help us to understand and even to navigate the political situation in which we find ourselves. Even though this volume is anchored in the philosophical past, the hope is that it can point to a different political future.

Bibliography

Ansell-Pearson, Keith (Ed.) (2013): *Nietzsche and Political Thought*. London: Bloomsbury.
Appel, Frederick (1999): *Nietzsche contra Democracy*. Ithaca: Cornell University Press.
Connolly, William E. (1989): *Political Theory and Modernity*. Hoboken: John Wiley & Sons.
Detwiler, Bruce (1990): *Nietzsche and the Politics of Aristocratic Radicalism*. Chicago: University of Chicago Press.
Dombowsky, Don (2004): *Nietzsche's Machiavellian Politics*. Basingstoke: Palgrave Macmillan.
Drochon, Hugo (2016): *Nietzsche's Great Politics*. Princeton: Princeton University Press.
Hatab, Lawrence J. (1995): *A Nietzschean Defense of Democracy: An Experiment in Postmodern Politics*. Chicago: Open Court.
Knoll, Manuel and Barry Stocker (Eds.) (2014): *Nietzsche as Political Philosopher*. Berlin: Walter de Gruyter.
Losurdo, Dominic (2020): *Nietzsche: The Aristocratic Rebel*. Translated by Gregor Benton. Leiden: Brill.
Richardson, John (1996): *Nietzsche's System*. Oxford: Oxford University Press.
Siemens, Herman, and Vasti Roodt (Eds.) (2008): *Nietzsche, Power and Politics*. Berlin: Walter de Gruyter.
Warren, Mark (1988): *Nietzsche and Political Thought*. Cambridge: MIT Press.

Part 1 **Politics and Difference**

Alan Watt
Nietzsche, Rancière and the Disputation of Politics

Abstract: This chapter approaches Nietzsche's politics through the thought of Jacques Rancière. To help us resolve the recurring question of whether Nietzsche is a political thinker we should also ask "what is politics?", and Rancière's novel answer to the latter question allows a new way of affirming the political relevance of Nietzsche's thought. Much of what is conventionally understood as politics is re-framed by Rancière as 'the police', his term for any order which puts all social actors in their supposedly 'proper place'. Politics, on the other hand, takes place when the order is challenged by those who claim they are not properly counted, and is thus a radical form of dispute. Nietzsche, I claim, outlines just such a 'different count' in GM I, since the slave revolt in morality renames the parties and challenges the aristocratic count.

1 Introduction

On the face of it, Jacques Rancière is an unlikely foil for a discussion of Nietzsche's politics. In the two major Rancière texts on which I primarily draw for my characterisation of his political thinking in this chapter – *La Mésentente* (*Disagreement*) and the essays published in English as *Dissensus* – there are only a couple of brief mentions of Nietzsche. Unlike many other contemporary French thinkers, then, Rancière cannot be classified as a "reader" of Nietzsche in any standard sense. There is no "Rancière's Nietzsche" to speak of, and I am not seeking in this chapter to discover or invent one.

Rancière's importance for interpreting Nietzsche's politics lies rather in his unorthodox understanding of what politics is – relative to the mainstream western tradition of political philosophy. This matters because from the standpoint of the philosophical mainstream it is highly contestable whether Nietzsche counts as a political thinker at all. Martha Nussbaum, after all, suggests that he fails to meet most of the criteria she proposes for counting a thinker as a serious political theorist, provocatively claiming that 'on six of the seven issues, Nietzsche has nothing to offer that is not utterly childish' (Nussbaum 1997, p. 2)[1]. Of course,

---

[1] Nussbaum's seven criteria are: 1) material need – showing awareness of basic human requirements and proposing an allocation to meet them; 2) procedural justification – proposing how to

Nietzsche has plenty of modern defenders, but most try to prove his seriousness as a political thinker by showing that he is far from "childish" on some of the topics Nussbaum lists as constitutive of serious political thought, such as proposing criteria for distributing resources, procedures that legitimate a political structure, and the role and limits of the State. Adopting a Rancièrian approach to politics, by contrast, offers the possibility of a completely different strategy, one that does not attempt to reconstruct a "political Nietzsche" that will fit the template proffered by traditional political philosophy but rather rips up that template, asserting a radically different view of the political from the traditional one articulated by Nussbaum, and aligning Nietzsche to this alternative understanding.

In this chapter, I offer a first attempt at viewing Nietzsche's politics through a Rancièrian lens. This leads to a relocation of attention from the second essay of *On the Genealogy of Morals*, on which recent political readings of Nietzsche have often concentrated (see, for instance, Conway 2008), to the first, because 'the slave revolt' (GoM I, 7) is the most obvious point of contact between Rancière's view of politics and Nietzsche. I will argue that there are several significant affinities between the two thinkers' approaches. This is not to say that I am characterising Nietzsche as a proto-Rancièrian, or conversely that Rancière expresses Nietzsche's sense of the political in a modern idiom. There are some very important differences between the two, despite the affinities, and I do not intend to gloss them over. However, I do believe that Rancière's new conception of politics is a fruitful one to apply to Nietzsche and may help to articulate why attempts to read Nietzsche as a political philosopher so often seem to be putting him in a straitjacket.

The chapter has four main sections. In section 2, I articulate some of what I take to be the key features of Rancière's approach to politics, emphasising particularly how it differs from mainstream traditions of political philosophy. In section 3, I highlight what I take to be some of the key ways in which such a Rancièrian perspective can influence a reading of Nietzsche's politics – here I am looking primarily for affinities. In section 4, I consider some of the obstacles to aligning Nietzsche and Rancière, and in the final section I summarise what

---

legitimise political decisions, e.g., Rawls' Original Position; 3) liberty and its worth – providing an account of human liberty and its relationship with the political sphere; 4) racial, ethnic and religious difference – proposing how to deal politically with such differences; 5) gender and the family – proposing how political institutions should relate to family structures and gender roles; 6) justice between nations – proposing what nations owe one another; and 7) moral psychology – having an account of human psychology, and how it impacts the political. Only on the last point, moral psychology, does Nussbaum award Nietzsche a passing grade.

overall benefits I see in bringing the two thinkers together and what politics becomes when viewed along these alternative lines. As I hint in the title, 'dispute' (understood in a particular, Rancièrian way) moves centre stage in this approach to Nietzsche's politics.

2 Rancière's Approach to Politics

I will begin with an articulation of Rancière's unusual definition of 'politics' (*la politique*), alongside the antagonistic term 'the police' (*la police*) – in his thought, the two cannot really be understood without reference to one another. This will include some discussion of how such an unorthodox conception can be defended, with a brief detour through Rancière's subversive reading of Aristotle. Next, I fill out the position with discussion of Rancière's take on 'democracy', another key term in his lexicon; and I conclude this first part of the chapter with a reflection on the implications of his position for "political philosophy".

The most obvious and heavily discussed element of Rancière's approach to politics is that it involves a radical re-definition of terms. Most of what standard definitions and university courses on politics cover – such things as the (proper) forms of government of organised communities – is re-labelled by Rancière as the police, while he reserves the term politics for a certain kind of challenge to these police structures. A quotation from Rancière can help to illuminate the point:

> The essence of *the police* lies in a partition of the sensible that is characterized by the absence of void and of supplement: society here is made up of groups tied to specific modes of doing, to places in which these occupations are exercised, and to modes of being corresponding to these occupations and these places. In this matching of functions, places and ways of being, there is no place for any void. It is this exclusion of what 'is not' that constitutes the police-principle at the core of statist practices. The essence of *politics* consists in disturbing this arrangement by supplementing it with a part of those without part, identified with the whole of the community. Political dispute is that which brings politics into being by separating it from the police.... Politics, before all else, is an intervention in the visible and the sayable. (Rancière 2010, pp. 44–45, emphasis added)

It should be clear already that what Rancière means by the police has little to do with people in uniforms carrying truncheons. They are just one part of a much larger system which puts everything and everyone in their 'right place'; it is the system, not its functionaries, to which Rancière wishes to draw attention. It would also be a mistake to think that Rancière's police refers to regimes in which the State is particularly powerful and individual liberty curtailed. He does not mean anything like a "police State" as it is understood in ordinary parlance, as a particular type of (totalitarian) regime: when Rancière talks about 'the police-principle at the core of statist practices' he means this to apply quite generally to liberal-democratic as much as to authoritarian regimes.

If the scope of the police is much broader than in common usage, the scope of politics is, correspondingly, much narrower. As Rancière puts it in *Disagreement*, 'politics doesn't always happen – it actually happens very little or rarely' (Rancière 1999, p. 17). Rancière's politics is essentially tied to dispute (*litige*), but not to everyday disputes over the distribution of resources. As he puts it, 'political conflict does not involve an opposition between groups with different interests. It forms an opposition between logics that count the parties and parts of the community in different ways' (Rancière 2010, p. 43).

At various points, Rancière elucidates what counts for him as politics via some historical examples. A particularly important one, which he discusses at some length, was the confrontation between the Roman plebeians and the consul Menenius Agrippa in 494 BCE, described by Livy and later re-characterised (in 1829) by the French historian Pierre-Simon Ballanche. For Rancière, what matters is that the plebs did not simply 'revolt', as escaped domestic animals might do, they set up a rival community outside the city and Menenius was forced to recognise their ability to speak and to negotiate with them. The revolutionary change is that these people, who for the Roman patricians did not count because they were not considered to have intelligent human speech, only an animalistic noise that could express nothing but immediate wants and needs, have 'given themselves names' and shown through their actions that they too are 'men' (Rancière 1999, p. 25). Menenius delivers to them an *apologia* for the class division of Rome and their exclusion from power, but by virtue of their being able to understand it they are already at odds with its content. As Rancière explains:

> from the moment the plebs could understand Menenius's apologia – the apologia of the necessary inequality between the vital patrician principle and the plebeian members carrying it out – they were already, just as necessarily, equals. The apologia implies an inegalitarian partition of the perceptible. The sense necessary to understand this division presupposes an egalitarian division that puts paid to the former. (Rancière 1999, p. 25)

A little later on, Rancière generalises the lessons about how the situation became a case of politics:

> Politics exists because those who have no right to be counted as speaking beings make themselves of some account, setting up a community by the fact of placing in common a wrong that is nothing more than this very confrontation, the contradiction of two worlds

in a single world: the world where they are and the world where they are not, the world where there is something 'between' them and those who do not acknowledge them ... and the world where there is nothing. (Rancière 1999, p. 27)

It is important to note that not every slave revolt achieves this breakthrough – Rancière provides a contrasting case with the revolt of the Scythian slaves who were briefly successful in military terms but were (according to Hesiod) cowed back into submission when the masters got out their whips: the Scythian slaves did not yet believe they were the equals of those against whom they had revolted, and were unable to 'make themselves of some account' (Rancière 1999, p. 12).

Now, at this point, one may well ask what could justify Rancière's highly specific and seemingly idiosyncratic understanding of politics. If it were no more than Humpty Dumpty's retort to Alice that 'when I use a word it means just what I choose it to mean' (Carroll 2018, p. 71), then it would have only modest significance, and not pose any significant challenge to traditional understandings of the type articulated by Nussbaum. But while Rancière never produces a formal defence of his usage, it is promulgated in connection with a serious engagement with Aristotle's *Politics*, such that it might be labelled a kind of subversive Aristotelianism. Right at the start of *Disagreement*, Rancière highlights a famous passage from Book I of the *Politics* in which Aristotle characterises the distinctiveness of the 'political animal' as defined by his possession of the logos, intelligent speech rather than mere 'voice', which allows the human (alone) to 'have perception of good and evil, just and unjust, etc. It is the sharing of a common view in these matters that makes a household and a state' (Aristotle 1962, I, ii, 1253a7–17. Whatever is incapable of participating – a dumb animal for instance – 'is not a part of the state at all' (Aristotle 1962, I, ii, 1253a18–28). A little later, though, Aristotle discusses the slave, characterising him as one who has only partial, limited access to reason: 'he that participates in reason so far as to recognize it but not so as to possess it' (Aristotle 1962, I, v, 1254b16–31). As we have seen with his discussion of the first secession of the plebs, Rancière considers that this definition contains a crucial contradiction that will inevitably be exposed at a certain point through action, when those who are excluded insist that their equal ability to understand must entail a part within the political community. As Rancière puts it:

> There is order in society because some people command and others obey, but in order to obey an order at least two things are required: you must understand the order and you must understand that you must obey it. And to do that, you must already be the equal of the person who is ordering you. It is this equality that gnaws away at any natural order. (Rancière 1999, p. 16)

Given that Rancière ties politics to "interruptions" of supposed hierarchical orders, it is natural that he also connects it strongly to democracy, or at least to the struggle for democracy, since democracy abolishes any natural right to rule of any section of the community and insists on the capacity of all to both rule and be ruled. He states, for instance, that 'democracy is the institution of politics as such' (Rancière 2010, p. 58). Given the prevalence of democratic regimes, this might seem to contradict his insistence on the rarity of politics, but it must be kept in mind that when he says "democracy" he is not referring to a particular institutional structure. Democracy, for Rancière, is 'neither a form of government nor a form of social life'; it is in fact 'a paradox' (Rancière 2010, p. 58). It is paradoxical because it purports to provide an answer to the fundamental question about the grounds of rule in the community, yet the 'answer', Rancière thinks, is 'an astonishing one: namely, that the very ground for the power of ruling is that there is no ground at all' (Rancière 2010, p. 58). There is no ground because in a democracy anyone and everyone can rule and be ruled; there is no "natural" division of rulers and ruled based on any inherently superior quality the rulers may be thought to possess (whether that quality be in terms of wealth, the wisdom of age, scientific expertise, noble birth, etc.). In several places, Rancière notes that Plato's characterisation of the democratic ruling principle was the drawing of lots,[2] which for Rancière is the clearest expression of what he believes to be democracy's an-archic logic. In ancient democratic Athens, this procedure of sortition was the main one for selecting officials, and on Rancière's account it was distress at this absence of ground in democratic practice that motivated Plato's search for a rationally defensible ruling principle in his *Republic*.[3] Modern democracies, which tend to elect officials rather than selecting them via the drawing of lots, are less clearly incompatible with a ruling principle (*arkhe*), because the candidates may put themselves forward on the basis that they are best qualified to rule. Thus, sortition makes far more tangible

---

[2] The Plato passage of recurring fascination to Rancière is the *Laws*, Book III, 690c. It is discussed at length, for instance, in *Dissensus*, pp. 58–60.

[3] Rancière claims at one point that '"political philosophy" begins with the revelation of this scandal, and this revelation is conducted by means of an idea presented as an alternative to the unfounded state of politics. It is the watchword Socrates uses to express his difference from the men of the democratic city: to really do politics, to do politics in truth, to engage in politics as a way of bringing off the exclusive essence of politics.... It is first in relation to politics that philosophy, from the very beginning, "comes too late". Only for philosophy this "lateness" is the wrong of democracy. In the form of democracy, politics is already in place, without waiting for its theoretical underpinnings or its *arkhe*' (Rancière 1999, p. 62).

the absence of ground for ruling and the rejection of any logic that would claim a right to rule.

Since Rancière ties politics so strongly to democracy and its absence of ground, he is on a collision course with (traditional) political philosophy, which for the most part has attempted to provide a firm ground for a political order, its *arkhe* or underlying (legitimate) source. Rancière indeed considers political philosophy to be fundamentally anti-political in intent. Inaugurated by Plato, 'the program of political philosophy ... is ... to achieve politics by eliminating politics, by achieving "philosophy" in place of politics' (Rancière 1999, p. 63).[4] It is important to understand that this characterisation is not just directed against overt anti-democrats such as Plato. It applies just as readily to advocates of liberal democratic regimes if their procedure is to posit an ideal regime type that political practice should then follow. This is so because it reduces politics to an enactment of philosophy and is inherently un-democratic insofar as it would leave philosophy running the show. It would be, as he puts it, 'a theoretical idyll of a philosophical determination of the good that the political community would then have the task of achieving: a political idyll of achieving the common good by an enlightened government of elites buoyed by the confidence of the masses' (Rancière 1999, p. 93). It seems to me that this would also do pretty well as a characterisation of the serious political thinker set up by Nussbaum as the ideal to which Nietzsche is compared, one who should do things such as give 'an account of distributive justice, including an account of the institutional structures required by justice' and 'give an account of the procedures through which a political structure is determined, procedures that legitimate and/or justify the resulting proposals' (Nussbaum 1997, p. 2). The unspoken assumption, here as in the whole philosophical tradition, is that such a political thinker would be setting out the model for a 'community strictly defined as a common body' and demonstrating a 'desire to give to the community a single foundation' (Rancière 2010, p. 49). Rancière sets himself implacably against all such politics of the philosophers. He aims at precisely the opposite, a separation of politics from the police, and he insists that politics occurs precisely as a *disturbance* of any police arrangement and cannot be assimilated to a just order of any kind. Rancière can, then, be used to counter those such as Nussbaum who would deny Nietzsche entry to the realm of serious political thinking, by critiquing their grounding assumptions about what constitutes a serious philosophical engage-

---

4 Rancière devotes a whole chapter of *Disagreement* ("From Archipolitics to Metapolitics") to the various modulations of "political philosophy" from Plato to modern times, distancing himself there not just from Plato and Aristotle but from a range of modern political philosophers, including Hobbes, Rousseau and Marx.

ment with politics. However, this will be of limited value unless it can be shown that there are some significant commonalities between Rancière's view of politics and Nietzsche's, and it is to this question that I now turn in the next two sections of the chapter.

3 Elements of a Rancièrian Politics in Nietzsche

How might a Rancièrian perspective allow us to see Nietzsche's politics in a different light? I will begin, in this section, by looking for points of commonality or compatibility – aspects of Nietzsche's approach that harmonise with Rancière's perspective – before considering the obstacles to any attempt to harmonise the two in the next section.

A first approximation between Rancière's and Nietzsche's approaches to politics I see in the general issue of how they conceive its scope and scale. As we have seen, Rancière narrows the scope of politics to situations in which the very nature and composition of the community is at stake, when fundamentally antagonistic views about what counts as "just" are in competition with one another. As he puts it at one point, 'The essence of politics is dissensus. Dissensus is not a confrontation between interests or opinions. It is the demonstration of a gap in the sensible itself' (Rancière 2010, p. 46). Politics may happen only rarely, but when it does happen it involves a battle over fundamentals. Nietzsche, for his part, displays a disdain for what he terms 'petty politics' and at one point (in *Ecce Homo*) provides a redefinition of politics that takes it close to Rancière's revolutionary conception:

> When truth steps into battle with the lie of millennia we shall have convulsions, an earthquake spasm, a transposition of valley and mountain such as has never been dreamed of. *The concept politics has then become completely absorbed into a war of spirits*, all the power-structures of the old society have been blown into the air. (EH "Destiny" 1, emphasis added)

In this passage, Nietzsche is, of course, looking to the future, but I would suggest that the history he provides, in the first essay of *On the Genealogy of Morals*, of the struggle between Rome and Judea could be read as an imaginative account of the history of this politics of a 'war of spirits'. This account has some notable overlaps with Rancière's view.

This type of politics begins when there is what Nietzsche elsewhere calls a 'slave uprising [*Sklaven-Aufstand*] in morals' (BGE 195). As we have seen, Rancière is also extremely interested in the historical uprisings of slaves, plebeians and others who are assigned no part in hierarchical orders, and he connects the inauguration of politics with them. However, as we saw, for Rancière not just any old slave revolt is political, and Nietzsche's conception of *Sklaven-Aufstand* is much closer to the (political) conflict of the Roman plebs than the pre-political revolt of the Scythian slaves. The key difference, for Rancière, is that the Scythian slaves were not capable of challenging their masters at the level of the *logos*. On their failure, he comments that 'when [the masters] once more show the signs of their difference in nature, the rebels have no comeback. What they cannot do is transform equality in war into political freedom' (Rancière 1999, p. 13). He further explains that 'politics comes about solely through interruption [of the supposed "natural" order], the initial twist that institutes politics as the deployment of a wrong or of a fundamental dispute' (Rancière 1999, p. 13).

Nietzsche's *Sklaven-Aufstand* is very much about 'the deployment of a wrong or of a fundamental dispute', since it involves a thoroughgoing re-description and re-evaluation such that the misfortunes suffered by the lower orders will no longer be accepted as part of their naturally inferior standing but will be regarded instead as an injustice visited on them by the masters, now characterised not as the natural and rightful rulers but as oppressors, who do wrong to the weaker members of their societies. Nietzsche ironically characterises participants in the *Sklaven-Aufstand* as reframing their situation as follows: '"We good men – we are the just" – what they desire they call, not retaliation, but "the triumph of justice"; what they hate is not their enemy, no! they hate "injustice"' (GoM I, 14). Here, there is a fairly close match with Rancière's conception of the inauguration of politics. Aristotle asserted that it is 'the sharing of a common view' in 'perception of good and evil, just and unjust' that 'makes a state' (Aristotle 1962, I, ii, 1253a7–17), but Rancière's twist is that while such a common view can establish the police, *politics* only begins when those who have been refused a part re-characterise their situation in a way that sets up an implacable dispute – implacable because, whereas an appeal to an agreed-upon notion of justice might allow for a distribution of shares that all sides could agree on, in politics the question becomes 'whose justice?'

As we saw, Rancière asserts that 'politics, before all else, is an intervention in the visible and the sayable', and Nietzsche's *Sklaven-Aufstand* clearly makes new things visible and sayable, things that could not be said or seen from within the framework of master morality. This is, of course, entirely consistent with his general view of the material power of naming – as he says elsewhere, 'it is enough to create new names and estimations and probabilities in order to create in the long run new "things"' (GS 58). When Rancière describes the secession of the Roman plebeians and seeks to characterise what made their uprising attain to the level of politics in a way that the Scythian slaves did not, he too has recourse to the language of name-giving:

> Through transgression, they find that they too, just like speaking beings, are endowed with speech that does not simply express want, suffering, or rage, but intelligence. They write ... 'a name in the sky': a place in the symbolic order of the community of speaking beings, in a community that does not yet have any effective power in the city of Rome. (Rancière 1999, p. 24)

With their different ways of naming and evaluating after the *Sklaven-Aufstand*, masters and slaves effectively occupy different worlds, a point that Nietzsche expresses vividly with his reinterpretation of Hesiod's division of the ancient epochs into gold, silver and bronze. Whereas they purported to be historically distinct, successive periods in human history, Nietzsche suggests that Hesiod was actually describing the same period from radically different perspectives, so far apart that they effectively saw different events: one world is split into two (GoM I, 11). Interestingly, Nietzsche had already expressed a very similar idea in *Daybreak* 189, in a passage entitled – even more interestingly – On grand politics (*Von der grossen Politik*):

> In the fable of the ages of mankind, Hesiod has depicted the same age, that of the Homeric heroes, twice and made *two ages out of one:* from the point of view of those who had to suffer the terrible iron oppression of these adventurous *Gewaltmenschen* ... it appeared *evil*; but the posterity of this knightly generation revered it as the *good* old happy times. (D III, 189)

As we have seen, Rancière uses similar language, at one point asserting that 'the essence of politics is the manifestation of dissensus as the presence of two worlds in one' (Rancière 2010, p. 45). Nietzsche's shorthand for this "dissensus", this "two worlds in one" is 'Rome against Judea' (GoM I, 16).

As well as these various specific commonalities of Nietzsche's account of the *Sklaven-Aufstand* and Rancière's concept of politics, I would like to emphasise one other important structural parallel, namely, the recourse to history, to what could be called the 'historicity' of their accounts. Samuel A. Chambers, in his interesting commentary on Rancière, emphasises how distant his approach to politics is from the patterning of social science and much political philosophy that would box the political into a regular structure. Rather, events matter, and as such politics is both 'untimely' and 'unpredictable' (Chambers 2012, p. 8). By the same token, Chambers contends, Rancière's politics cannot be assimilated to any approach that prioritises 'territoriality', that sees it in terms of a sphere or space within society (Chambers 2012, p. 46).[5] Nietzsche's account

---

[5] Chambers explicitly criticises efforts to align Rancière with Arendt because he believes there can be no 'pure politics' for Rancière (Chambers 2012, pp. 45–50).

of the Rome v. Judea conflict is also far from envisaging a stable structure or predictable pattern; at the end of the first essay of *On the Genealogy of Morals*, he rather looks forward to a re-opening of the conflict, a new event: 'Was that the end of it? Had that greatest of all conflicts of ideals been disposed of for all time? Or only adjourned, indefinitely adjourned? Must the ancient fire not some day flare up much more forcibly, after much longer preparation?' (GoM I, 17). If (grand-scale) politics is understood first and foremost in terms of periodically occurring historical events, past and future, it becomes much clearer why the kind of structural account of the political demanded by Nussbaum is not provided. Rancière can give Nietzsche an important alibi here, since he offers an account of the absence of an account, namely, that the event that ruptures the 'logic of the *arkhe*' cannot be captured in advance by a theoretical framework (Rancière 2010, p. 39).

4 Problems for an Alignment of Nietzsche and Rancière

In the previous section, I tried to bring out potential similarities between Rancière's approach to politics and Nietzsche's. In this section, I will examine the other side of the ledger and look at what in Nietzsche seems a poor fit with Rancière or even to contradict his approach.

Rather than discuss a number of smaller issues, I will focus on detailed consideration of a large and obvious problem for any attempt to align the two thinkers, which will likely have occurred by now to anyone familiar with the first essay of *On the Genealogy of Morals*. In simple terms, it is that whatever agreement there might potentially be between the two regarding the origins of politics in an insurrectionary movement in which the lower orders give themselves (re-) naming rights, they are – to put it rather freely – on opposite sides of the barricades, which drives them in very different directions once they progress past the first awakening of politics in the *Sklaven-Aufstand*. For Rancière, politics is intrinsically tied to democracy (as process or event, not regime); although the risk is always that it will be absorbed back into a hierarchy, that politics will disappear and there will only be the police. For Nietzsche, at the end of the first essay of *On the Genealogy of Morals*, the risk seems to be the polar opposite, namely, that hierarchy, order of rank, will be liquidated and equal rights will have fully materialised.[6] Likewise, both thinkers see later upsurges of politics

---

6 Nietzsche effectively provides a scorecard of how the Rome v Judea conflict has worked out

in more recent times, but with different polarities. For Rancière, on the one hand, they are always bottom-up, for instance, a worker claiming the universality of the proletariat or a woman claiming the universality of the Declaration of the Rights of Man.[7] Dissensus arises, in other words, in a moment of resistance to an exclusionary natural order of society. For Nietzsche, on the other hand, the heroic events come from above – Napoleon, for instance (GoM I, 16) – seeking once more to re-impose an order of rank on a levelled-down society. So, the question is, does this major contrast effectively ruin any attempt to draw parallels between the two, or can it be finessed somehow so that it does not refute such efforts? There are, I think, a couple of ways of trying to counter this objection, which I will explore below.

First, whereas above I have characterised Rancière and Nietzsche as being on opposite sides of the barricades, there is a case to be made that both are more interested in promoting struggle than in victory for their side. In Rancière's case, the distinction can be brought out by contrasting the readings of two of his prominent English-language interpreters, Todd May and Samuel Chambers. May is an anarchist and reads Rancière's ultimate objective as being the complete abolition of the police, that is, any hierarchical order involving domination, and the total victory of politics (May 2008). Chambers, by contrast, insists that for Rancière there is no thought of a total victory[8]: politics, for Rancière, is impure and, as Chambers reads him, necessarily (not contingently) so; it will always be involved in the interplay with a police order and we cannot and should not dream of a pure politics somehow cleansed of the police. In making his case, Chambers draws attention to a passage from *Disagreement* that does indeed seem strongly to support his interpretation:

> We should not forget … that if politics implements a logic entirely heterogenous to that of the police, it is always bound up with the latter. The reason for this is simple: politics has no objects or issues of its own. Its sole principle, equality, is not peculiar to it and is in no way in itself political. All equality does is lend politics reality in the form of specific cases

---

historically, and concludes that 'Rome has been defeated beyond all doubt', vanquished by Christianity and more recently the French Revolution. Nor is this just at the level of ideals; it also involves societal structures: with the French Revolution, 'the last political noblesse [*die letzte politische Vornehmheit*] in Europe, that of the *French* seventeenth and eighteenth century, collapsed beneath the popular instincts of *ressentiment*' (GoM I, 16).

7 Two such cases are discussed at length in Rancière 1999, pp. 37–42.
8 His case against May's interpretation is laid out at length in Chapter 2 of his book. See Chambers 2012, pp. 75–87.

to inscribe, in the form of dispute,⁹ confirmation of the equality at the heart of the police order.... Politics runs up against the police everywhere. We need to think of this encounter as a meeting of the heterogenous. (Rancière 1999, pp. 31–32)

At least in this passage, Rancière does seem to be articulating a view that the police will always be with us, and politics always playing off against it. And even if he is promoting the latter, it seems it is not with the purpose of ultimately abolishing the former.

A similar case could be made with regard to Nietzsche, drawing on a couple of considerations. Firstly, there are his general martial principles: the need for enemies, for strong enemies, opposing whom calls for a maximum of strength.¹⁰ Applied to the context of the first essay of *On the Genealogy of Morals*, this could be taken to imply a preference for the struggle, the ongoing ideological combat against this opponent, rather than for a new world order from which the opponent has been removed. Secondly, there is the more concrete feature that the closing section of the first essay of *On the Genealogy of Morals*, when expressing Nietzsche's aspirations for the future, does not look forward to the re-instatement of an order of rank but to a renewal of hostilities; as he puts it: 'Must the ancient fire not some day flare up much more terribly?' (GoM I, 17). Here, at the end, it seems that it is the fire that Nietzsche longs for, the *conflict* between ideals, rather than the triumph of his preferred one.¹¹

A second way in which the opposition is blunted may be found in their apparent endorsement of mixed types, neither pure anarchist rebel in the case of Rancière nor pure master in the case of Nietzsche. Rancière indicates the ambiguous nature of political action when he notes that 'What is specific to politics is the existence of a subject defined by its participation in contraries. Politics is a paradoxical form of action' (Rancière 2010, p. 37). What kind of paradox? It is clear that Rancière's thinking on this point, as so often, is influenced by Aristo-

---

9 The English translation renders *litige*, here and indeed throughout, as 'litigation', but I consider this unfortunate given the legalistic connotations of the English term and prefer 'dispute' or 'contestation'.
10 I am thinking in particular of principles set out in Z I, War, and in EH, Wise, 7.
11 It may perhaps seem somewhat paradoxical to suggest that Nietzsche both advocates the Roman ideal of an order of rank and the continuation of conflict between this ideal and its implacable opponent, but in my view this is consistent with a general tendency in Nietzsche to combine particular first-order valuations with a meta-level preference for unresolved tension and conflicts between first-order values. Thus, in GoM I, we find advocacy of the (first-order) values opposed to 'the levelling and the decline and twilight of mankind' (GoM I, 16), especially in sections 11, 12, and 16, while the (meta-level) advocacy of conflict between radically opposed values can be found primarily in section 17.

tle, specifically in this context his idea that a good citizen is one who is 'able to rule and be ruled well' (Aristotle 1962, III, iv, 1277a25–28). Rancière believes that radical implications follow from this: it strikes at the very possibility of founding a society on an *arkhe*, a principle that would divide it into segments and assign separate functions, ordaining some to rule and others to be ruled. Citizen-rule means rule of all and none, it 'suspend[s] all logics of legitimate domination' (Rancière 2010, p. 41). Moreover, people who experience political subjectification become multiple in Rancière's view: they dis-identify with the natural position that the police order assigns to them; and the new situation of political disorder, created when people identify additionally as, say, proletarian, 'inscribes a subject name as being different from any identified part of the community' (Rancière 1999, p. 37).[12] Politics can thus never be identity politics for Rancière, since the process of becoming political pulls the subject away from any definite, socially assigned position; it multiplies and complicates rather than essentialising.

Now, it might be thought that this kind of "different subject" is missing from Nietzsche's sense of politics, which at times seems uniquely determined to bind identities into differentiated social spaces.[13] Still, it is fascinating that late in the first essay of *On the Genealogy of Morals*, after seemingly going out of his way to differentiate master and slave moralities as associated with different (higher and lower) social orders, Nietzsche offers an important caveat:

> The two opposing values 'good and bad' and 'good and evil' have been engaged in a fearful struggle on earth for thousands of years; and although the latter value has certainly been on top for a long time, there are still places where the struggle is as yet undecided. One might even say that it has risen ever higher and thus become more and more profound and spiritual: *so that today there is perhaps no more decisive mark of a 'higher nature', a more spiritual nature, than that of being divided in this sense and a genuine battleground of these opposed values.* (GoM I, 16, emphasis added)

This would seem to place a major obstacle in the way of a reading of Nietzsche's politics as concerned with the establishment of a society based on order of rank, since, as we have seen, the good and evil value is intimately connected with the *Sklaven-Aufstand*. A politics of people divided in this sense is going to look very different from one that is composed of separate social orders, one of which com-

---

12 Chambers (2012) has a discussion of 'disidentification' and Rancière's ideas on political subjectivity in the Introduction, p. 22.
13 Perhaps the most extreme example of this tendency is in A 57, when Nietzsche seems to offer a full endorsement of the rigid caste system of the Manu Law-Book.

prises people fully committed to Rome, the other those fully committed to Judea – it will certainly be much closer to Rancière's approach.[14]

5 Conclusion: Nietzsche, Rancière and the Politics of Dispute

So, in the end, how should the relationship between Rancière's and Nietzsche's politics be characterised, and what overall value can come from bringing Rancière into discussions of Nietzsche's politics? What I consider the most essential connection between the two is their understanding of politics as inexorably tied to dispute and dissensus, to dispute of a fundamental nature, which goes well beyond the differences between interest groups theorised by pluralist democrats. Ultimately, nothing less than the struggle between hierarchical order and its dissolution is at stake. Neither of these thinkers understands politics in terms of the creation of ideal constitutions, even as distant goals, and indeed they do everything to undermine such "architectural" political thinking. I have also suggested that they have similar views about the origins of politics in a *Sklaven-Aufstand*, and the struggle it inaugurated over naming rights within society. However, their sympathies concerning this struggle fall in different places, and their diagnoses of the modern situation are almost polar opposites: whereas for Nietzsche the levellers and their equalising doctrine have triumphed and advocates of an order of rank are lacking, for Rancière the police is ever-recurring, and a patterned ordering of societies into hierarchies is ever in need of disruption by those who have no part in it. Though I have argued that this opposition is not quite as stark as it may at first seem, there are certainly fundamental normative divergences, such that if Rancière is to be considered in any way Nietzschean it is more at a deeply structural level, as, for instance, Finnish and Hungarian have common structural roots as Finno-Ugric languages despite the lack of overt similarity in their vocabularies.

As for what a juxtaposition with Rancière can bring to thinking about Nietzsche and politics, I would suggest three main things. Firstly, beyond all is-

---

14 It may seem that I am putting a lot of weight on a single short passage of text, but it is not unique. In the passage of *Beyond Good and Evil* in which Nietzsche discusses master morality and slave morality he makes a similar point regarding mixing: 'I add immediately that in all higher and more mixed cultures there also appear attempts at mediation between these two moralities … and at times they occur directly alongside each other – even in the same human being, within a *single* soul' (BGE 260).

sues of content, Rancière's approach to politics suggests a political value of Nietzsche's provocative, polemical style, which actively disrupts consensus. Informed by the political philosophy tradition, Nietzsche's philosophical readers have often attempted to distil a more treatise-like underlying political theory from Nietzsche's polemics (*Streitschriften*), but reading Rancière should make us suspicious of any such operation, which is liable to 'efface the dispute constitutive of politics' (Rancière 2010, p. 48). Secondly, as I have emphasised at a number of points in the chapter, I think that reading Nietzsche through the prism of Rancière suggests a greater significance for Nietzsche's politics of the first essay of *On the Genealogy of Morals* and especially the *Sklaven-Aufstand*, and I have attempted to sketch out what this version of Nietzsche's politics looks like. Finally, for those who find Rancière's approach to politics interesting, it may provide a new critical lens on Nietzsche's politics, and indeed possibly broader aspects of his thought. For if one accepts Rancière's suggestion that politics itself is always a kind of *Sklaven-Aufstand*, then Nietzsche's generally hostile attitude towards it (and it is generally hostile, for all the qualifications I have noted) may come to seem deeply problematic, and perhaps ripe for a new critique.

Bibliography

Aristotle (1962): *The Politics*. Edited by Trevor J. Saunders and translated by Thomas A. Sinclair. London: Penguin.
Carroll, Lewis (2018): *Through the Looking Glass*. Global Grey ebooks. https://www.global greyebooks.com/through-the-looking-glass-ebook.html, visited on 31 May 2022.
Chambers, Samuel (2012): *The Lessons of Rancière*. Oxford: Oxford University Press.
Conway, Daniel (2008): "The Birth of the State". In: Herman Siemens and Vlasti Roodt (Eds.): *Nietzsche, Power and Politics: Rethinking Nietzsche's Legacy for Political Thought*, pp. 37–67. Berlin: de Gruyter.
May, Todd (2008): *The Political Thought of Jacques Rancière: Creating Equality*. Edinburgh: Edinburgh University Press.
Nietzsche, Friedrich (1964): *Thus Spoke Zarathustra*. Translated by R. J. Hollingdale. London: Penguin.
Nietzsche, Friedrich (1966): *Beyond Good and Evil*. Translated by R. J. Hollingdale. New York: Random House.
Nietzsche, Friedrich (1967): *On the Genealogy of Morals*. Translated by Walter Kaufmann and R. J. Hollingdale. New York: Random House.
Nietzsche, Friedrich (1968): *The Antichrist*. Translated by R. J. Hollingdale. London: Penguin.
Nietzsche, Friedrich (1974): *The Gay Science*. Translated by Walter Kaufmann. New York: Random House.
Nietzsche, Friedrich (1979): *Ecce Homo*. Translated by R. J. Hollingdale. Harmondsworth, Middlesex: Penguin.

Nietzsche, Friedrich (1982): *Daybreak*. Translated by R. J. Hollingdale. Cambridge: Cambridge University Press.
Nussbaum, Martha (1997): "Is Nietzsche a Political Thinker?" In: *International Journal of Philosophical Studies* 5. No. 1, pp. 1–13.
Rancière, Jacques (1999): *Disagreement*. Translated by Julie Rose. Minneapolis: University of Minnesota Press.
Rancière, Jacques (2010): *Dissensus*. Edited and translated by Steven Corcoran. London: Bloomsbury.

Tracy Colony
Composing Time: Stiegler on Nietzsche, Nihilism and a Possible Future

> [W]e who are Nietzsche's heirs, and who find ourselves in the very heart of this nihilism that was promised for two centuries through his warning. (Stiegler 2011a, p. 55)

Abstract: This chapter argues that Nietzsche can be seen as one of Bernard Stiegler's key philosophical interlocutors, from the first volume of *Technics and Time* to his late works. Stiegler develops Nietzsche's notion of tragedy, understanding it as involving 'compositional' rather than oppositional thinking. Accordingly, Nietzsche's genealogy of guilt is able to articulate an originary default prior to the metaphysical and Christian understandings of an original fall. Moreover, this understanding of an originary sense of difference is important for tracing Stiegler's engagement with Deleuze's reading of Nietzsche. This chapter looks at Nietzsche in Stiegler's *Technics and Time* series, his 2004 text *The Decadence of Industrial Democracies*, and in his later work. It reveals that Stiegler is an important reader of Nietzsche, and that both philosophers are resources for thinking a politics of difference.

1 Introduction

Bernard Stiegler is unquestionably one of the most important philosophers to have worked on the theme of technicity. Stiegler's thought of originary technicity is able to overturn and reconceptualise many traditional metaphysical determinations of technical phenomena. His novel understanding of the radical co-origination of technics and the human as such also opens up a perspective for rethinking the history of metaphysics. One of the most important aspects of Stiegler's genealogy of metaphysics is his account of its origin in the obfuscation of a more original tragic form of thinking. This dissimulation of the tragic first occurs in Plato, who attempted to dispel its excess by reducing it to a more original unchanging form. Prior to the simple logic of opposition, which can be seen as defining metaphysics, tragedy gave expression to a composition of terms which are at once irreducible to one another, yet mutually articulated on the basis of their difference. For Stiegler, this tragic figuration of an insoluble, yet constitutive excess prior to the apparently discrete elements of metaphysics, is expressed in the Prometheus-Epimetheus myth at the centre of his understanding of technics. As I will argue, this is also the perspective from which Stiegler can be seen as reading Nietzsche as a key interlocutor.

With the growing reception of his work, Stiegler's engagements with principal philosophical sources such as Derrida, Heidegger and Gilbert Simondon have been well documented and such studies have helped shed light on the ways in which he both appropriated and moved beyond traditional forms of philosophy.[1] However, to date there has not been a single treatment of Stiegler's relation to Nietzsche.[2] This absence is remarkable in that Stiegler often indicates an important proximity to Nietzsche and also explicitly appropriates elements of Nietzsche's thought into his own. And yet, Stiegler's references to Nietzsche are, comparatively, far fewer than those to his many other interlocutors. There has only been one essay by Stiegler devoted to Nietzsche, which appeared in 2016, in a volume titled *Pourquoi nous sommes nietzschéens* (Stiegler 2016a). However, as I will argue, Stiegler's allusions to Nietzsche, although infrequent and often brief, should not be understood as merely ancillary. Rather, by drawing together Stiegler's references to Nietzsche and contextualising them within his wider trajectories, a rich and singular dialogue with Nietzsche can be traced in Stiegler's thought. Moreover, this often-overlooked reception is one which opens up many new points of departure for returning to and re-reading Nietzsche as a resource for diagnosing contemporary forms of nihilism and, perhaps, envisaging an alternative.

This chapter is structured in four sections. In the first section, I give a brief introduction to Stiegler's concept of originary technicity. Since Stiegler's understanding of Nietzsche's radicality lies in his account of him as a tragic thinker, I also refer to Stiegler's sense of the particular ability of tragedy to articulate the condition of originary technicity. In the second section, I trace the way Stiegler presents Nietzsche in the first three volumes of *Technics and Time* series, which originally appeared in 1994, 1996 and 2001 (Stiegler 2018a). In the third section, I look at the period of the early 2000s when Stiegler's dialogue with Nietzsche is increasingly pronounced. In particular, I focus on the first volume of his *Disbelief and Discredit* series, *The Decadence of Industrial Democracies* (Stiegler 2011a), which was originally published in 2004. In the final section, I conclude by using this background to demonstrate the significance of Stiegler's engagement with Nietzsche in some of his later works. With the reception of Stiegler's relation

---

[1] See, for example, the contributions in Christina Howells and Gerald Moore (2013). See also Ross Abbinnett (2018).
[2] Although it appeared too recently to be addressed in this chapter, see Ashley Woodward's (2019) excellent treatment of this theme.

to Nietzsche just beginning, my intention here is not to critically evaluate his readings but, rather, to trace out some of the important terms and themes of this overlooked yet compelling engagement with Nietzsche's thought.

2 Originary Technicity

Stiegler's understanding of originary technicity is first presented in the initial volume of *Technics and Time*, titled *The Fault of Epimetheus* (Stiegler 1998). For Stiegler, one of the most pervasive aspects of metaphysics has been the depiction of human being as simply given prior to any constitutive relation to technics. This division has traditionally defined technological beings as both fabricated and wholly determined by an anterior human intention. Challenging this logic of a pure origin and simple opposition, Stiegler returns to the original divergence of human being from non-technical forms of life and reconceptualises anthropo-genesis and techno-genesis as coincident. The appearance of the first tool is not the product of fabrication or the expression of a creative intelligence, but rather a process of exteriorisation through which life is transformed into something beyond a merely biological order. However, this process of exteriorisation is not preceded by any prior state of interiority. Instead, it must be seen as aporetic and immemorial. The conjugation of life with a technical supplement marks the transformation from merely organically ordered life to a form of life that Stiegler terms 'organological'. Life become organological, that is, ruptured and reorganised by a technical supplement, is inexorably prosthetic and artificial. The aporia of originary prostheticity opened up by the grafting of life on to technics is the matrix of hominisation. This absence of a pure origin and the awareness of an originary excess as constitutive of identity is what tragedy was able to articulate prior to the attempted dissolution of these aporias in the categories of metaphysics.

The new term Stiegler introduces to describe technical beings as arising with the process of exteriorisation is 'organized inorganic beings' (Stiegler 1998, p. 17). Neither biologically organised entities nor simply inanimate matter, technical beings can be seen to constitute a third order of entities which were simply unthinkable within the conventional concepts of metaphysics. Traditionally, the formed matter of a technical being was understood as merely inert and dependent upon a prior human intention for both its creation and operation. Moreover, technics as such was interpreted as a fallen and contingent sphere which marked the corruption of a metaphysically privileged term conceived as beyond any essential relation to technicity. Accordingly, technics was seen as a secondary realm of mere epistemic distortion which constituted a threat to philosophy and knowledge proper. As the devalued term in a binary opposition, technicity was construed within metaphysics essentially as a defect or instance of alienation. However, this deficiency could be philosophically resisted and eliminated by returning to the privileged and non-technical term in the opposition. This obfuscation of the aporia of originary technicity by the metaphysical logic of a pure origin and subsequent fall into technicity can be traced in traditional philosophical accounts of time and memory.

As the title of Stiegler's series announces, and against the metaphysical history of their division, technics is to be thought as properly constitutive of time. For Stiegler, the rupture of life into technical supplementation first opens up the possibility for the articulation of time and space. However, the metrification or calculation of time is not a material taint that distorts a more original purity. The opening of the possibility of temporal articulation is predicated on the inscription supported precisely by the materiality of technical beings. Technically formed matter and temporality are inextricably composed from out of the accident of life become technical. Rather than technics being understood simply as objects within time – as they were seen in the history of metaphysics – they are properly constitutive of temporality itself. This original technical supplementarity to time was not visible in the concepts of traditional philosophy, as inaugurated by Plato, because it opposed a non-technical purity of time to a fallen realm of contingent becoming and history. The attempt to overcome the fallenness of time and return to its plenitude will be a central trope of metaphysics from Plato to Heidegger. Stiegler's understanding of originary technics can also be seen as rethinking the meaning of memory beyond its traditional philosophical determinations.

Prior to the technical mediation of purely biological forms of life, memory was only possible either as a genetic programme or in the epigenetic memories of an individual's experience. With the technical supplement, a new artificial form of memory is conjoined to life. In purely natural forms of life, the experiences and memories of an individual are lost with the death of that individual. However, the inorganic matter of the tool is able to retain the experiences of the individual beyond its demise. Stiegler describes this third form of memory which technics makes possible as 'epiphylogenetic' memory. Yet, this opening of the capacity for an artificial memory is also coincident with an equally original, and inextricable, aspect of loss and forgetting. Tragic figurations of memory were able to indicate this originary aporia. However, with the inauguration of metaphysics in Plato, the meaning of forgetting becomes a now correctable lack with respect to the more original pure presence of thought to itself. Plato distinguished between the soul's pure memory which was untainted by forgetting, and a corrupted memory which relied upon artificial technical supports.[3] This division between an unmediated presence and a fallen realm of imperfect knowledge is one of the most pervasive aspects of metaphysics. For tragic forms of thought, at the origin is not an ontological plenitude but an original condition of excess or fault. This tragic sense of fault is not enacted upon an earlier state of purity. Rather, it indicates an original difference that is both constitutive of and insoluble in the terms it makes possible. It is this tragic sense of originary fault and attending de-fault of origin (*défaut d'origine*) that Stiegler finds expressed in the fault of Epimetheus, in his reading of the Prometheus-Epimetheus myth.

In its most basic form, this myth tells the story of the Titan Prometheus being given, by Zeus, the task of distributing capacities to all the animals, including humans. However, Prometheus unwisely hands over this task to his forgetful brother Epimetheus, who, having distributed all the capacities, when it came to the humans, no longer had any capacities left to give out. This forgetting of the human then leads Prometheus to commit the crime of stealing fire – *technē* – from the gods, in order to compensate this lack of attributes for human beings. On Stiegler's reading, the forgetfulness of Epimetheus and the Promethean supplement of stolen *technē* are faults that express the originary absence or de-fault at the origin of human beings. The fault of Epimetheus is not the forgetting of an already given positivity or original nature. Technical supplementation which occurs in the wake of this first fault is not the falling away from a more original human proper. The tragic fault is originary and the appendage of stolen *technē* does not augment or distort an already given nature. In terms of this tragic myth, technics is an originary aporetic supplement that is coincident with the genesis of the human as such.

While this tragic myth describes existence as the result of a fault and thus as inherently excessive and hubristic, this is not to be understood as a consequence of any human fault or a moralistic sense of fall. Rather, in the tragic mythology the fault belongs to the gods, and the character of excess is not a redeemable infraction but one which determines existence as an inexorable hubristic condition. For Stiegler, Nietzsche is a thinker who, because of his return to this pre-

---

[3] For a wider treatment of this theme, see Stiegler (2006). The question of memory is also related to Nietzsche in that essay: 'Nietzsche, the conceiver of trace and inscription in his Second dissertation of the *Genealogy of Morals*, is the philosopher who introduces the *genealogical* and thereby *organological* question of selection' (Stiegler 2006, p. 35n17). The second essay in *On the Genealogy of Morals* will be a key reference point in Stiegler's orientation to Nietzsche vis-à-vis its themes of mnemotechnics, retention and promise (cf. Stiegler (2014, p. 89); Stiegler (2016a, pp. 94 and 97); Stiegler (2016b, p. 102); and Stiegler (2018b, p. 193)).

metaphysical tragic form of thought, reaches earlier than Plato and beyond Heidegger, who both, in many ways, remained within moralistic logics of culpability, opposition and falling.[4] And yet, this sense of return to the tragic is never understood by Stiegler in his reading of Nietzsche as a nostalgic invitation to replicate elements from a previous historical period. Rather, this sense of Nietzsche as a tragic thinker is seen as an invitation to re-read and pass through his thought as a resource for diagnosing reactive discourses and imagining ones beyond the constraints of mere resistance and adaptation. For Stiegler, Nietzsche exceeds traditional metaphysics, and his sense of nihilism is able to illuminate aspects of our contemporary situation. While Stiegler will also articulate the limits of Nietzsche's tragic thought against the wider background of his own understanding of technics, the importance of Nietzsche as a point of orientation can already be seen in his earliest works.

3 Nietzsche in *Technics and Time*

Stiegler's proximity to Nietzsche is already announced in the preface to the first volume of *Technics and Time:*

> *Ressentiment* and denegation are factors of ruin as well as irreducible tendencies, which Nietzsche and Freud placed at the heart of their reflections a century ago. They will never have been exemplified so diversely as today. The reader will know, then, that these authors, if seldom quoted in these pages, form the vanishing point of the perspectives I have attempted to open. (Stiegler 1998, p. x)

And indeed, the explicit references to Nietzsche in this initial volume are rather scarce. Firstly, there are three references to *Human, All Too Human* (Stiegler 1998, pp. 84, 103, and 112). These references are clearly to Nietzsche's understanding of the human as a question that must be posed beyond static categories and in terms of becoming and process. Secondly, there is a reference to technological constitution as always re-constitution, which is described as genealogical in Nietzsche's sense (Stiegler 1998, p. 252). There is one reference to *Thus Spoke Zarathustra* in which the question of the human is seen to be more radically posed as the question of who overcomes the human (Stiegler 1998, p. 103). This is then

---

[4] However, regarding the point of transition from a tragic era to that of metaphysics, Stiegler will disagree with Nietzsche. While Nietzsche locates this shift in the figure of Socrates, Stiegler understands Socrates as still very close to the pre-Socratic and tragic forms of thought. For Stiegler, the end of the tragic epoch and the birth of metaphysics, i.e., philosophy in its traditional sense, is to be found in Plato.

supported by reference to Deleuze's reading of Nietzsche, in his *Nietzsche and Philosophy*, where the overhuman is described as not just a logic of intensification, but rather, as a new way of thinking (Stiegler 1998, p. 103; Deleuze 1983, p. 163). There is also a Nietzsche quote used as an epigraph to the second half of the text: '"What then?" I exclaimed with curiosity. "*Who then?* you should ask!" Thus spoke Dionysus' (Stiegler 1998, p. 185). Although Stiegler does not give the source – a notebook fragment from early 1886 (KSA 12, 4 [4]) – this quote is also a key citation in Deleuze's *Nietzsche and Philosophy* (Deleuze 1983, p. 76). More than any other work on Nietzsche, Deleuze's *Nietzsche and Philosophy* is an important point of reference in Stiegler's reception of Nietzsche. In particular, this can be seen with regard to Deleuze's account of Nietzsche as a tragic thinker and the role of the question 'who?' in Nietzsche's thought.[5]

One aspect of Deleuze's reading that clearly resonates in Stiegler's engagement is his account of the transformation of philosophical questioning that arose from Nietzsche's understanding of power as a differential process. In traditional metaphysics, proper philosophical questioning had the static form of asking 'what is it?' On Deleuze's account, Nietzsche can be seen to pose the more original and dynamic question as to 'who?' (*qui?*), which is translated in Deleuze's text, with his approval, as 'which one?' Beyond any mere personalism, or prosaic subjectivity, the question of 'which one?' represents for Deleuze Nietzsche's explicit strategy of asking, in every case, which dynamic configuration of forces or tendencies is being expressed here. As he states in the Preface to *Nietzsche and Philosophy*, the question 'does not refer to an individual, to a person, but rather to an event, that is, to the forces in their various relationships in a proposition or a phenomenon, and to the genetic relationship which determines these forces (power)' (Deleuze 1983, p. xi). Directly after the quote which Stiegler uses as the epigraph, Deleuze continues: 'According to Nietzsche the question "which one?" [*Qui?*] means this: what are the forces which take hold of a given thing, what is the will that possesses it?' (Deleuze 1983, p. 76; and Deleuze 1962, p. 118). This reference to forces is not based on an ontology of physical elements, but rather, must be understood in terms of an earlier inherently differential origination of forces.

On Deleuze's reading, prior to any apparently isolated force is its differential and constitutive relatedness to other forces. This differential is what opens the

---

[5] These themes in Stiegler's reading can be traced in many texts: 'This is why Prometheus is the tragic god par excellence, as Deleuze too underlines in relation to Nietzsche' (Stiegler 2011a, p. 51). '[A]s Nietzsche said, the first question posed by the philosopher is "who?"' (Stiegler 2009b, p. 6). 'The *We* having become *One*, is without a future: a-personal, it no longer knows who it is nor that there are others; it no longer knows how to ask "*who?*"' (Stiegler 2011b, p. 102).

possibility for the individuation of forces and is not reducible to any instance of an isolated element or logic of pure opposition. For Deleuze, this differential of forces is also what is indicated by the sense of constitutive difference and necessary excess in tragic figurations of force and will. Not simply discrete elements, but rather, dynamic configurations of the differing of forces: 'And so the question "which one?" reverberates in and for all things: which forces, which will? This is the *tragic* question' (Deleuze 1983, p. 77). Moreover, on Deleuze's account, Nietzsche had an awareness of the tragic sense of fault in which guilt was not firstly a human trait, as in Christianity, but instead, was attributed to a more original Promethean excess (Deleuze 1983, pp. 21–22). In the second volume of *Technics and Time*, titled *Disorientation* (Stiegler 2009a), Stiegler can also be seen as reading Nietzsche as a resource for tracing the dissimulation of the tragic not only in metaphysics but also in Christian accounts of guilt and falling.

After charting Heidegger's attempted recovery of an authentic time from its fall into technicity, Stiegler identifies this same logic of pure origin and subsequent fall as what limits Heidegger's ability to read Nietzsche, whom Stiegler then describes as 'the most profound thinker of power, that is to say technics' (Stiegler 2009a, p. 10). The example Stiegler then points to is the tragic experience of the Greeks that Nietzsche presents in *On the Genealogy of Morals*. Stiegler quotes from the second essay of that text: 'In this way the gods served in those days to justify man to a certain extent even in his wickedness, they served as the originators of evil – in those days they took upon themselves, not the punishment but, what is nobler, the guilt' (Stiegler 2009a, 10; GM II, 23). The original French word translated here as 'guilt' is *la faute* (Stiegler 2018a, p. 325). While Stiegler connects Nietzsche's tragic sense of fault to his own reading of the Prometheus-Epimetheus myth, this can also be seen as another point of engagement with Deleuze's reading: 'The Greeks themselves interpreted and evaluated existence as excess [*démesure*]' (Deleuze 1983, p. 19; and Deleuze 1962, p. 30). Moreover, 'When the Greeks spoke of existence as criminal and "hubric" they thought that the gods had driven men mad; existence is blameworthy *but it is the gods who take upon themselves the responsibility for the fault [la faute]*' (Deleuze 1983, p. 21; and Deleuze 1962, p. 33). What is significant in both accounts is that, for Nietzsche, the fault is original and not a flaw that could be expunged. When viewed tragically, it indicates that the very possibility of thought arises from an indissoluble co-incidence of measure and excess, good and evil.

In the third volume of *Technics and Time, Cinematic Time and the Question of Malaise* (Stiegler 2011b), Stiegler's references to Nietzsche, although brief and few in number, are significant and can be seen as looking forward to the themes he takes up in his more extensive engagement with Nietzsche in the period directly following this text. Two key aspects of this engagement which are announced in this work are his re-reading of Nietzsche's sense of will, and his concept of nihilism as illuminating aspects of our contemporary period. Stiegler specifically describes our period as the non-epoch of disorientation, articulated in the second volume of *Technics and Time*. Although Nietzsche, as a herald of nihilism, has perhaps been implicit throughout this series, and was signalled at the opening with regard to *ressentiment*, in the third volume this role is more explicitly invoked through the figure of a spreading desert, to which Stiegler will often return in later works. Both of these closely related themes of willing and nihilism are aspects of Stiegler's engagement with Nietzsche that can be understood in terms of his account of Nietzsche as a tragic thinker.

When viewed tragically, and beyond the traditional categories of static identity and mere opposition, forces or tendencies are never simply given. Rather, they are always the expression of an earlier processual configuration through which they are co-constituted by their differing from other forces or tendencies. A key term articulated in the *Technics and Time* series which will be important for tracing Stiegler's dialogue with Nietzsche as a tragic thinker is 'composition'.[6] This term will appear in crucial passages, sometimes referring to Derrida's thought of *différance* (cf. Stiegler 1998, p. 141), and at other times to a tragic figuration of difference which is also more originary than the metaphysical concepts of simple identity and opposition (cf. Stiegler 1998, p. 186). In contrast to metaphysics, which defines a counter-tendency as a mere opposition to be removed, the tragic sense of process as compositional understands counter-tendencies as inherently dependent upon, and constitutive of, each other.

In general, the danger of oppositional forms of thought is that they see a counter-tendency as a defect to be removed – the fault is seen as a flaw for which guilt is to be assigned or as an epistemic defect to be philosophically transcended. This framework of pure elements within a system of oppositions leads to merely reactive forms of thinking which Nietzsche diagnosed as *ressentiment*. While tendencies are conjoined in an inherently compositional process, the attempt of one tendency to become hegemonic and eliminate its counter-tendency indicates a de-composition which is the expression of passivity and reactivity. Stiegler's understanding of opposition as more originally the de-composition of a tragic composition elaborates a key facet of Nietzsche's sense of nihilism. This differential within process as composition also opens the possibility of creating in the sense of re-composing, and inventing. This sense of re-composing

---

[6] Stiegler will later specifically attribute this important aspect of his thought to his reading of Derrida and Nietzsche: 'Reading Jacques Derrida, along with Nietzsche (the genealogist), initiated me into what I here call composition – beyond what metaphysics constitutes as a play of oppositions' (Stiegler 2011a, p. 155).

from out of the irreducible difference between tendencies will be seen in terms of what Stiegler describes as 'individuation'.[7] Accordingly, composition as a form of thinking the possibility of individuation beyond mere opposition and reactivity can be seen at the centre of some of Stiegler's most important passages.[8] This sense of composition will often be expressed in Nietzschean vocabulary as active adoption in contrast to passive adaptation. Most importantly, it will also be the site where Stiegler reads Nietzsche's sense of willing as a struggle for the possibility of exceptional and affirmative instances of individuation. Stiegler's engagement with Nietzsche's sense of the will in the third volume of *Technics and Time* is first announced in terms of the necessity to move beyond oppositional forms.

With respect to the merely reactive 'opposition between technology and subjectivity' today, Stiegler states:

> It can only be thought *beyond*, passing by Husserl and Heidegger in their difficult relationship to Kant, while coming slowly back to us through Nietzsche. In 'subjectivity,' we must come to understand ... the *will* to which we hold beyond this subjectivity.... Nietzsche is the great interrogator of power, as technical power becomes a capitalistic and technological industry, asking: what do 'we' want? This 'we' is called into question by the question itself. (Stiegler 2011b, p. 177)

The way in which Stiegler can be seen to pass through Nietzsche is via a figure of the will that is not simply a faculty of subjectivity but, rather, one that is thought from out of a difference that opens earlier than any volitional capacity of a subject. This sense of willing is understood in terms of a figuration of becoming as intrinsically duplicitous. For Nietzsche, this difference could be seen as a tragic composition which articulated becoming as an interminable struggle for transformation, adoption and invention. The question of 'who?' – which puts itself into question by the question itself – is the demand that philosophy always be, properly, a struggle for individuation.

---

[7] This term should be understood firstly in the context of Stiegler's engagement with Gilbert Simondon. However, Nietzsche will often be read in proximity to some of Simondon's key concepts: 'Now, what Nietzsche thinks under this name of becoming is a *process*, that process of *individuation* of which Simondon, in the twentieth century, takes up the torch' (Stiegler 2011a, p. 57; cf. pp. 58, 97, 163n3).

[8] For example, 'This negentropic difference, which cannot be a simple opposition, is a relationship in which the terms of the relationship itself are composed, and in which that relationship would disappear if the terms were confused. This relationship is necessarily dynamic, activating the composing – without confusion – of the *who?* and the *what?*, the probable and the improbable, the synchronic and diachronic, calculation and undetermined, perception and imagination, *I* and *We*, past and future, future and to-come' (Stiegler 2011b, p. 171).

Stiegler's elaboration of Nietzsche's understanding of nihilism as a de-composition of tendencies and an obfuscation of the capacity to create and sustain a relation to the exceptional is announced in this text by the image of a spreading desert: '"The desert grows", says Nietzsche, the philosopher of the future' (Stiegler 2011b, p. 102). And he elaborates, 'there would no longer be any possible criterion of orientation within this area of becoming other than calculation itself – other than a growing entropy – or what Nietzsche calls *the desert*' (Stiegler 2011b, p. 171). These references look forward to the way in which Stiegler will read Nietzsche as diagnosing the current period of nihilism characterised by the spreading incapacity for individuation. Stiegler will refer to this as a period of de-composition in which the ability to compose and sustain a relation to the exception is systemically dissimulated and neutralised in the now hyper-industrial production of reactivity and *ressentiment*. Stiegler's reference to Nietzsche at the outset of *Technics and Time* as opening up the vanishing point of his reflections can be confirmed by a close reading of the few explicit indications of this important, although most often implicit, contiguity with Nietzsche as a tragic thinker. This is also the best introduction to what can be seen as the next phase of Stiegler's engagement, in which the tragic modes of Nietzsche's thought will be more expressly unfolded.

4 Nietzsche as a Tragic Thinker

The growing prominence of Nietzsche in Stiegler's work in the period directly after the publication of the third volume of *Technics and Time* can be seen in a series of interviews with Élie During in 2002.[9] Although Nietzsche is mentioned in relation to many different themes, the focal point of this engagement is, once again, the interpretation of Nietzsche as a tragic thinker:

> Moderation [*mesure*] and immoderation [*démesure*] are indissociable. It therefore requires us to return to the tragic sense: something that Nietzsche had already invited us to do…. The tragic philosophers thought without opposition, this is what Nietzsche taught us: they thought the tragic situation as composition, or, to put it differently, the irreducibility of fiction. (Stiegler 2017, p. 94)

---

9 This can also be seen in other texts from this period, for example: 'We live in a herd-society, as comprehended and anticipated by Nietzsche' (Stiegler 2009b, p. 48); and 'Nietzsche saw very clearly this lost capacity to produce a difference and the tendency of societies falsely named "individualistic" to deny the exception' (Stiegler 2009b, p. 76).

This condition of irreducible fiction can be understood in light of the way that Stiegler reads Nietzsche's experience of the death of God as entailing a reinterpretation of the meaning of becoming. In classical metaphysics and Christianity, the state of becoming was simply opposed to the unchanging truth of being. Becoming was wholly subsumed in its meaning to the other-worldly truth of the Platonic form or Christian God. The object of philosophical and religious desire was maintained through the devaluation of the realm of contingent becoming in favour of the projected ultimacy of an unchanging and unmediated truth.

For Stiegler, one aspect of Nietzsche's sense of the death of God is that the opposition between truth and fiction is no longer able to structure thought or desire and is exposed, in its own terms, as increasingly unsustainable. The sense of truth that Nietzsche returns to – prior to the simple oppositions of being and becoming, essence and accident, which have structured metaphysics – is a tragic awareness of knowledge and desire as only possible within the condition of inexorable intermittency. Rather than attempting to segregate truth from fiction, the challenge becomes one of distinguishing between affirmative and merely reactive fictions. For Stiegler, this is understood with regard to caring for the conditions of individuation which requires the ability to preserve a relation to exception and indetermination. However, this exceptionality is precisely what is being dissolved in the increasingly synchronised and homogeneous orders of contemporary life. In 2004, Stiegler presents this crisis of individuation in *The Decadence of Industrial Democracies* as a crisis of belief, will and futurity as such. At the nexus of these themes, Stiegler can be read as carrying out a sustained dialogue with Nietzsche.

Clearly informing this engagement is, once again, the understanding of Nietzsche as re-opening, beyond its occultation in the history of metaphysics, the possibility of tragic figurations of thought: 'Nietzsche is a tragic thinker and his most powerful thought is that a tendency only exists as that which constitutes the *condition* of its counter-tendency, which it cannot therefore be a matter of eliminating' (Stiegler 2011a, p. 55). One of the most important ways in which Nietzsche can be seen as passing beyond the oppositional logic of metaphysics is regarding the meaning of becoming itself. On Stiegler's reading, becoming is itself to be conceived tragically as the site of an insoluble duplicity, 'becoming insofar as it is always duplicitous [*duplice*], that is, tragic' (Stiegler 2011a, p. 57; and Stiegler 2004, p. 87). Thought in terms of a difference which opens up exactly within becoming in which tendencies and counter-tendencies are mutually articulated in relation to one another, becoming is inherently the site of a continuous struggle. For Stiegler, this understanding of becoming as an intrinsic struggle has been lost in those readings of Nietzsche which have been content to simply invert the traditional opposition of becoming to being and now privilege a prosaic conception of becoming as a positivistic continuity. This reading simply hypostasises becoming and turns it into a series of mere alterations within being. The further framing of this reactive sense of becoming – as what Nietzsche called on to be affirmed – introduces a passivity that neutralises the resources of Nietzsche's thought. Perhaps the most dangerous implication of such a reading is the simple equation of this flow of becoming with the future itself. On the contrary, Nietzsche's understanding of affirmation is not acquiescence to a mundane determination of becoming but, rather, must be understood as a struggle, Stiegler will even say combat, within the duplicity of a tragically composed dimension of becoming.

For Stiegler, the form of becoming which characterises the nihilism of the current period is a 'becoming-herdish' which reactively tends towards the levelling of all instances of singularity and exception: 'Today, *ressentiment* is what is produced, and on a massive scale, by technical becoming' (Stiegler 2011a, p. 54). Stiegler will also frame this sense of becoming-reactive as the de-composition of an earlier composition of tendencies within becoming: 'nihilism tends, as becoming-herdish, to stifle its counter-tendency, that is, to *decompose* becoming' (Stiegler 2011a, p. 57). While nihilism is diagnosed in terms of decomposition, a potential response that would not be simply another opposition is intimated in the thought of re-composition. This could be seen as an active struggle carried out within becoming for the invention of exceptions. This sense of re-composition as a struggle for exception was expressed in the duplicity of the tragic Greek sense of *eris*, or good discord. The projection of singularities which are capable of supporting aspiration is made possible only as a re-composition of the inherent strife of counter-tendencies. Stiegler refers to *Thus Spoke Zarathustra* as expressing a similar awareness: 'man has need of that which is worst in him if he wishes to reach what is best' (Stiegler 2011a, p. 50). While the dissimulation of difference by the tendency to level and neutralise all exceptions can be traced in many contemporary phenomena, one of the most dangerous can be seen in the decomposition of the duplicity which opens up our relation to time, and in particular, to the future.

The tendency towards levelling and the elimination of the exception, the attempt to determine the indeterminate, is paradigmatic of the current stage of capitalism, which is '*essentially computational*, and as such tends to eliminate those singularities that resist the calculability of all values' (Stiegler 2011a, p. 37). One of the most threatening aspects of this computational model is that it structurally and in advance attempts to synchronise temporality into increasingly ordered and homogeneous forms. For Stiegler, temporality can be articulated as a meta-stable composition of what he terms the diachronic and the synchronic. The sense of diachronic here indicates that one is never wholly present but always inhabited by an earlier difference and is always inherently out of phase. The counter-tendency towards equilibrium is indicated by the synchronic. Both tendencies are co-constitutively entwined with each other and are inseparable. However, the increasing hegemony of the synchronic leads to the attempted elimination of the diachronic and to the very decomposition of time: 'decomposition principally resides in the tendency of capitalism to hyper-synchronize the temporalities of consciousnesses, to eliminate their diachronies' (Stiegler 2011a, p. 49). Perhaps the most ominous implication of this decomposition of the meta-stability that conjoins these tendencies is the loss of the ability to invent and sustain a relation to the singularity and indeterminacy of the future.

With respect to the future, the attempt to turn *trust* into an object of calculation has the effect of occulting its necessary relation to belief. Here, the importance of belief is that it is able to preserve an experience of the future as indeterminate. Trust as such is only possible within a horizon of belief that is in excess of calculation and predictive determination. The term that Stiegler uses for this projection of what passes through, yet is irreducible to, calculation and existence itself is 'consistence'. This term describes the structure of a promise which is composed with and preserves the indeterminate always to-come of the future. This indeterminacy holds open the possibility of trust beyond the nihilistic synchronisations of time, which attempt to reduce the improbable to predictive control. The attempt to calculate trust 'contributes to the liquidation of belief as the experience of the indeterminacy of the future [*avenir*], beyond becoming [*devenir*], the openness of a future irreducible to calculation, and that can only be the object of a *will*' (Stiegler 2011a, p. 16). The obfuscation of the indeterminate in the attempt to reduce the meaning of promise to prediction also results in the liquidation of belief.

In distinction to the tendency towards levelling and standardisation, Stiegler reads Nietzsche as witness to the need for an element of radical incommensurability, 'which Nietzsche affirms as the exception countering the herdish massification inducing the adaptation in which the reign of nihilism consists' (Stiegler 2011a, p. 89). One instance of this exceptionality is the ability of belief to sustain a relation to the future as indeterminate: 'If nihilism, in fact, is this destruction of all belief, that is, also, of all exception ... Nietzsche calls for another belief' (Stiegler 2011a, p. 89). Stiegler will echo Nietzsche's call for a new belief in describing what is needed for the inauguration of another epoch of individuation: 'only a *new belief* in this possiblitiy *could* make it possible' (Stiegler 2011a, p. 96). At the basis of this sense of belief, which is able to hold open a relation to the future as indeterminate, is Stiegler's understanding of the will. This figure of the will is not traditionally defined, but explicitly rethought from out of the differential at the heart of a processual composition. It is perhaps when the figures of belief and willing are thought as forms of relation to time, and most importantly to the possible opening of a future as indeterminate, that Stiegler's passage through Nietzsche in this period is most pronounced.

Throughout *The Decadence of Industrial Democracies*, Stiegler describes the possibility of articulating a new epoch beyond our current non-epoch (which he later terms the absence of epoch) in relation to willing, 'our capacity to will a new epoch of the individuation process – that is, to *invent* it' (Stiegler 2011a, p. 30). This is also described as one 'that affirms a new *will* for the future' (Stiegler 2011a, p. 12). Rather than a mere 'avatar of the metaphysics of representation' (Stiegler 2011a, p. 96), Stiegler rethinks willing as the affirmation of the struggle within becoming and what he describes in terms of process and individuation: 'And the will to believe, which belief presupposes, does not secrete a psychic *subject* but a *process* of psycho-social individuation' (Stiegler 2011a, p. 96). Understood from this perspective, the will can be seen as a means of struggle against the *ressentiment* which prevents a thinking of the composition of tendencies. This sense of willing as a resource for countering decomposition beyond mere reaction is articulated as a question at the heart of Nietzsche's experience of nihilism:

> The Nietzschean question of nihilism, however, is more profoundly that of will, and of thinking will *after* the liquidation of the onto-theologico-political – of a will to power of which the operational concept is here, for us, individuation as process. Because, according to my proposed reading of the Nietzschean question of nihilism, this question of will, which is not at all outmoded, is that which the de-composition of tendencies, that is, the ruin of individuation, tends to liquidate, at the precise point where it is a matter of *engaging in combat*, of opposing this hegemony. (Stiegler 2011a, p. 96)

This question of will and belief, which is usually eliminated in nihilistic decompositions, is understood as articulating a compositional site in which struggle as transformation and invention could be opened up for the cultivation and projection of singularities. This projection could be seen as preserving a dimension of indeterminacy within its composition of a futurity beyond reduction to prediction, calculation and mere becoming.

This return to the question of will and belief, in passing through these themes in Nietzsche, is of course not an invitation simply to repeat any specific instance of these elements in his work. Rather, revisiting these questions can be seen to offer a resource for thinking a sense of struggle against hegemony that would not be a simple protraction of nihilistic forms of opposition. The figure of struggle in Nietzsche's sense of will is one in which the struggle is carried out precisely within becoming, that is, within the meta-stable compositions of process and individuation. The tragic dimension of excess inhabiting these articulations of measure is not a difference that could ever be eliminated. Rather, this excess indicates an irreducible differential which also opens up the possibility of singular re-compositions. The themes of spreading nihilism and the challenge of composing a sense of futurity which could preserve thought and desire are at the centre of Stiegler's work on the Anthropocene. These themes are elaborated in relation to what can also be seen as the later phase of Stiegler's dialogue with Nietzsche.

5 Reading Nietzsche in the Anthropocene

A key focus of Stiegler's later works is his interpretation of the Anthropocene and the question of thinking beyond this apparently terminal culmination of nihilism. This crucial theme was announced in a lecture presented in 2014, titled "The Anthropocene and Neganthropology" (Stiegler 2018b, pp. 34–50). An initial figuration of the question of the Anthropocene and the futurity which could be thought as opening up beyond it is presented by Stiegler in explicitly Nietzschean terms: 'If we are to think the Anthropocene as giving rise to the devaluation of all values, then we must think it with Nietzsche: the vital task for all noetic knowledge in the Anthropocene is the transvaluation of all values.... We must think the transvaluation of becoming into future by reading Nietzsche' (Stiegler 2018b, p. 38).[10] The task of thinking the devaluation of all values in the Anthropocene with Nietzsche is not simply an invitation to translate this situation back into specific concepts taken from Nietzsche's work, but rather, to think with and beyond Nietzsche. Unquestionably, one aspect of contemporary nihilism that Nietzsche is able to diagnose is the reactivity at the basis of the hegemonic reduction of all value to computation. While the extent of contemporary algorithmic computation is nothing that Nietzsche could have imagined, the necessity of composing a response beyond mere opposition as transvaluation remains a point of departure for re-reading Nietzsche outside the scope of his original formulations.

Although Nietzsche's concept of transvaluation is employed as an initial description of what is demanded by the sense of nihilism unfolding in the Anthropocene, this is not simply taken over by Stiegler but, instead, must be seen as a point of re-elaboration. The challenge that Stiegler enunciates regarding this in-

---

[10] This orientation can also be seen in other texts from this period: 'It is with Nietzsche that, after the Anthropocene event, we must think the advent of the Neganthropocene, and it must be thought as the transvaluation of becoming into future' (Stiegler 2016b, p. 10).

itial call for transvaluation is the task of transvaluing Nietzsche's sense of transvaluation:

> To think care-fully [*panser*] in the Anthropocene is to *evaluate and transvaluate disruption* as the *final extremity* of nihilism – an evaluation carried out from the perspective of a *transvaluation of that transvaluation* of all values that Nietzsche affirmed as the urgent need to leap (*Sprung*) beyond the 'last man'. And it is to do so beyond the nihilism that has led to the global spread of *ressentiment* in the hegemony of levelling and the calculation of averages. (Stiegler 2018b, p. 209)

This doubling of transvaluation is of course not a mere intensification of Nietzsche's original sense but the expression of the need to pass through and beyond Nietzsche while in dialogue with him, 'a transvaluation of what Nietzsche himself called transvaluation' (Stiegler 2018b, p. 225). One important aspect of Stiegler's formulation is his understanding of Nietzsche's sense of transvaluation as also the question of a new belief: 'I take extremely seriously the Nietzschean statement that, describing capitalism as nihilism ... that what is required beyond nihilism, and as the transvaluation of all values, is a new belief' (Stiegler 2018b, p. 67). This question of a new belief is returned to in Stiegler's own descriptions of the need for transvaluation in contrast to Heidegger: 'It is not a new god who alone could still save us ... but the new belief required for the transvaluation of all values, which presupposes that we "transvalue" Nietzsche himself' (Stiegler 2019, p. 304). What Stiegler intends by this sense of belief is not the awaiting of a future which is simply distanced from actuality by a chronological duration. What is at issue here is the structure of belief as such which, as a form of promise, both requires and preserves an element of indeterminacy.

The theme of promise can be seen as a point of re-reading in which Nietzsche's experience of nihilism and its possible implications for politics are brought together. With reference to algorithmic governmentality and its 'annihilation of political promise and of politics insofar as it promises', Stiegler continues: 'Here more than anywhere we must investigate Nietzsche's thinking of nihilism, which is also and fundamentally a thinking of the promise' (Stiegler 2016b, p. 102; cf. Stiegler 2013, p. 133). The decomposition of time and the obfuscation of capacities for composition are instances of nihilism which are not restricted to the sphere of economics. These forms of reactivity can also be seen at the centre of the question of politics today. While it is beyond the scope of this chapter to develop this, many of Stiegler's invitations to re-read Nietzsche can be seen to trace the implications of the inability of current decompositions of time to preserve the indeterminancy in relation to which politics could articulate promise. In this sense, one could speak of Stiegler's engagement as also opening the question of Nietzsche and a politics of difference. However, this initial proximity is passed through from the perspective of a difference which, according to Stiegler, remained unthought in Nietzsche.

Stiegler reads Nietzsche as a witness to the need for transvaluation in the service of preserving the possibility of exception, especially in relation to the future. However, he passes beyond this initial sense of transvaluation via the concept of negative entropy or negentropy. This concept is central to Stiegler's own thought and also a key point of reference in tracing his understanding of the limits of Nietzsche's witnessing. Stiegler stresses that the question of nihilism in relation to entropy and negentropy was not visible to Nietzsche in his historical period.[11] For Stiegler, the completed nihilism of the Anthropocene in which all values are computationally levelled is a form of becoming which must be interpreted as entropic. This systematic unsustainable production of entropy, which Stiegler also describes as the Entropocene, is a becoming without future. The new revaluation criteria from which to think a transformation of becoming into future is the concept of negentropy. In general, this term indicates the ability of life to differ and defer the degenerative process of entropic decay over time. On this basis, Stiegler will then think the possibility of the advent of what he terms the Neganthropocene and the Neganthropos. While there are points of resonance with Nietzsche in terms of nihilism as decomposition and the need for a new belief, the thought of the Neganthropocene opens up beyond any strictly Nietzschean sense of overcoming or leap and, instead, is composed via the concept of negentropy as a promise of what is always to come.

In many ways, Stiegler's dialogue with Nietzschean themes in his later works continues to build upon his earlier engagements. From the beginning, Stiegler can be seen as a careful reader of Nietzsche who thinks with him in terms of *ressentiment*, the tragic and the struggle for exception beyond the spreading desert of nihilism. His latter phase of thinking the anthropic devaluation of values with Nietzsche articulates the necessity of a criterion that would open up beyond the reduction of value to computation. This question of a beyond, when posed in terms of the need for a new belief which could preserve the experience of the future as indeterminate, can be seen as a point of re-elaboration where Stiegler thinks with Nietzsche while also passing beyond him. Stiegler's passage through Nietzsche convincingly re-reads him as a witness to nihilism. It also compellingly

---

11 'Nietzsche was able to think nihilism only within the framework of a physics within which the concept of negative entropy was yet to be incorporated. This is why we must today think Nietzsche *beyond* Nietzsche' (Stiegler 2019, p. 342n18). A similar assessment is given in Stiegler's essay on Nietzsche, "La grande bifurcation vers le *néguanthropos*", in which Nietzsche is described as a thinker of *hubris*; however, two crucial concepts which remained unthought in his work are exosomatisation and entropy (cf. Stiegler 2016a, p. 100).

transforms these themes against the background of Stiegler's own thought and the current absence of epoch. In this way, Stiegler returns to Nietzsche as a resource for thinking in a time that Nietzsche clearly foretold, but also in a future that he could never have predicted.

Bibliography

Abbinnett, Ross (2018): *The Thought of Bernard Stiegler: Capitalism, Technology and the Politics of Spirit.* London: Routledge.
Deleuze, Gilles (1962): *Nietzsche et la philosophie.* Paris: Presses Universitaires de France.
Deleuze, Gilles (1983): *Nietzsche and Philosophy.* Translated by Hugh Tomlinson. New York: Columbia University Press.
Howells, Christina, and Gerald Moore (Eds.) (2013): *Stiegler and Technics.* Edinburgh: Edinburgh University Press.
Nietzsche, Friedrich (1989): *On the Genealogy of Morals.* Edited by Walter Kaufmann and translated by Walter Kaufmann and R. J. Hollingdale. New York: Vintage Books.
Stiegler, Bernard (1998): *Technics and Time, 1: The Fault of Epimetheus.* Translated by Richard Beardsworth and George Collins. Stanford: Stanford University Press.
Stiegler, Bernard (2004): *Mécréance et discrédit 1. La décadence des démocraties industrielles.* Paris: Galilée.
Stiegler, Bernard (2006): "Anamnēsis and Hypomnēsis: The Memories of Desire". In: Arthur Bradley and Louis Armand (Eds.): *Technicity*, pp. 15–41. Translated by François-Xavier Gleyzon. Prague: Litteraria Pragensia.
Stiegler, Bernard (2009a): *Technics and Time, 2: Disorientation.* Translated by Stephen Barker. Stanford: Stanford University Press.
Stiegler, Bernard (2009b): *Acting Out.* Translated by David Barison, Daniel Ross and Patrick Croga. Stanford: Stanford University Press.
Stiegler, Bernard (2011a): *The Decadence of Industrial Democracies.* Translated by Daniel Ross and Suzanne Arnold. Cambridge: Polity.
Stiegler, Bernard (2011b): *Technics and Time, 3: Cinematic Time and the Question of Malaise.* Translated by Stephen Barker. Stanford: Stanford University Press.
Stiegler, Bernard (2013): *What Makes Life Worth Living: On Pharmacology.* Translated by Daniel Ross. Cambridge: Polity.
Stiegler, Bernard (2014): *Symbolic Misery, 1: The Hyper-industrial Epoch.* Translated by Barnaby Norman. Cambridge: Polity.
Stiegler, Bernard (2016a): "La grande bifurcation vers le *néguanthropos:* Exceptions et sélections dans la noodiversité". In: Dorian Astor and Alain Jugnon (Eds.): *Pourquoi nous sommes nietzschéens*, pp. 87–108. Brussels: Les Impressions Nouvelles.
Stiegler, Bernard (2016b): *Automatic Society, 1: The Future of Work.* Translated by Daniel Ross. Cambridge: Polity.
Stiegler, Bernard (2017): *Philosophising by Accident: Interviews with Élie During.* Edited and translated by Benoît Dillet. Edinburgh: Edinburgh University Press.
Stiegler, Bernard (2018a): *La technique et le temps, 1. La Faute d'Épiméthée – 2. La Désorientation – 3. Le Temps du cinéma et la question du mal-être.* Paris: Fayard.

Stiegler, Bernard (2018b): *The Neganthropocene*. Edited and translated by Daniel Ross. London: Open Humanities Press.
Stiegler, Bernard (2019): *The Age of Disruption: Technology and Madness in Computational Capitalism*. Translated by Daniel Ross. Cambridge: Polity.
Woodward, Ashley (2019): "Nihilism, Neonihilism, Hypernihilism: 'Nietzsche aujourd'hui' Today?" In: *Nietzsche-Studien* 48. No. 1, pp. 244–264.

Part 2 **Politics and Identity**

Glen Baier
Nietzsche's Diagnosis of Socrates in *The Birth of Tragedy:* Voyeurism and the Denigration of Difference

Abstract: This chapter contends that Nietzsche's commitment to the politics of difference commences with *The Birth of Tragedy*. At the core of that work is an assessment of Socrates which highlights his eagerness to denigrate difference. The chapter links this characterisation of Socrates to Nietzsche's analysis of the model of "vision" which dominates the Socratic perspective: Socrates is a voyeur seeking fulfilment of a personal erotic fantasy. As voyeur, Socrates demands to see all, and to "correct being". The chapter analyses how Nietzsche explains this fantasy as symptomatic of Socrates' deep-seated unwillingness to face the actuality of ontological diversity and thus denigrates difference.

1 Introduction

This chapter is informed by the presupposition that Nietzsche's commitment to the politics of difference commences with *The Birth of Tragedy*. At the core of that work is an assessment of Socrates which highlights his eagerness to demean difference. In particular, Nietzsche frames Socrates' distrust of tragic wisdom as a consequence of a deep-seated dread of ontological diversity. As I make evident, Nietzsche proposes that Socrates is suspicious of the world as it stands because being as a whole is 'so varied and multifarious' (BT 14). Socrates' response to this overwhelming heterogeneity is to act as if 'what exists is inwardly wrong and objectionable' and to assume that he personally 'was obliged to correct existence' (BT 13). For Nietzsche, Socrates sets the stage for a narrowing of the intellectual and political future of Europe, one in which sameness is favoured at the expense of difference. Socrates is accused of prescribing a stifling worldview, which limits diversity and privileges uniformity. As the prototype of what Nietzsche calls 'theoretical man', Socrates inspires a far-reaching devotion to homogeneity, in the form of the 'universality' of 'a common network of thought' which has 'stretched over the whole globe' (BT 15). As a result, any departure from what is instantiated in the "ideal" of theoretical man is denigrated because 'every other form of existence has to fight its way up alongside it, as something permitted but not intended' (BT 18). In other words, the world may be such that it contains difference, and we may not be able to eliminate difference, but we should in no way rest content with this circumstance. Socrates thus is ill-disposed to heterogeneity, and therefore he seeks to impose restrictions on being.

Historically speaking, Nietzsche thinks that Socrates serves as 'the forerunner of a completely different culture, art and morality' because of the manner in which he 'condemns existing art and existing ethics in equal measure' (BT 13). The ascendency of Socrates, as an inspirational figure, is coextensive with the victory of science in a manner consistent with 'its purpose, which is to make existence appear comprehensible and thus justified' (BT 15). Science, so understood, seeks to enshrine its explanatory prowess through the provision of 'reasons and knowledge' (BT 15). However, for Nietzsche, the influence Socrates wields is not itself rooted in the methods of science. Here Nietzsche questions the role Plato assigns Socrates as 'the dialectical hero' called on to 'defend his actions with reasons and counter-reasons' (BT 14). For Nietzsche, the better way to conceive of Socrates is as peculiar and unique, an unjustifiable perturbance upsetting the existing order of things. The Socratic project thus commences without recourse to 'reasons and knowledge' (BT 15), and Socrates' arrival on the cultural scene is not a rational response to some recognisable demand. It is, rather, a contingent occurrence, a function of Socrates himself. For Nietzsche, Socrates' nature makes him stand apart from the conventions and expectations of his communal circumstance.[1] In this way, Socrates counts as someone who is decidedly different, yet who, in the end, implores us to strive to defeat difference. Such a portrayal of Socrates is conspicuously ironic. He is depicted as a proponent of a sameness that is belied by his very being.

In terms of the politics of difference, Nietzsche's analysis of Socrates and his legacy alerts us to the real costs incurred by the rejection of difference. Socrates invites us to view difference as a problem, as something that needs to be overcome. To adopt Socrates' position is to agree that difference is eliminable and should be treated as such. The tradition which Nietzsche associates with the ascendency of theoretical man is, in part, a political tradition, one which strives actively to negate human difference and to extol narrow uniformity as a goal. Such uniformity limits our possibilities and restricts us to a life of sameness. In *The Birth of Tragedy*, Nietzsche, in effect, initiates a reversal of the Socratic mandate. He shows us that Socrates is the problem and that we must, in fact,

---

[1] In *Twilight of the Idols*, Nietzsche ascribes to Socrates an awareness of his idiosyncratic nature. However, in that context, Nietzsche contends that Socrates also came to realise that he was not the only one suffering from such deficiencies, and he began to view his fellow citizens as having the same nature: 'But Socrates suspected even more. He looked *behind* his noble Athenians; he understood that *his* case, his idiosyncrasy of a case was not an exception any more' (TI Socrates, 9).

overcome him by embracing difference. Moreover, the welcoming of difference in this fashion may appear daunting, but it requires little more than an acceptance of the world as heterogeneous and varied. My intent is to bring to the fore Nietzsche's suspicions regarding Socrates to show how Nietzsche gives us the starting point for a genuine politics of difference.

In what follows, I explore Nietzsche's characterisation of the distinctiveness of Socrates, as formulated in *The Birth of Tragedy*, in order to establish that he introduces Socrates in terms most befitting someone suffering from a psychosexual disorder. In section two, I liken Socrates to a voyeur seeking fulfilment of an erotic fantasy. I conclude that Socrates is comparable to a voyeur because he calls for being to show itself fully and completely; it is a case of Socrates commanding that the world lay itself bare. In setting up this position, I address Nietzsche's labelling of the Socratic 'gaze' as 'probing' (BT 13). This designation, I assert, marks Socrates as voyeuristic to the extent that he wishes to see that which is normally and properly concealed. I then comment on how Socrates is said to possess a 'great Cyclopean eye' (BT 14). This description indicates that Socrates' gaze is gauged in terms of its intensity, invasiveness and singularity. As voyeur, Socrates demands to see all, as closely and directly as possible. To this end, the world must reveal its nature without reservation, and this disclosure serves as a precondition for the world's correction. The world is required to denude itself so as to demonstrate that it is in need of regulation. In other words, the world must consent to being intrusively inspected so as to be redeemed through the intervention of Socrates, who only finds value in things which comply with his strict expectations.

In section three, I situate Nietzsche's remarks regarding Socrates from *The Birth of Tragedy* in relation to themes in some of his other works. My intent is to demonstrate that the judgement made about Socrates' voyeuristic disposition resonates in these texts and is not merely confined to Nietzsche's first major work. It will become evident as this chapter unfolds that Nietzsche thinks that there is something indecent at the heart of Socrates' desire, in that insisting to see everything is inappropriate and in poor taste. On this level, *The Birth of Tragedy* introduces us to a methodological prescript which re-emerges in Nietzsche's later work. In the Preface to the second edition of *The Gay Science*, Nietzsche refers to the example of 'those Egyptian youths who make temples unsafe at night, embrace statues, and want by all means to unveil, uncover, and put into bright light whatever is kept concealed for good reasons' (GS Preface, 4).[2] He goes on to

---

2 This example appears to be a reference to 'the temple in the Egyptian city of Sais', where

say: 'Today we consider it a matter of decency not to wish to see everything naked, to be present everywhere, to understand and "know" everything' (GS Preface, 4). In this regard, it is possible to assert that Nietzsche's preoccupation with Socratic voyeurism is not a passing concern. The charting of Socrates' tendencies in *The Birth of Tragedy* sets the stage for a Nietzschean critique of philosophy and science which resurfaces in later works.

If my interpretation of *The Birth of Tragedy* succeeds, then it is safe to say that Nietzsche is classifying Socrates as a kind of pervert.[3] This outcome is not startling, given that subsequently in his writings, Nietzsche declares that 'Socrates is a moment of the *deepest perversity* in the history of men' (LNB, 14 [111], 255). By itself, this claim merely entails that Socrates qualifies as unusual because his slavish commitment to reason comes at the expense of all other drives or instincts. He is a 'decadent',[4] and he should strike us as unnatural, as monstrous,[5] because he is the full embodiment of an abnormal extreme. Decadence of this sort, as per its definition in *Twilight of the Idols*, results in a 'negative attitude toward life' because it is a consequence of physiological and psychological decline (TI Socrates, 2). In this way, both Socrates and Plato are 'symptoms of decay' (TI Socrates, 2), and in the case of Socrates, his decadence is 'exaggerated' due to 'the admitted chaos and anarchy of his instincts' and 'the hypertrophy of logic ... as in his emblematic rachitic spite' (TI Socrates, 4). So, Socrates' decadence results from the disarray of his instincts and his logical fervour. Moreover, Socrates' ability to sway his audience reflects the spread of decadence in

---

'there was a veiled statue of the goddess Isis with the inscription "I am everything that is, that was, and that will be and no mortal <ever> raised my veil"' (GS Preface, 4n5).

[3] Throughout this chapter it will be clear that I shy away from Walter Kaufmann's (1948) appraisal of the portrait of Socrates in *The Birth of Tragedy*. While it may be true that Nietzsche does not detest Socrates, he is not overly enamoured with him either. So, Kaufmann's assertion that 'Socrates became little less than an idol' for Nietzsche appears to miss the mark (Kaufmann 1948, p. 474).

[4] In this context, we can deal with the complex matter of Nietzsche's conception of 'decadence' quite swiftly. Decadence is associated with a decline in physiological well-being that is sustained by psychological disorders. In *Nietzsche Contra Wagner*, decadence is equated with '*hatred* of life or *superabundance* of life', resulting in the 'will to the end' of life as a kind of nihilistic imperative (NCW Antipodes, 272). For more on this topic, see Daw-Nay Evans, who argues that Socrates, according to Nietzsche, counts as a decadent because he 'is misled by a single instinctual drive into psychological, moral and physiological decline through the worship of ideas that are nihilistic and inimical to life' (Evans 2010, p. 342).

[5] Nietzsche raises the problem of Socrates' 'monstrousness' in *Twilight of the Idols*, where he asks about the 'criminality' of Socrates: 'Anthropologists specializing in crime tell us the typical criminal is ugly: *monstrum in fronte, monstrum in animo* [monster in face, monster in soul]' (TI Socrates, 3).

his culture: 'Socrates understood that the world *needed* him, – his method, his cure, his personal strategy for self-preservation…. Everywhere, instincts were in anarchy' (TI Socrates, 9). Even though Nietzsche's later writings pay more attention to this decadence than his earlier ones, in the end, he does not stray far from the prognosis laid out in *The Birth of Tragedy*. There he notes how Socrates conveniently benefitted from a situation in which the 'Marathonian toughness of the body and soul was falling victim increasingly to a dubious enlightenment, and that physical and spiritual energies were atrophying progressively' (BT 13). Socrates, then, can be labelled a 'seducer' because of his knack for exploiting the decadence of his contemporaries (BT 13). His perversity thrives because he exists in a milieu which is receptive to what he has to offer.

I do not wish to rest content with the standard reading of Nietzsche, where Socrates' perversity is viewed as a consequence of his decadence alone. I seek to add the idea that Socrates is perverse in a more ordinary sense in that his orientation towards the world is reminiscent of those plagued by intense sexual desire. It is this aspect of Socrates that Nietzsche hints at by calling him a 'true eroticist' (BT 13),[6] an indirect reference to Plato's *Symposium* where Socrates is described as such. However, Nietzsche does not fully welcome the Platonic validation of Socrates, which is couched in 'divine naïveté and certainty' (BT 13). Nietzsche counters Plato by highlighting 'the enormous drive-wheel of logical Socratism behind Socrates' (BT 13), implying that Socrates is governed by forces which may not be immediately discernible. Hence, in order to see his actual state, 'one must look through Socrates as if through a shadow' (BT 13). In terms of my position, the lesson to heed here is that even though Socrates claims his mandate is entirely philosophical that should not obscure its actual source, namely, the unusual and distorted urge motivating him. Hence, the more we explore Nietzsche's commentary on Socrates in *The Birth of Tragedy*, the more we will see how consistent his description of Socrates is with that of a sexual pervert. Moreover, I contend that Nietzsche knowingly presents Socrates as a pervert of this sort for the sake of highlighting the particularity and strangeness of his desire. Nietzsche's investigation of Socrates is meant to demonstrate that Socrates' scorn for the world is an expression of an erotic idiosyncrasy. Again, this treats the opponent of difference in a manner which, ironically, brings his difference to the foreground.

---

6 In *Twilight of the Idols*, Nietzsche accepts this evaluation: 'Socrates was a great erotic too!' (TI Socrates, 8). Nietzsche holds that this is a factor to keep in mind when one tries 'to explain the fact that he fascinated' those around him (TI Socrates, 7).

2 Socrates as Voyeur

My overall contention is that the problem of Socrates is best viewed as a matter of erotic dysfunction. To sustain the view that Socrates is a pervert in a sexual sense, I turn to the concluding stages of *The Birth of Tragedy*, where Nietzsche spells out the preconditions for the return of "tragic culture", a culture capable of overcoming the limits legislated by theoretical man. In the modern circumstance, as noted, theoretical man is the 'highest ideal', and is seen as 'equipped with highest powers of understanding and working in the service of science' (BT 18). On the surface, this description is somewhat benign. It just establishes the conditions under which theoretical man operates. However, Nietzsche quickly transitions into an emotionally charged evaluation of the motives shaping modern culture. On the very same page, he speaks of 'the Socratic lust for knowledge' (BT 18). The stage for this dramatic designation is set earlier in the text. There we were informed that Socrates is 'the mystagogue of science' (BT 15). Such science, 'with Socrates at the head of it', is declared to be 'insatiable' (BT 16). Subsequently, we are told that the German attitude in the nineteenth century is dominated by 'the same excessive lust for knowledge' which proved to be the undoing of Greek culture (BT 23). While it is clear that these comments underscore Nietzsche's concern with Socrates' intellectual "perversity", in the guise of his overactive love of reason, they also suggest something about Socrates' desire. He is someone who has made the search for knowledge into more than an ordinary quest for truth. Nietzsche's vocabulary when describing Socrates makes him out to be engaged in an erotic pursuit and, in the process, Nietzsche highlights how we should view him as unseemly and treacherous.[7]

Nietzsche adeptly contrasts Socrates' worrying form of desire with one deemed more worthwhile. In addressing the insights made available through tragic wisdom, Nietzsche charts the means by which we can come to grasp the nature of the world itself. On this level, the 'innermost core of things' is made immanent through Dionysiac art:

> In Dionysiac art and its tragic symbolism this self-same nature speaks to us in its true, undisguised voice: 'Be as I am! – the primal mother, eternally creative beneath the surface of incessantly changing appearances, eternally forcing life into existence, forever satisfying myself with these changing appearances!' (BT 16)

---

[7] In a notebook entry from the same time period as *The Birth of Tragedy*, Nietzsche draws a direct connection between the 'drive for knowledge' and unseemly sexual impulses. He writes: 'The drive for knowledge without choice is on a par with the indiscriminate sexual drive – a sign of *coarseness!*' (ENB, 19 [11], 95).

This awareness is facilitated by the dissolution of individual identity which allows us to become one with the world as a totality. Such an experience is only temporary and fleeting: 'For brief moments we are truly the primordial being itself' (BT 17). We may have misgivings concerning the suitability of Nietzsche's metaphysical assertions in this context,[8] but we can still appreciate what he is saying about desire. He states, in reference to the primordial being, that 'we feel its unbounded greed and lust for being' (BT 17). It is important to compare this issue with the mentality of Socrates. In Socrates, greed and lust are for knowledge, and they are reduced to the interests of a specific individual. In regard to the primordial being, its greed and lust are for existence itself. Moreover, it is not a case of what a given individual desires. In fact, it is the opposite. The desires of the primordial being are felt in 'the uncountable excess of forms of existence' (BT 17). In other words, the primordial being wants to create; it wants to bring an indefinite number of diverse beings into existence. This point is reiterated when Nietzsche concludes that tragic art brings human beings together 'as the *one* living being, with whose procreative lust we have become one' (BT 17). The allusion to the world as the "primal mother" thus carries forward into the description of the primordial being. With this characterisation, there is the opening for a more, in the literal sense, productive model of desire. So, whereas the aim of Socrates' desire is the supposed validation of the world through its *correction*, the desire associated with the primal mother is more organic and authentic. It entails an acceptance of the world as evident in its countless changing manifestations.

As I have indicated, Socrates' attitude towards the world is one of metaphysical hostility. Socratism, which comes to fruition in the dispositions of theoretical man, is marked by a stunning disregard for the world as it actually is. It enters the world with 'a look of disrespect and superiority' and, as noted earlier, it assumes that 'what exists is inwardly wrong and objectionable' (BT 13), and therefore in need of correction. And it is in this context where Nietzsche indicates that Socrates' dissatisfaction with existence is manifest as a dread of difference. Socrates is unable to consider the diversity conspicuous in the world as worthy of

---

8 Nietzsche himself expresses misgivings regarding the metaphysical assumptions informing *The Birth of Tragedy*. In his "Attempt at Self-Criticism", added to the text in 1886, he admits to relying too heavily on a naïve conception of 'metaphysical solace' (ASC 7), which he thinks hamstrings the book. A little later in his re-evaluation, he points to his later 'teachings', such as those contained in *Thus Spoke Zarathustra*, which extol the curative power of laughter, and voices a hope that such laughter will put an end to metaphysics: 'Perhaps then, as men who laugh, you will some day send all attempts at metaphysical solace to Hell – with metaphysics the first to go!' (ASC 7).

his approval. He is 'debarred from ever looking into the abysses of the Dionysiac with pleasure' (BT 14). In respect to the world as revealed by tragedy, Socrates, as noted before, only saw 'the whole as so varied and multifarious' such 'that it was bound to be repugnant to a reflective disposition' (BT 14). Hence Socrates' distrust of tragedy is a symptom of his disregard for the world as it is and with the difference it engenders.

Now we can move on to address the erotic nature of Socrates' gaze. Nietzsche makes it evident how Socrates brings his gaze to bear on the world. He insists that the world show itself. His intent is for the world to match his ideal and thus it must *reveal* itself fully. If we take this to be a mode of voyeurism, it is the sort that calls for the one *watched* to expose themselves. They must show themselves totally and without resistance in order for the voyeur to exercise control over them. In this way, Socrates does not look away from the world, but instead "gazes" into it to exact what he wants. For Nietzsche, Socrates' probing gaze is taken to be a function of his 'one great Cyclopean eye' (BT 14).[9] It is this eye in which 'the lovely madness of artistic enthusiasm never glowed' (BT 14). The question arises as to what having a Cyclopean eye entails in terms of Socrates' orientation to being. Obviously, it implies that there is a singularity to Socrates' vision. He only "looks" with one thing, and that is his eye as directed by his desire. In addition, the exaggerated nature of his eye makes it invasive in that it constantly probes the world. He wants to see the entirety of being up close so that he can detect its flaws and orchestrate its redemption; and there seems to be an intensity in this mode of sight, in that it is unrelenting and continuous. The eye of Socrates is very much an extension of his temperament, that of the man who felt 'obliged to correct existence' so as to meet the conditions set by his desire.

We can tie this probing gaze of the sexual voyeur to the mode of vision most typical of theoretical man. As Peter Warnek notes, 'the peculiar Cyclopian illumination enacted by Socrates continues to operate today in the ideal of science' (Warnek 2014, p. 233). So, theoretical man, as the practitioner of science, relies on a gaze which seeks full disclosure. Nietzsche, in relation to this point, once more employs a contrast with the activities of tragic artists. In terms of the pur-

---

[9] Here we can gain assistance from Nietzsche's subsequent utilisation of a similar designation in *Thus Spoke Zarathustra*. There he refers to those he deems 'inverse cripples', and, as a classification, it pertains to those 'human beings who were missing everything except the one thing they have too much of – human beings who were nothing more than one big eye, or one big maw or one big belly or some other big thing' (Z II, Redemption, 109). Such a designation fits with the characterisation of Socrates in *The Birth of Tragedy*, both in respect to his nature being inverted and his Cyclopean eye being his dominant trait.

suit of truth, artists are willing to leave some things hidden. They do not wish to see everything. In this manner, they follow the edicts of Apollo. Apollo represents 'measure' (BT 4), such that when it comes to knowledge, there is a fundamental limit. Even the search for knowledge of oneself has to be tempered, as is indicated by 'the demands: "Know Thyself" and "Not too Much!"' (BT 4). Through the metaphor of the veil, Nietzsche expands on this theme: 'Whenever truth is unveiled, the ecstatic eyes of the artist remain fixed on what still remains veiled, even after the unveiling' (BT 15). Theoretical man, by contrast, differs because he 'enjoys and satisfies himself with the discarded veil, and his desire finds its highest goal in a process of unveiling' (BT 15).[10] As such, there is no measure in the pursuits of theoretical man, and for this reason he is unable to rest content with the idea of anything remaining hidden. Everything must be revealed.

It may seem as if I am reading too much into this idea of the Cyclopean eye. However, I think my position is supported by the contrast between Socrates' gaze and that of the artist who properly understands tragedy. The description given by Nietzsche of Socrates' gaze stands in firm opposition to that of the 'tragic poet', which is said to be 'unmoved' and 'fearless' (BT 18). Moreover, the poet's gaze has definitive intentional content, namely, 'the total image of the world' (BT 18). Those who would be the vehicles of tragic insight, the artists capable of conveying such wisdom, are comparable to the poet who views the world with a 'contemplative eye' (BT 8). Poetic insight, when utilised in the composition of drama, arises from the writer being able to 'gaze' into the 'innermost essence' of the characters in their plays (BT 8). In the end, the true master of this art form, relying on language with Apolline 'definiteness and clarity' (BT 9), makes us feel as if we are 'looking straight into the innermost ground of its being' (BT 9). Thus, the artist is confronting, and reckoning with, the actuality of existence, instead of inspecting and regulating it.

A similar distinction is to be noted when it comes to the role of the audience in tragic drama. Its gaze is demarcated in a fashion that sets it apart from the Socratic. We have seen how Socrates' gaze is associated with lust and greed. It seeks satisfaction through the mastery of being and takes "unveiling" to be a precondition for the philosophical salvation of the world. In terms of the properly responsive audience, they take in the spectacle of the drama with a 'sated gaze' (BT 8), a gaze which does not seek or need more than what has been given to it. In addition, the experience of oneness arising from the encounter

---

10 This passage hearkens back to the beginning of this chapter, in that we find, once again, that Nietzsche deploys the metaphor of a veil.

with the Dionysiac makes the audience part of the tragic chorus itself. In this condition, the audience does not have to have everything disclosed. In fact, it is Euripides' mistake to accept the 'rationalist method' of 'aesthetic Socratism' (BT 12) and ensure that the unfolding of the drama and its resolution is stipulated in advance to the audience. There is to be nothing left mysterious or hidden from the spectator. Euripides, Nietzsche argues, wrongly assumes that the 'greatest obstacle' standing in the way of the audience's appreciation of a tragic drama is 'some missing link, some gap in the texture of the story preceding the action' (BT 12) and his remedy for this shortcoming is the 'prologue' (BT 12). The 'prologue' consists of a single person on stage', there to 'explain at the beginning of the play who he is, what precedes the action, what has happened so far, indeed what will happen in the course of the play' (BT 12). Euripides, as a consequence, forces his art to conform to the dictates of Socratism, by obeying Socrates' command that all must be revealed. Lost in the process, according to Nietzsche, is the genuine experience of the tragic, which alerts us to the way the world is as such. Thus, we learn, once again, that the voyeuristic impulse informing Socrates' project places us at odds with the world and ourselves. If we continue, in the wake of Socrates, to impose our desire on the world in this manner, we are merely reinstating his perverse pattern.

3 *Situating* The Birth of Tragedy

There are interpretative advantages to be had by indulging in the idea that Nietzsche sees Socrates as akin to a sexual pervert. To begin with, the reading I am proposing removes some of the confusion surrounding Nietzsche's critique of Socrates. It is clear that in *The Birth of Tragedy* Nietzsche casts Socrates in the role of the 'villain',[11] the ne'er-do-well who teams up with Euripides to *kill* Greek tragedy by enticing it to commit suicide.[12] This "crime" has serious and irrever-

---

[11] Carl Pletsch provides context for the casting of Socrates as a villain. Pletsch notes, with respect to Nietzsche's 1870 Basel lecture, "Socrates and Tragedy", that 'Socrates was already the villain' (Pletsch 1991, p. 127). Nietzsche, in a letter to Rohde, remarked on how this lecture had 'incited terror and incomprehension', because, as Pletsch puts it, 'No one in Basel expected Socrates to be portrayed as the villain of Western Civilization' (Pletsch 1991, p. 127). Paul Daniels offers a similar appraisal: 'Socrates is an ambiguous character for Nietzsche's philosophy on many counts, but in *The Birth of Tragedy* his role is as the villain of our philosophical story' (Daniels 2013, p. 4). For more on Socrates as villain, see Christopher Raymond, who provides added detail on the "Socrates and Tragedy" lecture (Raymond 2019, p. 842–846).

[12] 'Greek tragedy perished differently from all other older sister arts: it died by suicide' (BT 11). This death is precipitated by the 'aesthetic Socratism', which provides 'the murderous principle'

sible repercussions, in that it opens up the opportunity for Socrates to become the beacon guiding western philosophy and culture. Thus, he emerges as the blueprint for a new human ideal, that of theoretical man, which ushers in a "theoretical optimism" donning the mantle of science.[13] For Nietzsche, Socrates' triumph over tragedy is a calamity in that it not only deprives us of the curative powers of tragedy,[14] it dooms us to existential alienation. The cementing of the dispositions of theoretical man ensures that we are dominated by a pernicious delusion, which is the erroneous belief that human life and suffering can be understood as serving a greater purpose. The overarching telos, postulated by theoretical man, is that individual contentment is obtainable, and that the acquisition of knowledge is the means for achieving this goal.[15] According to Nietzsche, this perspective is one of shallow optimism, exploiting the misguided pretences that he thinks tragic art guards against. With the ascendency of the Socratic perspective, we lose touch with the underlying reality of our existence, and we wrongly anticipate that the world will be hospitable to our being and our happiness. It is this tendency which Nietzsche thinks is spawned by Socrates' campaign against the world as it is, the world of difference which needs correction.

So far, I have only discussed the negative dimensions of Nietzsche's account of Socrates in *The Birth of Tragedy* by focusing primarily on his role as villain.

---

which puts an end to tragic art (BT 12). As for the murderousness of Socratism, Daniels nicely captures Nietzsche's intent by suggesting that 'The sections on Euripides and Socrates ... are laid out like a murder mystery, carrying with them all the suspense of that genre' (Daniels 2013, p. 128).

13 'Socrates is the archetype of the theoretical optimist whose belief that the nature of things can be discovered leads him to attribute to knowledge and understanding the power of a panacea' (BT 15). Alexander Nehamas provides an apt summary of what Nietzsche identifies as quintessentially optimistic about Socrates. Socrates 'rejected the idea that the world cannot be finally understood, that it was not made for us, that nothing we can do, as tragedy showed, can change that world effectively and for the better' (Nehamas 1998, p. 135).

14 'We shall never comprehend the supreme value of tragedy until, like the Greeks, we experience it as the essence of all prophylactic healing energies' (BT 21).

15 Nietzsche gives the following description of the outcome of the 'limitless' theoretical optimism at the heart of Socratism: 'We should not now take fright when the fruits of this optimism ripen, when the acid of this kind of culture trickles down to the very lowest levels of our society so that it gradually begins to tremble from burgeoning surges and desires, when the belief in earthly happiness of all, when the belief that such a general culture of knowledge is possible, gradually transforms itself into the menacing demand for such Alexandrian happiness on earth' (BT 18). M. S. Silk and J. P. Stern give a nice synopsis of Nietzsche's reflections on such an expansive optimism: 'The Socratic dialectic tendency, found alike in Euripides and Plato, is inherently untragic because it is inherently optimistic: it presupposes that essential problems of existence can be solved by the activities of the rational mind' (Silk and Stern 1981, p. 94).

However, that is not all there is to this account. Socrates is, at times, praised for his cultural contributions. For example, Jeffrey Church sets out the complex and positive way Nietzsche uses Socrates as 'the "supreme teacher" for the new culture' (Church 2006, p. 696), and Drew Hyland emphasises how Nietzsche credits the Socratic 'incessant and optimistic drive for knowledge at any price' for saving us from more pessimistic impulses (Hyland 2015, p. 4).[16] In this regard, *The Birth of Tragedy* is the beginning of what is said to be Nietzsche's ambiguous relationship with Socrates. Again, Church and Hyland can be of service here in that the former rightly remarks that 'Nietzsche's judgment of Socrates is complex and ambivalent' (Church 2006, p. 689), and the latter highlights how 'Nietzsche really was torn in his attitude toward Socrates' (Hyland 2015, p. 4), even in the text which contains his harshest criticisms. We can ask of *The Birth of Tragedy* the question many scholars come to ask of Nietzsche's work in general: Who is Nietzsche's Socrates?[17] Is he the diabolical mastermind who bars us from recognising the genuinely dire and tragic aspects of our existence? Or is he the misunderstood champion who saves us from the worst of our impulses? In terms of *The Birth of Tragedy*, much of this supposed ambiguity dissipates if we observe that there is more than *one* Socrates presented in that particular work. This claim is not intended to saddle Nietzsche with the burden of incoherence. I am not suggesting that Nietzsche gives us competing versions of Socrates; rather, I am asserting that he gives an account of Socrates which unfolds in distinct steps. In other words, the story of Socrates in *The Birth of Tragedy* is just that – a story. It has the regular and discernible features of a story: a beginning, a middle and an end. This insight should not surprise us, since that is the structure of the book itself. So, just as Nietzsche tells us about the birth, life and death

---

[16] Both Church and Hyland rely on the passage from *The Birth of Tragedy* in which Nietzsche names Socrates as 'the vortex and turning point of so-called world history' (BT 15). In this section of the text, Nietzsche imagines what would have happened if 'the quite incalculable sum of energy' that had been 'placed at the service of understanding' was 'applied instead to the practical, i.e., egoistical goals of individuals and nations' (BT 15). The chief consequence of such a use of this energy is, for Nietzsche, 'a practical pessimism which could generate a horrifying ethic of genocide out of pity' (BT 15). So, Socratic optimism is thought to save us from a murderous pessimism and on these grounds, Socrates protects us from a terrible fate. However, as I make clear in this chapter, this praise of Socrates does not mitigate the pernicious effects of the fundamental Socratic mindset. In other words, we may be lucky that Socrates' mandate distracted us from worse pursuits but that does not mean he is not culpable for the death of tragedy and what follows from it.
[17] My use of this question here is meant to invoke Sarah Kofman's (1991) paper "Nietzsche's Socrates: 'Who' is Socrates?" which provides an intriguing overview of the numerous ways Socrates is represented in Nietzsche's works.

of tragedy,[18] he gives us three corresponding stages in the life of Socrates. Obviously, he does not limit himself to a literal account of Socrates' birth or a strict biographical record of his life and death.[19] Nevertheless, he does give us something similar, a tale of Socrates' career as a philosopher, divided into three chapters. First, Nietzsche charts Socrates' emergence as a leading intellectual figure in Athens. Second, Nietzsche addresses Socrates' subsequent activities, culminating in his acceptance of his death sentence and his execution. Third, Nietzsche turns his attention to the meaning attached to Socrates after his death, especially in relation to theoretical man. Some of these details are, at times, overlooked when interpretative emphasis is placed solely on Socrates' legacy. In this chapter, I concentrate on Socrates' "birth", his beginning as a philosopher, and it is this phase I identify with the proclivities of a pervert. Socrates, then, is more than the 'archetype and progenitor' of theoretical man (BT 18). He takes other forms, such as the enthusiastic pursuer of a singular erotic fixation.[20]

---

18 Robert John Ackermann provides a helpful overview of the structure of Nietzsche's text. He identifies three themes which segment the book accordingly. The first theme is 'Greek tragedy as arising out of Apollinian and Dionysian forms of art' (sects. 1–10), the second is 'the destruction of the tragic outlook by Socratic optimism and rationality' (sects. 11–15) and the third is that 'hopes for a rebirth of something like Hellenic tragedy can be established on the basis of the nature of German music' (sects. 16–25) (Ackermann 1990, pp. 14–23). In terms of these sections, my chapter is confined almost entirely to the second.

19 The observations Nietzsche makes regarding Socrates as a person are not presented as purely factual. Nietzsche obviously embellishes and adds details for stylistic effect. As Christopher Vasillopulos points out, Nietzsche is not 'trying to present an accurate portrait of Socrates' (Vasillopulos 2011, p. 133). However, I do not think Vasillopulos is correct to think this means that Socrates is a metaphor and that when Nietzsche refers to him, or to Euripides, he does not intend to 'signify men that once lived in fifth-century Athens' (Vasillopulos 2011, p. 133). Regardless of how fanciful his description of Socrates seems, I think Nietzsche believes that it has some connection to the human individual known as Socrates. It may help here to keep in mind Nietzsche's claim in *Ecce Homo* that he tends to 'treat people as if they were high-intensity magnifying glasses that can illuminate a general, though insidious and barely noticeable predicament' (EH Wise, 7). Nietzsche, in this context, is rejecting the idea that he attacks people; we may have reasons to doubt whether that claim is sincere or accurate, but that does not matter here. What is telling is that Nietzsche affirms the idea that he addresses specific individuals in ways that make them something other than mere metaphors.

20 Eva Brann stresses how the application of the term 'erotic' to Socrates is 'no metaphor at all' and that in Plato's works 'the soul is presented in a figure of erotic arousal' such that *philosophos* becomes 'erotikosophos' in the form of 'an erotic lover of wisdom' (Brann 2014, p. 31). It is surprising, however, that Brann juxtaposes this erotic Socrates with the 'Socrates of Nietzsche's *Birth of Tragedy*' which she characterises as 'the antitragic Socrates invented in modernity'. For Brann, 'This portrait happens to be a brilliant travesty' (Brann 2014, p. 31). I think on this front Brann misses the clues Nietzsche drops regarding the erotic tendencies he is attributing

When approached in this manner, Socrates is granted a degree of psychological complexity that is not available when we reduce him to the content of his philosophical agenda alone. In other words, there is more to Socrates than the residue that persists in the form of theoretical man. So even though Nietzsche claims that 'one cannot do other than regard Socrates as the vortex and turning point of so-called world history' (BT 15), he is still a person and a distinct individual. Here, then, we need to take advantage of Nietzsche's later willingness to claim the appellation of 'psychologist'[21] and in his psychological examination of Socrates, in *The Birth of Tragedy*, we encounter many clues for supposing Socrates suffers from a kind of mania or compulsion of an erotic sort. I will address these details later, but for now, we need to recognise that Nietzsche is inviting us to "psychoanalyse" Socrates.[22]

My interpretation, on this level, takes seriously C. C. Evangeliou's complaint regarding Nietzsche's overall characterisation of Socrates. Evangeliou castigates Nietzsche for indulging in 'a non-philosophical treatment of Socrates' (Evangeliou 2003, p. 38). As such, Nietzsche assumes the 'role of the diagnostician of Socrates', investigating his 'soul and physiognomy' (Evangeliou 2003, p. 33).[23] In phrasing this as a criticism, however, Evangeliou misses the point. Nietzsche's intent is to diagnose Socrates. James Porter, by contrast, correctly observes that Nietzsche in his later works 'returns to the intense psychological analysis he had given to Socrates in *The Birth of Tragedy*' (Porter 2009, p. 409). Porter, however, needlessly tempers this claim by adding that Nietzsche's 'analysis

---

to Socrates. She takes Nietzsche's claim that Socrates lacked an enthusiasm for the Dionysian to be equivalent to the claim that he lacks enthusiasm entirely. She writes of Socrates that 'Not only is he not one in whom "enthusiasm has never glowed" – he is the very incarnation of enthusiasm' (Brann 2014, p. 32). On my reading, Nietzsche's does not deny that Socrates has such passion; he just sees Socrates as having a misplaced and misdirected passion.

21 In *On the Genealogy of Morality* and *Beyond Good and Evil*, Nietzsche frequently refers to himself (and to his readers) as 'psychologists'. See GM III, 19–21 and BGE 269.

22 As Kaufmann rightly notes, in Nietzsche's works, 'The irrational springs of human behavior are uncovered expertly, and the self-styled vivisectionist cuts mercilessly through prejudices and conventions to lay bare the hidden motivations of our actions. In the course of these investigations, which extend into his later works, Nietzsche frequently offers suggestions that one would today associate with psychoanalysis' (Kaufmann 1974, p. 181).

23 Here Evangeliou actually captures the basic framework of Nietzschean psychology, namely, his reliance on morphology: 'To grasp psychology as morphology and the *doctrine of the development of the will to power*, which I have done – nobody has ever come close to this' (BGE 23). Christian Emden is helpful when it comes to unpacking this notion of morphology. He shows that what Nietzsche 'had in mind was a "genuine physio-psychology", that is, a morphology of mental forms and intellectual configurations, which is already linked to the material world since it is embedded in the body' (Emden 2014, p. 40).

was never really aimed at Socrates as a person so much as at Socrates as an event or (better yet) an *idea*' (Porter 2009, p. 409). I think Porter's qualification of his initial thought is unnecessary because there are ample grounds for supposing that Nietzsche is intrigued by Socrates psychologically, even if the scope of this concern will expand to include thinking of him as an event and idea.

Holding that the treatment of Socrates offered in *The Birth of Tragedy* is fundamentally personal should not surprise us given the trajectory of Nietzsche's later works. After all, he famously proclaims in *Beyond Good and Evil* that he has 'gradually come to realize what every great philosophy so far has been: a confession of faith on the part of its author, and a type of unself-conscious memoir' (BGE 6). Such a formula for understanding a philosopher captures exactly the method Nietzsche uses to make sense of Socrates in *The Birth of Tragedy* and, as a formula, it appears to sanction psychoanalysis in that it becomes a matter of going past the surface of consciousness to discover what lies – *beyond* or beneath it.[24] Moreover, when clarifying what it means to read philosophy as memoir, Nietzsche exclaims that 'the moral (or immoral) intentions in every philosophy constitute the true living seed from which the whole plant has grown' (BGE 6), implying that there is an intention other than 'a drive for knowledge' (BGE 6) underlying the engagement in philosophy. In other words, philosophers have a hidden motive which directs their activities, and this motive is not equivalent to the one they confess to having. A philosopher purports to be dedicated to the acquisition of knowledge, yet Nietzsche contends this pursuit of knowledge is a by-product of something else which remains concealed. As such, Nietzsche argues that he uncovers, and brings to light, the impulses which lurk under the surface of the philosopher's own self-awareness. Therefore, the reading of philosophy as memoir makes interpretation a matter of psychological investigation, the search for unconscious motives. Thus, in relation to *The Birth of Tragedy*, it is plausible to suggest that Nietzsche gives us his initial foray into reading unconscious memoirs, and uncovering hidden motives, well before the publication of *Beyond Good and Evil*.

In the thematic convergence of Nietzsche's earlier and later works, another relevant point surfaces. In his provocative opening remarks in *Beyond Good and*

---

24 In the *Genealogy*, Nietzsche makes a similar explanatory manoeuvre and exploits the metaphor of digging beneath the surface to set up the idea that moral ideals are a consequence of concealed drives. It requires looking 'into these dark workplaces' (GM I, 14), and it is part of the challenge he issues for the psychologist willing to take the risk of exposing the source of moral prejudices: 'Would anyone like to go down and take a little look into the secret of how they *fabricate ideals* on earth? Who has the courage to do so?' (GM I, 14).

Evil, Nietzsche comments on the resistance conventional philosophers have to the idea that something could arise from its contrary. He introduces this problem through a rhetorical question: 'How *could* anything originate out of its opposite?' (BGE 2). He goes on to a list a number of instances of what he takes to be cases of such occurrences. For example, he raises the possibility of a 'will to truth' arising from a 'will to deception' (BGE 2). What is of particular importance, however, is the last opposition he mentions. Nietzsche juxtaposes 'the pure, sun-bright gaze of wisdom' with the 'covetous leer' (BGE 2), where the latter is presented as the actual source of the former. So, the stance of scientists, as self-declared impartial servants of truth, is more closely aligned with a lustful gaze than they would dare to admit. In the conclusion of this chapter, I will make clear that this is the dynamic Nietzsche highlights in his overview of Socrates in *The Birth of Tragedy*. Theoretical man, the exemplar of scientific wisdom, is brought into being by what counts as its strict negation, namely a strange erotic orientation which is inimical to rational knowledge. As such, Socrates, despite claims to the contrary, is driven by that which he denounces.

4 Conclusion

At this point, the connection Nietzsche draws between musical dissonance and human existence proves relevant. In the final pages of *The Birth of Tragedy*, he remarks on 'the wonderful significance of *musical dissonance*' (BT 24). This significance is a result of dissonance being able to replicate 'the effect of tragedy' (BT 24), but that observation is not my concern here. What is most intriguing, from my perspective, is when Nietzsche prompts us to 'imagine dissonance assuming human form', and then interrupts this thought with the rhetorical question: 'and what else is man?' (BT 24). Hence Nietzsche suggestively defines a human being as dissonance, as a coming together of that which is disparate and contrary. In this context, Nietzsche's critique of Socratic culture and theoretical man appears to be motivated by a fundamental disagreement over the nature of human existence. Any culture which is hostile to difference is, in essence, opposed to human beings. The need, then, is for a culture which embraces difference as intrinsic to human being. Instead of seeking to regulate being and human existence, to make it conform to philosophical dictates, human existence should be seen as an actualisation of difference. In short, human beings exist as difference.

To return to the theme of a politics of difference, one of the main lessons to be derived from *The Birth of Tragedy* in this regard is that it tells of the risks incurred by the fear of difference. Today we find ourselves in historical circumstances where the dominant ideals are often predicated on a deep-seated hostility towards heterogeneity. If we acknowledge that the human being is an instantiation of dissonance, we have the means for reconfiguring our political situation. Nietzsche's critical analysis of Socrates enables an overcoming of a pernicious political legacy initiated by the Socratic attack on tragedy. However, if we seek to overcome the limits Socratism has imposed on us culturally, we cannot think that the solution to the problem of Socrates rests in the reconciliation of oppositions. There is no optimistic remedy. In this regard, unlike Socrates, Nietzsche thinks we need to look into the 'abysses of the Dionysiac' (BT 14) with pleasure instead of dread. To do so is to accept the lessons of the Attic Greeks. It is to gaze upon 'all the unmeasurable excess in nature' as seen in the Dionysiac festival where '*Excess* revealed itself as the truth; contradiction, bliss born of pain, spoke of itself from the heart of nature' (BT 4). It is to recognise, through the chorus of satyrs, 'a truer, more real, more complete image of existence' (BT 8), one which is consistent with the tragic experience of 'Dionysiac man', who has 'gazed into the true essence of things' (BT 7). Individuals of this sort find it 'laughable or shameful that they should be expected to set to rights a world so out of joint' (BT 7). In other words, they reject the naïve pretence that existence can or should be corrected. Instead, they accept the world as it is and as a whole, which Socrates deemed 'so varied and multifarious' (BT 14).

Bibliography

Ackermann, Robert John (1990): *Nietzsche: A Frenzied Look*. Amherst: The University of Massachusetts Press.
Brann, Eva (2014): "Socrates: Antitragedian". In: *Philosophy and Literature* 38. No. 1, pp. 30–40.
Church, Jeffrey (2006): "Dreaming of the True Erotic: Nietzsche's Socrates and the Reform of Modern Education". In: *History of Political Thought* XXVII. No. 4, pp. 685–710.
Daniels, Paul Raymond (2013): *Nietzsche and* The Birth of Tragedy. Durham: Acumen Publishing.
Emden, Christian J. (2014): *Nietzsche's Naturalism: Philosophy and the Life Sciences in the Nineteenth Century*. Cambridge: Cambridge University Press.
Evangeliou, C. C. (2003): "Nietzsche on Tragedy and Socrates". In: *Phronimon* 1, pp. 18–39.
Evans, Daw-Nay (2010): "Socrates as Nietzsche's Decadent in *Twilight of the Idols*". In: *Philosophy and Literature* 34. No. 2, pp. 340–347.
Hyland, Drew A. (2015): "Nietzsche's 'Love' for Socrates". In: *Humanities* 4, pp. 3–16.
Kaufmann, Walter A. (1948): "Nietzsche's Admiration for Socrates". In: *Journal of the History of Ideas* 9. No. 4, pp. 472–491.

Kaufmann, Walter A. (1974): *Nietzsche: Philosopher, Psychologist, Antichrist*. 4th ed. Princeton: Princeton University Press.

Kofman, Sarah (1991): "Nietzsche's Socrates: 'Who' is Socrates?" In: *Graduate Faculty Philosophy Journal* 15. No. 2, pp. 7–29.

Nehamas, Alexander (1998): "A Reason for Socrates' Face: Nietzsche on 'The Problem of Socrates'". In: Alexander Nehamas: *The Art of Living*, pp. 128–156. Berkeley: University of California Press.

Nietzsche, Friedrich (1995): *The Pre-Platonic Philosophers*. Edited and translated by Greg Whitlock. Urbana Champaign: University of Illinois Press.

Nietzsche, Friedrich (1998): *On the Genealogy of Morality*. Translated by Maudemarie Clark and Alan J. Swensen. Indianapolis: Hackett Publishing Co.

Nietzsche, Friedrich (1999): *The Birth of Tragedy and Other Writings*. Edited by Raymond Geuss and Ronald Spiers and translated by Ronald Spiers. Cambridge: Cambridge University Press.

Nietzsche, Friedrich (1999): "An Attempt at Self-Criticism". *The Birth of Tragedy and Other Writings*, pp. 3–12. Edited by Raymond Geuss and Ronald Spiers and translated by Ronald Spiers. Cambridge: Cambridge University Press.

Nietzsche, Friedrich (2001): *The Gay Science*. Edited by Bernard Williams and translated by Josefine Nauckhoff and Adrian Del Caro. Cambridge: Cambridge University Press.

Nietzsche, Friedrich (2002): *Beyond Good and Evil*. Edited by Rolf-Peter Horstmann and Judith Norman and translated by Judith Norman. Cambridge: Cambridge University Press.

Nietzsche, Friedrich (2003): *Writings from the Late Notebooks*. Edited by Rudiger Bittner and translated by Kate Sturge. Cambridge: Cambridge University Press.

Nietzsche, Friedrich (2005a): *Ecce Homo*. In: *The Anti-Christ, Ecce Homo, Twilight of the Idols and Other Writings*, pp. 69–151. Edited by Aaron Ridley and Judith Norman and translated by Judith Norman. Cambridge: Cambridge University Press.

Nietzsche, Friedrich (2005b): *Nietzsche Contra Wagner*. In: *The Anti-Christ, Ecce Homo, Twilight of the Idols and Other Writings*, pp. 31–282. Edited by Aaron Ridley and Judith Norman and translated by Judith Norman. Cambridge: Cambridge University Press.

Nietzsche, Friedrich (2005c): *Twilight of the Idols*. In: *The Anti-Christ, Ecce Homo, Twilight of the Idols and Other Writings*, pp. 53–229. Edited by Aaron Ridley and Judith Norman and translated by Judith Norman. Cambridge: Cambridge University Press.

Nietzsche, Friedrich (2006): *Thus Spoke Zarathustra: A Book for All and None*. Edited by Adrian Del Caro and Robert Pippin and translated by Adrian del Caro. Cambridge: Cambridge University Press.

Nietzsche, Friedrich (2009): *Writings from the Early Notebooks*. Edited by Raymond Geuss and Alexander Nehamas and translated by Ladislaus Löb. Cambridge: Cambridge University Press.

Pletsch, Carl (1991): *Young Nietzsche: Becoming a Genius*. New York: The Free Press.

Porter, James (2009): "Nietzsche and 'The Problem of Socrates'". In: Sara Ahbel-Rappe and Rachana Kamtekar (Eds.): *A Companion to Socrates*, pp. 406–424. Oxford: Wiley-Blackwell.

Raymond, Christopher (2019): "Nietzsche's Revaluation of Socrates". In: Christopher Moore (Ed.): *Brill's Companion to the Reception of Socrates*, pp. 837–880. Boston: Brill Publications.

Silk, M. S., and J. P. Stern (1981): *Nietzsche on Tragedy*. Cambridge: Cambridge University Press.
Vasillopulos, Christopher (2011): "Euripides and Socrates: Nietzsche's Unnatural Enemies". In: *Skepsis: A Journal for Philosophy and Interdisciplinary Research* 21. No. 2, pp. 122–140.
Warnek, Peter (2014): "*Fire from Heaven* in Elemental Tragedy: From Hölderlin's *Death of Empedocles* to Nietzsche's Dying Socrates". In: *Research in Phenomenology* 44. No. 2, pp. 213–239.

William A. B. Parkhurst
Ecce Homo – Notes on Duplicates: The Great Politics of the Self

> "Starting with me, the earth will know *great politics* –" (EH Destiny, 1)

Abstract: It seems to have gone unnoticed until now that none of Nietzsche's self-quotations in *Ecce Homo* are identical to the original quoted material. This chapter argues that these misquotations are intentional. Nietzsche's self-misquotations performatively undermine authorial identity by means of self-parody and, through this, metaphysics itself is undermined. Nietzsche's understanding of Kant's *Critique of Pure Reason* came through Eduard von Hartmann and Gustav Gerber. Both argued that the foundation of the *Critique* is a historically contingent linguistic illusion, the unity of consciousness. Nietzsche furthers these arguments against the transcendental unity of apperception at the foundation of Kant's work. He argues that nothing is truly original or self-identical but always a re-performance, a re-quotation, and a re-appropriation within language. The chapter argues that *Ecce Homo* performs this critique and undermines the metaphysics of self-identity.

1 Introduction

As Alexander Nehamas has convincingly argued, Nietzsche sees the world, and us with it, as a kind of literary text. He writes, 'Nietzsche ... looks at the world in general as if it were a sort of artwork; in particular, he looks at it as if it were a literary text ... including his view of human beings' (Nehamas 2002, p. 5). I argue that just as we might think of texts having a singular author behind them, we analogously think of persons having a unitary self behind our actions. Just as we need what Michel Foucault calls an 'author function' to hold together the unity of a text, so too do we need a similar author function, the "I", "self", "soul", or "subject" to unify the manifold of experience into cognition (Foucault 1977, p. 127). Nietzsche holds that the unitary self, the soul, is something which was created (GM II, 16). This unitary self, the subject, is a 'false changeling' created out of the vengeful *ressentiment* of slave morality and the seductions of language (GM I, 13). The unitary self was created in order to make bodies accountable, and therefore punishable (GM I, 13; and GM III, 13). The creation of the unitary self was an act of a 'truly *great* politics of revenge' (*einer wahrhaft grossen*

Politik der Rache [GM I, 8, translation modified and emphasis added]).[1] Nietzsche sees Kant as continuing the Christian tradition of the unitary self (see, e. g., TI Reason, 6; GM I, 13; GM II, 6; and GM III, 25). In Nietzsche's *Ecce Homo*, I hold that he is parodying the unity of authorship and, through that, the unity of the self at the foundation of Christian and, continuing that tradition, Kantian morality.[2] Nietzsche's parody, then, replaces the unitary self with a performative enactment of the multiplicitous self. In this way, Nietzsche has enacted a form of 'great politics' (*grosse Politik*), as he claims in *Ecce Homo*, by inverting the millennia-long 'great politics of revenge' (*grosse Politik der Rache*) which created the unitary soul and bad conscience (EH Destiny, 1).

In the *Critique of Pure Reason*, Kant argues that there are two types of self-consciousness: empirical apperception (inner sense) and pure apperception (original or transcendental apperception). Empirical apperception, on the one hand, is simply the consciousness of ourselves and our inner states. In this we find knowledge of ourselves as we exist purely as phenomena (B 132). Pure apperception, on the other hand, is transcendental consciousness, a consciousness that produces the representation 'I think' (B 132), that is, transcendental consciousness is not experienced but is the condition for the possibility of experience. It is only based on the unity of pure apperception that we can synthesise the manifold of experience. Put more plainly, in order to unify varying experiences, one after another, there needs to be a unitary self that has those experiences. That is, as Kant suggests, if the I think did not accompany representations, those representations could not be thought at all, and therefore knowledge would not be possible (B 131–133). For Kant, without a unity of self, an I think, cognition would be impossible.[3] The point is that the transcendental unity of apperception which holds together the manifold of experience is functionally analogous to the unity of authorial intention that holds together the coherence of a text. If there is any kind of text we would expect to be held together by the unity of authorship,

---

1 For consistency, I will be translating *gross* and cognates as 'great' across translations.
2 It is important to note from the beginning that there is no evidence Nietzsche read the *Critique of Pure Reason* itself. All of his quotations from the *Critique* can be traced to secondary sources he was reading. Therefore, I will be making Nietzsche's argument against Kant from those readings as strong as possible. However, it must be admitted, it does not seem that Nietzsche was completely clear about the difference between empirical and transcendental apperception. Such a difference, if applied carefully, can probably get around Nietzsche's argument. References to the *Critique of Pure Reason* are cited by reference to the A and B pagination of the original 1781 and 1787 editions.
3 I am grateful for Zach Vereb's assistance with this brief summary of Kant.

it would be an "autobiography" such as *Ecce Homo*.[4] In *Ecce Homo*, however, we find that Nietzsche challenges the unity of authorial intention, and therefore the unity of the self, through his consistent and intentional self-misquotation. Nietzsche challenges the unity of the self by performatively presenting a multiplicitous self.

One of the most striking facts about *Ecce Homo* is that every single one of its self-quotations is inaccurate. This fact, previously unnoticed by scholars, is central to understanding how we ought to make sense of this work. I demonstrate through archival, historical and genetic evidence that Nietzsche's self-misquotations are intentional. I then argue that Nietzsche is making use of a performative self-parody to undermine the unity of authorial identity and the metaphysics of the self.

Nietzsche's rejection of the unity of authorial intention began early in his career. On May 28, 1869, Nietzsche delivered a lecture entitled "On the Personality of Homer" (*"Über die Persönlichkeit Homers"*). This lecture was published later that year as "Homer and Classical Philology" (*"Homer und die klassische Philologie"*). In it, Nietzsche deconstructs the idea of singular authorial intention. He contends that the singular individual "Homer" is a historical construction and fiction. Nietzsche, a scholar of philology at the time, goes into a technical and in-depth analysis of the philological and historical problems of claiming that there is a singular author or authorial intent behind any text. During that same period he goes even further, in the unpublished work "Zu einer Geschichte der litterarischen Studien im Alterthum und in der Neuzeit," and argues that 'every identity is imaginary' (BAW, vol. 3, 323; cf. Swift 2005, p. 80).

Nietzsche's early critique of the principle of identity concerns the identity of authorship. This was known at the time as the 'Homeric problem'. It concerns whether the writings we attribute to Homer had only one author, were the result of several authors, or perhaps had no individual author at all. On the one hand, we can treat the Homeric question by seeing 'the *Iliad* and the *Odyssey* as the creations of one single Homer' (HCP 152). On the other hand, we can approach historical texts without recourse to a single personality and treat them as 'the work of several different persons' (HCP 151). In the end, Nietzsche concludes there are no individual thinkers who write great works; rather, they emerge out of the expression of a 'mysterious impulse' of the unconscious mass of historical consciousness (HCP 156–159). This line of thought concluded at the end

---

[4] I will in general refer to *Ecce Homo* as an autobiography, but it is clear that it is much more than a mere autobiography.

of Nietzsche's productive life. His late performative autobiography, *Ecce Homo*, effectively undermines the unity needed for any sense of authorial intention.

Nietzsche scholars have noted that the styles he employs in the late works dissolve his authorial identity and intention in a variety of complex ways (see, e.g., Bernd Magnus 1988, p. 155; and Jacques Derrida 1986, p. 246–262). Nietzsche's translators have also noted that several of his self-quotations in *Ecce Homo* do not match the original material.[5] However, to my knowledge, no scholar has noticed that every single one of Nietzsche's self-quotations is actually a misquotation and none of them is identical to the original material. When I say they are not identical, I am specifically referring to their typographical identity. That is, some differ only in punctuation and typographical emphasis (*Sperrdruck*), while others insert content, rearrange paragraphs or erase intervening lines. As these self-misquotations are to support my thesis, I will first need to demonstrate that these misquotations are not simply accidents.

2 Evidence of Misquotation

Early in his career, Nietzsche chastised others for misquoting and complained that his critics misquoted his own work. In *Untimely Meditation I*, he attacks Strauss for misquoting Schiller and in his letters to Erwin Rhode he is furious that Ulrich von Wilamowitz-Moellendorff misquoted him in his attack on *The Birth of Tragedy* (UM I, 12; KGB II/3, Bf. 239). Later in his life, in *Human, All-Too-Human*, Nietzsche would argue that the only language original to Germany is ironic citation, but he also cautions young authors that if they do not take care in their citations, it can ruin an entire book (HH II, 228). Nietzsche continued thinking about the importance of quotation throughout the second part of *Thus Spoke Zarathustra*, in which he suggests that it is the thoughts that come within quotations that silently move the world (Z II, 22). This should pique our curiosity about the consistent self-misquotations in *Ecce Homo*. Were they simply mistakes?

Nietzsche sent a letter to Peter Gast on December 9, 1888, which makes it clear that Nietzsche edited the work closely and that he understood the work as doing something beyond common literature. He writes:

---

[5] See, e.g., the following editorial notes in Walter Kaufmann's (1989) translation of *Ecce Homo*: 234n3, 289n2, 298n2, 301n3, 306n5, 309n3, 327n1, 329n5, 329n6, and 330n10. See also the following editorial notes in Aaron Ridley and Judith Norman's (2012) translation: 110n43, 120n54. Cf. Duncan Large (2001, p. 99).

> I have good news too. *Ecce Homo* went off to C. G. Naumann [Nietzsche's publisher] yesterday, after I had put my qualms of conscience to rest for the last time by weighing every word again from beginning to end. It so transcends the concept of 'literature' that there is no parallel to it even in nature herself; it blasts, literally, the history of mankind in two – the highest superlative of *dynamite*... (SLN 331; Bf. An Peter Gast, 09.12.1888, KGB III/5 Bf. 1181)

This should give us pause and allow us to reflect that, first, if Nietzsche weighed every word that would include his quotations, and second, perhaps Nietzsche sees *Ecce Homo* as more than a simple autobiography.

In order to address whether Nietzsche is simply misquoting by mistake, we ought to first look at a few of these self-misquotations. One self-misquotation found in *Ecce Homo* misquotes from *Thus Spoke Zarathustra* (Z III, Tables). The quote in *Ecce Homo* reads: 'Good people never speak the truth. Good people have taught you false coasts and assurances; you were born and hidden in the lies of the good. The good lie about everything and conceal it completely' (EH Destiny, 4). He erases over 459 lines, or more than fifteen pages in the KGW, between the first sentence and the last two.[6] He gives no indication to the reader that he is radically misquoting himself. Nietzsche repeats this kind of erasure in EH Books: Zarathustra, 3 where he misquotes *Thus Spoke Zarathustra* III, 9 and erases approximately 28 lines of text, joining the two lines quoted in *Ecce Homo* (KGW VI/1, 227). Furthermore, Nietzsche also changes punctuation and words in the quotes he does include. Again, he gives no indication that he is misquoting himself.

However, in another misquotation a few pages later (EH Books: Z, 6), Nietzsche does indicate to the reader that he is making an erasure. He does this by separating his quotations with an ellipsis to indicate an erasure of text between the two.[7] Nietzsche erases approximately 35 lines, from between the lines quoted in EH (KGW VI/1, 204). This indicates that Nietzsche was perfectly capable of indicating when he was altering his self-quotations but chose not to.

Nietzsche's misquotations in *Ecce Homo* also get more complicated. For example, in his quotation of *Zarathustra*, III, 12 in *Ecce Homo*, Destiny, 4, he not only changes words, emphases and punctuation, but also has reorganised the order of the argument. He takes the three lines that end the section "Old and New Tables" from *Zarathustra* and places them at the beginning of the quotation in *Ecce Homo*. He then adds a fourth line to end the quote that was from the be-

---

6 The first part of the quotation in *Thus Spoke Zarathustra* starts in subsection 7 and ends with sentences from subsection 28 (KGW VI/1, 247–263).

7 So we find the following: 'das ungeheure unbegrenzte Ja- und Amen-sagen…. In alle Abgründe trage ich noch mein segnendes Jasagen' (EH Books: Z, 6).

ginning of the original section in *Zarathustra*. He is drastically misquoting this section and reorganising its structure. These are merely a few examples of how Nietzsche misquotes himself in *Ecce Homo*. The question remains, could these be simple errors?

When we examine the history of Nietzsche's published canon, we do find errors for a variety of reasons. For example, due to his poor eyesight, Nietzsche asked his publisher to correct a few misspellings which he did not catch in the proofing process of *Twilight of the Idols* (Bf. An Constantin Georg Naumann, 25.11.1888, KGB III/5, Bf. 1156 cf. KGW III/5, 486–488). Some errors were even discovered after a work had already been printed. In the case of the first edition of HH 431, one can see where the 'eere' was itself pasted in on top of the incorrectly typeset 'enon'. One thousand little rectangles of paper with 'eere' printed on them were cut out and glued into the first edition to correct the error (Schaberg 1995, p. 63).[8] Furthermore, we can demonstrate a history of Nietzsche making errors in his self-quotations which he then double-checked, identified and ordered his publisher to make corrections (Bf. An Ernst Schmeitzner, 11.03. 1878, KGB II/5, Bf. 691). This demonstrates that Nietzsche is surely capable of making mistakes in the publication process, including self-misquotations. However, it also suggests that he closely edited his proofs with the help of others to identify errors and he also double-checked his self-quotations. When misquotations were identified, he ordered them to be corrected.

3 Genetic Evidence

One kind of evidence that bears on questions of intentionality is genetic evidence, that is, evidence such as drafts and corrections pages that aid in reconstructing the genesis of a work. The early editions of *Ecce Homo* inadvertently lead the reader to the conclusion that Nietzsche did not cite his quotations. The first edition was edited by his sister Elisabeth and Peter Gast and clearly left out content (Montinari 2003, p. 105). It is only later that scholars such as Erich Podach, Raoul Richter, Karl Schlechta, Mazzino Montinari and Walter Kaufmann would attempt to rectify Elisabeth Nietzsche's distortions. Much of this early work was done by Karl Schlechta. However, Schechta's edition of *Ecce Homo* gave the reader a distorted assumption about Nietzsche's self-quotations, namely, Schechta's misrepresentation of Nietzsche's citations suggested that

---

[8] For an image, see William A. B. Parkhurst (2020), 241.

Nietzsche was not using his personal copies for reference. This might lead the reader to the assumption that the citations were added by his editors.

Nietzsche's personal library, stored in the *Herzogin Anna Amalia Bibliothek* (Weimar), contains Nietzsche's personal copies of his own books. If Nietzsche was double-checking his self-quotations in his own personal copies, we would expect his citations to track to those paginations. However, as Kaufmann has pointed out, Schechta's reproduction of Nietzsche's citations in the first edition are inaccurate (Kaufmann 1989, p. 275n6). These inaccuracies might lead the reader to think that Nietzsche was not checking his quotations in the personal copies he had on hand. That is, if Nietzsche pulled his personal copy off the shelf to check his quotations and citations, we would expect the citations to line up with his own copy. Schlechta's editorial choices make it look like this could not be the case. However, when we compare Nietzsche's citations in the first edition to the copies in his personal library, many of the citations in *Ecce Homo* track to the paginations of Nietzsche's personal copies of his own work.

More evidence comes from the proof sheets for *Ecce Homo* that are archived at the *Herzogin Anna Amalia Bibliothek*. They are not complete and only include up to the third section of the second chapter (excluding the Preface; HAAB – C 4626).[9] According to Kaufmann, Nietzsche had corrected and authorised the sheets at least up to this point (Kaufmann 1989, p. 243n6).[10] The rest of the correction sheets are nowhere to be found. These proof sheets contain edits by both Nietzsche and Gast (Oehler 1997, "K 14" (S) *Z-9994 + [Index]; cf. Kaufmann 1989, p. 243n6).[11]

The page proofs include the section of *Ecce Homo* "Why I am so Wise", 8 that contains a misquotation of *Zarathustra* II, 6. Interestingly, in the page proofs, punctuation and spelling was added that makes the finished text more closely correspond to the original material quoted.[12] This conclusively proves that the self-quotations were not simply skipped over through the proofing processes. Having multiple people, including his publisher, Gast and Nietzsche himself, ed-

---

9 Nietzsche's personal Library, including his own works and proof sheets are stored at Der Herzogin Anna Amalia Bibliothek (HAAB). Each item is given a shelf number. Thus, HAAB – C 4626 indicates it is stored at the Herzogin Anna Amalia Bibliothek and has shelfmark C 4626.
10 It is of course possible that Nietzsche would have continued editing had he not collapsed.
11 The microfilm index, "*Z-9994+Index" was created when Nietzsche's documents were put onto microfilm and sent to the New York Public Library. It is one of the only indexes that is included on these documents. A hard copy is available at the New York Public Library under the title "Verzeichnis der Erstdrucke von Nietzsches Werken in der Folge auf den Microfilmen". This seems to be an internal publication for Herzogin Anna Amilia Bibliothek in 1997.
12 Kaufmann claims that coloured pencil in the manuscripts is from the printer, Kaufmann (1989, p. 325n8). This quote contains both pen as well as red and blue pencil.

iting the quotations in *Ecce Homo* and having these misquotations not come to their attention is unimaginable.¹³

There also exists another important document discovered within Peter Gast's estate in 1969. Between October and November 1888, Gast made a handwritten copy of *Ecce Homo* which is much more complete than the correction pages. This is available in the Goethe and Schiller Archive (GSA 71, 33, "Ecce Homo"; cf. Montinari 2003, p. 104). What is important in this copy is that citations, with page numbers, are given for almost every single self-misquotation. Some of these citations are in-text while others are marginal. The marginal citations could have been added by Gast and therefore may not have been in Nietzsche's original text. However, the in-text citations are likely Nietzsche's. This indicates, first, that Nietzsche's in-text citations track to the pagination in his personal library. Second, even if Nietzsche did not include some in-text citations, Gast was double-checking them and writing them down in the margins. It is unfathomable that these radical misquotations would go unnoticed.

Furthermore, we find new evidence from KGW IX/10 (2015) and KGW IX/11 (2017) that Nietzsche is not quoting from memory. Some of Nietzsche's drafts, which contain the self-misquotations in *Ecce Homo*, cite page numbers which were then crossed out (KGW IX/10 [W II 8], 37). These were not included in the older KGW due to its editorial practice of linear transcription which excludes crossed out passages.¹⁴ In other drafts where one would expect to find a self-quotation, Nietzsche simply leaves a quotation mark (") as a placeholder for the quote. By the first edition, we find that the place holder has been replaced with the self-misquotation (KGW IX/10, [W II 9], 13; cf. EH Books: BT, 3). This indicates Nietzsche did not write down all the quotes from memory but came back to insert them.

Another important piece of evidence from KGW IX is that Nietzsche wrote *Ecce Homo* in the same notebooks in which he had previously written *Twilight of the Idols*. In writing the drafts for *Ecce Homo*, Nietzsche wrote on the same pages that contain material from *Twilight of the Idols*. That very material was mis-

---

13 There exists another document, probably dating to 1888, that may corroborate my thesis which I was unable to access at the time of this paper. Cf. GSA 71, 32.
14 Linear transcription attempts to edit text into a readable linear format. KGW I–VIII systematically excluded lines that were crossed out, deemed personal, or were close repeats of other sections. It also organised the individual sections in Nietzsche's notebooks into what the editors believed was a linear progression. However, the new KGW IX represents the notebooks diplomatically. Diplomatic transcription tries to include all physio-textual features such as words' spatial relationships with one another and includes cross outs, colour variants, non-syntactic features (lines), and represents the notebooks page by page rather than organise sections linearly.

quoted in *Ecce Homo*. We can therefore conclude that Nietzsche literally had the page open to the quote while writing a draft in which he would later misquote it (cf. EH Books: BT, 3). This is perhaps one of the strongest pieces of evidence one could ask for that Nietzsche had the quote in front of him while writing *Ecce Homo* and nevertheless decided to alter it. All three of these points are strong evidence that Nietzsche is not simply quoting from memory and likely had the quoted text on hand in the publication process or literally right in front of him.

Another broad piece of evidence for the quotes being intentional is the documented history of Nietzsche reading his own works. Anyone who has attempted to quote a text from memory that had been read or that they themselves had written years previously will find themselves confronted with the finitude of human memory. However, evidence indicates that Nietzsche systematically reviewed and read his work between 1885–1888. In 1885–1886, Nietzsche clearly re-read *The Birth of Tragedy*, *Daybreak*, *Human, All too Human* and *The Gay Science* in preparation for his new prefaces. Evidence also suggests that Nietzsche re-read the following texts in 1887–1888: *The Birth of Tragedy* (read in 1888), *Untimely Meditations* (1888), *Human, All too Human* (1888), *Daybreak* (1887), *The Gay Science* (1888), *Thus Spoke Zarathustra* (1888), *Beyond Good and Evil* (1888), *On the Genealogy of Morals* (1888), and various prefaces (1888).[15] Additionally, Nietzsche's annotations in two of his own copies of *Menschliches, Allzumenschliches* stored in his personal library can also be dated to 1885 and 1888 (NPB 418; KGW IV/4, 108; NPB 420; HAAB C 441 2 [1]; KGW IV/4, 108).[16] The historical facts bear out that he had many of the books available and was re-reading them while writing *Ecce Homo*. All of this genetic and historical evidence points to the conclusion that Nietzsche is not simply accidentally misquoting from memory but intentionally misquoting himself. Now I will turn to other examples of Nietzsche using misquotation, and self-misquotation, intentionally.

---

15 *The Birth of Tragedy* (1888) (Bf. An Peter Gast, 22.12.1888, KGB III/5, Bf. 1207), *Untimely Meditations* (1888) (Bf. An Peter Gast, 09.12.1888, KGB II/5, Bf. 1181), *Human, All too Human* (1888) (Bf. An Peter Gast, 09.12.1888, KGB II/5, Bf. 1181), *Daybreak* (1887) (Bf. An Theodor Fritsche, 23.03.1887, KGB II/5, Bf. 819), *The Gay Science* (1888) (Bf. An Peter Gast, 09.12.1888, KGB II/5, Bf. 1181; Bf. An Carl Spitteler, 11.12.1888, Bf. 1189), *Thus Spoke Zarathustra* (1888) (Bf. An Peter Gast, 09.12.1888, KGB II/5, Bf. 1181; Bf. An Peter Gast, 22.12.1888, KGB III/5, Bf. 1207), *Beyond Good and Evil* (1888) (Bf. An Carl Spitteler, 11.12.1888, Bf. 1189), *On the Genealogy of Morals* (1888) (Bf. An Meta von Salis, 22.08.1888, KGW III/5, Bf. 1094; BF An Carl Spitteler, 11.12.1888, Bf. 1189), and various prefaces (1888) (Bf. An Peter Gast, 09.12.1888, KGB II/5, Bf. 1181).
16 See footnote 10 for citation scheme.

4 Nietzsche's Use of Misquotation

In *Twilight of the Idols*, "The Problem of Socrates", written around the same time as *Ecce Homo*, Nietzsche misquotes Plato's account of Socrates' last words: 'living – that means being sick for a long time: I owe Asclepius the Saviour a Rooster' (TI Socrates, 1). The actual passage from the *Phaedo* is simply: 'Crito, we owe a cock to Asclepius; make this offering to him and do not forget' (*Phaedo* 118a). Nietzsche's misquotation of Socrates supports an interpretation he made years earlier in *The Gay Science* (GS 340).

The misquotation in *Twilight of the Idols* is clearly intentional. Nietzsche was very familiar with the *Phaedo*, having taught a course on it for six separate semesters at Basel's Pädagogium.[17] He also taught the *Phaedo* in his university-level course on the Platonic dialogues in the winter of 1871–1872. He would teach this course another three times under variant titles (cf. Janz 1973, p. 202).[18] His course notes include seven pages in KGW on the *Phaedo*, quoting in the original Greek (KGW II/ 4, 85–91). The last line of Nietzsche's lecture concerns Socrates' last words about a cock.[19] This is strong evidence that Nietzsche had read and was very familiar with the line. This suggests that the misquotation in *Twilight of the Idols* is a blatant and intentional misquotation. Here, Nietzsche is not craftily trying to deceive his reader in a way that would involve a lack of scholarly integrity. Given his audience, they would know it was a misquotation as every undergraduate philosophy student would. However, this misquotation is doing interpretive philosophical work in the section.

What Nietzsche is suggesting is that this is what Socrates *really* meant with his reference to Asclepius: that he saw life as a sickness. Given the close proximity to Nietzsche's writing of *Ecce Homo*, this is positive evidence that Nietzsche is playing with the philosophical and rhetorical uses of misquotation. In this case it is certainly not an error.

Furthermore, in works written around the same time as *Ecce Homo*, Nietzsche explicitly tells his readers that he is intentionally misquoting himself. *Nietzsche Contra Wagner* is mostly composed of quotations from previous works. Nietzsche explicitly tells his readers that he is intentionally misquoting himself.

---

17 Spring 1869, Winter 1870–1871, Winter 1871–1872, Spring 1873, Winter 1875–1876, and Spring 1876. See Janz (1973, p. 202); cf. Bf. An Friedrich Ritschl, 10.05.1879, KGB II/1, Bf. 3.
18 Winter 1873–1874, Summer 1876 and Winter 1878–1879.
19 'Der geschichtliche Schluß: er badet sich, spricht [mit] seiner Familie, trinkt das Gift, nachdem der Wärter Abschied genommen, ungeheurer Schmerz, die letzten Worte über den Hahn' (KGW II/4, 91).

He writes the following in the foreword: 'The following chapters have all been selected from my earlier writings, and not without some caution – several of them date from 1877 –; I have made some clarifications, and above all abbreviations' (NCW 265). However, Nietzsche's self-misquotations are not as innocent as he claims. The self-misquotations are used as a support for the thesis of the work. Nietzsche writes, 'Read one after the other, [the quotations] will leave no doubt about either Richard Wagner or me: we are antipodes' (NCW 265). Nietzsche's misquotations corrupt the original meaning of the text in order to support this thesis.

For example, in an altered quote from *The Gay Science*, Nietzsche notably changed his putative need for 'tender harmonies' (GS 368), as expressed in the original quote from *The Gay Science*, to 'oil-smooth melodies' (NCW 267). This is a subtle but important change because it distanced him from Wagner. While Wagner could very powerfully use harmony, it was a widely held view at the time that Wagner could not write melodies to save his life.[20] Nietzsche was aware of this and mocked him for it in *The Case of Wagner* (CW 6). As a final and dramatic change to the quotation, Nietzsche adds: 'But Wagner has a sickening effect' (NCW 267).[21] Clearly, this last addition greatly alters not just the style but the content of the quotation. The fact that Nietzsche intentionally misquoted his own work during the time of *Ecce Homo* is undeniable since even Nietzsche admits it in print (NCW 265).

While I have presented evidence from a variety of approaches, I find the most intuitive proof that Nietzsche is intentionally misquoting himself to come from the very first self-misquotation in *Ecce Homo*. He highlights the importance of quotation here in the very first quote, which, aside from a comma replacing a full-stop, is identical to the original. He writes, 'It is the stillest words that bring on the storm, the thoughts that come on doves' feet are the ones that guide the world' (EH Preface, 4). As Graham Parks notes, 'Doves' feet' (*Taubenfüsse*) is actually the German expression for quotation marks (cf. Parkes 2008, p. 307n127).[22] This suggests that Nietzsche's self-misquotations in *Ecce Homo* are intentional and that he is actively drawing our attention to this.

---

20 '"Let us slander melody!", Nietzsche cried. "Nothing is more dangerous than a beautiful melody. Let us dare to be ugly, my friends! Wagner dared!". Written five years after Wagner's death, this was hardly an enviable epitaph for a composer of opera. Nietzsche's barb paraphrased the widely-held view that the master of Bayreuth could not write melodies as such' (Trippett 2013, p. 1).
21 Cf. GS 368 to NCW 266.
22 Supposedly because quote marks look something like the footprint of a dove.

5 Parody and Authorial Identity

At the end of the fourth book of *The Gay Science* (1882), the final section contains a variant of the beginning of *Thus Spoke Zarathustra*, entitled, 'Incipit tragoedia [the tragedy begins]' (GS 342). However, in the Preface to the second edition (1886), Nietzsche writes, '*Incipit tragoedia*, we read at the end of this suspiciously innocent book. Beware! Something utterly wicked and mischievous is being announced here: *incipit parodia* [the parody begins], no doubt' (GS Preface, 1). Since then, scholars have claimed that a number of Nietzsche's works are a form of parody, including *The Birth of Tragedy*,[23] *The Gay Science*,[24] *Thus Spoke Zarathustra*,[25] *Beyond Good and Evil*,[26] *On the Genealogy of Morals*,[27] his 1886 Prefaces,[28] *Twilight of the Idols*,[29] his poetry,[30] as well as his philosophical writing more broadly.[31]

It is a widely accepted claim that *Ecce Homo* is a parody of some sort. Most notably, it is thought to be a parody of Christianity because the title of the work parodies Pontius Pilate's introduction of Jesus to the people with the words 'Ecce homo' (behold the man [John 19:5]). Others hold that the parody is a two-fold self-parody in which Nietzsche is parodying himself parodying Christianity (Megill 1996, p. 121). This is similar to suggestions Nietzsche himself made about one possible interpretation of Wagner's *Parsifal* as self-parody that contains Wagner's 'secret laugh of superiority at himself' (GM III, 3).

Scholars have previously argued that Nietzsche makes use of misquotation as a form of parody (see, e.g., Griffin 1994 and Large 2001). Indeed, it has even been suggested that Nietzsche's self-misquotation in other works is a kind of self-parody intended to make the active reader think carefully (Marsden 2006, p. 34). *Ecce Homo* itself has been identified by scholars as a self-parody.[32] Furthermore, in work on Nietzsche's use of misquotation as a form of parody, it

---

[23] Conway (1992, p. 347).
[24] Gilman (1974, p. 291); Magnus and Higgins (1996, pp. 39 and 44); and Gooding-Williams (2001, pp. 21, 52, 55, 57, 80, and 290).
[25] Griffin (1994, p. 346); Nelson (1973, pp. 175–188); Solomon and Higgins (2000, pp. 59–60 and 155); Del Caro (2004, p. 61); Large (2001, pp. 88–115); and Conway (1988, 257–80).
[26] Cox (1999, p. 72).
[27] Inkpin (2018, 140–166).
[28] Conway (1992, p. 343–357).
[29] Cox (1999, p. 72).
[30] Griffin (1994, p. 343); Grundlehner (1986); and Gilman (1974, p. 291).
[31] Klossowski (1963, pp. 185–228); Kunnas (1982); and Shapiro (1989, pp. 97–123).
[32] Conway (1993, pp. 67 and 70); cf. More (2014, p. 27); and Meyer (2012, pp. 32–43).

has been pointed out that Nietzsche also misquotes himself in *Ecce Homo* (Large 2001, p. 99). However, even in that instance, the idea that Nietzsche may be parodying himself is not raised.

As I noted at the beginning of this chapter, no scholar seems to have yet noticed that every single one of the self-quotations in *Ecce Homo* is inaccurate. If these misquotations are intentional, as I demonstrated above, then one explanation is that Nietzsche is parodying the unity of authorship itself. I hold that this parody of unitary authorial intention mirrors Nietzsche's view of the self, which he believed undermined the Christian and Kantian foundations of the self. These foundations, Nietzsche argues, were created as a kind of great political revenge that came out of a desire to punish, to harm, and to create festivals of cruelty. *Ecce Homo*, then, through the undermining of the unitary self, inverts this great politics and allows the innocence of becoming to flourish once again. In this sense, *Ecce Homo* is specifically a political text. As Martha Nussbaum argues, 'Nietzsche claimed to be a political thinker in *Ecce Homo* and elsewhere. He constantly compared his thought with other political theorists, chiefly Rousseau, Kant and Mill, and he claimed to offer an alternative to the bankruptcy of Enlightenment liberalism' (Nussbaum 1997, p. 1). Furthermore, Nietzsche lays at least part of the blame for what he calls 'the most anti-cultural sickness and unreason', nationalism, at the feet of Kant (EH Books: CW, 2).

Nietzsche did, of course, state his opposition to petty politics, such as nationalism, in *Beyond Good and Evil*, writing, 'the time for petty politics is over: already the next century will bring the struggle to rule the earth – the *compulsion* to great politics' (BGE 208; cf. EH Clever, 10). In *Ecce Homo* itself, Nietzsche writes in the final part, "Why I am Destiny", 'Starting with me, the earth will know *great politics* –' (EH Destiny, 1).

Nietzsche sees great politics not as a short-lived political movement but something subterranean which happens over long periods of time. Nietzsche's most prominent example of this is the creation of the soul or the self that is unitary, responsible for its actions, and is then forced to feel guilt. Nietzsche has in mind the slave revolt in morality which he describes as 'the secret black art of a truly *great* politics of revenge, a far-sighted, subterranean, slow-working and pre-calculating revenge' (GM I, 8; cf. GM I, 7; and GM II, 16). This great politics of slave morality created the subject (or the *soul*) which underlies all human action and can therefore bear blame (GM I, 13). According to Nietzsche, Kant places this subject, or soul, beyond the reach of reason along with God, freedom and immortality (GM III, 25). The soul, which is sheltered by Kantian ignorance of thing-in-itself, was then used to justify festivals of cruelty which Nietzsche explicitly associates with Kant's categorical imperative (GM I, 13 and GM III, 25).

Nietzsche, however, rejects the soul-atom hypothesis as merely a 'synthetic concept "I"' about which we are deceiving ourselves regarding our constitution (BGE 19). This false unity is a fabrication based on a seduction of language and grammatical habit (BGE 19 and 56). Nietzsche calls this 'soul atomism' (BGE 12). He holds that we should reject any belief according to which 'the soul [is] something ineradicable, eternal, indivisible, a monad, an *atomon*' (BGE 12).

For Kant, the rejection of the grounding of the unity of apperception would be a disaster. Nietzsche's early knowledge of the importance of unity and identity in Kant's work is exemplified in his early drafts from 1868 of his incomplete dissertation on Kant (COK 89 and 91). Soon after, his knowledge of the synthetic unity of apperception (*synthetische Einheit der Apperception*) is demonstrated in a letter dated March 19, 1874 (Bf. An Erwin Rohde, 19.03.1874, KGB II/3, Bf. 353).

By 1885 Nietzsche argues that 'The assumption of the single subject is perhaps unnecessary…. *My hypothesis:* the subject as multiplicity' (LNB 40 [42], p. 46). His notebooks of 1888 demonstrate his very serious attacks on the unity of the singular subject as simply a fiction of language and grammar: 'We have borrowed the concept of unity from our concept of "I" – our oldest article of faith…. Now, rather late in the day, we have become quite convinced that our concept of "I" guarantees nothing in the way of a real unity' (KGW VII/3, 14 [79]; LNB 14 [79], 246). Nietzsche, however, has a ready-made replacement. He suggests in *Beyond Good and Evil* that if we get rid of such a superstition, we do not need to get rid of the soul all together. Instead, we can understand 'soul as subject-multiplicity' (BGE 12), as 'A social structure of many souls' (BGE 19), or 'as social structure of drives and affects' (BGE 19). That is, we can understand the self not as a unity but as an economy within experience with warring drives with different goals. Just as the slave revolt that created the concept of a unitary soul was a kind of great politics, so too Nietzsche sets out to wage great politics by demonstrating the multiplicitous self.

During his mature period, Nietzsche's notes demonstrate that he is becoming more and more interested in the foundations of the self in Kantian philosophy. For example, following a section on Kant, Nietzsche writes in 1886–1887:

> Must not all philosophy finally bring to light the assumptions on which the movement of *reason* depends? *Our belief in the I* as substance, as the only reality on the basis of which we attribute reality to things in general? At last the oldest 'realism' comes to light: at the moment when the whole religious history of humanity recognizes itself as the history of the soul superstition. *Here there is a barrier:* our thinking itself involves that belief…, abandoning it means no longer being allowed to think. (KGW VIII/1, 7 [63]; LNB 7 [63], 140)

Nietzsche again argues that the I, as the basis of being, is the ground of knowledge, writing:

> If our 'I' is our only *being*, on the basis of which we make everything *be* or understand it to be, fine! Then it becomes very fair to doubt whether there isn't a perspectival *illusion* here – the illusory unity in which, as in a horizon, everything converges…. Finally, assuming that everything is becoming, *knowledge is only possible on the basis of belief in being*. (KGW VIII/1, 2 [91]; LNB 2 [91], 77)

For Nietzsche, as for Kant, the I is the originary unity upon which all other knowledge rests, including the ability to synthesise the manifold of experiences and posit objects or things. Nietzsche writes:

> We have borrowed the concept of unity from our concept of 'I' – our oldest article of faith. If we didn't consider ourselves to be unities, we would never have created the concept of 'thing'. Now, rather late in the day, we have become quite convinced that our concept of 'I' guarantees nothing in the way of real unity. (KGW VIII/3, 14 [79]; LNB 14 [79], 246)

Nietzsche develops a conceptualisation of the I as a pragmatic regulative fiction that is a condition of life. He writes in 1885:

> What separates me most deeply from the metaphysician is: I don't concede that the 'I' is what thinks. Instead, I take the *I itself to be a construction of thinking*, of the same rank as 'matter', 'thing', 'substance', 'individual', 'purpose', 'number', in other words to be only a *regulative fiction* with the help of which a kind of consistency and thus 'knowability' is inserted into, *invented into*, a world of becoming…. Something can be a condition of life and *nevertheless be false*. (KGW VII/3, [35]; LNB 35 [35], 20)

Not only is the unitary self, the I, a useful fiction and a condition of life, but also one of the prerequisites for a text having a unified authorial intention. That is, how could one write an autobiography that itself undermines the prerequisite of an autobiography: the unity of authorship?

Nietzsche is very clear about his plan for multiplicitous authorial intention in one of his first outlines of *Ecce Homo*. Notebook W II, 9 contains drafts of *Ecce Homo* and *Twilight of the Idols*. In that notebook we find an outline entitled "Ecce Homo: Notes on Duplicates [*Vielfaches*]" and then goes on to list six different internalised characters/authors who speak in the text (GSA 71, 165, [W II 9], 132; KGW VIII/24 [3], 3). This includes the psychologist, the philosopher, the poet, the musician, the writer and the educator. This multiplicitous self needs no single I, self, or soul to ground it. These different selves, this social structure of many souls, need not have a single unitary author. The multiple selves, these multiple subjects, might too be fictions without any singular author. It is only based upon our faith in grammar, in the grammatical subject, that we suggest that a single author, a single cause, to a text is necessary. In *Beyond Good and*

Evil, Nietzsche suggests that works of fiction need no author and responds to an objection, writing:

> And whoever were to ask: 'but doesn't an author belong with a fiction?' – could we not flatly respond: *why?* Does this 'belong' perhaps also belong to fiction? Is it not permitted by now to be a bit ironic towards the subject, as we are towards the predication and the object? Shouldn't the philosopher be permitted to rise above faith in grammar? (BGE 34)

Ecce Homo, then, is a project precisely along these lines to parody the unity of authorial intention and undermine the unity of the self. Nietzsche's inversion of the soul created out of slave morality's great politics of revenge, is then itself a form of great politics. Nietzsche's multiplicitous conception of self, performatively played out in *Ecce Homo*, undermines the unity of the self in Christianity which later manifested in Kantian philosophy, and in so doing opens our eyes to a new vision of personhood.

Bibliography

Campioni, Giuliano, Paolo D'Iorio, Maria Christina Fornari, Andrea Orsucci, Francesco Fronterotta (Eds.) (2003): *Nietzsches persönliche Bibliothek*. Berlin: De Gruyter.

Conway, Daniel W. (1988): "II. Solving the Problem of Socrates: Nietzsche's Zarathustra as Political Irony". In: *Political Theory* 16. No. 2, pp. 257–280.

Conway, Daniel W. (1992): "Nietzsche's Art of This-Worldly Comfort: Self-Reference and Strategic Self-Parody". In: *History of Philosophy Quarterly* 9. No. 3, pp. 343–357.

Conway, Daniel W. (1993): "Nietzsche's *Doppelgänger:* Affirmation and Resentment in *Ecce Homo*". In: Keith Ansell-Pearson and Howard Caygill (Eds.): *The Fate of the New Nietzsche*, pp. 55–78. Aldershot: Avebury Press.

Cox, Christoph (1999): *Nietzsche: Naturalism and Interpretation*. Berkeley: University of California Press.

Del Caro, Adrian (2004): *Grounding the Nietzsche Rhetoric of Earth*. New York: Walter de Gruyter.

Derrida, Jacques (1986): "Interpreting Signatures (Nietzsche/Heidegger): Two Questions". In: *Philosophy and Literature* 10. No. 2, pp. 246–262.

Foucault, Michel (1977): "What is an Author?". In: *Language, Counter-Memory, Practice*, pp. 113–138. Edited by Donald F. Bouchard and translated by Donald F. Bouchard and Sherry Simon. Ithaca: Cornell University Press.

Gilman, Sander L. (1974): "Nietzsche and the Pastoral Metaphor". In: *Comparative Literature* 26. No. 4, pp. 289–298.

Gooding-Williams, Robert (2001): *Zarathustra's Dionysian Modernism*. Stanford: Stanford University Press.

Griffin, Drew E. (1994): "Nietzsche on Tragedy and Parody". In: *Philosophy and Literature* 18. No. 2, pp. 339–347.

Grundlehner, Philip (1986): *The Poetry of Friedrich Nietzsche*. Oxford: Oxford University Press.

Inkpin, Andrew. (2018): "Nietzsche's *Genealogy:* A Textbook Parody". In: *Nietzsche-Studien* 47 No. 1, pp. 140–166.
Janz, Curt Paul (1973): "Friedrich Nietzsches Akademische Lehrtätigkeit in Basel 1869–1879". In: *Nietzsche-Studien* 3. No. 1, pp. 192–203.
Kant, Immanuel (2017): *Critique of Pure Reason.* Edited and translated by Paul Guyer and Allen Wood. Cambridge, New York: Cambridge University Press.
Klossowski, Pierre: (1963): *Un si funeste désir,* pp. 185–228. Paris: Gallimard.
Kunnas, Tarmo (1982): *Nietzsches Lachen: Eine Studie über das Komische in Nietzsches Werken.* Edition Wissenschaft und Literatur. München: Flade and Partner.
Large, Duncan (2001): "Nietzsche's Use of Biblical Language". In: *Journal of Nietzsche Studies* 22. No. 1, pp. 88–115.
Magnus, Bernd (1988): "The Deification of the Commonplace: *Twilight of the Idols*". In: Robert Solomon and Kathleen Higgins (Eds.): *Reading Nietzsche,* pp. 152–181. New York: Oxford University Press.
Magnus, Bernd, and Kathleen M. Higgins (1996): "Nietzsche's Works and Their Themes". In: Bernd Magnus and Kathleen M. Higgins (Eds.): *The Cambridge Companion to Nietzsche,* pp 21–68. Cambridge, New York: Cambridge University Press.
Marsden, Jill (2006): "Nietzsche and the Art of the Aphorism". In: Keith Ansell-Person (Ed.): *A Companion to Nietzsche,* pp. 22–38. Oxford: Blackwell Publishing.
Megill, Allan (1996): "Review: Historicizing Nietzsche? Paradoxes and Lessons of a Hard Case". In: *The Journal of Modern History* 58. No. 1, pp. 114–152.
Meyer, Matthew (2012): "The Comic Nature of *Ecce Homo*". In: *Journal of Nietzsche Studies* 43. No. 1, pp. 32–43.
Montinari, Mazzino: (2003) *Reading Nietzsche.* Translated by Greg Whitlock. Chicago: University of Illinois Press.
More, Nicholas D. (2014): *Nietzsche's Last Laugh:* Ecce Homo *as Satire.* Cambridge, New York: Cambridge University Press.
Nehamas, Alexander (2002): *Nietzsche: Life as Literature.* Cambridge: Harvard University Press.
Nelson, Donald F. (1973): "Nietzsche, Zarathustra, and the Jesus Redivivus: The Unholy Trinity". In: *The Germanic Review: Literature, Culture, Theory* 48. No. 3, pp. 175–188.
Nietzsche, Friedrich (1869): *Homer und die klassische Philologie.* Basel: Bonfantini.
Nietzsche, Friedrich (1909): "Homer and Classical Philology". In: *On the Future of our Educational Institutions: Homer and Classical Philology,* pp. 145–170. Translated by J. M. Kennedy. Edinburgh, London: T. N. Foulis.
Nietzsche, Friedrich (1967-): *Kritische Gesamtausgabe Werke.* Begründet von Giorgio Colli, Mazzino Montinari, weitergeführt von Volker Gerhardt, Norbert Miller, Wolfgang Müller-Lauter and Karl Pestalozzi. Berlin: Walter de Gruyter.
Nietzsche, Friedrich (1975–1984): *Sämtliche Briefe. Kritische Studienausgabe in 8 Bänden.* Edited by Giorgio Colli and Mazzino Montinari. Berlin, New York: Walter de Gruyter; Munich: DTV.
Nietzsche, Friedrich (1988): *Ecce Homo: Wie man wird was man ist.* Frankfurt a.M: Insel Verlag.
Nietzsche, Friedrich (1989): *On the Genealogy of Morals and Ecce Homo.* Edited and translated by Walter Kaufmann. New York: Vintage Books.

Nietzsche, Friedrich (1994): *Frühe Schriften*, vols. 1–5. Edited by Hans Joachim Mette and Karl Schlechta. München: Verlag C. B. Beck.
Nietzsche, Friedrich (1995a): *Human, All Too Human*. In: *The Complete Works of Friedrich Nietzsche, Vol 3*. Edited by Bernd Magnus and translated by Gary Handwerk. Stanford: Stanford University Press.
Nietzsche, Friedrich (1995b): *Unfashionable Observations*. In: *The Complete Works of Friedrich Nietzsche, Vol 2*. Edited by Alan D. Schrift and translated by Richard Gary. Stanford: Stanford University Press.
Nietzsche, Friedrich (1996): *Selected Letters of Friedrich Nietzsche*. Edited and translated by Christopher Middleton. Indianapolis: Hackett Publishing Co.
Nietzsche, Friedrich (1997): *Untimely Meditations*. Edited by Daniel Breazeale and translated by R. J. Hollingdale. Cambridge, New York: Cambridge University Press.
Nietzsche, Friedrich (2003a): *The Gay Science*. Edited by Bernard Williams and translated by Josefine Nauckhoff and Adrian Del Caro. Cambridge, New York: Cambridge University Press.
Nietzsche, Friedrich (2003b): *Writings from the Late Notebooks*. Edited by Rüdiger Bittner and translated by Kate Sturge. Cambridge, New York: Cambridge University Press.
Nietzsche, Friedrich (2005): *Thus Spoke Zarathustra: A Book for All and None*. Translated by Clancy Martin. New York: Barnes and Noble.
Nietzsche, Friedrich (2010): "On the Concept of the Organic since Kant". Translated by Th. Nawrath. In: *The Agonist: A Nietzsche Circle Journal* 3. No. 1, pp. 86–110.
Nietzsche, Friedrich (2012a): *The Case of Wagner*. In: *The Anti-Christ, Ecce Homo, Twilight of the Idols and Other Writings*, pp. 231–262. Edited by Aaron Ridley and Judith Norman and translated by Judith Norman. Cambridge, New York: Cambridge University Press.
Nietzsche, Friedrich (2012b): *Ecce Homo*. In: *The Anti-Christ, Ecce Homo, Twilight of the Idols and Other Writings*, pp. 69–152. Edited by Aaron Ridley and Judith Norman and translated by Judith Norman. Cambridge, New York: Cambridge University Press.
Nietzsche, Friedrich (2012c): *Nietzsche contra Wagner*. In: *The Anti-Christ, Ecce Homo, Twilight of the Idols and Other Writings*, pp. 69–152. Edited by Aaron Ridley and Judith Norman and translated by Judith Norman. Cambridge, New York: Cambridge University Press.
Nietzsche, Friedrich (2012d): *Twilight of the Idols*. In: *The Anti-Christ, Ecce Homo, Twilight of the Idols and Other Writings*, pp. 153–230. Edited by Aaron Ridley and Judith Norman and translated by Judith Norman. Cambridge, New York: Cambridge University Press.
Nietzsche, Friedrich (2013): *Human, All Too Human II*. In: *Human, All Too Human II and Unpublished Fragments from the Period of Human, All Too Human II (Spring 1878–Fall 1879). The Complete Works of Friedrich Nietzsche, Vol 4*, pp. 3–396. Edited by Alan D. Schrift and translated by Gary Handwerk. Stanford: Stanford University Press.
Nietzsche, Friedrich (2014a): *Beyond Good and Evil*. In: *Beyond Good and Evil, On the Genealogy of Morality. The Complete Works of Friedrich Nietzsche, Vol. 8*, pp. 1–206. Edited by Alan D. Schrift and translated by Adrian Del Caro. Stanford: Stanford University Press.
Nietzsche, Friedrich (2014b): *On the Genealogy of Morality*. In: *Beyond Good and Evil, On the Genealogy of Morality. The Complete Works of Friedrich Nietzsche, Vol 8*, pp. 207–352. Edited by Alan D. Schrift and translated by Adrian Del Caro. Stanford: Stanford University Press.

Nussbaum, Martha (1997): "Is Nietzsche a Political Thinker?" In: *International Journal of Philosophical Studies* 5. No. 1, pp. 1–13.
Oehler, Max (1997): *Bibliothek Nietzsches: Verzeichnis in systematischer Anordnung nach Oehler.* Weimar: Herzogin Anna Amalia Bibliothek.
Parkhurst, William A. B. (2020): "Does Nietzsche have *a Nachlass?*" In: *Nietzsche-Studien* 50. No. 1, pp 216–257.
Plato (1997): *Phaedo.* In: *Complete Works*, pp. 49–100. Edited by John M. Cooper and D. S. Hutchinson and translated by G.M.A. Grube. Indianapolis: Hackett Publishing Co.
Schaberg, William H. (1995): *The Nietzsche Cannon: A Publication History and Bibliography.* Chicago: University of Chicago Press.
Shapiro, Gary (1989): *Nietzschean Narratives.* Bloomington: Indiana University Press.
Solomon, Robert, and Kathleen M. Higgins (2000): *What Nietzsche Really Said.* New York: Schocken Books.
Swift, Paul (2005): *Becoming Nietzsche: Early Reflections on Democritus, Schopenhauer, and Kant.* New York: Lexington Books.
Trippett, David (2013): *Wagner's Melodies: Aesthetics and Materialism in German Musical Identity.* Cambridge, New York: Cambridge University Press.

Niklas Corall
Voluntary Submission and the 'Politics of Truth': Nietzsche and Foucault on the Danger of the Fully Normalised 'Last Human'

Abstract: Nietzsche and Foucault offer critical genealogies of how an important narrative promising the emancipation from sovereign power through truth has instead led to the opposite, a voluntary submission under the "true discourse" and what is declared to be normal. In the centre of this development lies the assumption of an essential identity which makes the "discovery" of its true self through scientific and rational reflection the most adequate approach to secure individuality and autonomy. A dystopian horizon of full normalisation is portrayed with the parable of the Last Human's voluntary submission in *Thus Spoke Zarathustra*. The chapter explores a theoretical response to this dystopian scenario with Nietzsche's praxeological model of identity. It suggests the combination of actions and different procedures of memory constituting a dynamic, non-essential but constantly actualised individual.

1 Introduction

Nietzsche and Foucault seek to understand why modern humanity, having emancipated itself from disempowering superstition and the patronising rule of metaphysical shepherds, does not try to 'expand what the concept "human" might encompass' (HL 2), but instead becomes complicit in the development towards a 'normal human type' (GS 143). Instead of exploring humanity's capacity continually to overcome itself, modern societies attempt to fix what is to be considered a normal human being and normal human behaviour. The process of Enlightenment was expected to ferment a liberation from external expectations and the rule of others. It must now be investigated why, even now that 'God is dead' (GS 125), modern humanity appears to be voluntarily working towards a self-understanding and self-modelling that ensures its efficient and easy governability.

In this chapter, I will argue that in order to understand the modern development of 'voluntary submission' (section 2),[1] it is crucial to understand the analysis of the effects of power surrounding the establishment of what Foucault labels 'true discourse' (Foucault 1981, p. 54) and the essential qualities of Nietzsche's idea of the 'will to truth' (GM III, 24) (section 3).[2] The phrase true discourse describes a specific form of discourse in which the value of a statement is not based on who speaks or under what circumstances, but whether or not it can be assumed that the statement is true (or scientifically valid) by the participants of the discourse (Foucault 1981, pp. 54–56). The phrase 'Politics of Truth' is used to express both the influence of power over what can be established as truth and the effects resulting from what is established as truth (Foucault 2007, p. 47). It is this which for Foucault offers the most efficient means of enforcing a normal human type and thus making political subjects calculable and governable in a modern society (section 4).

While Foucault brilliantly applies Nietzsche's critique to modern societies (section 5), it is worthwhile to return to Nietzsche's *Thus Spoke Zarathustra*. Its fictional narrative philosopher presents a discursive framework that aims at what could be labelled a 'politics of difference'. The term 'narrative' is used here to denominate discursive frameworks that are not in relation to a 'truth-maker', meaning any form of foundation that seemingly guarantees the truth of the framework as a whole, such as recollection of eternal ideas, empirical evidence, insight into theological revelation or deduction from a priori concepts or laws. Instead, narrative discursive frameworks provide the recipients with a consistent, yet contingent perspective – be it a system, a method, a story, a future, an ideal – in which they can locate themselves. While I consider it to be the case that all discursive frameworks are narratives – including the narrative that truth is the only valid source of value and mere narratives are not worthwhile pursuing – I will use the term 'narrative philosophy' to specify a philosophical approach that is aware of the narrative dimension of philosophical discourses and deliberately and openly aims at providing narratives. Zarathustra's philosophy introduces a twofold narrative that challenges the ideas of normality and 'true identity' (section 6).

---

[1] The term 'voluntary submission' is used here to counterpose Foucault's definition of critique as 'voluntary insubordination' from "What is Critique?" (Foucault 2007, p. 47).

[2] Regarding modern forms of power, many interpreters focus on Nietzsche's ideas of incorporation and corporeal "mnemonics" from *On the Genealogy of Morals* (GM II, 1–14), which is also an important line of argument. For example, see Butler (1997, pp. 63–78). Foucault also has a strong focus on this aspect of Nietzsche's philosophy in his essay "Nietzsche, Genealogy, History", see Foucault (1984).

2 The Last Human and Voluntary Submission

To illustrate the potential effects of a Politics of Truth, the parable of the 'Last Human' in *Thus Spoke Zarathustra* provides a metaphorical depiction of a fully normalised human society.[3] It is important to note that the Last Human is not introduced as a parody. In *Human, All-Too Human*, Nietzsche even considers a model of tempered passions and contemplative happiness as a positive response to the fast-paced and overstimulating modern condition (HH 34).[4] At the centre of humanity's self-understanding lies the idea of freedom from any enforced external rule. The Last Human proclaims, 'No shepherd and one herd! Each wants the same, each is the same, and whoever feels differently goes voluntarily into the insane asylum' (Z I, Prologue, 5). The Last Human is not oppressed by anyone,[5] nor does he function within any hierarchical structure of asymmetric distribution of power, instead he freely chooses the happiness he 'invented' (Z I, Prologue, 5).

In *Zarathustra*, this future narrative of the Last Human is affirmed by the post-theological, post-metaphysical humans in the marketplace, who – while laughing at Zarathustra's plurality-based agonistic model of the 'Overhuman' (Z I, Prologue, 3) – aspire to develop towards this Last Human (Z I, Prologue, 5). This is understandable, as central social human ideals, such as happiness, health, security or the fulfilment of basic needs, are provided for in the depicted society (Z I, Prologue, 5). There is no struggle, as the self-proclaimed inventors of happiness have achieved universal peace and a non-hierarchical social order. Scientific progress, mainly understood as historical and medical knowledge, is well developed. The survivors of times in which 'the whole world was insane' understand themselves as the creators of their own positive fate (Z I, Prologue, 5).

---

[3] 'Last Human' will be used instead of Adrian Del Caro's translation 'Last Human Being'. Also, 'Overhuman' will be used for *Übermensch*.
[4] In *Nietzsche's Search for Philosophy*, Keith Ansell-Pearson considers this 'wise Humanity' as the 'free spirit', which further underlines the ambivalence in the portrayal of the Last Human: 'Nietzsche's model of the free spirit at this time is a specific and a curious one. He posits a "free" and "fearless hovering" above all things, including human beings and their customs, laws and traditional evaluations as the most desirable condition (HH 34). In addition, the free spirit has purified itself of the affects and communicates the "joy" of this elevated condition of passionless contemplation' (Ansell-Pearson 2018, p. 31).
[5] Thus, the Last Human is not an example of developed slave morality, as the latter requires an outside oppression to originate and persist. Slave morality is understood as a "no" to the predominant power-structures. The Last Human does not understand itself in opposition to external oppression and appears to be without any form of *ressentiment*.

However, Zarathustra depicts a humanity that developed into a 'herd' (Z I, Prologue, 5) in the apparent absence of shepherds. Individuals who deviate from the emotional, cognitive or discursive norm judge themselves to be unfit for human society, as simple deviation from an expected norm is reason enough for self-marginalisation and even self-admittance to psychiatric or medical correctional facilities. This metaphorically predicts a distinctive feature of modern societies described by Foucault. The government of a population through normalisation allows for a subject not visibly oppressed to act voluntarily and to function efficiently in a provided framework of normality – a framework of complete voluntary submission. The norm has been incorporated and is constantly performed, reiterated and reproduced. As the connection between the belief in truth as the singular possible measurement of value and the Last Human's submission to normality are not directly presented in the passage from *Thus Spoke Zarathustra*, I will first establish this connection with recourse to passages from *The Gay Science*.

3 The Essence of the Will to Truth

Almost a century before Foucault built upon Nietzsche's terminology to analyse true discourse, his German precursor questioned the value of modernity's will to truth. Nietzsche's investigation is neither solely an attempt to refute the epistemological possibility of truth, nor a critique of specific concepts that are believed to be true. Instead, the essence of the will to truth (GM III, 27), that is, the belief in truth as the only legitimate source of value concerning knowledge, emotions or identity, is put into question. On the one hand, a quasi-pragmatic line of argument questions the efficiency of discourses based on truth. If the scientific discourse cannot offer values and goals that positively overcome the superstitious interpretations it devalues, the assumed progress of science is not necessarily beneficial for humanity.[6] In the final passages of *On the Genealogy of Morals* (GM III, 24–27),[7] Nietzsche investigates why humanity continues this pursuit of truth at every cost, despite the lurking threat of nihilism through the devaluation of the highest ideals and the inability of science to produce new ideals (GM III, 27). I will focus on an adjacent line of argument that unravels intrinsic differences between a discourse based on an assumed truth – however such an as-

---

[6] The second *Untimely Meditation*, "On the Uses and Disadvantages of History for Life", is also an example of this. See n. 15, below, for a more extensive example.

[7] In part quoting himself from the second edition of the *Gay Science* (GS 344; GS Preface, 4).

sumed truth is established – and different forms of discourse, in relation to social subjectivation.

In section 143 of *The Gay Science*, titled "The greatest advantage of polytheism", Nietzsche points out an essential characteristic of true discourse that distinguishes it from other forms of valuing, such as tradition, developmental perspectives or vitalism. He shows a direct connection of true discourse and standardisation through a critical study of two different applications of the norm 'human' within the religious belief-systems of polytheism and monotheism.[8] Within polytheistic narratives, this norm is based on the dynamic of situational-perspectival needs and goals of a people, while in monotheistic narratives, the norm is based on its assumed truth, established through true discourse as warranted by the true god.

With polytheism, on the one hand, Nietzsche describes the agonistic coexistence of peoples with their respective folk gods, which represent their worshippers' self-conceptualisation and their conditions of survival and growth within given circumstances. Neighbouring folk gods are considered real, yet inferior or malevolent towards one's own gods. The proclaimed 'advantage' of this form of polytheism lies in the idea that the mythological act of creating one's folk gods offered both an apology for egocentrism and for creating an individual ideal breaking with the ideas of the herd (GS 143). Adopting the perspective of a higher being enabled the individual metaphysically to alienate themselves from formerly self-evident cultural practices, and thus facilitated the re-evaluation and eventual abandonment of familiar sets of values formerly shared with the group. In this polytheistic framework, the norm human is used pluralistically, individualistically and constructively. Nietzsche writes, 'There was only one norm, "*the* human being" – and every people believed itself to have this one and ultimate norm. But above and outside oneself, in a distant overworld, one got to see a *plurality of norms*, one god was not the denial of or anathema to another god!' (GS 143). In each tribe, the aspired or enforced norm is presented as singular and necessary but functioning within a pluralistic setting of competing norms.[9] Nietzsche writes that the 'invention of gods, heroes, and over[humans] [*Übermenschen*] of all kinds' within polytheism allowed for the recognition of an out-

---

[8] Nietzsche uses the term 'polytheism', but it should be noted that he describes a belief-system in which each individual tribe has a singular god and not a pantheon of gods. The label 'henotheism' would thus be more appropriate, as it describes a system of belief in which your god is not the only one, yet it is merely considered the best, strongest or most fruitful of gods. Nevertheless, in this chapter, I will maintain the vocabulary Nietzsche uses.

[9] See Z I, Goals, for another metaphorical depiction of norm as both singular and necessary within a tribe and agonistic and pluralistic in regard to humanity as a whole.

side of the respective norm of a people, in which additional personified norms – other god figures – were not negated but merely disdained (GS 143). The norm demands absolute devotion, yet it is subordinated to the prerequisites for survival that reality dictates. If the values represented by one's folk god did not allow for a positive development of a people, the god's capabilities, rather than its reality, were put into question. The mythical agonism between these different personifications of an ideal humanity remained dependent on the mundane agonistic struggle for tribal development. In cases of a detrimental development within the people or a subjugation by other peoples, it was assumed that the triumphant gods represented superior sets of values and were often adopted as new gods to worship in place of the evidently inferior gods that were worshipped before. Thus, in polytheism, the gods are challenged and judged based on the development of the corresponding people, not by the supposed truth of their divine or metaphysical representation. The metaphysically represented norms are upheld or abandoned based on their impact on mundane developments.

Monotheism, on the other hand, is introduced as the direct antithesis of polytheism. It is understood as the 'rigid consequence of the teachings of a normal human type – that is, the belief in a normal god next to whom there are only false pseudo-gods' (GS 143). This assumption is considered to be the 'greatest danger to humanity so far, it threatened us with ... premature stagnation' (GS 143). As in polytheism, a singular norm is applied, yet the framework surrounding this norm is fundamentally reinterpreted. While polytheism allowed for plural interpretations of what the idea human can encompass, monotheism aims for a convergence towards a 'normal human type'. The value of the monotheistic norm does not derive from its applicability in any given circumstances, nor does it depend on a positive development of a people, but it is based solely on its assumed truth, excluding pseudo-gods and their sets of ideals from even competing for efficiency with the true ideal represented by the true God (GS 143). In a case where the belief in the true God results in suffering and enslavement, it is not the God's capabilities that are questioned, but the life circumstances are reinterpreted as a form of punishment or test (A 25). In contrast to the polytheistic model, in which reality serves as an anchor critically to assess the quality of the ideal represented in the people's god, the metaphysical truth of the monotheistic God instead serves as an anchor to interpret reality in a way that is compatible with the true discourse. The value deriving from the truth of the worshipped God is rated as more fundamental than the idols leading other people to positive developments or superiority. The idea of humanity as developing through overcoming burdens and challenges is replaced by a normal human type bearing the consequences of their true fate. Nietzsche understands the summary of this development as a 'two-thousand-year discipline *towards truth*' as the most adequate description of Christian dominance in occidental culture (GM III, 27, translation modified, emphasis added).¹⁰ He also considers this path of standardisation of humanity through an unconditional attachment to the value of truth as the greatest danger humanity faces.

The dichotomy between the monotheistic and polytheistic traditions illustrates essential differences in the use and consequences of discourses, based either on life experience or on the assumption of truth or its substitutes. However, this conceptual framework is limited neither historically nor systematically to the idea of a true God vouching for the true discourse. In the case of Christianity, Nietzsche acknowledges the extraordinary scale on which true discourse is applied yet does not attribute any originality to Christianity concerning the use of an assumed true world devaluing a world of mundane experience. Instead, the "Christian" idea that truth has an intrinsic value warranted by the true God was originally introduced by the 'proleptically Christian', Plato (TI Ancients, 2). As Nietzsche illustrates in "How the 'true world' finally became a fable", Christianity and rationalism are primarily sophistications in the reiteration of the Platonic distinction between the true world and our mundane reality of mere appearance (TI, Fable).¹¹ While monotheism has produced the most impactful consequences, this critical analysis is not limited historically to monotheistic truth-based interpretations of reality.

As was metaphorically hinted at in the initial interpretation of the Last Human, Nietzsche extends this critique of extensive devaluation of experienced life to other areas in which true discourse is applied. This especially applies to the seemingly post-metaphysical modern scientific discourse. This appears counterintuitive, as modern science, instead of claiming to produce absolute truths, understands itself as providing approximations towards a more objective and cohesive understanding of reality and refrains from ever assuming the ability to explain reality from the outside (GS 344). Science could thus be understood as overcoming metaphysics and the idea of absolute truth altogether. Nietzsche anticipated this contestation and, while much of his critique is focused on Christianity, he discusses scientific method specifically in light of its self-perception of refraining from assuming truths, and instead working with hypotheses (GS 344).

---

10 Italics mark my modified translation. Carol Diethe's translation reads: 'two-thousand-year discipline in truth-telling', which reduces the passage to the active dimension of deception. As the German passage is more ambiguous, mentioning solely a general 'Zucht zur Wahrheit' (GM III, 27), it is not valid to drop the aspect of not wanting to be deceived in this passage without changing the meaning of Nietzsche's line of argument.
11 In this passage, 'INCIPIT ZARATHUSTRA' is marked as the end of the old narrative (TI, Fable).

Nietzsche tentatively introduces science as overcoming the ascetic ideal and as the cornerstone of a new ideal for human society in the third essay of *On the Genealogy of Morals* – quoting the fifth book of *The Gay Science* in important steps of the argument. He arrives at the conclusion that 'even we knowers of today, we godless anti-metaphysicians' still base our hypothetical method on nothing but a metaphysical prejudice assuming the absolute superiority of truth over superstition and deceit (GS 344). As agents of the modern scientific discourse, we 'still take our fire, too, from the flame lit by the thousand-year old faith, the Christian faith which was also Plato's faith, that God is truth; that truth is divine' (GS 344). Overcoming Christianity and the true God vouching for the true world is considered merely another step in our worship of truth and enlightenment over illusion and falsehood in general (GM III, 24), thus a final result of the aforementioned two-thousand-year discipline towards truth. Focusing on hypotheses and refraining from producing "truths" is unravelled as a moral imperative forbidding oneself to use narratives and falsehoods or subjective speculations; and – as truth is no longer an option – an imperative at least not to lie.[12] While we might think that we do not believe in the superiority of truth anymore, we still believe in the inferiority and damnability of lies, deceit, errors and falsehoods.

The objects of Nietzsche's critique are not the epistemological possibilities of modern science, but the uninterrupted belief in a metaphysical order of values. It is the will to truth, which has not lost its influence over humanity, that is put into question. It is therefore important to note that Nietzsche's critique does not encourage relativism. On the contrary, his critique of the will to truth shows that the ostensible dichotomy of either truth-based value or relativism is itself based on the belief that truth is the only possible source of value, while, as Nietzsche points out on several occasions,[13] there have always been alternative foundations for values in human societies. The assumption of a missing third option is itself a discursive strategy to stabilise the perceived necessity of some form of truth, be it vouched for by a true God or the most precise hypothetical

---

[12] Nietzsche focuses on this moral imperative in GS 344 and GM III, 24 – 27, and he understands questioning the value of the will to truth as the final step towards its 'self-overcoming' (GM III, 27). I consider the basic argument of a metaphysical hierarchy of values still being in place as sufficient and will not discuss the moral imperative in this chapter.

[13] The strongest example is discussed in the second *Untimely Meditation*, "On the Uses and Disadvantages of History for Life". Nietzsche presents the *monumental*, the *antiquarian* and the *critical* historical perspectives in opposition to his contemporary '*demand that history should be a science*' (HL 4). He describes the three non-scientific perspectives as the 'natural relationship of an age, a culture, a nation with its history' (HL 4). Despite them being detrimental to historical truth, they function as productive horizons for future developments.

approximation provided by the scientific methods we have at our disposal. Challenging the will to truth thus does not release us from social responsibilities, but instead presents them as our responsibilities.

Nietzsche's more systematic analysis and critique of the will to truth remained a desideratum due to his productive period being drastically cut short (GM III, 24). However, even though there is no systematic elaboration of what might fill the void left by the true God vouching for absolute truth, I will argue that his analysis of the Last Human allows for an understanding of how the metaphysical ideas of a shared and normal true human nature, of a true order of things, of a true set of values and identities have been substituted by what can be measured and formulated within scientific discourse. As there is no further ulterior, metaphysical or theological measure against which we can hold ourselves, it is only the interrelation of measurable aspects of humanity that can be scientifically fixed. Science may not go beyond perceivable and quantifiable aspects of known humanity – and it often does not go beyond contemporary humanity (HH 2) – but it can build upon measurable aspects and their interrelation to formulate precise normal expectations in central aspects of human life, establishing average or normal regulating expectations in areas such as happiness or health. In this way, happiness was 'invented' (Z I, Prologue, 5).[14]

The Last Human allows for a visualisation of how a society might function in which normality is not derived from approximating the likeness of a metaphysically personified true human self as revealed by metaphysical shepherds, but from the scientific anchor per se, in which individual humans are understood in reference to interrelated measures of normality and deviations from it. Voluntary exclusion or marginalisation of oneself or others as abnormal, "untrue to oneself", or rationally unaccountable is based on the standardising reduction of individual qualities to a "true identity" which can be expressed within a grid of scientifically produced knowledge. Following Nietzsche and Foucault, it is not "truth" or "knowledge" that needs to be criticised, but the unconditional will to truth that holds on to normality as the scientific substitute for truth.

The connection between the Last Human and true discourse is thus clear in the context of the human condition after the death of God, as a combination of accepting the absence of absolute metaphysical measure and the need for re-stabilising the order of things. However, following this line of argument, it appears that the focus on scientific method is nothing more than the result of a habitu-

---

14 The word 'invention' is well chosen, as it is used in both processes of narrative fabrication and processes of scientific developments.

ation to the formerly predominant true discourse of monotheism, nothing but another 'shadow of God' within which we still attempt to function (GS 109). Indeed, Nietzsche uses this terminology when criticising the unconditional pursuit of the will to truth and considers the scientific prejudice against falsehood a moral imperative (GS 344). As I believe that this explanation falls short of accounting for the unquestioned acceptance of the rapid and widespread extension of true discourse within modern societies, I will follow Foucault's genealogy of the 'Platonic myth' as a more fruitful basis on which to understand the success of the scientific substitutes for truth beyond the death of God.[15] As I will show, the alternative genealogy does not only illustrate the ways in which true discourse was applied, but also the hopes and aspirations that are connected with realigning different discourses according to true discourse from the perspective of modern subjects.

4 From the Great Myth of Plato towards a Politics of Truth

The expression will to truth is used differently by Nietzsche and Foucault. While Nietzsche uses it to describe the unconditional belief in an intrinsic value of truth, and truth as the exclusive measure of values, Foucault builds on this concept and establishes an understanding of how such true discourse is used to realign discursive practices and to legitimise and enhance social power. Both thinkers deliver analyses of the importance of truth in the Christian tradition and the Christian application of power, yet both remain vague in their genealogies regarding the means with which true discourse was originally established and what allowed it to evolve into the discursive hegemony it remains today. The common ground of their analyses of the historical origin of true discourse is that both consider Plato's philosophy to have started the process through which most societies and social institutions have instituted a version of the true discourse as the predominant form of valuing.[16]

---

[15] I will refer to it as the Platonic Myth, although Foucault does not use this exact expression.
[16] While Nietzsche mentions in one of the most important sections that it was Plato's faith, 'that God is truth; that truth is divine' that was driving the unconditional belief in truth over deceit (GS 344), Foucault describes very abruptly that finalised with Plato, 'a certain division was established, separating true discourse from false discourse' (Foucault 1981, p. 54).

In *Truth and Juridical Forms*, Foucault offers an interpretation of Nietzsche's "On Truth and Lies in an Extra-moral Sense".[17] He concludes that Nietzsche was the first philosopher to work towards destroying the predominant philosophical narrative in western culture, which he labels the 'great myth' established by Plato:

> The West would be dominated by the great myth according to which truth never belongs to political power.... With Plato there began a great Western myth, that there is an antinomy between knowledge and power. If there is knowledge, it must renounce power. Where knowledge and science are found in their pure truth, there can no longer be any political power. (Foucault 2000, p. 32)

According to Foucault, Plato's philosophy constitutes an ostensible change from a discourse of power to a discourse of truth (Foucault 1981, p. 54). The Platonic myth implies that the sphere of truth cannot be penetrated by power, that truth can function as a shelter from mundane hierarchy,[18] and that power can be judged, delegitimised and potentially regulated from a perspective based on truth. Once true discourse is established within a society, power must answer to questions of legitimacy, and any false claims of authority can be rejected based on the disciplinary requirements of truth, be it rational reflection, scientific examination or religious revelation. The perceived value of truth for the individual lies in its potential for self-governance unhindered by the possible influences of others. Sovereign rule, the abusive and arbitrary use of power, and pre-existing hierarchical structures must now answer to, and be formulated within, the true discourse. Critical and constructive potential has henceforth shifted from the performative word of a powerful group or individual to the true discourse: 'the highest truth no longer resided in what discourse was or did, but in what it said' (Foucault 1981, p. 54).

The focus on truth thus provided an important means to break open rigid social hierarchical structures, especially regarding justice and morals.[19] In most western societies, the blatant discourse based on displays of sovereign

---

17 The close reading of Nietzsche's text by can be found mainly in Foucault (2000, pp. 6–15).
18 In the dystopian novel *Nineteen Eighty-Four*, George Orwell exemplifies the application of the Platonic myth. As the protagonist is tortured to submit to the party on both the conscious and subconscious, emotional level, the protagonist holds on to the mathematical formula 'two plus two make four' as an anchor to resist the intrusion of power (Orwell 2000, p. 226). The protagonist assumes that, as logical truth cannot be altered by power, one needs to hold on to truth in order not to become the submissive subject of sovereign power.
19 While I will focus on Foucault's genealogy, noble morality as described by Nietzsche is a good example of the discourse of power discussed by Foucault.

power had successfully been overcome by the discourse of truth, largely unrelated to the status of the persons involved in it. Before widespread establishment of this true discourse, justice or legitimacy was regulated through a performative act by the sovereign, a proof of testimony by the invoked God, or by challenges in the manner of duels (Foucault 2000, pp. 37–42). These exemplary measures are based upon power or status. In contrast, the narrative of a non-hierarchical true discourse provided the possibility of disentangling justice from power by linking justice to truth instead. This does not mean that there has not been a ritualised apparatus established around juridical decisions, as I will discuss later. Rather, it means that, ideally, neither status nor position determines innocence or guilt. Indeed, the analysis of the true course of events provides the basis for judgement. In *Truth and Juridical Forms*, Foucault illustrates how the intertwining of justice and truth has both helped us to rid ourselves of the arbitrary rule of sovereign power, and also allowed for further entry points into spheres of individuality previously understood as impenetrable by power.

Within the discourse of power, the word or performative gesture of the sovereign constituted what shall be considered justice and legal jurisdiction. This drastically changed with the implementation of true discourse. It suddenly became necessary to investigate the respective course of events, circumstances and participants in order to derive a truth-based foundation on which to base objective verdicts. Through meticulous inquisition and investigation, through the testimonies of witnesses, and through employing a scientific apparatus, it now became necessary to unfold motives, the course of events, circumstances and biographical backgrounds, in order adequately to judge the situation. Additional psychological profiles, the medico-chemical investigation of a crime scene or a body might be consulted before any judgement – not considered an act of declaring the right, but instead as concluding remarks of the ongoing investigation – could be delivered.[20] This truth-based judicial system was formed around an idea of justice as part of a non-hierarchical discourse in which an impartial judge functioned as an extension of true justice manifesting itself in the given juridical context.[21] This ideally resulted in sovereign power being restricted from performing any acts of justice that were not publicly justifiable, thus radically liberating subjects of sovereign power from experiencing its arbitrary and intrusive exercise. However, while the adoption of the true discourse within jurisdiction is of utmost importance in defence against the arbitrariness of the sovereign use of power, the perceived liberation entails problematic effects.

---

[20] See, for example, Foucault (1978, pp. 31–32).
[21] See Foucault (2000, pp. 42–45).

Firstly, while a duel or an ordeal by battle had been cruel and unfair procedures for determining justice, the involved individuals' personal lives, emotions, motivations, constitutions or thoughts remained in the private domain. The power applied was able to have a drastic impact on the individuals' external circumstances yet had no valid and voluntarily provided point of entry into the individuals' inner life. The habits, biographies and motivations of the concerned individuals remained outside the grasp of power until they were willingly presented to the public domain in order to allow for truth to prevail and the non-hierarchical discourse to function. By contrast, with the discourse of truth, while liberating itself from the intrusive abuse of power, the individual surrenders its private domain and is drawn into the sphere of public examination (Foucault 1978, pp. 60–64).[22] As modern subjects liberate themselves from the blatant discourse of power, they voluntarily submit their previously private sphere to the true discourse and the rules of its (social) genesis. Even in an ideal scenario, in a discourse free of hierarchical structures, in which there was an identifiable truth untouched by power, it would still be debatable whether or not the unconditional submission to the true discourse would be a step towards liberation from power or rather a step towards further submission.

Secondly, the adoption of the true discourse as a basis of jurisdiction introduced a plethora of applied scientific tools and theoretical frameworks into the equation, serving to guarantee the best approximation to what happened and why it happened, assuring adequate juridical measures could be taken. While truth may or may not be considered impervious to power, the scientific and bureaucratic apparatus certainly is not. Foucault does not consider the ideal scenario of a true discourse free from power plausible. Instead, he contrasts the Platonic myth and the narrative of liberation through truth with an alternative genealogy of truth and power, depicting the 'instinctive' pursuit of truth as a guided and widely enforced 'Politics of Truth' (Foucault 2007, p. 47). His genealogy shows the apparent emancipation as resulting in a fundamental and voluntary submission to the producers of the seemingly emancipating truth. He illustrates how modern subjects are encouraged or even forced to speak the truth, which goes beyond the general agreement on a common usage of vocabulary (which Nietzsche understands as the productive understanding of truth and lie; see TL I). Foucault discusses religious and juridical confessions, investigative practices, and modern medical therapies, and he thereby describes the development of the modern subject towards a 'confessing animal' (Foucault 1978, pp. 59). The insights provided by these polymorphic encouragements publicly

---

22 For more extensive clarifications on a more general level, see Foucault (1995, pp. 170–174).

to provide true information about oneself allow for a more detailed knowledge base about the social body, which greatly facilitates its regulation and governance (Foucault 2007, p. 43). Through the precise and rigid distinction between what is and is not rightfully understood as scientific discourse, the production of truths and their substitutes can be orchestrated. Guiding paradigms, exclusive disciplines, or imperatives for the scientific agents to adjust to the current state of scientific discourse allow for the disqualification of knowledge which is not in accordance with the pre-determined instruments of its valid construction (Foucault 2003, p. 10). Thus, hegemonic knowledge-structures are not only allowed to persist but gain further legitimacy through the true discourse they organise (Foucault 2007, p. 59). The resulting truths provide a comprehensive categorial grid, which allows for, and encourages, the acquisition of identity through pre-existing formats.[23] Modern subjects are provided with the means to understand the truth about their sexuality, mental or bodily health, or the real motivations behind their actions, and identity becomes something that can be pronounced and represented in scientific terms (Foucault 1978, p. 42). In modern society, this enforcement is not ostensibly repressive, but merely advocates valid paths towards happiness. Subjects rejecting the established categories find themselves marginalised and appear as dysfunctional within the social body. Accepting one's true identity allows for orientation and empowerment within society, as long as the advocated categories are adopted and reproduced. Foucault's genealogy of the will to truth describes a system of exclusion and a means of introducing structure into possible discourses, differentiating what can reasonably be expressed in a given discourse. As the establishment of the true discourse is contingently based on its 'historical a priori' (Foucault 2002, p. 143), it allows for pre-existing hegemonic power to manifest and legitimise itself through the true discourse.

It is important not to understand Foucault's critique as being limited to a critique of the construction and manipulation of truth. Foucault is aware that such a limitation would mean a simple reproduction of what he previously described as the Platonic myth; it would only re-establish the value-distinction between knowledge-corrupted-by-power and absolute truth outside the sphere of power on a different level of analysis. Voluntary submission to the true discourse

---

[23] Zarathustra discusses a similar process regarding virtues and the transformation of individual concepts into possession of the monitoring power. If the individual is not content with simply performing their virtue in private but tries to express it in a pre-established framework of understanding, the formerly experienced aspect of individuality develops into an objective and quantifiable commonplace: 'Now you have [the virtues'] name in common with the people and have become the people and the herd with your virtue' (Z I, Passions).

should always be understood as both liberation, emancipation and empowerment, on the one hand, and submission, normalisation and becoming a social subject of power, on the other. Truth must be understood as a contingent concept which allows for emancipation from forceful subjugation through voluntary submission to the producers of the true discourse. Foucault's genealogy of the will to truth shows how subjects are tempted towards the true discourse by the Platonic myth, how it is expanded through different sorts of enforcement, and how the seemingly independent concept of truth is orchestrated by power. He explains how this Politics of Truth was so easily accepted, and how it is used as an efficient tool for governing modern societies.

The Platonic myth has not disappeared since antiquity, but instead can be found in multiple forms and functions, many of which were described in great detail by Nietzsche and Foucault: be it the Christian narrative of an eternal true world, from which mundane human struggles can be interpreted (A 15); the narrative of progress through scientific method (GM III, 24–27); the modern sciences of confession which suggest that one can only help oneself with a self-examination derived from the scientific analysis of previously disclosed aspects of one's inner life (Foucault 1978, pp. 64–69); or the idea that machine-learning-based algorithms provide objective grounds for actions, thus liberating us from the human, all-too-human biases of judgement. These examples can be considered different reiterations of the Platonic myth, suggesting to the individual that an established rational, scientific or spiritual discourse allows for liberation from unjust and arbitrary uses of power and for an autonomous and emancipated life. Even though modern science is considered to have overcome the pursuit of absolute truth, we have become even more fixated on examining, measuring and understanding ourselves as a prerequisite to forming autonomous decisions. Be it through analysis, quantitative measurement or normalised expectations, modern humans have learned how to reflect upon themselves and their behaviour to choose freely and without foreign influence.

In the next section, I will briefly introduce Foucault's idea of disciplinary societies as the modern equivalent of Nietzsche's society of the Last Human. As I believe that Gilles Deleuze's distinction between a disciplinary society and societies of control provides further clarity and applicability to Foucault's terminology, I will use his 1992 paper "Postscript on the Societies of Control" as the basis for exploring Foucault's ideas.

5 Disciplinary Societies and Societies of Control – The 'Dividual'

In Deleuze's terminology, subjects of disciplinary societies are constituted and identified through 'signature' and 'administrative numeration' (Deleuze 1992, p. 5). The first term suggests a strong emphasis on the examination and monitoring of individuals, drawing their individuality, mental states and even perversions into the light of scientific discourse (Foucault 1995, pp. 170–175). However, as the metric dimension of the second term implies, individuals are then understood and referred to in constant consideration of their numerically derived, statistical relations to the population as a whole. They are treated according to their degree of deviation from the norm they can reasonably be expected to meet (Foucault 1995, pp. 177–184). The ostensible paradox of individualization and dissolution of individuals into numerical relations is a twofold process. As the tools for measuring the human mind and body grow in capabilities and applicability, additional aspects of the individuals become measurable and quantifiable and are subsequently evaluated in relation to each other.[24] This facilitates the constitution of precise normalised expectations and allows for more efficient monitoring and disciplinary intervention in additional areas of social life, such as education, healthcare or political participation. Knowing about possible deviations and rules of their appearance, the constitution and sub-classification of a population becomes practicable. In areas in which the human mind would otherwise remain impervious to scientific examination, the human sciences developed into confessional sciences, extracting knowledge about individual qualities and converting it into quantifiable data (Foucault 1978, pp. 64–67). The extracted scientific "confessions" and their functional translation into measurable and quantifiable terms concerning one's emotional state, convictions, or general self-examinations, allow for the reduction of the individual's most personal experiences to measurable data and knowledge that can be interrelated, or related back to the population as a whole. Personal experiences dissolve into symptoms, irregularities, or other explanatory variables. While confessions still had to be extracted with a certain amount of persuasion or enforcement in early Christianity, social institutions based on the Platonic myth of emancipation through truth have established an omnipresent narrative, suggesting that speaking the truth

---

[24] See the chapter "*Scientia Sexualis*" for an extensive example of how a scientific discourse and scientific techniques are established in an area of human behaviour that was not previously treated as a scientific topic in Foucault (1978, pp. 53–73).

as often and as extensively as possible allows for non-hierarchical democratic processes. Through the application of such narratives, subjects of western societies have developed into 'confessing animals', providing social institutions with sufficient data to function efficiently (Foucault 1978, p. 59). In disciplinary societies, understanding the individual thoroughly is the key to sub-classifying and regulating the population as a whole. The quantifiable traits of individuals are used to constitute the norm, which is then used to categorise and discipline individuals with regard to their deviations. The more individuals are investigated or provide insights into their practices, choices and preferences themselves, the less important the individual becomes as an individual and the more it is reduced to a mere constituent of normality within the population.

Although a strong initial emphasis is placed on analysing and monitoring individuals, they become less relevant as individuals and are participants of society only as carriers of their quantifiable traits. Deleuze explains that disciplinary societies have reached a point at which whole individuals are no longer considered, but the extraction and evaluation of isolated actions and traits is sufficient. In the resulting political body which Deleuze labels 'societies of control' (Deleuze 1992, p. 4), human or political sciences are not established on the analysis of individuals, but rather based on the idea of 'dividuals' (Deleuze 1992, p. 5). Modern subjects are no longer more than the sum of their isolable and quantifiable parts, but on the contrary, rather much less. There is no "core identity" represented in the modern idea of individuality, as sets of traits are automatically combined from large pools of impersonal data and used to define characteristic behaviour in given circumstances. This allows for the sub-classification of subjects into easily governable groups. Regarding risk-management, political participation or consumerism, the individual described in the dominant post-Enlightenment narrative has become virtually irrelevant.

While a possible final state of such human society was illustrated by Nietzsche in the parable of the Last Human, he also provides an image for the current state of humanity that comprises a state of fragmentation analogous to the societies of control described by Deleuze. In the following, I will provide a reading of Zarathustra's walk among 'fragments of human beings' through the terminology of Foucault and Deleuze (Z II, Redemption). I will then discuss his counter-narrative that aims at preventing societies of 'dividuals' – a counter-narrative the two French philosophers omitted to provide.

6 Fragments of Human Beings – Two Readings

In response to a hunchback claiming that it is the philosopher's duty to cure cripples, Zarathustra indicates that he is not interested in the further normalisation of humans. Removing the hunchback's hump would be taking away his soul, meaning that even a perceived 'cripple' would lose something by approximation to an assumed normality (Z II, Redemption). Instead, Zarathustra begins a critique of the fact that only isolated qualities are positively sanctioned – such as the big-eared genius with the pitiful body (Z II, Redemption) – while the development of whole individuals is disregarded. Curing cripples would mean feeding individuals to a system that produces 'reversed cripples' (Z II, Redemption) and uses isolated 'fragments and limbs of human beings' (Z II, Redemption) to constitute a norm to be aspired to.

Three statements Zarathustra makes in "On Redemption" are especially important. He first states, 'I walk amongst men as amongst the fragments and limbs of human beings! This is the terrible thing to mine eye, that I find man broken up, and scattered about, as on a battle- and butcher-ground [*Schlacht- und Schlächterfeld*]' (Z II, Redemption).[25] He refines this statement by adding a future perspective: 'I walk amongst men as the fragments of the future, that future which I contemplate' (Z II, Redemption). A further statement points to the narrative approach of his philosophy, which unfortunately gets lost in English translations. In reference to the section "On Poets", Zarathustra again characterises himself as a 'poet' (Z II, Redemption). This self-characterisation was used in the earlier section as a response to a statement attributed to him, claiming that 'the poets lie too much' (Z II, Poets). Zarathustra replies, 'But Zarathustra too is a poet.... But supposing that someone said in all earnestness that the poets lie too much: he is right – *we* lie too much' (Z II, Poets). In "On Redemption", it is shown that his "poetry" encompasses a philosophical approach that does not aim for truth, but rather focuses on the narration of contingent but impactful future perspectives. As the main translations use creative terms to translate the verb corresponding to the noun 'poet' (*Dichter*), I have added the German term to the passages: 'And it is all my poetisation [*Dichten*] and aspiration to compose [*dichten*] and collect into [one] what is fragment and riddle and fearful chance. And how could I endure to be a man, if man were not also the composer

---

25 I am using the Thomas Common translation for passages from the chapter "Redemption" in this section, as it is much more precise than the Cambridge edition. Unless otherwise indicated, I follow the Del Caro translation when discussing *Thus Spoke Zarathustra*.

[*Dichter*], a riddle-reader, and redeemer of chance!' (Z II, Redemption).[26] Zarathustra does not characterise himself as a philosopher trying to uncover the truth, but as a poet narrating what reality could be. He thus characterises himself as a narrative philosopher, who does not deduce his statements from a truth-maker, but who establishes contingent narratives with social and individual implications for the recipients[27] – namely, narratives such as the Overhuman or Eternal Recurrence. I will describe two major dimensions of this alternative narrative, understanding the diagnosed fragmentation as a philosophical problem with social implications on the one hand and with individual implications on the other.

The social reading is based on Zarathustra's statement that he aims at bringing together present fragments of humans 'into one' with the help of an alternative social narrative. Modernity is interpreted as a 'butcher-ground' (*Schlächterfeld*), which could be interpreted as meaning that external force is applied to dissolve individuals into fragments then to be consumed within society (Z II, Redemption).[28] Subjects are salvaged for their quantifiable traits and actions while their individuality dissolves into interrelations and measures of deviation from the norm. The means to find orientation are provided through measured data that must be extracted. Modern subjects in the post-theological condition are prone to this quantification as they have no meaningful system of orientation outside current society. Since there is no absolute sacred and indisputable orientation to follow, regarding how to act and appear, the only possible orientation revolves around the capacity that helped overcome the theological superstition in the first place – reason and scientific method. Modern subjects continue examining themselves, sharpening their self-understanding by means of measuring their individual qualities in relation to the population as a whole, and strive to establish a normal and rational ground to stand on. Thus, even though the theological perspective is widely disregarded as stable ground, the path towards the previously described greatest danger of monotheism – the final development into a fully normalised human being (GS 143) – is now continued and intensified by means of a self-examination focused on what is normal or rational. In *Thus*

---

26 I have changed 'into unity' to 'into One', as the German reads 'in Eins zusammendichten' (KSA, 4, Z, 179). The Common translation in this case is much more accurate than the Cambridge edition, in which *dichten* is translated as 'creating' by Del Caro and Pippin, which strips away the narrative component of Zarathustra's approach. However, Common translates *in Eins zusammenbringen* as 'bringing into unity', which in my view is too harmonious in this context, as I will discuss below.
27 And in this case a therapeutic dimension for the philosopher himself.
28 Also see, Z I, Idol.

Spoke Zarathustra, the picture of a fully normalised society is introduced in the future narrative of the Last Human, in relation to which the present situation of fragmented human beings in the "On Redemption" passage should be read as the dangerous intermediate stage at which modern humanity finds itself.

In his narrative of a possible alternative future, Zarathustra formulates a unified goal, namely the overcoming of 'the human' towards the Overhuman (Z I, Prologue, 3). Overcoming the human can be read as a post-humanist or even anti-humanist project. However, I would argue that it is not "humans" or "humanity" that must be overcome,[29] but rather the normalised and normative idea of the human. The imperative to overcome the human appears in close proximity to the critical depiction of a society of the Last Human in which everyone knows what it means to be human. In order to avoid the Last Human, to avoid a stagnation in the otherwise constant development of humanity, the idea of a normal human type is challenged by the imperative to overcome the human. Zarathustra responds to the needs produced by two thousand years of the monotheistic narrative while teaching people not to say 'God' when looking towards the future, but 'Over[human]' (Z II, Isles). The Overhuman, as a new singularity of purpose, does not entail the assumption of a normal or right path for overcoming the human, but justifies constant experimenting through wilfully becoming what one is within the agonistic context of other experimental concepts of what the human might encompass. When Zarathustra introduces the Overhuman as the counter-narrative (Z I, Prologue, 3), he pledges his love for various different contemporary social misfits, while he places no constraints on how human beings are supposed to develop. The Overhuman serves as the one goal and remains 'a ghost running in front of you' (Z I, Neighbour), which needs to be equipped with the blood and bones of anyone who feels addressed by the narrative. The relation between identity and normality is thus reversed in comparison to the disciplinary societies and societies of control. Zarathustra breaks with the assumption of normal identity that can be projected on to social subjects in order to integrate and discipline them based on their deviation from the norm. Instead, social subjects are compelled to project their self-experience into the agonism of experiments towards a future not based on the idea of an objective norm. The idea of the Overhuman and of overcoming the human allows the narrative philosopher to "poeticise" the seemingly displaced fragments into one. The first part of Zarathustra's narrative, the social dimension, provides a common goal for humanity and extends an invitation to identify oneself as more

---

29 In the German text, the word *Mensch* is not used in the plural, while in the Cambridge edition it is translated as plural (Z I, Prologue, 3).

than a quantifiable part of society, but instead as a necessary agent to establish a future society not focused on one normal human type. In this social dimension of the narrative, the individual is addressed as an agent of social order.

In addition to the social dimension of Zarathustra's narrative, he also offers a dimension that is directly addressed to the understanding of the individual as an individual. While the social dimension of the fragmented individual can be explained through the lens of his French successors, the problematic situation of the individual as an individual is more open to interpretation. In order to keep a concise line of argument, I will focus on the individual as it experiences itself confronted with a social order.[30] On the one hand, one can directly relate the state of the individual to the social perspective as described above. The individual is aware of being defined in terms of nothing more but the sum of its character fragments. However, this experience would mean that a critical perspective towards society had already been acquired. Much more problematic (at least within this line of argument) is the experience of being confronted with the 'new idol' (Z I, Idol), meaning the modern state and its scientific, juridical and political apparatus that assumes a quasi-objective status.[31] As the ideas of personal immortality and any metaphysical moral order become implausible, no higher entity can be addressed when going against the truth-based social order of things[32] – whoever thinks otherwise voluntarily admits themselves to an 'insane asylum' (Z I, Prologue, 5). Confronted with the persistent order of society, the individual experiences itself as a passive recipient of circumstances, illness or political spheres of influence. Zarathustra includes himself in this battlefield of fragmentation and states it was only possible to bear being human as a poet of the future. Thus, to confront fragmentation caused by external pressure, modern individuals must assume – or even poetise (*dichten*) – a narrative suggesting a stable personal identity. To provide the individual with such a non-ob-

---

30 In this chapter, I will not go into detail regarding other possible and less socially-related aspects of problematic individuality. One could follow the destruction of the transcendental subject with the 'death of God' (GS 125), the experience of vanity in a world of 'sovereign becoming' (HL 1, 10), the experience of fatigue regarding the cultural process of becoming a tame animal (GM I, 11)
31 The speech of the "great Dragon" in "On the Three Metamorphoses" also offers an example of the struggle of the individual striving for their own perspective: 'the value of all things – it gleams in me. All value has already been created, and the value of all created things – that am I. Indeed, there shall be no more "I will!"' (Z I, Metamorphoses). Zarathustra's first speech is aimed mainly at morality but can serve as an analogy for society as a reality without alternatives.
32 The former advantages of polytheism do not offer a valid path after the death of God. See GS 143.

jective anchor of self-experience, Zarathustra considers the will and passion as the only legitimate foundations from which to confront the security of normality. However, while the prospect of possible eternal suffering or eternal happiness of monotheist religions added the necessary weight to processes of moral decision-making, the fleeting experience of happiness or sadness does not carry enough weight to turn the balance against a society that 'invented happiness' and provides the individual with guidance on how to act (Z I, Prologue, 3).

This new narrative of identity is established in two steps. To counteract the assumption of identity as the sum of fragments, Zarathustra first proposes a praxeological model of experience and identity in contrast to self-examination through isolated qualities. This means a model in which it is not a stable and predeterminable identity from which to predict rational future decisions,[33] but actions and decisions which determine identity in the process or in hindsight. In this perspective, identity is the reflective state of taking responsibility and ownership of one's actions. Instead of acting according to one's predeterminable character, the praxeological understanding of identity suggests that one can only 'become what one is' (EH Clever, 9).[34] This act of becoming oneself is thus not a rationally predeterminable right action according to quantifiable character traits, but a retrospective contemplation in which the individual considers the self it created through actions in its lifetime. However, as the most important facet of individuality is will, which is considered to be an intentional capacity directed at the present and the future, mere retrospection does not provide sufficient counterweight to become active against better reasoning in the first place. As the will is the most important vehicle, a merely retrospection-based model of identity would require the impossible, as it would need the will to be able to 'want backwards' (Z II, Redemption). The second step of the praxeological narrative of identity thus requires the interpretation of reality as eternal return – which is only hinted at in the section "On Redemption". Through the idea of eternal return, the individual is not limited to a retrospective unity of identity, but the will can aspire to the recurrence of every otherwise fleeting instance of action or emotion that is produced. Instead of deciding between a quasi-objective happiness within the social order and a retrospective identity constructed of short-lived experiences, the addition of eternal return shifts the balance between indi-

---

[33] In this case referring to decisions that are true to one's character. As Nietzsche describes with very radical examples in *On the Genealogy of Morals*, there is no actor behind action, thus a 'strong character' acting weakly does not exist, but rather shows weakness (GM I, 13).
[34] In the Cambridge translation by Judith Norman, the passage reads 'how you become, what you are'. I changed it to 'what one is', as the German passage is kept impersonal with the German word *man* (EH Clever, 9).

viduality and social reason. The individual now decides between the recurring experience of simply functioning within the grid of the social order or re-experiencing the emotions of individual and possibly irrational decisions. Zarathustra not only offers a future perspective that allows for individual action, but also offers an interpretation of reality that makes each personal decision as significant as all values produced in the quasi-objective structure of society.

7 Conclusion

While much of critical social philosophy has arrived at the conclusion that absolute truth-makers are beyond our epistemological capabilities in regard to the human sciences, I believe it is important to follow Nietzsche and Foucault in their claims that truth in the strong sense of the word is by no means necessary to produce a discourse that functions as a true discourse. Much of the above has been very abstract, but true discourse in the forms described here has very tangible effects on social life. Historically, ostensibly rigid objective knowledge concerning biological sex, somatic or mental health and economic laws have rightly been critically challenged as results of contingent scientific production. While these steps have been very important for giving previously marginalised groups – especially those not able or willing to identify with what they are supposed to be "scientifically" – a voice within political discourse, it is now important to realise that the processes associated with the will to truth have in no way abated, but still pervade large parts of our daily lives. While (post)modern philosophers such as Foucault and Deleuze have surpassed the German philosopher with regard to critical analyses, it is possible that Nietzsche introduced the only philosophical approach that is able to do more than point out systematic injustices and call for responsible action. The narrative philosophy presented by Zarathustra allows one to re-evaluate one's individual perspective not based on truth or normality, but in regard to possible personal or social futures.

Lastly, it is important to understand how Nietzsche's narrative philosophy, as developed in *Thus Spoke Zarathustra*, opens up new opportunities for counteracting a Politics of Truth by allowing the participants to rethink themselves in relation to the current and to a future society and to rethink their identity on a praxeological instead of an essentialist foundation. Nietzsche, much more so than Foucault, understands that even if one 'suddenly awoke in the middle of this dream', it is the philosopher's responsibility to 'prolong the earthly dance', to 'sustain the universality of dreaming ... and thereby also the duration of the dream' (GS 54) – but to give it a direction for which the philosopher can and must take responsibility. The narrative philosophy he devises is an attempt to understand the social world as a discursive order of things with no true world behind it. For Nietzsche, it is much more important to introduce the possibility of difference through philosophical narratives, allowing further space for different identities and actions. Zarathustra's narrative philosophy should thus be read as an attempt to counteract the Politics of Truth with a Politics of Difference.[35]

Bibliography

Ansell-Pearson, Keith (2018): *Nietzsche's Search for Philosophy: On the Middle Writings.* London, New York: Bloomsbury.

Butler, Judith (1997): *The Psychic Life of Power – Theories in Subjection.* Stanford: Stanford University Press.

Deleuze, Gilles (1992): "Postscript on the Societies of Control". In: *October* 59. Winter, pp. 3–7. Translated by Martin Joughin.

Foucault, Michel (1978): *The History of Sexuality I – An Introduction.* Translated by Robert Hurley. New York: Pantheon Books.

Foucault, Michel (1981): "The Order of Discourse". Translated by Ian McLeod. In: Robert Young (Ed.): *Untying the Text, A Post-Structuralist Reader*, pp. 48–78. Boston: Routledge & Kegan Paul.

Foucault, Michel (1984): "Nietzsche, Genealogy, History". Translated by Donald F. Bouchard and Sherry Simon. In: Paul Rabinow (Ed.): *The Foucault Reader*, pp. 76–100. New York: Pantheon Books.

Foucault, Michel (1995): *Discipline and Punish – The Birth of the Prison.* Translated by Alan Sheridan. New York: Vintage Books.

Foucault, Michel (2000): "Truth and Juridical Forms". Translated by Robert Hurley. In: James D. Faubion (Ed.): *Essential Works of Foucault 1954–1984 – Power*, pp. 1–89. New York: New Press.

Foucault, Michel (2002): *The Archaeology of Knowledge.* Translated by A. M. Sheridan Smith. New York: Routledge.

Foucault, Michel (2003): *Society Must be Defended – Lectures at the Collège de France 1975–1976.* Edited by Mauro Bertani and Alessandro Fontana. General Editors: Francois Ewald and Alessandro Fontana. English Series Editor: Arnold I. Davidson. Translated by David Macey. New York: Picador.

Foucault, Michel (2007): "What is Critique?" Translated by Lysa Hochroth. In: Sylvère Lotringer (Ed.): *The Politics of Truth*, pp. 41–82. Los Angeles: Semiotext(e).

Nietzsche, Friedrich (1909): *Thus Spake Zarathustra.* Translated by Thomas Common. Edinburgh and London: T.N. Foulis.

Nietzsche, Friedrich (2002): *Beyond Good and Evil.* Edited by Rolf-Peter Horstmann and Judith Norman and translated by Judith Norman. Cambridge: Cambridge University Press.

---

35 I am deeply grateful to fellow Nietzsche researcher Richard Elliot for twice proofreading this chapter and for providing constructive criticism and insightful comments.

Nietzsche, Friedrich (2005a): *The Anti-Christ*. In: *The Anti-Christ, Ecce Homo, Twilight of the Idols and Other Writings*, pp. 1–67. Edited by Aaron Ridley and Judith Norman and translated by Judith Norman. Cambridge: Cambridge University Press.

Nietzsche, Friedrich (2005b): *Ecce Homo*. In: *The Anti-Christ, Ecce Homo, Twilight of the Idols and Other Writings*, pp. 69–151. Edited by Aaron Ridley and Judith Norman and translated by Judith Norman. Cambridge: Cambridge University Press.

Nietzsche, Friedrich (2005c): *Twilight of the Idols*. In: *The Anti-Christ, Ecce Homo, Twilight of the Idols and Other Writings*, pp. 153–229. Edited by Aaron Ridley and Judith Norman and translated by Judith Norman. Cambridge: Cambridge University Press.

Nietzsche, Friedrich (2006): *Thus Spoke Zarathustra*. Edited by Adrian del Caro and Robert B. Pippin and translated by Adrian Del Caro. Cambridge: Cambridge University Press.

Nietzsche, Friedrich (2007a): *The Birth of Tragedy and Other Writings*. Edited by Raymond Geuss and Ronald Speirs and translated by Ronald Speirs. Cambridge: Cambridge University Press.

Nietzsche, Friedrich (2007b): *On the Genealogy of Morality*. Edited by Keith Ansell-Pearson and translated by Carol Diethe. Cambridge: Cambridge University Press.

Nietzsche, Friedrich (2007c): *Human, All Too Human*. Translated by R. J. Hollingdale. Cambridge: Cambridge University Press.

Nietzsche, Friedrich (2007d): "On the Uses and Disadvantages of History for Life". In: *Untimely Meditations*, pp. 57–124. Edited by Daniel Breazeale and translated by R. J. Hollingdale. Cambridge: Cambridge University Press.

Nietzsche, Friedrich (2008): *The Gay Science*. Translated by Josephine Nauckhoff. Cambridge: Cambridge University Press.

Orwell, George (2000): *Nineteen Eighty-Four*. London: Penguin.

Andrea Rehberg
Towards Immanence – A Nietzschean Trajectory

'Our masters are slaves that have triumphed'
(Deleuze 2001, p. 76)

Abstract: This chapter seeks to explain populism as it presented itself in recent history; but it then goes beyond the mere phenomena of populism by considering a number of explanations for them. It then enters a philosophical terrain by turning to a Nietzschean reading of reactivity in terms of nobility and slavishness, and of the ascetic ideal, as analysed by Nietzsche in *On the Genealogy of Morality*. Next, it discusses the import of Nietzsche's physiological thinking for these analyses. The chapter concludes with an exploration of Nietzsche's and Deleuze's concept of immanence, since it is arguably only on this terrain that the phenomena of reactivity, specifically, the phenomena of populism, can ultimately be overcome. Hence, this chapter progresses from the most immediately given, through increasingly complex levels of analysis, to an ever more comprehensive understanding of the structures and forces involved in the current political situation.

Introduction

This chapter draws out the politically and philosophically significant features of populism as it presented itself at a particular – and particularly critical – moment in recent history (section 1); but it then goes beyond the mere phenomena of populism by, first, considering a number of – sociological, political, economic and psychological – explanations for them (section 2). It then enters a philosophical terrain by turning to a Nietzschean reading of reactivity in terms of nobility and slavishness, and of the ascetic ideal, as analysed by Nietzsche in *On the Genealogy of Morality* (section 3). Next, it discusses the import of Nietzsche's physiological thinking for these analyses (section 4). The chapter concludes with an exploration of the philosophical issue of immanence, as conceived by Nietzsche and Deleuze (section 5), since it is arguably only on this terrain that the phenomena of reactivity, here, specifically, the phenomena of populism, can ultimately be overcome. That is to say that this chapter progresses from the most immediately given, the phenomena, through increasingly complex levels of analysis, to an ever more comprehensive understanding of the structures and forces involved in the current political situation.

1 The Phenomena of Populism

Roughly since the beginning of the current millennium, the political ground in many parts of the world has shifted dramatically. The extreme right has crept into democratic institutions and is daily insinuating itself into consciousness through its statements and actions. The tone and style of extremist politicians and demagogues is often highly aggressive and hostile to whomever is projected as their enemy. Undoubtedly, democratic state forms are intrinsically adversarial, conflictual and confrontational spaces. In fact, the very space of democratic society is itself contested and only arises in and as contest.[1] But what has been happening over the last few decades or so – and what is usually discussed under the heading of right-wing populism – is of a different nature than what went before, not least because so-called "social" media facilitate and circulate propaganda in word and deed in real time. Such propaganda does not just take the form of hostile verbal confrontations, but frequently tips over into actual physical violence against individuals and groups, especially if they belong to identifiable minorities or are easily interpolated as "enemies of the people". The salient points in recent history were of course Brexit and the election of Trump in 2016,[2] but also the long-term after-effects of German reunification, the election of Jair Bolsonaro in 2018,[3] and the right-wing regimes in Eastern Europe and beyond.

Politicians' rhetoric and agitation against such groups has had terrible consequences. As of 2019, the dire litany of events of this nature includes attacks on Jews and Muslims throughout the US, Europe and Asia[4]; violence against, and

---

[1] See, e.g., Lefort (1988, especially ch. 1, "The Question of Democracy").
[2] Lest it be thought that this populist moment has now passed, we should remember that even if Trump was ousted in 2020, and even when Johnson is replaced as Tory leader and PM, the threat of populism has not abated as the next populist strongman (or Trump himself) is always just waiting in the wings, ready to use democratic institutions and conventions to undo democratic structures from within.
[3] Cf. the chapter by Valladão Silva in this volume.
[4] In 2017, the Pew Research Centre reported that, between 2015 and 2016, the number of assaults against Muslims in the US rose significantly, easily surpassing the modern peak reached in 2001, the year of the September 11 terrorist attacks. See https://www.pewresearch.org/fact-tank/2017/11/15/assaults-against-muslims-in-u-s-surpass-2001-level/ (visited on 4 August 2021). In its latest currently available annual report, of 2018, the UK NGO 'Tell MAMA' (Measuring Anti-Muslim At-

murders of, asylum-seekers[5]; daily attempts to intimidate and silence, often by means of death-threats, moderate MPs who support immigration or champion other "liberal" causes; and even occasional assassination attempts on moderate politicians by right-wing fanatics, which sometimes result in actual deaths – witness the murder of the Labour MP Jo Cox in the UK in 2016,[6] and of the CDU politician Walter Lübcke in Germany in 2019.[7] Dreadful though the attacks evidenced here are, they only represent the tip of the iceberg of the violence daily perpetrated against individuals and groups by the adherents of right-wing populism.[8]

---

tacks) recorded 1,072 verified anti-Muslim or Islamophobic hate crimes and incidents in England, 745 of which occurred at street-level and 327 of which occurred online. A significant spike occurred in August 2018, after the then foreign secretary Boris Johnson published a column referring to veiled Muslim women as 'letterboxes' and 'bank-robbers' (*Daily Telegraph*, August 5, 2018). In the week following his article, anti-Muslim incidents increased by 375%. Most of the recorded anti-Muslim hate incidents in the first week following Johnson's comments were directed at visibly Muslim women who wore the face veil (niqab) or other types of veil. 'Tell MAMA' recorded a total of 57 incidents in the three weeks following the column's publication, 32 of which were directed at visibly Muslim women. In August of that year, 42% of the street-based incidents reported to 'Tell MAMA' directly referenced Johnson and/or the language used in his column. Throughout 2018, 'Tell MAMA' recorded the details of 1244 victims and 1196 perpetrators. Of the known/disclosed victims, the majority were female at 57% (721). The majority of known perpetrators were male (73%, 482 of 663), and 61% were white men (404 in 663). See https://tellmamauk.org/tell-mama-annual-report-2018-_-normalising-hate/ (visited on 3 August 2021). See also https://www.bbc.co.uk/news/uk-politics-45083275 (visited on 4 August 2021).

5 Probably the most notorious of these to date was the NSU case (National Socialist Underground, or German: *Nationalsozialistischer Untergrund*). This was a German neo-Nazi terrorist group which, between 2000 and 2007, committed a series of xenophobic murders which left ten people dead and one wounded. The primary targets were ethnic Turks and Kurds, though the victims also included one ethnic Greek and one German policewoman. See https://en.wikipedia.org/wiki/National_Socialist_Underground_murders (visited on 6 August 2021). The German interior ministry reported 3,533 attacks on migrants and asylum seeker hostels in 2016 alone. See, e. g., https://www.bbc.co.uk/news/world-europe-39096833 for horrific incidents (visited on 6 August 2021).
6 On 16 June 2016, Cox died after being stabbed and shot multiple times by a neo-Nazi who had a history of psychiatric problems and links to the US-based neo-Nazi group National Alliance. He shouted 'Britain first' as he carried out the attack.
7 A moderate, centre-right politician, he was murdered at his home, on June 2, 2019, with a single shot to the head by a neo-Nazi extremist. See https://www.zeit.de/thema/walter-luebcke (visited on 6 August 2021).
8 These adherents of right-wing populism have been venting their spleen against state-mandated public health measures since the beginning of the pandemic, their ire fuelled by internet-promulgated conspiracy theories.

But aside from these extremist groupings and their violent effects in society, parties like the right-wing AfD in Germany and Ukip/the Brexit Party in the UK seek to shift the political discourse to the far right and to normalise quasi-fascistic views and practices within democratic institutions, such as the national parliament and regional assemblies of their respective countries.[9] In the UK, so-called Brexiters, led by Boris Johnson (PM at the time of writing), have been agitating against the EU and against foreigners in general. Although Brexit was supposedly about political and economic withdrawal from the EU, since the vote street attacks against Muslims, as one of the most visibly (ethnically and culturally) different groups, have risen by 30% in the UK,[10] thus exposing the xenophobic ideological essence of the Brexit project.

This list of right-wing populist incidents, parties, policies and leaders could be extended to many other countries also in thrall to the forces of reaction; it could be extended to include incidents of murderous assaults and slanderous attacks, and by innumerable cases indicating a threat to liberal democratic civilisation. What all these examples document is the seamless slide from rhetorical violence, as practiced by right-wing demagogues (whether in government or in opposition), to the verbal and physical violence perpetrated by their followers in public places and online. That is to say, the phenomena of right-wing populism have to be understood on a continuum, for example, from Trump's tweets to the killings perpetrated by white supremacists throughout the US; and from Johnson's newspaper articles to an increase in incidents of hate-crimes in the UK. What this means is that the phenomena of populism are widespread, deadly serious and deserving of extensive theoretical analysis. In the following, we will approach the more deep-seated structures of populism that lend themselves to theoretical (section 2) and philosophical analysis (sections 3–5).

---

9 *Alternative für Deutschland* was founded in September 2012 (then called Electoral Alternative 2013 [German: *Wahlalternative 2013*]). Early in 2013, the group decided to found a new party to compete in the 2013 German federal elections, and called themselves AfD. The party's stance has variously been described as ultra-nationalist, right-wing populist, Eurosceptic, anti-immigration, anti-feminist and participating in climate change denial.

10 See the 'Tell MAMA' report of June 2018, https://tellmamauk.org/wp-content/uploads/resources/Gendered%20anti-Muslim%20Hatred%20and%20Islamophobia%20-%20Tell%20MAMA%20Interim%20Report.pdf (visited on 8 August 2021).

2 Theories of Populism

Although the question of what the socio-political and economic causes of these phenomena are is both important and fascinating, and has, especially over the last few years, been investigated by a host of social scientists,[11] this is not my question here. Not only would an investigation of this kind go far beyond the scope of this chapter, but it would divert us from our path, which leads to Nietzsche. Equally, indications of how populists should and could be effectively counteracted politically by and in democracies, whilst an equally important question, will not be addressed here, and for the same reasons.[12] Nonetheless, the sociological attempts to explain the logic and the *modi operandi* of populism, as discussed in this section, are instructive here, since they pave the way for a Nietzschean interpretation of the phenomena of populism.

Although in the theoretical literature on populism, many social scientists talk both about a populism of the left and a populism of the right (mainly because they see a continuum of means between them, or a "logic" that spans right-wing and so-called left-wing populism[13]), in this chapter, what is being referred to as populism is meant as a collective term for the anti-pluralistic, racist, xenophobic, often authoritarian, often repressive regimes of the extreme right, even and especially where they have been democratically elected, for example, in the US (2016–2020), UK, Hungary, Poland, Turkey, India, and many other countries. Where they have not (yet) come to power, we see the same mindsets in parties and groupings in a host of other countries, such as Germany (Pegida, AfD, NPD), France (FN/NR), Austria (FPÖ), the Netherlands (PVV), etc. The two reasons that motivate me in what may initially seem a restrictive terminological choice are these: firstly, it is these forces that encourage xenophobic, racist and all-too-often murderous tendencies in their followers and those parts of the population receptive to their anti-pluralist rhetoric. Secondly, these forces all

---

[11] As early as 1986, Helmut Dubiel published a collection of papers on the theme of Populism and Enlightenment. In 2007, Ivan Krastev published a famous article titled "The Populist Moment". Seminal is Jan-Werner Müller's *What is Populism?* (2017). Other important contributors are Isolde Charim, *Ich und die Anderen: Wie die neue Pluralisierung uns alle verändert* (2018) and Didier Eribon, *Returning to Reims* (2019). Theoretical approaches to populism are legion, too many to adduce here.
[12] Both of these issues are covered with admirable clarity in Müller (2017, especially chs. 1 and 3).
[13] See, e.g., Dubiel (1986, pp. 33–50), Karin Priester, quoted in Müller (2017, p. 117n12).

evince an orientation towards a more or less rapacious capitalism,[14] so much so that I consider the appellation "left-wing populism" a contradiction in terms,[15] as varieties of it share a profound anti-capitalist stance and so are in essence liberatory rather than repressive, even where their chosen political means are illiberal.

Despite various disagreements (Müller 2017, p. 2),[16] most commentators concur on a few features of populism, which I will briefly aim to chisel out in the following. The first point to emphasise is that the "new" populist politicians, in contrast to their 1930s forebears, are not so much anti-democratic as illiberal, a point stressed by Ivan Krastev (2007, pp. 1–2).[17] These politicians disavow the representative nature of modern democracy without rejecting (the veneer of) democracy altogether; they disregard the democratic obligation to protect the rights of minorities and are always avowedly anti-pluralistic and xenophobic (Krastev 2007, pp. 1–5).[18] Populist ideologies are rigidly dualistic, espousing the idea that society is composed of two essentially 'homogeneous and antagonistic groups: "the people as such" and "the corrupt elite"' (Krastev 2007, p. 3).[19] They tend to suggest that politics is the expression of the general will of a known and well-defined, easily identifiable and self-identical group: "the people". By contrast, a nebulous but hostile, immoral, corrupt and self-serving (globalised) elite are portrayed as working against the people; and this elite, they say, needs to be eradicated in order to bring about the will of the people (Krastev 2007, p. 3). Who or what do populists mean by these two groups, though, and how are they supposedly composed?

If populists are in power, then by the "corrupt elite" they do not mean themselves, that is, powerful rulers but, variously, "experts",[20] the judiciary,[21] even

---

[14] Politicians' populism should be seen as the denial of community, society, the State, and as the culmination of rapacious capitalism, i.e., as the expression of a desire for self-enrichment and at the same time clientelism, but contingent on citizens' support. In this regard, Erdogan's regime is typical of mass clientelism. See Müller (2017, pp. 44–47).
[15] Usually applied to Chavez, Maduro and other Latin-American leaders.
[16] As Müller avers, there is no comprehensive theory of populism agreed upon by social scientists investigating it, only a series of – often mutually contradictory – explanations of it.
[17] But see Müller (2017, p. 118n26) for a different, albeit now generally discredited, view.
[18] See also Müller (2017, p. 20).
[19] See also Müller (2017, pp. 2–3 and 87–88).
[20] Cf. the famous slur, in a 2016 TV interview, by Oxford-educated Conservative cabinet minister Michael Gove, in which he claimed that 'the people ... have had enough of experts' (https://www.theguardian.com/politics/2016/dec/28/brexit-campaigner-michael-gove-defends-nhs-funding-pledge, visited on 8 August 2021). See also Müller (2017, p. 108), where the same pronouncement is (mis-)quoted.

Parliament itself,[22] and, from a reactionary UK perspective, so-called EU "plutocrats". Because, crucially, populists are always virulently anti-pluralistic (Müller 2017, p. 3), it should also be stressed that this nebulous category of the "elites" includes any individuals or groups who share certain "pluralistic" features, or who practise "pluralistic" – e.g., LGBTQ+, XR, anti-Capitalist, internationalist, feminist, etc. – life-styles.[23] So, the 'line of identification' does not just run between populists and their opponents (see Müller 2017, p. 20), let alone between those in power and those in opposition, but between populists (whether in power or not) and pluralists, although even this is a little too crude.

The Austrian writer Isolde Charim offers a more subtle analysis of the conflict between populists and their opponents. The upshot of her analysis is that, although populist propaganda tends to be anti-modernist (and, indeed, anti-postmodernist),[24] the real fault-line runs between those who oppose pluralisation and those who inhabit it affirmatively, or between (pre-individualised) instances of resistance to pluralisation and (pre-individualised) instances of its affirmation. This latter view has the advantage of de-personalising the issue of populism, thereby moving the discussion into the vicinity of a philosophical approach.

As spurious as the idea of these putative "elites", though for different reasons, is the idea of a homogeneous people. Given the multicultural, pluralistic societies that make up most of the Western world, in which every supposedly unified national culture is permeated by other cultures, the very idea of national cultural homogeneity is purely imaginary.[25] In fact, even before any influx by mi-

---

21 "Enemies of the People" was the headline of an article in the right-wing British newspaper *The Daily Mail* in November 2016, after three judges had ruled that the UK government would require the consent of Parliament to go ahead with Brexit.
22 Cf. Johnson's attempt to prorogue the UK Parliament in the autumn of 2019, so he could dictate Brexit unopposed.
23 For this reason, George Monbiot, in an otherwise excellent article in *The Guardian*, is only half correct when he says that 'When [populists] deride "elites", they don't mean people like themselves – the rich and powerful. They mean teachers and intellectuals. They are creating an anti-intellectual culture, to make people easier to manipulate' ("Out of this darkness we must find the will to fight back", para. 9). But it is not even intellectuals, it is, on one level, simply anyone opposed to populists, and "elites" is simply code, used by populists when addressing their adherents, to indicate, ultimately, "those who are not with us". More on this below and in sect. 3. See https://www.theguardian.com/commentisfree/2019/dec/13/fight-back-recrimination-blame, visited on 13 December 2019).
24 Charim (2018, esp. ch. 4, "The Hostile Takeover of Modernity by Tradition").
25 See Charim (2018, esp. ch. 2), on these issues. The imaginary character of the nation was analysed as long ago as 1983 by Benedict Anderson in his (2006) *Imagined Communities: Reflections on the Origin and Spread of Nationalism*.

grants – who are themselves, of course, a greatly diverse group – from a putative "outside", every culture is always already differentiated according to the political, psycho-sexual and ethnic diversity of its population (Charim 2018, ch. 2). In other words, it is not a matter of a homogeneous national culture being confronted by a self-identical group of immigrants – although that is exactly the fiction populists like to peddle to their adherents – but rather a series of complex encounters between heterogeneous multiple micro-identities. In fact, the rhetoric of an "influx" of "immigrants" from the "outside" is really only a symptom of a nostalgic longing for a simpler world, in which personal and political identity felt more like a full subjectivity, in contrast to today's split, fragmented, pluralist subjectivities (see Charim 2018, ch. 4, esp. pp. 104–108). Charim explains that the actual line of demarcation runs not between natives and foreigners, but between opponents of migration and those who accept it as an ineluctable feature of contemporary society (Charim 2018, pp. 108 and 212–214). Predictably, the former tend to embrace the ideology of capitalism whereas the latter tend to critique it.

A number of commentators have also pointed out a common denominator of those whom populists refer to as "the people", namely, the factor of a perceived grievance or slight (German: *Kränkung*) and the reaction to it, being aggrieved, feeling slighted (German: *gekränkt sein*).[26] Formerly, those who harbour this feeling assumed themselves to be constituting the unquestioned (white, male, heterosexual) societal norm, whereas now they suffer from a 'precarious identity' (Charim 2018, pp. 151–152), only existing alongside notionally equal others who do not conform to this norm. This newly arisen vacuum of identity arouses in them an intense desire for recognition, and it is this desire to which populists respond, by styling themselves as advocates of the aggrieved, against "elites" from "above" and migrants from "below" (Charim 2018, p. 137). Populists thereby respond to a classic, deep-rooted emotional need no longer fulfilled in pluralistic societies, a need for a stable identity, which is felt all the more urgently the less such an identity is available. It should be remembered that populists thrive on this sense of grievance, whether real or imagined, in their supporters and it is this which sustains them (Charim 2018, p. 163); a sense of grievance, above all, of the socio-economically left-behind, white, often poorly-educated, economically unproductive or underproductive males (Charim 2018, pp. 201 and 204–206). Whoever promises them a restitution of their masculinity and their lost social status more generally will get their support. The points made in this section

---

26 See Charim (2018, pp. 141, 151–152, 163, 202, 204 and 207). See also Dubiel (1986, pp. 44–45) and Müller (2017, p. 1).

obviously only provide a brief sketch of what is in fact the much more complex socio-economic, psycho-sexual and historical constellation in which we find ourselves today, but they provide the backdrop for the following sections.

3 Nietzsche on Reactive Types

At the end of the previous section, we saw the issue of grievance or slight playing a role in populists' machinations. A number of studies have set out to dissect this phenomenon of political resentment and to map the Nietzschean notion of *ressentiment* on to contemporary populism.[27] But for reasons that should become apparent below, in the following the emphasis is not primarily on the affect of *ressentiment* and its political effects as on certain structural features of populism and the types that populate its narratives. Although *ressentiment* is no doubt the central affective aspect of populism, reducing populism to this affective issue risks overlooking the persistent structural problems it harbours. It is therefore here not chiefly a question of mapping the Nietzschean notion of *ressentiment* on to those who feel aggrieved or slighted,[28] but of showing how populism shares certain structural features with what Nietzsche analyses, in *On the Genealogy of Morality*,[29] as the reactive types that he thematises in terms of slavishness and the ascetic priest. Nietzsche knew that phenomena of reactivity had their own specific breeding-ground, and in the *Genealogy* he explains in quasi-systematic fashion what this breeding-ground is and through what mechanisms reactive forms of life are generated from it.

First of all, then, a reminder of the points made by Nietzsche in the *Genealogy* that are relevant to this discussion. Nietzsche carries out a genealogy (a radicalised critique) of the moral values that have sustained 'every kind of "Europe"' (GM III, 14), as he calls it. In particular, the value of these values for life is the crucial issue which must be examined (GM Preface, 3 and 6). He does this in terms of the physiological question, namely, whether our values have 'hitherto hindered or promoted human flourishing', whether they are

---

27 E.g., Abbas (2015); Birns (2005); Fassin (2013); Illing (2017); Olschanski (2015); Small (1997); and Ure (2015).
28 Müller (2017, pp. 15–16) warns against using resentment or *ressentiment* to explain populism since he sees it as psychologising and, ultimately, simplifying a complex socio-political phenomenon. He mentions Nietzsche and GM by name but without employing a properly philosophical hermeneutic to it.
29 Unless otherwise noted, quotations from the *Genealogy* are from Maudemarie Clark and Alan Swensen's translation.

'signs of distress, of impoverishment, of the degeneration of life', or, conversely, whether they hint at 'the fullness, the strength, the will of life, its courage, its hopefulness [*Zuversicht*], its future' (GM Preface, 3, translation modified). The former kinds of values he calls 'slave morality' and associates with the project of self-protection and self-preservation; the latter he calls 'noble morality' and associates with the unguarded expenditure of self. An important proviso that must be noted here is that, although human beings are the carriers, conduits and perpetuators of values, for Nietzsche, they are not the causes or grounds of these values. Why this is so will be explained in the following.

Now, Nietzsche's questions in the *Genealogy* concern *moral* values, and the religious regimes out of which they grew, but which they have largely left behind. But the question being raised here concerns not primarily moral or religious values, but merely the perspectives which Nietzsche had identified as propagating them, namely, those of nobility or slavishness, and their typical characteristics.[30] We recall that Nietzsche's genealogical enquiry traces the following development: firstly, how originally physiological values become symbolic ones, for example, 'pure' and 'impure' (GM I, 6); secondly, how these newly-minted symbolic values are co-opted by a hieratic elite, a priestly aristocracy, to take on religious signification (GM I, 6–8); and thirdly, how these religiously-inflected terms are in turn adopted by a numerically superior entity, whom Nietzsche calls 'the people, ... the slaves, ... the mob, ... the herd' (GM I, 9). Thereby these values become entirely disconnected from their physiological provenance and their previous religious signification, diluted to their merely moral meaning and widely disseminated to justify the "natural" tendencies of the slaves. But here, to emphasise, it is not this development which is central, nor the genealogy of the moral values it traces, but only the perspectives which Nietzsche chisels out in the process, namely, nobility and slavishness, and the question is whether, to what extent and in what way they can help us understand the inner workings of populism.

To recap Nietzsche's key points about each tendency, nobility is characterised above all by an original, spontaneous affirmation of itself, by a profound yes-saying to itself (GM I, 10), by a contempt for security and comfort, and even by an indifference towards the preservation of its – bodily, or "personal" – integrity. If it notices an other at all, this is an afterthought, and a matter of

---

[30] It should be remembered that nowadays, when slavishness has a tendency to invoke religious values to furnish a pretext for its nefarious activities, this is at best quaint, in the era of the death of God, and should be treated for what it is, namely, a set of rhetorical devices employed by ascetic priests in order to manipulate the herd.

indifference to it. Moreover, throughout the *Nachlass*,[31] Nietzsche associates nobility with the desire or even the need for expenditure, which he sees as the fundamental trait of a living being (see, e.g., WP 650; NL1885–1886 KSA 12, 2[63]). By contrast, slavishness is characterised by its original act of no-saying to everything that is different, that is positioned as other, as outside, as not-self. In fact, slavishness needs such an outside, needs to interpolate it, we might say, in order to develop a sense of identity in the first place. It needs to posit an enemy in order to be itself, a "not-I" or "not-we", in contradistinction and opposition to which it derives its "I" or "we". Its original act is one of negation, and if it becomes creative of values at all, it does so out of *ressentiment* against otherness (GM I, 10). Nietzsche adds that, 'physiologically speaking, [slavishness] needs external stimuli in order to act at all; its action is fundamentally reaction' (GM I, 10 translation modified).[32] Whereas nobility is necessarily active and finds its happiness in activity, steered by the powerful regulating unconscious instincts of which it is the carrier (*Träger* [GM I, 11]),[33] the happiness of slavishness lies in inactivity, in 'narcosis, anaesthetic, quiet, peace, "sabbath"' (GM I, 10), in short, in an emasculated passivity,[34] of the impulse towards which it is the carrier (GM I, 11). Nobility only uses its enemies as a way of acting out its natural impulses of joyful destructiveness, beyond which they are insignificant to it. By contrast, slavishness constructs the image of an enemy through a sophistical, moralistic syllogism and then cleaves to its conclusion unswervingly: "they are evil, I am not them, therefore I am good" (GM I, 7, 10, 13). Even more fundamentally, we could add what could be termed the ontological version of this syllogism, concluding in the existential tautology typical of reactive types: "they are other, I am not them, therefore I am what I am" – hence there occurs not a spontaneous self-affirmation but the reactive insistence on self-identity and the refusal of self-transcendence.

---

31 The largely untranslated notes and fragments from the notebooks Nietzsche kept between 1850 and his collapse in January 1889, see KSA vols. 7–15.
32 Bizarrely, as happens at times with translations of Nietzsche's text, where it says 'physiologisch', i.e., 'physiological/ly' in the original, this is rendered as 'psychological/ly' in the translation. Clark and Swensen commit this error in their translation of GM I, 10, Kaufmann and Hollingdale do not, in theirs. But then Kaufmann commits this error in his translation of WP 227.
33 GM I, 11 has 'bearers'.
34 Through this it becomes clever (*klug*), since in the absence of external expenditure its violent and aggressive impulses become internalised, so much so that Nietzsche calls cleverness a condition of its existence (see GM I, 10, translation modified).

Nietzsche's analysis of the phenomena of slavishness culminates in what Deleuze later identifies as the Nietzschean critique of paralogistic thinking,[35] in which an impersonal happening or event is first of all separated into a deed and its doer. An impersonal event is thereby "personalised" and turned into the activity of an agent (even if that "agent" is a force of nature, e. g., lightning [see GM I, 13]), meaning an agent of the action is posited as existing prior to, outside of and separate from the action. In actual fact, however, this is merely an instance of 'the seductions of language' drawing us into a way of thinking by hypostasising what is actually the merely grammatical subject of a verb into a substantive, independently existing agent (GM I, 13).[36] The distinction thereby arrived at – between a force and what it can do, between a doer and a deed – can then be turned by reactive forces into the whole nightmarish phantasmagoria of free will, responsibility, guilt, bad conscience, etc., that finally spawn their most reactive outcrop, namely, the 'sovereign individual' (GM II, 2),[37] as Nietzsche analyses it in the second essay of the *Genealogy*. In other words, slavishness can begin to dominate when it succeeds in the imaginary separation of an active force from what it can do (GM I, 13; see Deleuze 1983a, p. 57).

The turning-point in Nietzsche's dissection of reactivity, however, occurs when he begins to discuss the phenomena surrounding the ascetic ideal and, specifically, the ascetic priest. In GM III, the question of the value of our moral values for life leads Nietzsche to the investigation of ascetic values, whose meaning varies depending on which life-forms they inhabit (e. g., artists, philosophers, saints [GM III, 1]). It is only when ascetic values occupy priests that they become dangerous (GM I, 6), because then it becomes a question of the value of life itself, and not merely of this or that aspect of life. But because life means becoming, change, transitoriness (GM III, 11), as well as force, physicality (GM III, 11), and multiplicity (GM III, 12), against all of which ascetic priests polemicise, Nietzsche there observes the strange spectacle of what seems to be life turning against itself (GM III, 13). But because, physiologically

---

35 The philosophical analysis of paralogistic thinking in the modern period begins with Kant's critique of Descartes's psychological paralogisms in deriving the substantiality, simplicity, identity and relations of a thinking substance (*res cogitans*) from the "I think". See Kant, *Critique of Pure Reason*, A 341–405/B 399–432. Nietzsche extends this critique to all impositions of agency upon the impersonal flux of the will to power. That Nietzsche does this, in GM, was first made explicit in Deleuze 1983a, pp. 57, 66, and 87–89.
36 Nietzsche had already made this point with all-but explicit reference to Descartes in *Beyond Good and Evil* (BGE 16–19), by saying that it is not "I" who thinks, but that thinking occurs by itself, apart from, and before the imposition of any alleged "I" or subject (BGE 17).
37 See Christa Acampora (2006).

speaking, this is a nonsense (GM III, 13), Nietzsche finds that this can only be an apparent self-contradiction and, when thought within the immanence of life or will to power, he concludes that '*the ascetic ideal springs from the protective and healing instincts of a degenerating life* that seeks with every means to hold its ground and is fighting for its existence' (GM III, 13).

He observes that the ascetic ideal indicates a 'partial physiological obstruction and exhaustion' (GM III, 13[38]), against which the instincts that have remained intact battle by means of various devices and that the ascetic ideal is such a device (GM III, 13). Ultimately, then, the ascetic idea as channelled by the ascetic priest, far from being nihilistic, turns out – as a result of Nietzsche's transvaluation – to be a device for the preservation of life, which the ascetic priests unwittingly and paradoxically employ in their ardent desire for a beyond (GM III, 13). Nietzsche sums up the relation of the ascetic priest to their followers thus:

> The ascetic priest is the incarnate wish for a different existence, an existence somewhere else ... in this very process he becomes a tool that must work at creating more favourable conditions for being here and being human – with this very *power* he ties to existence the entire herd of the deformed, disgruntled, underprivileged [*Schlechtweggekommnen*], unfortunate, those of every kind who suffer from themselves. (GM III, 13)[39]

The overall effect of the ascetic ideal on the priests' acolytes is to alleviate their suffering for, as Nietzsche explains, the real burden is not suffering itself but the apparent meaninglessness of suffering, and the ascetic priests redirect what would otherwise be a 'suicidal nihilism' towards a 'purpose' (GM III, 28),[40] or, conversely, a cause (GM III, 15). This redirection is so crucial that Nietzsche says:

> if one wanted to compress the value of the priestly mode of existence into the briefest formula ... one would have to say ... : the priest *changes the direction of ressentiment*... every sufferer instinctively seeks a cause for their suffering; more precisely, a perpetrator [*Täter*] ..., a *guilty* perpetrator who is receptive to suffering – in short, some living thing on which, on some pretext or other, they can discharge their affect in deed or in effigy. (GM III, 15, translation modified)

The typical machinations of populist leaders were drawn out in sections 1 and 2, above, and it should now have become apparent that – mutatis mutandis – it is

---

38 Here, I am quoting Kaufmann and Hollingdale's translation, which strikes me as more forceful. The original is 'partielle physiologische Hemmung und Ermüdung'.
39 The translation given here is an amalgam of Kaufmann and Hollingdale's and Clark and Swensen's.
40 Here, I am quoting Kaufmann and Hollingdale's translation.

Nietzsche's figure of the ascetic priest who maps most closely upon them; just as it is Nietzsche's most overtly reactive types, the slaves, who correspond most closely to today's adherents of populism. Needless to say, in comparison to the awful grandeur of the gradual internalisation of human being and its Christian-metaphysical systematisation (as analysed by Nietzsche in the *Genealogy*), the paltry posturings of today's power-hungry populist politicians, and of the disenfranchised followers they galvanise, is but a faint, and faintly ridiculous, echo – but an echo that nevertheless shares certain of its central features. More specifically, populism can be understood as the most recent form of humanity's gradual slide into reactivity and nihilism, whose beginnings and key characteristics Nietzsche shows in the *Genealogy*.

Rather than striving to enlighten them about the inner workings of global capitalism and its devastating local effects, populists redirect their adherents' attention to, as we saw, chimerical identities and illusory oppositions, thus providing them with a – however misconceived – meaning to what might otherwise turn into bottomless despair at their own situation. Just as the priestly ascetic ideal, albeit on an infinitely grander scale, provides a screen from the intrinsic meaninglessness of suffering and a shelter for 'the sick animal' that is human being (GM III, 13), so populist propaganda provides both a screen from the vacuum of status and meaning experienced (however numbly) by their followers as a result of the contemporary global socio-economic upheaval and the accompanying pluralisation of all Western societies, as well as a screen on which to project their fears (as we saw, "elites" and migrants).

As is the case with Nietzsche's analysis of the priestly ascetic ideal's propaganda, understanding what might be called the "populist ascetic ideal" of an ethnically and culturally homogeneous ("pure") society is, however, not the end but only a stage of the investigation. These points are, I believe, incontrovertible from a contemporary political perspective and may help us to understand the mechanisms of populism. However, from the perspective of Nietzsche's philosophy – whose ultimate tasks are transvaluation and affirmation – it is necessary to explore two further levels in our burrowing into these matters, as the next two sections will do.

4 Physiological Aspects of Reactivity

Nietzsche's analyses of the logical operations of slavishness no doubt allow us to understand certain phenomena better, especially the prima facie incomprehensible phenomena of nationalism, racism, xenophobia, and related expressions of the hatred of otherness, since they all construct their image of the other as the enemy, and consequently their own identity, in a way that is typical of slavishness. In fact, as we saw, this dual construction (of other and self) is one of the core characteristics of slavishness, in tandem with a certain brooding and resentful inactivity. The types who indulge in this kind of operation, as we saw above (section 3), Nietzsche sometimes calls 'die Schlechtweggekommenen', which is a highly polysemic term and therefore difficult to translate. Literally, it means 'those who got away badly', but it is used to mean the disadvantaged, the underprivileged,[41] the left-behind.[42] Some of Nietzsche's most extensive ruminations on this type are to be found in the famous Lenzer Heide notes of 1887, where he explains that 'schlechtweggekommen' is above all a physiological, and not a political category, designating the unhealthiest kind of human being (NL1885–1886 KSA 12, 5[71], no. 14); where he predicts with uncanny accuracy what happens when this type is detached from all traditional (Christian) morality, how it then becomes the breeding ground of the most extreme form of nihilism, and becomes indiscriminately destructive, including of itself (NL1885–1886 KSA 12, 5[71], no. 12). Following Nietzsche's signposting of the essentially *physiological* character of these types of disturbance, it is this feature that will be briefly highlighted in the following.

Here it is helpful to recall Deleuze's observation that 'The Nietzschean notion of the slave does not necessarily stand for someone dominated ..., but also characterises the dominators as much as the dominated once the regime of domination comes under the sway of forces which are reactive and not active' (Deleuze 1983a, p. x). A similar point is made in the Deleuze quotation that forms the epigraph of this chapter, namely, that slavishness is not – not only, not primarily, or not at all – the state of being dominated by masters. Instead, slavishness indicates a certain constellation of forces, one in which slavish kinds of forces have triumphed, and this affects masters as much as slaves. It would then be an error, on a par with the paralogism (see section 3, above), to identify slavishness with, or reduce it to, those lifeforms that have obviously surrendered to that particular constellation, namely, the slaves, and not also to see it at work in the apparent masters. Instead, it is vitally important to remember that in a

---

41 This is how Kaufmann translates this term in GS 370, although he simply omits it in his translation of GM III, 15. Clark and Swensen translate it as 'the short-changed' (GM III, 15). Duncan Large, in his translation of TI, renders it as 'the botched' (TI Improvers, 4).
42 From today's point of view, this is a fortuitous expression, since those who got away badly literally managed badly or not at all to get away from their milieu, from their prejudices and literally from the piece of earth where they find themselves, and it is perhaps this physio-psychological parochialism that is another source of their resentment towards open-minded, globally-thinking internationalists.

Nietzschean understanding of this phenomenon, it is best viewed as the quality of a force (in contrast to the quality he calls 'nobility'). Simply put, it is not a matter of understanding slaves – or, for that matter, nobles – as individuals. Instead, slavishness (and nobility) should be seen as tendencies, eruptions, fluxes, and as the ineffable quality of forces, or, in sum, as types of will to power. This is difficult to accept for a culture as completely steeped in the prejudices of substance metaphysics as ours, but it is, I believe, the properly Nietzschean understanding of these phenomena.[43]

In GM II, 16, Nietzsche famously charts in phylogenetic terms the original physiological obstruction that paved the way for the internalisations of human being leading to the reactive phenomena of guilt and bad conscience. This was, in brief, the domestication of the human animal, making it fit for life in society, signalled by the shift from the dominance of instincts to the dominance of consciousness. But on an ontogenetic level, too, reactivity can be "bred" by environmental factors and circumstances, be they socio-economic, political, or even cultural. See, for instance, Nietzsche's claim that 'conscience changes according to the environment [*Umgebung*], insofar as the feeling of non-coincidence of evaluation generates the instinct of fear, scepsis' (NL 1883 KSA 10, 7[15], my translation). Both of these points, encompassing phylogeny and ontogeny, seem to indicate something like a fluid exchange between physiologies and their environments, even or especially when in the broadest sense environmental factors lead to physiological blockages. What they also show is that physiologies and the values they harbour are by no means fixed but instead mutable according to myriad environmental factors. Some of the environmental factors leading to the predominance of slavishness or, much more rarely, nobility, in any given physiology are outlined by Nietzsche, for instance, in *Ecce Homo*, in the chapter "Why I am so Clever". There he suggests that whether one or the other tendency dominates any given phenomenon is a question of innumerable, infinitely subtle, almost imperceptible interacting factors, such as diet, locale, climate, the relative humidity of the environment, the quality of the air and the direction of the wind (see especially sections 8–10) – a dynamic of factors almost too subtle for our organs of perception and consciousness.[44]

---

[43] It might be objected that ours is a "post-modern" culture, and that we are beyond substance metaphysics. It is true that, since Nietzsche's intervention, thinkers have sought to "destruct", "deconstruct", "transvaluate" or genealogically investigate metaphysics, but arguably that work has not (yet?) filtered down into contemporary culture, if it ever could.

[44] But see, e.g., Marsden (2018), which explores this perhaps more than any other contemporary text on Nietzsche.

As can be seen from these brief indications, Nietzsche's critique amounts to a thoroughgoing de-mythologising of the notions of cause, agency and subjectivity, such that any thinking in terms of stable identities – "slaves", "masters" – simply misses its mark. But it should be remembered that beyond the dismantling of our substantialist modes of thinking, Nietzsche ultimately aims at the restitution of the innocence of becoming and that to insert an allegedly self-identical agency into the ongoing impersonal event of becoming is nothing but a 'falsification' (*Fälschung* BGE 17). In a properly Nietzschean understanding, there are therefore only anonymous fluxes, impersonal forces, and the tendencies or fluctuations of the will to power, which is never "mine", but a pre-individuated economy of relatively active or reactive, ultimately libidinal, forces formative of phenomena.[45] This Nietzschean thinking in terms of a comprehensive, yet groundless, impersonal conative multiplicity is underscored by the use of the term 'carrier' (*Träger*), mentioned above. This term indicates that, for Nietzsche, human beings, even if construed in terms of – individual or collective – subjectivity, are never points of origin of occurrences or events, but only ever conduits or channels for the forces which seek to exert power; for instance, all manner of societal, moral or cultural values that both constitute and tug at the individual. These forces should in any event be seen as broadly "physiological", insofar as physiologies are the nodal points between such impersonal forces and their articulations, instantiations and perpetuations in the "human" realm.

What also follows from this is that crucially – even though this may be a hard pill to swallow – reactivity is never just out in the world, a feature of (other) individuals and (other) circumstances. To take it thus would amount to a repetition of the paralogism (discussed in section 3, above). Instead, reactivity is a stream that flows through everyone to different degrees at different times, a stream that ebbs and flows, according to the circumstances, the situation and the environment in which one finds oneself. Reactivity is not a doing (in Nietzsche's sense of an artificially separated doer and deed), but a happening, yet another ongoing impersonal event that we can only try to attenuate or mitigate or that we – whether deliberately or, more usually, unwittingly – buttress and intensify with the actions we perform, the conative milieu we cultivate.

From these points it becomes clear that the populist rhetoric of a (group-) identity (of "the people" or "the nation"[46]) merely transposes into the political realm an illusion that sustains thought more generally. Nietzsche never fails to

---

[45] See WP 1067; NL 1885, KSA 11, 38[12], for a summary of Nietzsche's understanding of will to power.
[46] For instance, "America", "Great Britain". See also Charim (2018, ch.1), which reminds us of the illusory nature of a homogeneous society.

point out what he succinctly sums up in the phrase: 'Everything that enters consciousness as "unity" is already tremendously complex: we always have only a semblance of unity' (WP 489; NL 1885–1886, KSA 12, 5[56]),[47] although the imaginary populist identities do not of course so much mark a failure of cognition or insight, but a physiological disturbance leading to the triumph of reactivity. For Nietzsche, not only is identity never unproblematically given, but it is only ever produced by complex synthetic operations of the will to power. More specifically, the "I" (whether singular or plural) is always already other to itself and never self-identical, so that all supposed pre-given self-identity is merely a chimera. Similarly, the opposition set up between this imaginary self-identity and the (plural or singular) non-I, produced through a concomitant act of othering, always only functions to obscure the infinitely greater complexity of forces within, across and between each of these two putative poles.

5 Towards Immanence

It has already been stated that Nietzsche's thinking revolves around the will to power and the economy and dynamic of forces it involves; that the decisive issue in each case is the physiological condition of the phenomena examined; that within the will to power we can at best discern rapidly fluctuating, differing degrees (e.g., of nobility and slavishness); and that the ultimate aim of Nietzsche's critique (e.g., of paralogistic thinking) is the transvaluation of values and the restoration of the innocence of becoming. All of these issues are indicative of Nietzsche's persistent effort to think through what we would now call 'immanence'.[48] In the previous section, we began the task of immanentising the notional opposition between slavishness and nobility within the Nietzschean physiological understanding of the will to power. This must now be made more explicit. In a sense, though, we have already been working towards an immanent philosophical reading of the phenomena of populism when they were shown to be no more than aspects of the will to power, and as such already freed from the

---

[47] See also, e.g., WP 490, 500, 501, and 512, as well as GM I, 12, and 16. For Nietzsche, identity, unity, etc. are always the products of the process of equalisation (see, e.g., WP 511; NL 1885–1886, KSA 12, 2[90]).

[48] Or – as Deleuze calls it – the 'plane of immanence'. Deleuze speaks of the 'vertigo of philosophy' (Deleuze 1997, p. 180); and he and Guattari claim that 'Spinoza is the vertigo of immanence' (Deleuze and Guattari 1994, p. 48). In the latter text, they also say that 'The plane of immanence is neither a concept nor the concept of all concepts' (Deleuze and Guattari 1994, p. 35). This, too, indicates an isomorphism between the will to power and the plane of immanence.

burden of their carriers' claims (to naturalness, veracity, etc.). Since we are always already in the immanence that is will to power it is in fact not a matter of a special effort to get to or into immanence, but rather of letting go, relinquishing the pre-conceived notions that bind us, even though consciousness is always too late, always lags behind and has to catch up with what is already underway, namely, a ceaseless, all-encompassing, impersonal becoming – the will to power, or immanence.

Just to clarify briefly, immanence is not a thing, entity, substance or ground, but should be understood as a movement, an economy, a ceaseless doing and being. Different kinds of forces can be understood in relation to and by their relation to it: namely, whether they resist it (reactivity) or whether are open to, drawn to, sustained and quickened by it (activity). In actual fact, everything and everyone is always already encompassed in it, but that does not, of course, mean that everything and everyone is always equally open to it. In this sense, the hostility certain phenomena and life-forms display towards otherness is always of a piece with their resistance to immanence or the impersonal happening of will to power.

Although it is ultimately not enough to understand immanence merely in opposition to transcendence, it is still worth remembering that both monotheistic religions and traditional metaphysics tend to start from transcendent "givens", which are not questioned or examined, but openly or clandestinely assumed to exist. These include, but are not limited to, God, spirit, subject, substance, cause, ground, *telos*, *arché*, etc. Nietzsche's – and much post-Nietzschean – thinking, by contrast, seeks to sustain (a plane of) complete immanence, with the result, as mentioned before, that we can only ever discern degrees and fluctuations within it, and that any absolute segregation – such as would characterise dualistic paradigms – becomes unsustainable once we attempt to think from and on the plane of immanence.

Moreover, as Nietzsche knew, and as Deleuze reminds us, radical immanence or will to power must not be thought as immanent *to* anything, such as a substance or subject, but instead all such identities are only ever immanent to and produced by it (WP 1067; NL 1885, KSA 11, 38[12]; Deleuze 2001, pp. 26–27), however they may be represented. What this also means is that both when a multiplicity is interpolated as other and when reactivity is presented as self-identical, both are in the manner of simulacra, that is, of simulations without an original, which call into question the entire order of (the metaphysics of) representation.[49]

For both Nietzsche and Deleuze, the meaning of a phenomenon, as well as the phenomenon itself, is only ever produced through a process of interpretation which seeks to dominate phenomena. Nietzsche says, 'The will to power interprets', meaning it determines differentials of power and thereby the quality of forces, that is, active or reactive, affirmative or negative (WP 643; NL 1885–1886, KSA 12, 2[148]; Deleuze 2001, pp. 72–73). And although both Nietzsche and Deleuze diagnose the – seemingly comprehensive – triumph of reactive forces (GM I, 9; III, 20; Deleuze 2001, pp. 74–82), both their interpretations find, at the very moment when this triumph seems to be complete, the point which the transvaluation can latch on to, from where it can commence, and this is what we saw Nietzsche discover with the spectacle of life ostensibly turning against itself in the ascetic ideal (see section 3, above; GM III, 11–13; Deleuze 2001, pp. 82–86). In fact, both Nietzsche and Deleuze suggest that the most extreme point of reactivity must be reached before the transmutation of values can proceed (GM III, 11; Deleuze 2001, p. 82), apparently in the manner of a metabolē (μεταβολή) or overthrow of one prevailing type or regime of will to power by another. We also saw (section 3, above), and Deleuze confirms, that nihilism's enmity is chiefly directed against multiplicity and becoming, and that these reactive forces become victorious by separating a force from what it can do (GM I, 13; Deleuze 2001, p. 78; see also Deleuze 1983a, pp. 49–57). And although Deleuze warns that we, who 'inhabit only the desolate surface of the earth' (Deleuze 2001, p. 84), may not know what affirmation looks like in practice (Deleuze 2001, pp. 83–84), he is clear that it 'is the highest power of the will', that what is affirmed is 'the earth, life',[50] and that this means 'elevat[ing] multiplicity and becoming to their highest power and mak[ing] them objects of…affirmation', because 'in the affirmation of the multiple lies the practical joy of the diverse' (Deleuze 2001, pp. 83–84). He concludes that to 'valorise negative sentiments or sad passions … is the mystification on which nihilism bases its power', whereas 'joy emerges as the sole motive for philosophising' (Deleuze 2001, pp. 83–84) – and, we might add, for living.[51] Hence, to show all phenomena as radically im-

---

[49] Deleuze (1983b, pp. 45–56). A different translation of this is Appendix I in Deleuze (1990, pp. 253–266).
[50] This is of course reminiscent of Z, Prologue, 3, when Zarathustra enjoins his followers to 'remain true to the earth'.
[51] Could this be an answer to Nietzsche's question when he asks where is the opposing will, ideal and goal to the will, ideal and goal expressed in the ascetic ideal? (GM III, 23).

manent, and thereby to affirm multiplicity and becoming, is both the first impulse and the goal of a politics of difference.

Bibliography

Abbas, Asma (2015): "*Ressentiment*". In: Michael Gibbons (Ed.): *The Encyclopedia of Political Thought*, pp. 1–5. Chichester: Wiley Blackwell.
Acampora, Christa Davis (2006): "On Sovereignty and Overhumanity: Why it Matters how we Read Nietzsche's *Genealogy* II, 2", In: Christa Davis Acampora (Ed.): *Nietzsche's* On the Genealogy of Morals: *Critical Essays*, pp. 147–161. Lanham: Rowman and Littlefield.
Anderson, Benedict (2006): *Imagined Communities: Reflections on the Origin and Spread of Nationalism*. Rev. ed. London: Verso.
Birns, Nicholas (2005): "*Ressentiment* and Counter-*Ressentiment:* Nietzsche, Scheler, and the Reaction against Equality" (unpublished manuscript, January 1, 2005), Portable Document Format. http://nietzschecircle.com/ResentimentMaster.pdf
Charim, Isolde (2018): *Ich und die Anderen: Wie die neue Pluralisierung uns alle verändert*. Vienna: Paul Zsolnay Verlag.
Deleuze, Gilles (1983a): *Nietzsche and Philosophy*. Translated by Hugh Tomlinson. London: The Athlone Press.
Deleuze, Gilles (1983b): "Plato and the Simulacrum". *October*, 27. Winter, pp. 45–56. Translated by Rosalind Krauss.
Deleuze, Gilles (1990): "Plato and the Simulacrum". In: *The Logic of Sense*, pp. 253–266. Edited by Constantin V. Boundas and translated by Mark Lester. New York: Columbia University Press.
Deleuze, Gilles (1997): *Expressionism in Philosophy: Spinoza*. Translated by Martin Joughin. New York: Zone Books.
Deleuze, Gilles (2001): *Pure Immanence – Essays on A Life*. Translated by Anne Boyman. New York: Zone Books.
Deleuze, Gilles, and Felix Guattari (1994): *What is Philosophy?* Translated by Graham Burchell and Hugh Tomlinson. London: Verso.
Dubiel, Helmut (Ed.) (1986): *Populismus und Aufklärung*. Frankfurt a. M.: Suhrkamp Verlag.
Eribon, Didier (2019): *Returning to Reims*. Translated by Michael Lucey. London: Penguin Books.
Fassin, Didier (2013): "On Resentment and *Ressentiment:* The Politics and Ethics of Moral Emotions". In: *Current Anthropology*, 54. No. 3, 249–267.
Illing, Sean (2017): Interview with Hugo Drochon. In: *Vox*, 11 June, https://www.vox.com/conversations/2016/12/20/13927678/donald-trump-brexit-nietzsche-democracy-europe-populism-hugo-drochon, visited on 14 August.
Kant, Immanuel (1964): *Critique of Pure Reason*. Edited and translated by Norman Kemp Smith. London: Macmillan.
Krastev, Ivan (2007): "The Populist Moment". In: *Critique and Humanism*, 23, pp. 1–5.
Lefort, Claude (1988): *Democracy and Political Theory*. Translated by David Macey. Cambridge: Polity Press.

Marsden, Jill (2018): "'The Immeasurable Fineness of Things': Nietzsche and the Quiet Machinery of Thought". In: Andrea Rehberg (Ed.): *Nietzsche and Phenomenology*, pp. 67–85. Newcastle upon Tyne: Cambridge Scholars Press.
Müller, Jan-Werner (2017): *What is Populism?* London: Penguin Books.
Nietzsche, Friedrich (1966): *Beyond Good and Evil*. Translated by Walter Kaufmann. New York: Random House.
Nietzsche, Friedrich (2014): *Beyond Good and Evil*. In: *Beyond Good and Evil, On the Genealogy of Morality. The Complete Works of Friedrich Nietzsche*, vol. 8. Translated by Adrian Del Caro. Stanford: Stanford University Press.
Nietzsche, Friedrich (2012): *Ecce Homo*. In: *The Anti-Christ, Ecce Homo, Twilight of the Idols and Other Writings*, pp. 69–151. Edited by Aaron Ridley and Judith Norman and translated by Judith Norman. Cambridge and New York: Cambridge University Press.
Nietzsche, Friedrich (1967): *On the Genealogy of Morals*. Edited by Walter Kaufmann and translated by Walter Kaufmann and R. J. Hollingdale. New York: Random House.
Nietzsche, Friedrich (1964): *Thus Spoke Zarathustra*. Translated by R. J. Hollingdale. London: Penguin.
Nietzsche, Friedrich (1998): *On the Genealogy of Morality*. Translated by Maudemarie Clark and Alan J. Swensen. Indianapolis: Hackett Publishing Company.
Nietzsche, Friedrich (1968): *The Will to Power*. Edited by Walter Kaufmann and translated by Walter Kaufmann and R. J. Hollingdale. New York: Random House.
Olschanski, Reinhard (2015): *Ressentiment*. Paderborn: Verlag Wilhelm Fink.
Small, Robin (1997): "*Ressentiment*, Revenge, and Punishment: Origins of the Nietzschean Critique". In: *Utilitas*, 9, No. 1, pp. 39–58.
Ure, Michael (2015): "Resentment/*Ressentiment*". In: *Constellations*, 22. No. 4, pp. 599–613.

Part 3 **Nietzsche and Deleuze on a New Politics**

Jonas Oßwald
Echoes of a New Politics: Deleuze's Nietzsche and the Political

Abstract: As Deleuze says in his essay "Nomadic Thought", it is Nietzsche's movement of uncoding which announces a "new politics". Nietzsche marks the beginning of a counter-culture in the effort "to get something through which is not encodable". In this way, Nietzsche establishes a different kind of philosophical discourse, a "counter-philosophy", inasmuch as its utterances are directed against philosophy conceived as the bureaucracy of pure reason. This chapter attempts to establish an *untimely* echo of Deleuze's essay, which aims at an actualised understanding of this rather enigmatically announced "new politics". It first illustrates how a recent strain of political thought, post-foundationalism, repeats the recoding of society. It then shows that these efforts of recoding are obsessive expressions of a figure which resembles the Nietzschean priest. Finally, it concludes with an outline of Nietzsche's "new politics".

1 Introduction

It is a timeless question with which Gilles Deleuze begins to think anew with Nietzsche in 1972, ten years after his seminal study *Nietzsche and Philosophy* (2006). 'What is Nietzsche today?', he asks in a talk called "Nomadic Thought" (Deleuze 2004b, p. 252). What is Nietzsche today? – one can almost hear all the echoes emanating from this question, then, before it and now. At the same time, Deleuze is quite specific: *What* is Nietzsche today? Not 'who is Nietzsche today?' or even simply 'Nietzsche aujourd'hui?' as the conference in Cerisy-la-Salle asked, where Deleuze gave this talk. What is Nietzsche today? – that implies at least that Nietzsche is relevant somehow, whereas 'Nietzsche aujourd'hui?' questions this relevance. So, what is Nietzsche in 1972? In France? After Heidegger's Nietzsche, after Pierre Klossowski's, Maurice Blanchot's and Georges Bataille's Nietzsche? After Deleuze's and Foucault's Nietzschean structuralism of the 1960s? What lesson is there still to be learned, once we got rid of the fascistic usurpation of Nietzsche and simultaneously positioned him as an anti-dialectical, anti-Hegelian thinker? Deleuze's answer to this question basically demarcates the scope of this chapter. 'Nietzsche' in 1972 mainly means conceiving of

---

Supported by the Faculty of Philosophy and Education, University of Vienna.

https://doi.org/10.1515/9783110688436-009

a counter-discourse to the discourse of philosophers, 'the bureaucrats of pure reason', as Deleuze says. Nietzsche's 'conspiracy against his own class' initiates a 'new politics' (Deleuze 2004b, p. 259).

This chapter tries to establish a resonance, an echo, by asking what it means to conspire, like Nietzsche, against one's own class, and what kind of (new) politics this involves. For this, in section 2, I reconstruct Deleuze's principal argument in "Nomadic Thought" and, in section 3, I confront it with the concept of political difference in contemporary post-foundationalist thought. Since the differences between Deleuze's Nietzschean thought and post-foundationalism appear to be very profound, in section 4, I propose to conceive of these in terms of opposed perspectives on power and sovereignty. I conclude, in section 5, with a brief sketch of some implications of the idea of a "new politics" that Nietzsche, according to Deleuze, made possible and that seeks to betray philosophy's fundamental bonds to power and the Sovereign. With Deleuze's Nietzsche, one could say that a politics of difference is understood as a radical counter-politics to any closure of the social field.

2 Nietzsche's Conspiracy

Besides the echoes that beg the question what Nietzsche's 'conspiracy against his own class' actually means, there are also those echoes that assume this conspiracy as already given and that concern themselves with the exploration of counter-discourses or counter-practices (e.g., arts-based philosophies).[1] Besides the strategy of refusal inherent in such a conspiracy, however, there is perhaps an even more profound scandal residing in the conspiracy against one's own class, namely, the subtlety of betrayal. In contrast to refusal, betrayal does not necessarily leave the territory of that which it betrays, it does not necessarily perform the grand and heroic gesture of publicly denouncing a demanded allegiance, it does not even necessarily call for an alternative. Betrayal is a silent, almost subterranean suspension of habits and beliefs that may become visible if it seems opportune, but for as long as it stays invisible and imperceptible, betrayal is a source of unrest immanent to a well-ordered system of habits and beliefs.[2] In contrast to the oppositional strategy of refusal, betrayal invokes parti-

---

[1] See, for example, Arno Böhler and Susanne Granzer (2020).
[2] From "Nomadic Thought" onwards the notion of betrayal regularly reappears in the work of Deleuze and Deleuze and Félix Guattari. See, for example, Deleuze and Claire Parnet (2007, pp. 40–41); Deleuze and Guattari (1987, pp. 358 and 377); or Deleuze (1997, p. 117). For an interpretation of this notion as a break in power relations, see Ronald Bogue (2004, pp. 143–160).

san tactics; the wisdom of the serpent rather than the lion's 'sacred No' (Z I, Metamorphoses). But why betray in the first place? And who exactly does Nietzsche betray if the betrayal is not about philosophy as such, but the discourse of the philosophers? Who are these philosophers if they do not exactly equal philosophy? To answer these questions, we need first of all to dwell on the positional problem indicated above. In other words, the question 'What is Nietzsche today?' needs to be understood in relation to the question of what role Nietzsche plays in modernity.

For Deleuze, the answer to the question of Nietzsche's role in modernity is quite simple. Regarding the habitual account, according to which modern critical thought begins with the trinity of Nietzsche, Freud and Marx, it may be that the latter two do play the role of founding figures, but this is not the case for Nietzsche, who in contrast marks the 'dawn of a counter-culture' (Deleuze 2004b, p. 253). This reading of Nietzsche's antagonistic position concerning – from Deleuze's perspective in the 1970s – an orthodox discourse of Freudo-Marxism, rests on the premise that 'our society does not function according to codes' (Deleuze 2004b, p. 253), but can be codified. De jure, there is no code whatsoever that would exhaustively explain a given society on all accounts, which nonetheless does not mean that there are no de facto attempts to do so. In fact, 'Marxists and Freudians' are constantly engaged in an effort not only to codify society but also Marx and Freud themselves:

> in the case of Marxism, you have a recoding by the State ('the State has made you ill, the State will cure you' – this cannot be the same State); and in the case of Freudianism, you have a recoding by the family (you fall ill *from* the family and recover *through* the family – this is not the same family). What at the horizon of our culture in fact constitutes Marxism and psychoanalysis as those two fundamental bureaucracies, the one public, the other private, is their effort to recode as best they can precisely that which on the horizon ceaselessly tends to come uncoded. (Deleuze 2004b, p. 253)

Marx and Freud have become the founding figures of an orthodox discourse inasmuch as they have become codified and institutionalised in a (philosophical) school which, in turn, serves as the doctrine or model according to which society is represented. Nietzsche's alterity in regard to philosophy resides not in showing the error of this movement or refusing its premises,[3] but in betraying the idea that everything is about finding the proper code, the proper formula that ex-

---

[3] This fundamental alterity is already implied in the 'and' in *Nietzsche and Philosophy*; it is not 'Nietzsche's philosophy' or 'Nietzsche against philosophy' or something similar; it is Nietzsche *côte à côte* with philosophy as well as Nietzsche vis-à-vis philosophy; a positional rather than propositional determination.

plains society. In contrast to denouncing a given code as false or insufficient and thereby implicitly accepting the conceptual validity of codes in relation to society, according to Deleuze, Nietzsche's strategy consists in 'getting something through in every past, present, and future code, something which does not and will not let itself be recoded' (Deleuze 2004b, p. 253). Basically, Nietzsche dares to pose a different problem rather than compliantly searching for the correct solution to a given problem (who posed it?) when the solution will always be determined by the problem posed.[4] He dares to create a novel perspective, a different position with respect to the question of society, instead of arguing about the correct elaboration of a perspective which everybody already knows is the right one.[5] While doubting the conceptual validity of codes in relation to society, Nietzsche does not simply refuse to deal with them, for his aim is to get something through 'which does not and will not let itself be *re*coded' (Deleuze 2004b, p. 253, emphasis added). Nietzsche is well aware of the de facto, we might say empirical, efficacy of codes; he is aware of the fact that these codes produce a specific social reality, which is why he tries to produce something which could escape the present as well as the future code, something which inherently takes flight despite any present or prospective attempts at codifying. Again, the possibility for this rests upon the premise that de jure 'society does not function according to codes', even more so that de jure society is 'that which on the horizon ceaselessly tends to come uncoded' (Deleuze 2004b, p. 253). In short, Nietzsche is aware of the empirical efficacy of codes but doubts their transcendental validity.

The differentiation between the empirical efficacy and transcendental doubtfulness of social codifications becomes more accessible if we take one of Deleuze's examples, namely, madness. It is, of course, not by chance that Deleuze chooses madness as an example, particularly in a Nietzschean context, a notion

---

4 Deleuze develops a theory of the problem following his earlier reading of Bergson in *Difference and Repetition* where the quality of the problem determines its solvability. A question would be regarded as the relation between a problem and an imperative from which the problem starts. This theory of the problem already implies a theory of thinking that postulates a fundamental encounter which forces one to think, giving this encounter a consistency in the form of a problem or an idea. See Deleuze (1994, pp. 168–208, esp. 197–198).

5 It is precisely this form of 'everybody knows', which, for Deleuze, is one of the most basic characteristics of a dogmatic, orthodox or moral image of thought and a discourse of the representative. This everybody knows does not only presuppose that thinking is the natural exercise of a faculty in accordance with a good will and a good nature of the thinker (rather than a fundamental encounter), it is first and foremost the decision to renounce any participation in the creation of a problem or problematisation and thus the decision to reduce oneself to the good-willed solving of already given problems. See Deleuze (1994, pp. 129–130).

which to a 1970s French intellectual audience must also have sounded very Foucauldian, since the general opposition of Nietzsche to Freud and Marx could arguably be regarded as a Foucauldian inspiration.[6] Besides this, "Nomadic Thought" was also written in the same year as *Anti-Oedipus* was published, which in turn also draws heavily on Foucault in crucial passages regarding the history of madness.[7] In any case, there are three ways of codifying or encoding madness, as there are in general, according to Deleuze, only three principles of codifying (Deleuze 2004b, p. 253). First, there are repressive codes that follow the principle of *law* and try to lock madness away, for example in an asylum. Second, there is psychoanalysis that establishes a special kind of contractual relation to some of the mad who were previously excluded from the bourgeois contract, namely, the neurotics, thus binding the neurotics by a *contract*. Third and quite vaguely, there are more recent attempts to capture madness by a code, 'whose political implications, and at times revolutionary ambitions, are clear; such attempts are called institutional' (Deleuze 2004b, p. 254). Law, contract, and institution are the means by which one can attempt to codify not only madness but society in general, and each is capable of capturing the residue of the previous one: those who could not be locked away in an asylum can be tied in a psychoanalytic contract; and those who cannot be contractual parties are encoded in institutional relations. Ideally, this series of codifications leaves no room for an outside. Factually, however, this never occurs, because there is always a non-encodable residue, and our societies always 'come uncoded, codes leaking away on every side' (Deleuze 2004b, p. 254). This, again, is the point of intervention for Nietzsche, the ceaseless uncoding of society, which he tries to accelerate by producing the absolutely uncodable.

Since Nietzsche shapes this uncodable in the textual form of the aphorism, there can no longer be any distinction between content and expression or even discourse and politics; rather, we are talking about 'style as politics' (Deleuze 2004b, p. 254), a style that is correlated with three relations a Nietzschean aphorism maintains (Deleuze 2004b, pp. 255–257). Besides the relations to humour and to the intensive (understood with Klossowski and Lyotard as a pre-subjective, uncoded stream of lived experience that is both the agent and object of

---

[6] See Foucault's "Nietzsche, Freud, Marx" (1998), which he initially presented at the Nietzsche conference in Royaumont organised by Deleuze in 1964 (published in 1967) and that, in turn referencing Deleuze's *Nietzsche and Philosophy*, claims a fundamental difference in the approaches to interpretation between Nietzsche, on the one hand, and Marx and Freud, on the other, despite their shared hermeneutical orientation. For Deleuze's reception of this juxtaposition, see his concluding remarks to the conference in Deleuze (2004a).
[7] See Deleuze and Guattari (1983, pp. 50, 92–93, 132, 197, 212, 271, 299, 303, 321, and 359).

the ceaseless uncoding of society itself, as we shall see later), 'style as politics' is probably best expressed in the relation to the outside which basically claims that an aphorism is, first of all, a configuration of forces originating not from the interiority of textual meaning, from its sense, but from outside the text, from the world of lived experience, so to speak. If the meaning of an aphorism is secondary to its being a configuration of forces, it follows that the reading should focus on finding the forces which made the aphorism possible, actualising some of them, and thereby constructing some sort of functional analogue to the pragmatic effect the aphorism had in Nietzsche's lived experience.[8] In sum, these three relations (to humour, to the intensive, to the outside) constitute what Deleuze calls the 'nomadism' of a Nietzschean aphorism, meaning its ceaseless opposition to the administrative machine constituted by the 'two fundamental bureaucracies', Marxism and Freudianism (Deleuze 2004b, p. 259). This nomadism is primary: it is only the ceaseless uncoding of society that necessitates the likewise ceaseless but ultimately futile attempts of recoding. If it were not for this primary taking flight, why bother to capture the lines of flight, why bother to find the master code of society? If there is no primordial code beforehand, but a ceaseless uncoding, this means that every attempt to encode the social field is not an explanation, but a prescription of its workings and structures, an ought disguised as an is.

3 The Orthodoxy of Post-Foundationalism

There is a contemporary example of said attempts at recoding that does essentially nothing other than Marxism and Freudianism despite its development in a post-Marxist and post-Freudian context and that additionally clarifies the important, yet still neglected, aspect of reduplication ('the State has made you ill, the State will cure you ... you fall ill *from* the family and recover *through* the family' [Deleuze 2004b, 253]) inherent in these attempts. It is what Oliver Marchart

---

[8] This is basically Deleuze's general approach to the history of philosophy *in nuce* and, besides, also the reason why there is an anti-Semitic possibility in Nietzsche, because late-nineteenth-century anti-Semitism is one of the forces that made Nietzschean aphorisms possible. For the problem of fascist or anti-Semitic resonances in Nietzsche, see Deleuze (2004b, p. 256). For a retrospective account of his approach to the history of philosophy that emphasises also its polemical and inventive characteristics, see Deleuze (2015, p. 86).

(2007) calls post-foundationalism.[9] With this label, Marchart tries to cover quite a heterogeneous ensemble of theoretical positions (Jean-Luc Nancy, Claude Lefort, Alain Badiou, Ernesto Laclau, but also Jacques Rancière, Chantal Mouffe and others), which are based on a crisis of the foundationalist paradigm without erasing the figure of the ground entirely, though relativising its aspirations substantially. The different positions, according to Marchart, are united by a shared 'Left Heideggerianism' as well as the differentiation between politics (*la politique*) and the political (*le politique*), which justify the subsumption under the label 'post-foundationalism' that Marchart elaborates systematically (Marchart 2007, pp. 11–34). So when I speak of 'post-foundationalism' in the following, I am referring to Marchart's systematisation, not to the theorists he discusses.

In contrast to foundationalism, post-foundationalism contends that there is no a-historical, necessary and ultimate ground, but only a potentially infinite series of contingent groundings that are still possible, and this would be one of the important distinctions from what Marchart calls anti-foundationalism.[10] For political thought, this means that there is a distinct domain, in contrast to empirical acts of politics (the day-to-day business of politics), called the political, that essentially constitutes the possibility of the grounding as well as the ungrounding of politics by its contingency, a ceaseless play of institutionalisations and de-institutionalisations. The difference between politics and the political is thought to be an absent cause that can only be negatively inferred. An absent cause that has to be assumed given the obvious gaps in political signification and the fact that every attempt at a closure of society, its definite and ultimate encoding or institutionalisation consistently fails. In short, it is the negativity of the political that always disrupts a given closure and simultaneously provides the means of grounding politics as contingent groundings.

---

[9] For a profound analysis of the political implications of Deleuze that situates his thought in relation to contemporary post-democratic, radical-democratic and post-foundationalist discourses, see Nathan Widder (2012).

[10] Anti-foundationalism would in its most simplistic form be the mere negation of or opposition to foundationalism. As such, it would contend that there are no possible grounds at all and thus it would be unable to abandon the foundationalist horizon as – and this would be the standard objection not just in political thought – it thereby postulates the definite and final foundation of the impossibility of grounds (Marchart 2007, p. 12). As true as this objection against very simplistic anti-foundationalisms may be, it remains disputable whether post-foundationalism itself can actually leave the foundationalist paradigm behind, as it is fundamentally fixated on the figure of the ground. It seems as if abandoning the foundationalist paradigm would require a fundamental shift or reformulation of the underlying problem of ground/grounding in general.

The political difference is modelled on Heidegger's ontological difference but with a transcendental spin since, as Marchart repeatedly maintains, a unifying element in the different positions mentioned above is the assumption of a quasi-transcendental distinction while differing in the concrete elaborations of the difference (Marchart 2007, pp. 6 and 154).[11] The quasi-transcendentality of the political difference again lies in a Heideggerian interpretation of the transcendental inasmuch as transcendental thought is understood as ontological thought in disguise (Marchart 2007, p. 24; Heidegger 1962, pp. 209–255). Basically, according to Marchart, post-foundationalist thought assumes that the transcendental does not just denote epistemological conditions of understanding but also ontological conditions of being. The political difference is transcendental inasmuch as it enables contingent groundings in an ontological sense.

Central to this idea is a specific notion of contingency that is not opposed to necessity but in accordance with it – the necessity of contingency – and thus essentially supra-historic (Marchart 2007, p. 29). If the crisis of foundationalism lies in the understanding of the absence of a necessary (a-historic, ultimate) ground, then this enables the post-foundationalist understanding of the necessity of contingency, for if contingency were not necessary there would still be the possibility of an ultimate, necessary ground, but this is not a problem in itself. The problem is that Marchart equates contingency with conflictuality, as his corresponding social theory shows more clearly (Marchart 2013, p. 51),[12] and hence the political with the agonal.

This is a crucial point, since it is not clear from the outset why the political should be agonal, though this idea expresses and reifies the old conception of the friend in the Greek *polis*, a friend who is an equal inasmuch he is a rival (Deleuze and Guattari 1994, pp. 4–7).[13] Notwithstanding the inherent traditionalism, where exactly does the agonism of the political come from? Why is contingency equal to conflictuality? The reason for this lies in another crucial decision that

---

11 This is also the reason why the political difference remains reserved for political theory: mere political empiricism (i.e., here, empirical political science) cannot elevate to the transcendental. See Marchart (2018, p. 4). This equation of empiricism and science disregards the philosophical tradition of empiricism, including the pragmatist critique and renewal at the end of the nineteenth century which is of great importance for Deleuze's whole philosophical work since it leads directly to his doctrine of transcendental empiricism. For Deleuze's relation to pragmatism, see Sean Bowden, Simone Bignall and Paul Patton (eds.) (2015).

12 Unfortunately, there is no English translation of Marchart's post-foundationalist social theory yet, which is why I will keep references to this work to a minimum.

13 For a discussion of Nietzsche's account of friendship, see also Willow Verkerk (2019) and, regarding the role of conflictuality in Nietzsche, see Herman Siemens and James Pearson (eds.) (2019).

differentiates contingency from arbitrarity: contingency is defined by the lack of necessity, not by chance. This means that a (social) fact is contingent because it has no necessary grounds, not because it is by chance. There are always reasons or grounds for facts, but contingent grounds that, for Marchart, imply a conflict (Marchart 2013, p. 32). The reasons why contingent grounds should imply conflicts remain somewhat unclear, but apparently Marchart presupposes that multiple contingent grounds contradict each other, or rather, that a fact can only relate to one ground. Besides that, there seems to be no other mechanism for the production of new grounds than the conflictuality of contingency, since the only other option that could account for non-necessary grounds would be chance. In other words, by excluding chance from the notion of contingency, Marchart is forced to equal contingency and conflictuality, because he still needs to explain the reason for the potentially infinite series of contingent groundings, which is the primordial conflictuality or agonism of the social. As a result, conflictuality or agonism becomes the central concept of post-foundationalist thought and consequentially also a transcendental.[14]

The centrality of conflictuality or agonism in Marchart's post-foundationalism thus results from a specific notion of contingency that is based on a differ-

---

[14] Agonism is, of course, thematically as well as structurally a central notion in Nietzsche, from the early essay "Homer's Contest" to the late work, and is predominantly conceived as a struggle of pluralistic forces, i.e., essentially non-dialectical. Besides, there is quite a diverse tradition of agonistic democratic theory (Chantal Mouffe, Ernesto Laclau, William E. Connolly, Foucault in some respects, etc.) that at least claims to operate with a non-dialectical notion of agon. While it is clear that the critique of agonism, as presented in this contribution, does not concern Nietzsche's pluralistic notion of agonism, it is applicable to agonistic democratic theories that actually operate with a notion of antagonism under the label of agonism, as is the case with Laclau, according to Marchart. See Marchart (2018). From a slightly different perspective, we could also say that the equation of contingency and conflictuality forces post-foundationalism to think difference, or in this case the novelty of grounds, in a way that is dependent on negation and contradiction and therefore inherently Hegelian, whereas the thought of a non-negative difference or rather difference in itself essentially needs the consideration of chance as the guarantee of the genuinely new. Contingency is equated with conflictuality because post-foundationalism cannot think difference other than in terms of negation, and the new other than in terms of contradiction and sublation. This sort of Hegelianism is also the reason for the inherent and sometimes explicitly formulated anti-pluralism of post-foundationalism, since a pluralistic approach would be based on an account (though not necessarily a Deleuzian one) of difference in itself. See, for example, Marchart (2007, p. 14): 'Hence, post-foundationalism does not stop after having assumed the absence of a final ground and so it does not turn into anti-foundationalist nihilism, existentialism or pluralism, all of which would assume the absence of any ground and would result in complete meaninglessness, absolute freedom or total autonomy' See also Marchart (2018, pp. 33, 83, and 135).

entiation from chance, but then we inevitably have the problem that the transcendental resembles the empirical. The postulate would be that politics as an agonal play of forces is possible because the political is essentially qualified by its conflictuality or agonism.[15] It is unproblematic that empirical politics is inherently conflictual and at the same time a sort of institutionalised mediation of conflicts, but it is problematic if it is claimed that empirical politics is conflictual by virtue of its conflictual conditions of possibility. It would be more or less the same as Nietzsche jocularly attributes to Kant in *Beyond Good and Evil:*

> How are synthetic judgments *a priori possible?* Kant asked himself, – and what really was his answer? *By virtue of a faculty,* which is to say: *enabled by an ability:* unfortunately, though, not in these few words, but rather so laboriously, reverentially, and with such an extravagance of German frills and profundity that people failed to hear the comical *niaiserie allemande* in such an answer. (BGE 11)[16]

This peculiar reduplication that Nietzsche finds in Kant's first *Critique* is structurally more or less identical to what Foucault described under the heading of the 'empirico-transcendental doublet' for the modern episteme (Foucault 1970, p. 347).

Deleuze generalises Foucault's historical account by specifying the structure of the empirico-transcendental doublet as a method already at work in Kant and which consists of 'tracing the transcendental from the outlines of the empirical' (Deleuze 1994, p. 144). As a method, the empirico-transcendental copy or tracing is not just a characteristic of a historical situation (e. g., the humanities, including philosophies after Kant) but an inherent element of a certain style of those transcendental philosophies which claim a specific a-historicity or universality in some or every aspect. These, in the terms of *Difference and Repetition*, non-genetic and non-differential representational transcendental philosophies, are apparently unable to avoid the integration of empiricities into their transcendental frameworks. In the case of Kant, for example, this would be the adoption of the

---

15 Conflictuality or agonism in their co-originality with contingency are also treated as transcendentals in Marchart's latest book. See Marchart (2018, pp. 63, 81, and 206). Marchart here eventually reinscribes his approach in a certain Hegelian-Heideggerian lineage à la Kojève as well. See Marchart (2018, pp. 53–54).
16 The translation struggles to convey the original conciseness that shows the emprico-transcendental copy very clearly: 'Wie sind synthetische Urtheile *a priori möglich?* fragte sich Kant, – und was antwortete er eigentlich? *Vermöge eines Vermögens:* leider aber nicht mit drei Worten, sondern so umständlich, ehrwürdig und mit einem solchen Aufwande von deutschem Tief- und Schnörkelsinne, dass man die lustige *niaiserie allemande* überhörte, welche in einer solchen Antwort steckt' (BGE 11).

empirical fact of subjectivity as transcendental subject or the subsumption of the three syntheses of the first edition of the first *Critique* under the empirical act of recognition. To be clear here, the problem is not that this procedure would be logically fallacious (for there is a difference between formal logic and transcendental logic, i.e., the empirico-transcendental reduplication is not equivalent to a tautology) or that one could disprove such a structuring of the transcendental. The problem is that a transcendental containing empirical remains, or being fundamentally modelled on the empirical, de-historicises and hypostatises the empirical and yet also imposes it on every possible future, since it expresses its conditions of possibility.

4 The Priest and the Discourse of the Sovereign

But let us come back to Deleuze and Nietzsche. As mentioned above, in dealing with Marchart's post-foundationalism, the focus is not on the demonstration of flaws or the contestation of its implementation but on the will that expresses itself in it. The circularity of the empirico-transcendental copy of conflictuality leads to the inevitability of grounding. The transcendental status of agonism may weaken the ontological status of the ground but it does not question the gesture of grounding at all. On the contrary, the political difference elevates grounding to the real political matter while ungrounding or destabilising movements are taken for granted and are incorporated into the concept of the political. The retreat into the exposition of the conditions under which acts of grounding can take place actually intensifies the thought of the ground because we always have to deal with it as there is no ultimate, a-historic, undisputable ground, but why this obsession with grounds and grounding in general? Why this loyalty to the thought of the ground? Is it not that what Deleuze described as recoding for the master-code of the ground or grounding is generally accepted though weakened in its ontological status? If Marxism replaced the problematic state with a different state and Freudianism replaced the sickening family with a curing family, then post-foundationalism replaces the no-longer-possible ultimate ground with the conditions of the still possible ground as contingent groundings.

So apart from the problem of the transcendentalisation of conflictuality, there is also the more important issue of what actually counts as a problem in political thought. Post-foundationalism seems to conceive society as something ungroundable that precisely therefore seeks an ever-new contingent grounding. This is perspectively the opposite to the Deleuzo-Nietzschean account of society as something which is de facto codifiable (groundable) but that de jure continually escapes being captured in a code. It is the perspectival opposite not in its premises (an ever uncoding or ungrounding society) but in its conclusions. It is *because* society is codifiable and groundable, Nietzsche and Deleuze would say, that we need to get something through that cannot ever be codified. While post-foundationalism is concerned with how it can legitimately capture the uncoding of society, the new politics that Deleuze, following Nietzsche, announces is concerned with how to escape this capture.

So, if we say that the circularity not only leads to a hypostatisation of conflictuality but also to the a-historic validity of the necessity of grounding which equals a recoding of society, we could conclude that post-foundationalist thought aligns itself with the aforementioned discourse of philosophers which Nietzsche, according to Deleuze, seeks to betray – but again: Who are the philosophers if they are not equivalent to philosophy? Who are the bureaucrats of pure reason? Or in our case: who accepts not only the problem of ground and grounding as valid but intensifies it?

Nietzsche would probably say 'the priest'. The priest would be the figure who negates this world in favour of a *Hinterwelt*,[17] a world beyond, that is purportedly the real world or at least the one with which we should ultimately concern ourselves. This postulation stems from a physiological need: the priests imagine being strong and healthy in the *Hinterwelt*, whereas they suffer in this world (A 15; and GM I, 15). The priests are particularly qualified by their will to power which enables them to rule over those who, like themselves, suffer from this world, but lack their specific will to power, that is, the herd (GM III, 13, 18). The priests are also instinctively aware that they need to avoid the unmasking of their lies, as Nietzsche says, since their power resides in the belief in them, which is why they teach their followers not to think (A 52). In a Deleuzeian understanding, we could also call this not letting oneself be affected by this world, to avoid a fundamental encounter with this world which forces one to think (Deleuze 1994, pp. 129–167). In this manner, the priests establish an unquestionable belief in a *Hinterwelt* to which they, as priests, have privileged access. The priest is not only the figure who denies this world in favour of a *Hinterwelt* and teaches this doctrine to his followers, but also the figure who reigns by this combination of denial and promise: he is the figure of the Sovereign. The crucial point here is that the priest is also the mask of the philosopher, as the philosopher is forced from time to time to disguise himself or herself as priest in order to survive (GM III, 4–11). The exceptional example of the priestly

---

[17] The notion of *Hinterwelt* is difficult to translate since it bears multiple connotations. Adrian Del Caro has 'Hinterworld'. See Z I, Hinterworldly.

philosopher for Nietzsche would be Kant, whose 'success is just a theologian success' (A 10),[18] as Nietzsche famously says, inasmuch as his distinction between appearance and thing-in-itself just repeats the priestly distinction between this false world and a real world (*Hinterwelt*). To be more precise, the priestly philosopher would even be a development of the priest since the corruption through the adoption of the priestly manner leads to the situation where he or she fights with the weapons of reason against reason (GM III, 12; and A 17). The demarcation of the limits of reason by understanding means playing off reason against itself since the realm beyond that which is legitimately accessible to reason becomes indisputable.

So, if we say that the philosophers whose discourse Nietzsche tries to betray more or less equal the priests, then it is important to point out that it is, first and foremost, the priests' rulership that is indicated here. When Deleuze, at the end of "Nomadic Thought", says that the discourse of philosophers was always essentially related to the three principles of recoding – law, contract, institution – he goes beyond the initial statement according to which Marxism and Freudianism in particular share this relation. In general, philosophers participate in a recoding of society, this is the normal case (Deleuze 2004b, p. 259); but law, contract and institution do not recode society by chance. In fact, all of these are 'the Sovereign's problems, traversing the ages of sedentary history from despotic formations to democracies' (Deleuze 2004b, p. 259). In every historical situation, the Sovereign is confronted with the problem of how to capture the ceaseless uncoding of society, how to capture legitimately the lines of flight that are inherent to the social field.

If the normal discourse of philosophers participates in this problem, if the priestly philosopher is basically an agent of the Sovereign,[19] then there is no other option than to abandon this discourse and to 'conceive of another kind of discourse, a counter-philosophy, in other words, a discourse that is first and foremost nomadic, whose utterances would be produced not by a rational administrative machine – philosophers would be the bureaucrats of pure reason – but by a mobile war-machine' (Deleuze 2004b, p. 259). When the discourse of philosophers is essentially the discourse of rulership, of power, then there is no other possibility of resistance than to betray this discourse, to conspire against one's own class. In this sense, Deleuze says, Nietzsche marks the dawn of a 'new politics' (Deleuze 2004, p. 259). So, regarding our initial question: to con-

---

18 For an instructive investigation on the role, meaning and implications of this diagnosis of Kant in Nietzsche, see Paul Loeb (2019).
19 We could also say the master-thinker inasmuch as they regularly constructs a distinct domain to which they alone have privileged – cognitive – access.

spire against one's own class means, for a philosopher, first of all to be done with the complicity with power, which means to be done with the Sovereign's problem of how to recode or ground a society. This does not mean that analyses of grounding or recoding, or power in general, are irrelevant or that one can ignore philosophy's habitual complicity with power. It means modifying the philosophical discourse itself rather than leaving it behind altogether; it means trying to stay inside philosophy while simultaneously aspiring to become its alterity and, by doing so, untying philosophy's primordial bonds with power and the Sovereign.

5 A New Politics

We could leave it there and contend that there are basically two positions or standpoints regarding the problem of grounding. On the one hand, we have a post-foundationalist thought which takes the crisis of foundationalism seriously and simultaneously tries to avoid the pitfalls of anti-foundationalism, and, on the other, a Deleuzo-Nietzschean thought which tries to cultivate tactics for the intensification of ungrounding. Looking more closely, however, this would presuppose that there is a symmetry between these positions, that it is just a matter of standpoints while the overall motivation is basically the same. For are we not working on the same problem, that is, of developing accounts that would allow a degree of institutionalisation of the social field without totalisation or anarchic dispersion? Are we not in the "same boat" after all?

We are in the same boat, but again the conclusions drawn from this situation differ fundamentally. Deleuze writes:

> We read an aphorism or a poem from *Thus Spoke Zarathustra*. But materially and formally, texts like that cannot be understood by the establishment or the application of a law, or by the offer of a contractual relation, or by the foundation of an institution. Perhaps the only conceivable equivalent is something like 'being in the same boat'. Something of Pascal turned against Pascal. We're in the same boat: a sort of lifeboat, bombs falling on every side, the lifeboat drifts toward subterranean rivers of ice, or toward rivers of fire, the Orenoco, the Amazon, everyone is pulling an oar, and we're not even supposed to like one another, we fight, we eat each other. (Deleuze 2004b, p. 255)

With this image of the lifeboat, Deleuze insists on the ontological primacy as well as – from the perspective of the nomad – the sufficiency of the uncoding of the techno-material flow. This flow is basically equivalent to the aforementioned intensity as non-subjective lived experience that is for itself both the agent and the object of uncoding. From this perspective, there is no need for a unity among those stuck in the boat that would exceed, ground or orient the fundamental unity given by being stuck in the boat. On the contrary, the new politics announced would try to use and intensify this uncoding, thereby constituting, as it were, an inverted teleology (not heading towards, but escaping from, something). It would not be about finding a common goal or ground for society, not even a contingent one. It would be about how to get away from something, namely micro-fascisms, planetary collapse, etc. In this proposed trajectory, every utterance, every action is important if it accomplishes the implementation of relations that cannot be subsumed under the three instruments of re-codification, but which nonetheless correspond to the fact that we are in the same boat.

Would that not mean that we are simply at the mercy of the primary uncoding flow, that we are blindly drifting towards uncertain ends? This objection would, again, presuppose that we could meaningfully assume a sort of *tabula rasa* situation where we could choose between a Deleuzo-Nietzschean new politics and the Sovereign's discourse. But this is de facto never the case; de facto, there is always a bureaucratic or despotic machine that produces an orientation for the lifeboat, independently of the ontological primacy of uncoding which does not imply a chronological primacy. On the contrary, the intensification of uncoding can only be thought in relation to a chronological primacy of recoding, since there would be no need to intensify the uncoding (as it is ontologically primary), had it not been recoded beforehand. In this sense, the aspirations of the proposed new politics are rather humble, for it does not present itself as an alternative to the discourse of the Sovereign, but as a tactical intervention in it. This new politics does not seek to reign, it seeks to weaken any reigning discourse. So, we could say that this is a sort of asymmetrical complement to political thought, for if political thought has always been concerned with ground and grounding, as it seems to have been, then the new politics would be a sort of counter-weight that receives meaning just in relation to the discourse of the Sovereign.

Let us now briefly ask what the Deleuzo-Nietzschean approach would mean, if we take seriously the problem of how to achieve a solidarity between various struggles without reinstating a bureaucratic or despotic machine and without an appeal to closure, in other words, if we take seriously the problem of how to share a common cause without sharing a telos (Deleuze 2004b, p. 260). One possibility would be the affirmation of the proposition 'everything is political' (Deleuze and Guattari 1987, p. 213),[20] which equals a betrayal of post-foundational-

---

[20] For a quite explicit demarcation of the threat of this proposition to Marchart's approach, see Marchart (2018, pp. 133 and 135).

ism's aspirations to the autonomy of the political domain. If everything is political, nothing is; a doctrine that Jacques Rancière – whom Marchart's post-foundationalism follows here – characterises as meta-politics (Rancière 1999, p. 86). Meta-politics would be the idea that the political difference is just an appearance of deeper structures (e. g., economic structures), that it has no a-historical content but always expresses an ideological distortion of social objectivities. According to Rancière, this would lead to the conclusion that there could be no other institutionalisation of the social field than in terms of totality or in terms of civil war, since there is no domain of mediated conflictuality. From the Sovereign's point of view this is probably true, but from the nomad's point of view the proposition 'everything is political' is most adequate if we take into account a not-so-recent shift in the history of power, a shift that William S. Burroughs called 'control' (Burroughs 1978, p. 38; see also Deleuze 1995).

From the perspective of the analysis of power relations, in contrast to other societies, societies of control rely inherently on a complicity of the controlled and the controlling, since, as Burroughs (just like Deleuze) says, both are stuck in the same boat. Due to this complicity, there is no real distinction between a public, political domain and a private, non-political domain, as every utterance is by definition part of control. Take the example of social media: every utterance on one of its platforms is per se political, either because it is prone to manipulation or because it is the basis of an algorithmic modelling of the possibilities of future utterances, and for the same reason it is not political (since the non-political no longer exists).

I hope to have clarified what it means, in politico-philosophical terms, to conspire against one's own class, why there is a need for it in the first place, and what kind of (new) politics this involves. At first glance, the conspiracy is necessary because we have the problem of the hypostatisation of the status quo in post-foundationalist thought by an empirico-transcendental reduplication. Beyond that, though, we have the more important problem of the loyalty of the priestly philosopher to the problem of grounding, which is essentially a problem of the Sovereign. This inherent complicity of the philosophers' discourse with power makes a betrayal of this discourse and the establishment of a counter-discourse inevitable. The counter-discourse thus settles itself within the philosophical discourse and hence refuses simply to refuse it. In the case of political thought, this betrayal of the political discourse would not only contest the validity of the problem of grounding, but also cast doubt on the political, or the autonomy of the political domain per se. In this sense we could say that a Deleuzo-Nietzschean new politics would be a politics of difference that acts as a counter-weight to or tactical intervention in the discourse of the Sovereign, a discourse in which post-foundationalism, for example, clearly partakes. However, we are not talking about a social theory that would be complementary to existing theories of the political. It would not be a theory of the ungrounding of the social that nonetheless needs a contingent grounding. It would be a counter-discourse in the originary domain of the political that doubts the political as a distinct domain and that would eventually lead, as it were, to the micro-dispersion of the political in the social. Only then would it be true to say that everything is political.

Bibliography

Bogue, Ronald (2004): *Deleuze's Wake: Tributes and Tributaries*. Albany: State University of New York Press.

Bowden, Sean, Simone Bignall and Paul Patton (Eds.) (2015): *Deleuze and Pragmatism*. New York, London: Routledge.

Burroughs, William S. (1978): "The Limits of Control". In: *Semiotext(e): Schizo-Culture*, 3. No.2, pp. 38–42.

Deleuze, Gilles (1994): *Difference and Repetition*. Translated by Paul Patton. New York: Columbia University Press.

Deleuze, Gilles (1995): "Postscript on Control Societies". In: *Negotiations: 1972–1990*, pp. 177–187. Translated by Martin Joughin. New York: Columbia University Press.

Deleuze, Gilles (1997): *Essays Critical and Clinical*. Translated by Daniel W. Smith and Michael A. Greco. London, New York: Verso.

Deleuze, Gilles (2004a): "Conclusions on the Will to Power and the Eternal Return". In: *Desert Islands and Other Texts, 1953–1974*, pp. 117–127. Edited by David Lapoujade and translated by Michael Taormina. Los Angeles: Semiotext(e).

Deleuze, Gilles (2004b): "Nomadic Thought". In: *Desert Islands and Other Texts, 1953–1974*, pp. 252–261. Edited by David Lapoujade and translated by Michael Taormina. Los Angeles: Semiotext(e).

Deleuze, Gilles (2006): *Nietzsche and Philosophy*. Translated by Hugh Thomlinson. New York: Columbia University Press.

Deleuze, Gilles (2015): *Lettres et autres textes*. Edited by David Lapoujade. Paris: Minuit.

Deleuze, Gilles, and Félix Guattari (1983): *Anti-Oedipus: Capitalism and Schizophrenia*. Translated by Robert Hurley, Mark Seem and Helen R. Lane. Minneapolis: University of Minnesota Press.

Deleuze, Gilles, and Félix Guattari (1987): *A Thousand Plateaus: Capitalism and Schizophrenia*. Translated by Brian Massumi. Minneapolis: University of Minnesota Press.

Deleuze, Gilles, and Félix Guattari (1994): *What is Philosophy?* Translated by Hugh Tomlinson and Graham Burchell. New York: Columbia University Press.

Deleuze, Gilles, and Claire Parnet (2007): *Dialogues*. Translated by Hugh Tomlinson and Barbara Habberjam. New York: Columbia University Press.

Foucault, Michel (1970): *The Order of Things: An Archeology of the Human Sciences*. Translated by anonymous. New York, London: Routledge.

Foucault, Michel (1998): "Nietzsche, Freud, Marx". In: *Essential Works of Foucault, 1954–1984*, vol. 2, *Aesthetics, Method, and Epistemology*, pp. 269–278. Edited by James D. Faubion and translated by Robert Hurley. New York: New Press.
Heidegger, Martin (1962): *Kant and the Problem of Metaphysics*. Translated by James S. Churchill. Bloomington: Indiana University Press.
Loeb, Paul (2019): "Nietzsche's Critique of Kant's Priestly Philosophy". In: Daniel Conway (Ed.): *Nietzsche and* The Antichrist: *Religion, Politics, and Culture in Late Modernity*, pp. 89–116. London, New York: Bloomsbury.
Marchart, Oliver (2007): *Post-Foundational Political Thought: Political Difference in Nancy, Lefort, Badiou and Laclau*. Edinburgh: Edinburgh University Press.
Marchart, Oliver (2013): *Das unmögliche Objekt. Eine postfundamentalistische Theorie der Gesellschaft*. Frankfurt a. M.: Suhrkamp.
Marchart, Oliver (2018): *Thinking Antagonism: Political Ontology After Laclau*. Edinburgh: Edinburgh University Press.
Nietzsche, Friedrich (1980): *Jenseits von Gut und Böse: Vorspiel einer Philosophie der Zukunft*. Edited by Giorgio Colli and Mazzino Montinari. Kritische Studienausgabe, vol. 5. Berlin, New York: de Gruyter.
Nietzsche, Friedrich (1998): *On the Genealogy of Morality: A Polemic*. Translated by Maudemarie Clark and Alan J. Swensen. Indianapolis, Cambridge: Hackett Publishing Co.
Nietzsche, Friedrich (2002): *Beyond Good and Evil: Prelude to a Philosophy of the Future*. Edited by Rolf-Peter Horstmann and Judith Norman and translated by Judith Norman. Cambridge: Cambridge University Press.
Nietzsche, Friedrich (2005): *The Anti-Christ: A Curse on Christianity*. Edited by Aaron Ridley and Judith Norman and translated by Judith Norman. Cambridge: Cambridge University Press.
Nietzsche, Friedrich (2006): "Homer's Contest". In: *On the Genealogy of Morality: A Polemic*, pp. 174–181. Edited by Keith Ansell-Pearson and translated by Carol Diethe. Cambridge: Cambridge University Press.
Nietzsche, Friedrich (2006): *Thus Spoke Zarathustra: A Book for All and None*. Edited by Adrian Del Caro and Robert B. Pippin and translated by Adrian Del Caro. Cambridge: Cambridge University Press.
Siemens, Herman, and James Pearson (Eds.) (2019): *Conflict and Contest in Nietzsche's Philosophy*. London, New York: Bloomsbury.
Verkerk, Willow (2019): *Nietzsche and Friendship*. London, New York: Bloomsbury.
Widder, Nathan (2012): *Political Theory After Deleuze*. London, New York: Continuum.

Lilian Kroth
The Topology of Difference: Deleuze's Nietzsche in his Politics of Folded Spaces and Subjects

Abstract: This chapter examines spatial aspects of the politics of difference by reading Nietzsche along with Foucault and Deleuze. Deleuze invokes Nietzsche with his concepts of power and force, considering them in terms of a topology of difference. Inspired by Nietzsche, Deleuze's concept of multiplicity generates a radical form of perspectivism, a productive form of critique and an opposition to territorial originality. Focusing on the political implications of Deleuze's understanding of spatiality, the chapter leads to a confrontation with postcolonial discourse that revolves around philosophical conceptions of space. In the 1980s, Spivak expressed strong criticisms of the underlying Eurocentrism of Deleuze's (and Foucault's) concepts of subjectivity, pluralism and power. By adapting this critique, this chapter argues that there is also a productive reading of Deleuze's politics of difference, which entails a counter-narrative to an essentialised Eurocentric subject.

1 Introduction

Foucault's remark that we find ourselves in an 'age of space' has been taken up no less often than his suggestion that one day the century may be 'Deleuzian' (Foucault 1986, p. 22 and Foucault 1998, p. 343). While Deleuze himself understood the latter as no more than a friendly ironic remark, it seems to be the category of the spatial which proves to be fundamental, for example, in the motif of the net-like rhizome, the de- and reterritorialisations, or the fold. These multiple spatialities, although often referred to under the label 'spatial turn',[1] do not ex-

---

[1] Deleuze is inscribed in a philosophical discourse on space and plays a role in the so called 'spatial turn' (see Casey 1997, p. 286). In addition to the question of whether this is actually a trend or an innovation, the search for the causes of the inflationary talk of space is also dominated by a looming disagreement. This is not necessarily about the category of space itself, which has come to the fore, but about a "double turn" for which the course has been set in the philosophy of difference. According to Dirk Quadflieg, this means that a turn is not spatial in the first place, but in the second, following the concept of difference. The spatial turn does not stand at the beginning of a new paradigm, but rather marks the threshold at which the previ-

https://doi.org/10.1515/9783110688436-010

clude temporality or time. Deleuze's categories of space are, furthermore, political insofar as they have proved to be influential and adoptable both in the social sciences, as well as beyond the realms of academia.[2] In Deleuze's work, the term 'topology' addresses a specific space-time that gains clear contours with the motif of the fold, which provides the paradigmatic differential to develop a materialised and relational concept of spatio-temporality (Saldanha 2017, pp. 196– 200). Crucial for his understanding of topology and the difference with which it operates is Nietzsche, as I will argue. Thinking a non-dialectical overcoming, a productive difference, *ressentiment* and its critique in the framework of a topology of forces emerges from his reading of *On the Genealogy of Morals* and *Beyond Good and Evil*. This aspect of Nietzsche's work can also be related to Postcolonial Theory. Without going into Nietzsche's concept of 'culture', the aspect of the overcoming of *ressentiment* is adaptable to Postcolonial Theory from another angle: that of the difference in a topological space.

Gayatri Chakravorty Spivak has famously criticised Deleuze and Foucault for the Eurocentrism of their philosophies of non-representationalism.[3] Spivak's relationship to Nietzsche is mostly mediated through Derrida and informed by a feminist Marxian perspective. The encounter between Nietzsche and postcolonial critique I will stage in order to approach the politics of difference is mediated by Deleuze. I will proceed in three steps: Firstly, I will briefly situate Spivak's discussion of Nietzsche's philosophy and assess to what extent the critique of *ressentiment* is a crucial and possibly misunderstood concept for engaging with problems of the post-colony (Naicker 2019, p. 75). Secondly, I will discuss Deleuze's reading of Nietzsche, which brings the latter's diagnoses of the economy of forces into a spatial setting and explicates a model of non-dialectical folding – a thread that he then spells out again in his later books on Foucault and Leibniz. With his concept of the 'outside', Deleuze develops a topology in which his Nietzschean reading of active and reactive forces plays a central role. Thirdly, I will engage with Spivak's criticism of anti-representationalism from the angle of Deleuze's Nietzsche. By targeting the outside and the 'other', the perspective of topology

---

ously set points towards thinking in spatial categories are reflected thematically and become manifest (Quadflieg 2011, p. 27).

2 Deleuze proves to be particularly relatable for spatial thinkers and designers – regarding, for example, the influence on the methodology of landscape architecture on the spatial strategies of the Israeli military and on the 'folds' in architecture (Frichot 2013, and Weizman 2006).

3 The problem of central philosophical concepts like 'representation' or 'outside' in relation to their political grounding can be extended to a broader context of French thinkers (Ott 2018, p. 10).

provides a generative source for approaching the politics of difference from what may be considered a postcolonial perspective on space and on the subject.

2 Nietzsche and the Politics of Difference – Engaging with Postcolonialism

Spivak's criticism of Nietzsche seems to come from several different angles. Before I attempt to bring Nietzsche into critical dialogue with Spivak through Deleuze's reading in the third section of this chapter, I would briefly like to discuss Spivak's own references to Nietzsche. Her perspective on Nietzsche is, firstly, influenced by a Marxian critique of value, when she points out that 'the Nietzschean enterprise has not worked out on what I call a "materialist" subject-predication of labor-power, but rather by way of a critique of the "idealist" subject-predication as consciousness' (Spivak 1996, p. 121). Secondly, Spivak's relationship with Nietzsche is mediated by Derrida, and her attempt to situate Derrida's reading of Nietzsche in relation to Heidegger led to a very differentiated discussion in her Translator's Preface to Derrida's *Of Grammatology* (Spivak 1976). Elsewhere, she points out that Derrida's modification of Heidegger's project ultimately also builds on his reading of Nietzsche and the role 'destruction' plays in his – Derrida's – work (Spivak 1999, p. 423). The way in which Spivak problematises Nietzsche, reading him through Derrida and what she embraces as a methodology of 'double displacement' can in fact be connected to the way in which Deleuze reads Nietzsche's topology of forces (Spivak 1983, p. 181). Deleuze's reading of Nietzsche can therefore be seen as a reconciliation with Spivak's critique and the attempt to double-displace the question of representation.

For the following points, I would like to draw on the politics of difference in Nietzsche regarding its implications for postcolonialism, especially, as will become clearer below, through its topological potential. The term topology here follows Deleuze's reading of Nietzsche, and Deleuze's idea of a space orchestrated by a topology of forces. This goes back to Nietzsche's description of a complex internalisation and inward-turning of instincts, which in *On the Genealogy of Morals*, he related to the becoming of the 'soul' and bad 'conscience':

> All instincts which are not discharged outwardly *turn inwards* – this is what I call the *internalization* [*Verinnerlichung*] of man: with it there now evolves in man what will later be called his 'soul'. The whole inner world, originally stretched thinly as though between two layers of skin, was expanded and extended itself and gained depth, breadth and height in proportion to the degree that the external discharge of man's instincts was *obstructed*. Those terrible bulwarks with which state organizations protected themselves against the

old instincts of freedom – punishments are a primary instance of this kind of bulwark – had the result that all those instincts of the wild, free, roving man were turned backwards, *against man himself.* Animosity, cruelty, the pleasure of pursuing, raiding, changing and destroying – all this was pitted against the person who had such instincts: *that* is the origin of 'bad conscience'. (GM II, 16, translation modified)

Generally, his concept of *ressentiment* has a critical potential for and within postcolonial theory. Veeran Naicker argues that it would be inaccurate to talk of a Nietzschean turn in postcolonial theory, even though Nietzsche's *ressentiment* has been widely adopted (Naicker 2019, p. 62). Before approaching difference on the level of topological forces, in the following I will try to point out the reasons why Naicker claims that Nietzsche has been misread in postcolonial theory.

After his naturalistic diagnosis of morality in *Beyond Good and Evil* had been misinterpreted, Nietzsche felt the need for clarification (Naicker 2019, p. 64). According to Naicker, there are three ways in which Nietzsche uses *ressentiment* in his early work: as an explanation of (1) 'how a healthy life-affirming will to power came to negate itself' (Naicker 2019, p. 64), (2) 'how suffering arises from a cause external to the subject which must be abolished' (Naicker 2019, p. 65), and (3) 'to account for the internalization of suffering, which meant that suffering is seen as internally produced by the subject's natural desires' (Naicker 2019, p. 65). Crucial for *ressentiment* is the specifically intertwined relationship between inside and outside, which inverts the performativity of the "healthy" will to power. *Ressentiment* is both characterised by externalisation and internalisation, but in seemingly opposite ways: it instinctively searches for an external agent as the cause of suffering (GM III, 15) and gives this external cause a moral value in a seemingly creative way (GM I, 7). At the same time, this logic would be internalised, which makes *ressentiment* a 'psychic and physiological condition enabling the slaves to justify their own weakness as chosen', and, furthermore, shifts the moral valuation 'from initially being applied to a particular rank of men to the moral worth of an individual being deciphered on the basis of the subject's intentions' (Naicker 2019, p. 66). According to Naicker, postcolonial theory missed the opportunity to apply the substantial points of Nietzsche's *ressentiment* to the problems of the post-colony (Naicker 2019, p. 67). Naicker identifies, for instance, in Frantz Fanon's work, 'a clear misunderstanding of *ressentiment* as the central psychic symptom of reactive force in an ontology of power' (Naicker 2019, p. 68). This, according to Naicker, derives from the deployment of Nietzsche and Hegel on the same ontological plane: 'This mistaken contradiction conflating the reactive internalisation of colonial morality as *ressentiment* and social, dialectical recognition as its solution will pervade postcolonial thinking until Achille Mbembe' (Naicker 2019, p. 68). Even though

Naicker complicates the problematic of *ressentiment* in regard to the work of Said and Mbembe, his point remains broadly the same: *ressentiment* would be shifted into a Hegelian framework and would therefore contradict Nietzsche's intent. Furthermore, how to 'overcome *ressentiment*', as Nietzsche's key question, would be lost (Naicker 2019, pp. 72–74). To approach the question of the non-dialectic overcoming of *ressentiment*, I will try to illuminate the economy of forces in Deleuze's reading of Nietzsche, shaping the outside and the other similarly topologically.

3 Deleuze and Nietzsche – the Topology of Inside and Outside

Deleuze's concept of topology has many facets, from an intermingling with Riemann's mathematics, Blanchot's void and Foucault's power, but it evidently arises from his reflections on the dynamic of forces. In *Nietzsche and Philosophy*, the 'topological' aspect of forces appears as a "raw state" or "pure matter", whereas the "typological" aspect takes advantage of it and makes the bad conscience take form (Deleuze 2006a, p. 124, referring to GM III, 20). The force shifts, reverses, becomes internalised, and only in this way does it create an interiority that gains 'depth, width, height' through this reversal (Deleuze 2006a, p. 129).[4] In Deleuze's Nietzsche, topology first appears as a formal aspect in its reversal of the power and creation of an "interior". In a second dimension – as a "typology" – it appears as the bad conscience and internalisation of suffering. The typology begins with a topology (Deleuze 2006a, pp. 105 and 110). Deleuze describes the same two aspects in regard to Nietzsche's concept of *ressentiment:*

> The one, topological, a question of animal psychology, constitutes *ressentiment* as raw content: it expresses the way in which reactive forces escape the action of active forces (*displacement* of reactive forces, invasion of consciousness by the memory of traces). The second, typological, expresses the way in which *ressentiment* takes on form: the memory of traces becomes a typical character because it embodies the spirit of revenge and engages in an enterprise of perpetual accusation; reactive forces are then opposed to active forces and separate them from what they can do (*reversal* of the relation of forces, *projection* of a reactive image). (Deleuze 2006a, p. 124)

---

4 Nietzsche himself describes this economy of forces, especially in the second and third treatises of *On the Genealogy of Morals*, elaborating the process of bad conscience and the internalisation (*Verinnerlichung*) of suffering, as well as in *Thus Spoke Zarathustra*, when, for example, he refers to chastity and the despisers of the body (Z I, 4 and I, 13).

This distinction, albeit in slightly different terms, also runs through Deleuze's later works on the folded topology of the outside, and the distinction between force as a pure element and the concrete formations and shapes it takes on. Deleuze's concept of topology does not primarily emerge from the consideration of space or mathematical set theory, but from the question of the modes, reversals and dynamic of forces in terms of "inside" and "outside" he finds in Nietzsche. Coming from the dynamics of agonal, non-dialectical forces, Deleuze is able to conceptualise relational, affective and full spatialities. His topology is not bound to the primacy of place over space by favouring locality over a generalisation of (a global) space; rather, topology describes the external spatio-temporal principles of force and power, constituting spaces of different scales, bodies, institutions, actions, etc.

Force itself is neither a substantialist concept, nor can its origin be traced back to its activity. Deleuze says, "Forces are inseparable from the differential element from which their quality derives" (Deleuze 2006a, p. 125). By emphasising this, Deleuze works towards a differential topology, rather than towards an ontologisation of force (Patton 2000, pp. 52–56 and 136). He furthermore picks up Nietzsche's 'power to organize' in connection to 'warlike organizations' [kriegerisch organisiert und mit der Kraft, zu organisieren] (GM II, 17). The exteriority of force and the agonal relationship between forces is a specifically Deleuzian-Nietzschean thread that is also further developed in *A Thousand Plateaus* in the context of the 'war machine', and that shows the strong connection between the philosophy of force, on the one hand, and a political spatiality, on the other hand (Deleuze and Guattari 1987, pp. 376–381).

The topology of the outside creates a spatial reference that can only distinguish the inside from the outside to the extent that it is permanently inverted.[5] With this, Deleuze establishes, broadly speaking, a counter-concept to a conception of space based on a container model, or the framework of clearly distinguishable limited territories. With the inversion, implication and explication based on an agonism of forces, he puts forward a productive difference, and avoids thinking dialectically – a practice Deleuze carries on from his philosophical investigation of Nietzsche.[6] Deleuze furthermore avoids a neutral perspective on space from the perspective of a non-involved observer. According to Claire Colebrook, Deleuze thinks that 'The idea of space as the effect of a radically absent force of spatialization that lies outside the field it spaces – even while this out-

---

[5] For example, *ressentiment* and bad conscience in Nietzsche (Deleuze 2006a, p. 124); the invagination of the outside of matter and the inclusions in Leibniz (Deleuze 2006b, p. 7); and the turning dynamics of the double in Foucault (Deleuze 1988, p. 97).
[6] Cf. dialectics as a form of *ressentiment* (Deleuze 2006a, p. 121); see also Patton (2000, p. 30).

side can only be thought *as* outside once terms are spatialized – is itself a peculiar event, affect and multiplicity' (Colebrook 2005, p. 199). The topology of the outside thus ultimately does not set itself apart spatially but differentiates immanently in its logic. It seems to be linked to the fold in particular insofar as its fundamental operator – the limit – appears to be less a territorial separation than a '*line* dividing the fields of force' (Badiou 1999, p. 86).

The exterior does not coincide with power, but comes from it. Power cannot be identified with a formation; it must be strictly treated as the unformed element of forces.[7] Here, Deleuze consistently upholds the distinction: the relation of forces to the outside is only agonistic within its own element – a force never occurs singularly, but only ever in relation. In distinction to what he considers Hegel's approach, Deleuze sees the relationality of forces in Nietzsche not as dialectical, but as a synthesis of unequal forces through disjunction (Widder 2012, pp. 65 and 68). As Deleuze puts it, 'Dialectic thrives on oppositions because it is unaware of far more subtle and subterranean differential mechanisms: topological displacements, typological variations' (Deleuze 2006a, p. 157). This means that forces are not in tension with their actualisations or forms, but only with other forces. In this sense, force possesses no other subject or object than force; it is not an attribute outside its relationality. As Deleuze says, "Power has no essence; it is simply operational. It is not an attribute but a relation: the power-relation is the set of possible relations between forces, which passes through the dominated forces no less than through the dominating' (Deleuze 1988, p. 27).

But where do these forces enter into a relationship – or, to put it more directly – where is the outside? The description of the outside aims at a function, but also at a 'pure unformed matter independent of the formed substances, qualified objects or beings which it enters: it is a physics of primary or bare matter' (Deleuze 1988, p. 72). According to Deleuze, Foucault's analysis of the Panopticon in *Discipline and Punish* is not a consideration of the forms that serve the purposes of education, punishment, care, etc., but rather a consideration of a pure disciplinary function that draws itself as a category of power through different formations of the eighteenth century. Deleuze understands Foucault's diagramme as this function, which is not only bound to specific substances, but also to specific modes of use. He states that 'We can therefore define the diagram in several different, interlocking ways: it is the presentation of the relations between forces

---

7 This unformed element of the outside finds a parallel in the concept of 'chaos' in *What is Philosophy?*, especially when Deleuze and Guattari describe the struggle with an 'oceanic chaos' and a fisherman who 'always risks being swept away and finding himself in the open sea when he thought he had reached port' (Deleuze and Guattari 1994, p. 203).

unique to a particular formation; it is the distribution of the power to affect and the power to be affected; it is the mixing of non-formalized pure functions and unformed pure matter' (Deleuze 1988, pp. 72–73).

Thinking the outside means illuminating this unformed element of forces, not its interaction in its actualisations or forms. The difference between the two dimensions is structurally insurmountable. Elsewhere, Deleuze also speaks of Foucault's functionalism as a 'new topology which no longer locates the origin of power in a privileged place, and can no longer accept a limited localization' (Deleuze 1988, p. 26). It is precisely the instability of power relations that distinguishes them from the layered connections of knowledge. Power relations are neither known nor layered, but mobile, and they cannot be localised. Knowledge is formed from these shaped elements, light and speech, seeing and speaking, which are distinguished from each other by the dimension of the outside to which they refer. This dimension – itself formless, unformed, consisting of undecomposable distances – is that of the relations of forces. Deleuze states that 'There is therefore an emergence of forces which remains distinct from the history of forms, since it operates in a different dimension. It is *an outside which is farther away* than any external world and even any form of exteriority, which henceforth becomes infinitely closer' (Deleuze 1988, p. 86).

With Foucault, Deleuze tries to locate power in or out of an outside that does not designate an empty surrounding space of localisable bodies and thus also detaches them from their forms. However, the outside is neither to be mystified nor to be understood as a transcendental moment. Deleuze inverts the absolute outside and turns it over into what then becomes 'infinitely closer' (Deleuze 1988, p. 86). This relates to what Naicker criticises as a lack of an account of 'overcoming' in the processes of internalisation described by postcolonial theorists with their references to Nietzsche's *ressentiment* (Naicker 2019, pp. 72 and 74). Deleuze's topology of the outside insists on a non-transcendent outside which refrains from being absorbed by dialectics. In this regard, it is not only the dual opposition of inside and outside that matters, but the distinction between inside, exteriority and outside which Deleuze depicts as a lineage from Nietzsche to Blanchot and Foucault (Deleuze 1988, pp. 86–98). In this context, the topology of the outside as a way of conceiving overcoming activates both space and time. As Deleuze elaborates:

> We will then think the past against the present and resist the latter, not in favour of a return but 'in favour, I hope, of a time to come' (Nietzsche), that is, by making the past active and present to the outside so that something new will finally come about, so that thinking, always, may reach thought. Thought thinks its own history (the past), but in order to free itself from what it thinks (the present) and be able finally to 'think otherwise' (the future). (Deleuze 1988, p. 119)

According to Deleuze, Foucault's writing went through a long period of silence to find the third dimension – the subject – beyond his work as an archivist and cartographer. Deleuze attributes its emergence to Foucault's impression that he was shutting himself in on power relations without having a 'line of flight' (Deleuze 1988, p. 92). With the subject, he succeeded in creating this third dimension alongside knowledge and power – and in doing so, he found something that is, as it were, outside the grasp of power. The motif of folding is brought into play in order to think subjectivity as 'coextensive' with an outside (Deleuze 1988, p. 114). This aspect resonates with Nietzsche's understanding of becoming oneself and individuation as interiorising exteriority, like climatic circumstances or nutrition (EH Clever, 2 and 3 and HH 224) – a way of thinking exteriority in relation to the subject which Deleuze picks up and carries further in his reading of Foucault. By understanding subjectivity as a process, Deleuze underscores that 'subjectivation' does not give the impression that Foucault intends a return to the subject or an interiority (Deleuze 1988, p. 105).[8] On the one hand, Deleuze describes the outside as a breaking in, bursting open and splintering the inside. On the other hand, the motif of the fold as an untransgressable line seems decisive for the relationship between outside and inside: 'The outside is not a fixed limit but a moving matter animated by peristaltic movements, folds and foldings that together make up an inside: they are not something other than outside, but precisely the inside *of* the outside' (Deleuze 1988, pp. 96–97).

According to Deleuze, Foucault seems in all his work to be haunted by this theme of an inside which is merely the fold of the outside, 'as if the ship were a folding of the sea' (Deleuze 1988, p. 97). This folding of the outside into an inside and by that constituting an inside, is Deleuze's attempt to understand Foucault's discovery of the Greeks' 'self' and 'auto-affection' (Deleuze 1988, pp. 107 and 118). For an understanding of the outside, the dynamics of internalisation coming from the topology of Nietzsche play a decisive role, as already stated. But Deleuze does not resort to a figure that feeds the outside into an interior or an inwardness. Neither is it a projection of the interior. He mobilises the notion of 'the double' as an internalisation of the outside:

---

8 At this point, one might see a fork at which Deleuze and Foucault may diverge. Deleuze follows Foucault's attempt to introduce a further dimension, the subject, in relation to power, but according to Deleuze's own philosophical background, he might not consider it necessary. While Foucault introduces a subject to power as a kind of self-empowerment, for Deleuze, this problem presents itself differently in the context of his concept of desire. This, in turn, becomes clear in the two very different concepts of resistance of the two authors (Smith 2017).

> the theme which has always haunted Foucault is that of a double. But the double is never a projection of the interior; on the contrary, it is an interiorization of the outside. It is not a doubling of the One, but a redoubling of the Other. It is not a reproduction of the Same, but a repetition of the Different. It is not the emanation of an 'I', but something that places in immanence an always other or a Non-self. It is never the other who is a double in the doubling process, it is a self that lives me as a double of the other: I do not encounter myself on the outside, I find the other in me. (Deleuze 1988, pp. 97–98)

To summarise briefly what has been elaborated so far, while at the beginning the outside appeared to be a distinguishing feature between knowledge and power, whereby power comes from the outside and is realised as an unstable balance of power, it then becomes even clearer that neither power nor the diagramme can be identified with the outside, but both come *from* the outside (Deleuze 1988, p. 89). This outside is folded in a specific way that is essentially geographical, historical and cultural. The conditions for the different ways of folding are not based on an external structure of possibility, but on the instability of power itself. The folds of the outside bring to light a third dimension that eludes power. Their folding causes a self-affection and accommodates a creative dimension.

Deleuze's topology in his reading of Leibniz is explicitly Nietzschean when it comes to the matter of perspectivism in relation to space. Deleuze's idea of a Leibnizian space is both bound to the perspective of place and goes hand in hand with a plurality and differentiation of the spatial. Perspectivism fulfils both the conditions of continuity and distance: the different points of view are thus a kind of singularity, but the distances between them are indivisible and without empty space. In this capacity, perspectivism is pluralism, but implies distance without discontinuity. Deleuze directly refers to Nietzsche when he claims that Baroque perspectivism cannot be described as a relativity of truth, but as the truth of relativity (Deleuze 2006b, pp. 22–24. Exactly this reversion of terms is what Spivak designates as a specifically Nietzschean intervention.[9] However, what matters for the argument here is that space can only be determined by what is happening in it, what is constantly changing its own structure. In *The Logic of Sense*, Deleuze works out in which way Nietzsche's perspectivism goes beyond Leibniz, insofar as he establishes a topology which entails the 'idea of positive distance' (Deleuze 1990, p. 173). With Nietzsche, 'the point of view is opened onto a divergence which it affirms' (Deleuze 1990, p. 174). According to

---

9 According to Spivak, the 'Nietzschean reversibility applies for instance for possible replacements like 'history of an error'/'error of a history', or 'Zur Genealogie der Moral' and 'Zur Moral der Genealogie'. She interprets this gesture as 'putting the author's place in question' (Spivak 1983, p. 181).

Deleuze, Nietzsche stands for a perspectivism through which 'divergence is no longer a principle of exclusion, and disjunction no longer a means of separation' (Deleuze 1990, p. 174). Generally, in Deleuze's conception there are no subjective perspectives *on space*, but only local perspectives *in space* that have a reciprocal relationship to what they order and structure. With the outside, Deleuze does not activate an operator which embodies the view from nowhere and therefore a possibly imperialist gaze. On the contrary, the implicated outside conceives a pluralist perspectivism which sticks to its aspiration of the multiple perspectives being immanent.

4 The Politics of Topology – between Space and Subject

As mentioned in the introduction, Deleuze's concept of space – especially what he and Guattari called 'smooth space' – has proven its impact both in and beyond academia. The politicality of Deleuze's topology and folded spaces has been discussed from different angles. Badiou, for instance, articulates strong doubts when it comes to the political potential of the fold (Badiou 1999, pp. 90–92) and thereby problematises the lack of a disruptive event, which touches upon general differences between his and Deleuze's philosophy regarding continuity and discontinuity. Slightly different from the centrality of immanence, Deleuze's folded topology centres around 'implication' (Deleuze 2006b, p. 25), to which Nietzsche contributes crucially. The 'dissolved self', embedded in its dynamics of implication and explication, belongs to the realm which Deleuze calls in *Difference and Repetition* the 'great discovery of Nietzsche's philosophy' (Deleuze 1994, p. 258).

The logic of implication itself has great potential when it comes to ontological questions of the political as implied. As Christiane Frémont underlines, through his concept of implication Leibnizian-Deleuze breaks with an image of necessary consequence in which contingency is based on unprovability (Frémont 1996, pp. 63–69). The model of the fold offers a general schema of how a point can imply others, or how the implication enables thinking several points in one (Frémont 1996, pp. 70–76). This resonates with several approaches to the status of the political in Deleuze's thought and its evident compatibility with heterogeneous political directions.[10] Deleuze's concept of difference oriented to-

---

10 See, for example, Patton (2000, p. 46), or Härle: 'The peculiarity of the political results from its tense relationship: it is not a region of being, but a zone of indifference, which is distinguish-

wards the fold is neither purely ontological in the sense of apolitical, nor in its political content expressively elaborated – which in the writings on Foucault, Nietzsche and Leibniz considered here does not necessarily seem to be Deleuze's claim. The politicality of Deleuze's philosophy, in which Nietzsche played a considerable role (Patton 2000, pp. 4 and 30), appears to be a counterweight to the identity politics under the broad heading of 'reason' (Ansell-Pearson 1997, p. 11). As I have tried to argue, for Deleuze's concept of topology Nietzsche is central from the beginning. The differential which defines the fold as an operative function for a folded space-time has an outstanding role for Deleuze.

Deleuze finds this radical pluralism in Foucault, but also in Leibniz and not least in Nietzsche, claiming that 'Nietzsche's philosophy cannot be understood without taking his essential pluralism into account' (Deleuze 2006a, p. 4). Reading Nietzsche, Deleuze discovers a differential topology which does not derive from monism or duality, but from a multiplicity itself. It is neither a dissolution from unity nor a step towards it. This radical multiplicity or pluralism touches upon a vocabulary which is highly political and opens up the question of this being grounded in a politicality with regard to postcolonial critique.

Various commentators have discussed to what extent Deleuze's (or Deleuze and Guattari's) philosophy has omitted to thematise political and anti-colonial movements of its time and stay, both in its philosophical and aesthetic references, within a classical western canon. According to Ott, it appears as if topics like the outside, the 'fission', the 'unsayable' ignored the needs of those who are actually affected by it (Ott 2018, pp. 171–175). A similar critique was famously raised by Spivak in regard to Deleuze's and Foucault's post-representationalist manners of speaking or 'speaking for' (Spivak 1988, p. 272–294). Deleuze's interpretation of Nietzsche is, as I argue, a crucial contribution to relating post-Nietzschean philosophy to postcolonial critique. Especially the concept of topology seems to encounter aspects in which Spivak's critique can in fact be reconciled with the lineage Deleuze draws from Nietzsche and Foucault.

In her famous text "Can the Subaltern Speak?", Spivak raises an outstanding criticism of Deleuze's and Foucault's approaches to pluralism and their reservations concerning representation (Spivak 1988). This critique relates to Nietzsche insofar as it expresses a deconstructive feminist reading of Nietzsche which she

---

ed by its urge, its insistence…. The way in which the real approaches thinking is political. The political pushes itself forward, intermittently and predictably, as an event, as that which is not thinking but from which thinking nevertheless cannot escape…. The political is not external to philosophy, as one phenomenon among others, it is internal to it, but not as a category or idea, but as an impulse that releases in it a force that is both critical and creative' (Härle 1996, pp. 136–137, my translation).

pursues in "Displacement and the Discourse of Woman" (Spivak 1983, p. 181). Spivak approaches 'Nietzsche's misogyny' as a displacement through Derrida's 'double displacement' (Spivak 1983, pp. 170–171). The latter text relates to "Can the Subaltern Speak?" in the context discussed here mainly in two regards: Firstly, it shows the extent to which Spivak's critique is motivated by a Derridean deconstructive reading, in which she draws on his reading of Nietzsche in regard to a critique of 'phallocentrism' and its 'masquerade'. As a deconstructive feminist strategy, she draws on a perspectivism which is doubly displaced (Spivak 1983, pp. 174–179). Secondly, the double displacement and its foldedness displays a certain parallel with the topology described by Deleuze. Through its alliance with the operative function of invagination, the fold appears to be the feminist operator par excellence, and furthermore inseparably constitutive of a topological space. The double displacement would allow 'double affirmation' and 'double invagination', a 'double turning-inside-out' (Spivak 1983, p. 188). According to Spivak, this 'creates a space which is larger than the whole of which it is a part, and allows "participation without belonging" (to the female sex?)' (Spivak 1983, p. 188). I will try to approach "Can the Subaltern Speak?" from the question of the compatibility between Spivak and Nietzschean Deleuze.

Without being able to do justice to all the arguments of Spivak's essay, I will try to sketch briefly her main themes and connect them to the topology of the fold. With her critique of Deleuze and Foucault, she mainly refers to a conversation between the two published as "Intellectuals and Power" (Deleuze and Foucault 2004, pp. 206–213). In this dialogue, Foucault and Deleuze negotiate the status of a theory beyond it being 'applied' to a practice (Foucault and Deleuze 2004, p. 206), as well as the question of who speaks, which ultimately includes the question of how many speak, how, from where and where one speaks. Deleuze formulates, relatively clearly, that there is no representation, but only action – 'the action of theory, the action of praxis, in the relations of relays and networks' (Foucault and Deleuze 2004, p. 207). He stresses the consequences of Foucault's books and his practical work as concerning 'the indignity of speaking for others' (Foucault and Deleuze 2004, p. 208). For Spivak, this conversation between Foucault and Deleuze is an occasion for friction, in regard to which I will concentrate on her considerations of representation and pluralism. Crucial is the recourse to her argument that 'Western intellectual production is, in many ways, complicit with Western international economic interests' (Spivak 1988, p. 271). Spivak critically assesses the demand to let people speak for themselves on several levels. In the conversation "Intellectuals and Power", Deleuze and Foucault focus on prisons, schools, barracks and factories as the places where 'reality happens' (Foucault and Deleuze 2004, p. 210). Spivak sees this as a turning point towards an 'advanced capitalist neocolonialism', in which precisely those places and situations are defined as what actually happens' (Spivak 1988, p. 275). According to Spivak, Foucault and Deleuze simultaneously 'valorise' the experience of the oppressed as well as the position of the intellectuals, whose position as a historical function they leave unchallenged. Regarding their specific involvement in the *Groupe d'information sur les prisons* (GIP), this has, however, not necessarily been taken for granted.[11] Spivak considers the critique of representation to be problematic for it encompasses different meanings:

> Two senses of representation are being run together: representation as 'speaking for', as in politics, and representation as 're-presentation', as in art or philosophy. Since theory is also only 'action', the theoretician does not represent (speak for) the oppressed group. Indeed, the subject is not seen as a representative consciousness (one re-presenting reality adequately). These two senses of representation – within state formation and the law, on the one hand, and in subject-predication, on the other – are related but irreducibly discontinuous. (Spivak 1988, p. 275)

Deleuze and Foucault's commitment to the principle that everyone should speak for themselves is developed in the framework of their understanding of radical plurality and reservations towards representation and the hierarchy it imposes. Spivak's criticism hits precisely this point by claiming that the problem of the Subaltern is the Subaltern's inability to speak – in the sense of not being able to be heard or to make oneself heard (Spivak 1988, p. 308). From this perspective, Deleuze and Foucault's position appears to be marked by utopianism or cynicism, as they seem blind to the need for political representation of people who cannot be heard by the public.

Spivak's postcolonial critique of Deleuze and Foucault is ignited by the question of a specifically Eurocentric constitution of the subject and the significance of the 'other'. Even though it is Deleuze's attempt to distance himself from a colonialist discourse by, for example, valorising nomadism in connection with smooth space (Deleuze and Guattari 1987, pp. 380–420), Spivak sees in Foucault and Deleuze the paradigmatic presentation of a Eurocentric subject-oriented thinking (Spivak 1988, p. 293). She argues that an individual subject and thus

---

11 According to Lawlor and Sholz, the GIP documents show clearly that 'Foucault and Deleuze have tried in a very specific way to allow the inmates to speak on their own account. In particular, ... Foucault made the GIP be independent of any political party and therefore any ideology. In this way, he tried to free the inmates from general concepts that would reduce them. They could appear as a singularity, as an event. More importantly, both Deleuze and Foucault were aware of the risks involved in the GIP's practice of allowing the inmates to speak on their own account. There is no guarantee of success, and that lack of guarantee seems to be what Spivak is really asking for' (Lawlor and Sholz 2017, p. 159).

a 'subjective essentialism' is reintroduced through totalising conceptions of power and desire (Spivak 1988, p. 279). Deleuze often contradicts this argument when, with Nietzsche, he consistently endeavours not to trace an outside back to the inwardness of a subject (Deleuze 2006a, pp. 44; 115–116; 123–124). Spivak's criticism touches upon Deleuze's reading of Nietzsche insofar as Deleuze stresses a critique of representation (Deleuze 2006a, pp. 80–85), which affected his thinking far beyond his work dedicated to Nietzsche. Nevertheless, the accusation of an essentialism of the subject in Deleuze's work can be profoundly questioned. Isolating a neutral subject with a free will from forces is, in Deleuze's reading of Nietzsche, repeatedly unmasked as an invention (GM I, 13; Deleuze 2006a, pp. 23 and 123).

Spivak furthermore problematises that an indefinite 'other', a non-European subject, seems to constitute a European subject. The Other emerges with a namelessness that contributes all the more to blurring the Other's actual economic or political situation. In this sense, Otherness is, according to Spivak, retroactively instrumentalised for the constitution of the European subject and economic analyses are 'ruthlessly dislocated' (Spivak 1988, p. 280). Despite this being a very important point on which to scrutinise French theory and Deleuze in particular, his work itself offers a reading that withdraws from being captured by one distinct concept of the other and the outside, so it can hardly be grasped as homogeneous. Moreover, Deleuze's understanding of space seems to be based on heterogeneity, on multiplicity itself (Buchanan and Lambert 2005, p. 7). The outside – similar to the other – proves its specificity in its constellation, configuration and use.[12] Thus, this concept proves to be more of an analytical tool that contributes to a thematisation of spatial sensitivity than to manifest 'a' space and its logic. When, in his reading of Nietzsche and Foucault, Deleuze repeatedly refers to the topological relationship between inside and outside (Deleuze 2006a, pp. 105; 110; 114–116; Deleuze 1988, p. 118), he introduces neither an essentialist subject, for whom the other serves only as a demarcation, nor a nameless Other. He seeks an outside that is farther than any outside world and thus closer than any inside world (Deleuze 1988, p. 86), through the concept of the double, the outside and the Other are surprisingly close to each other.

---

12 See also Widder: 'Otherness, for Deleuze, is precisely this kind of folding. It complicates relations of difference in such a way that the opposition between two things is never enough to delineate their respective meanings or senses: although two things may be distant and opposed in one respect, they may be much more intimately related in another, or even related in ways that are neither intimate nor opposed, and the full sense of something must refer to all these axes of difference taken together' (Widder 2012, p. 19).

What remains most 'unnamed' – to take up Spivak's term (Spivak 1988, p. 280) – is the 'inside'. Deleuze's Nietzsche seems to be much more likely to be connected with the folded topology of the outside than with the accusation of a projection and its culminations in a logic of assimilation. Another point that comes to bear especially in relation to topology is Spivak's allegation of 'dislocation' (Spivak 1988, p. 280). It is the merit of Deleuze's reading of Nietzsche and Foucault to link subject and power plausibly through the folding of power, and therefore to bring the most diverse scales of magnitude into relation with each other – in other words, to relate power in its largest and smallest forms. Deleuze thus develops a topology that conceptualises power not only apart from territoriality, but also as relatively independent of its concrete expansion. The problem of the topology of the fold lies in this ambiguous potential. On the one hand, it provides an explanation for the folded relations of power and force and puts their formation, their scale, their territoriality, if not completely into the background, then at least in a secondary position. With this, it opens topology to the critical aspects of dislocation which Spivak points to. On the other hand, it resonates with what she herself calls the double displacement in textual strategies. The foldedness of space appears in this context to be accessible especially from the feminist deconstructive position Spivak herself espouses.

5 Conclusion

Deleuze's topology of the outside is inseparably connected with the motif of the fold, to which his reading of Nietzsche regarding the topological aspect of forces, the conception of space, time and plurality, crucially contribute. Even though Deleuze relates the concept of topology in his later writings to its mathematical context, his early reading of Nietzsche show that his conceptualisation significantly derives from his reading of Nietzsche's economy of forces, *ressentiment* and the critique of subjectivity.

Given the problematics and misunderstandings with which Nietzsche's concept of *ressentiment* has been adopted by and adapted to postcolonial theory (Naicker 2019), Deleuze's reading of Nietzsche builds – through the concept of topology – a non-dialectical bridge to postcolonial theory. I have exemplified this with the critique Spivak raised concerning the question of pluralist perspectivism and representationalism. It reconciles strategies of double displacement with a non-dialectical overcoming of forces and power exactly through the lens of the topological space to which it opens up: a space of folds, displacements and invagination. Deleuze's topology of the outside *as folded* conceives subjectivity from spatialised forces rather than from human subjectivity itself. Without necessarily emphasising an ontologisation of forces, without necessarily claiming self-enclosed monads or dismissing any form of agency, Deleuze's attempt to undermine sovereign subjectivity is spelt out in terms of the outside as folded spatio-temporality.

The political dimension of the fold has, from a theoretical perspective, two dimensions. First, the politics of difference finds multiplicity and pluralism at its core, as well as the attempt to fight against the philosophical contribution to the politics of fixed identities (Ansell-Pearson 1997, p. 11). Second, the topological fold, as it is based on the logics of implication and explication, poses the question of philosophical antecedence and marks different approaches to Deleuze's political thought. The ontology of forces can, on the one hand, be regarded as prior to the political dimension of subjectivity and spatiality. This ontology therefore provides the option to find many political dimensions enveloped in Deleuze's work. Twisting the question of the politics of folded difference around, the political dimension would then, on the other hand, be prior to the philosophical concept of space and subjectivity, and therefore rather motivate the topology.

With a view to postcolonial theory, the folded topology bridges subjectivity and spatio-temporality to the degree that one may speak of a conceptual crossing of the outside and the 'other'. I have discussed three points of the Nietzschean-Deleuzian topology in regard to a postcolonial perspective. First, its preference for a non-territorial spatio-temporality is both capable of turning and twisting forces into power-structures, institutions and subjects, and is also exposed to the problem of losing its scale and drifting off into speculative assumptions about concrete historical power relations. In this sense, Spivak's allegation of dislocation also holds for relevant aspects of the topology of the fold. Second, the structure of the outside as folded forms part of a structure-other that is not totally assignable to an imperialist projection, but provides the possibility to convert the antecedence of the outside in a way that may be fruitful for a postcolonial reading of Deleuze. Furthermore, with Deleuze's concept of the fold it seems possible to think subjectivity without inevitable essentialisation and the capacity for action without inevitable identification (Robinson 2010, p. 199). Simone Bignall mobilises Deleuze's concepts – despite Spivak's and Hallward's doubts – for a 'post-colonial agency' and proceeds from the assumption that 'ontology shapes agency, while practice provokes thought' (Bignall 2010, pp. 2, 10, and 21).

Third, as the concept of the outside itself proves to be structurally heterogeneous, I have argued that the structural multiplicity of the folded outside provides the potential for a postcolonial perspective, as its structural malleability remains open to different ways of thinking the outside and the 'other'. Topology's foldedness opens up both to the feminist and postcolonial critique in Spivak. Thinking subjectivity from the topological angle shifts the problem of what Spivak thematised in relation to dislocalised manners of speaking for towards displaced or doubly displaced textual strategies.

Bibliography

Ansell-Pearson, Keith (1997): "Deleuze Outside/Outside Deleuze: On the Difference Engineer". In: Keith Ansell-Pearson (Ed.): *Deleuze and Philosophy: The Difference Engineer*, pp. 1–24. London: Routledge.
Badiou, Alain (1999): *Deleuze: The Clamor of Being*. Translated by Louise Burchill. Minneapolis: University of Minnesota Press.
Bignall, Simone (2010): *Postcolonial Agency: Critique and Constructivism*. Edinburgh: Edinburgh University Press.
Buchanan, Ian, and Gregg Lambert (Eds.) (2005): *Deleuze and Space*. Edinburgh: Edinburgh University Press.
Casey, Edward S. (1997): *The Fate of Place: A Philosophical History*. Berkeley: University of California Press.
Colebrook, Claire (2005): "The Space of Man: On the Specificity of Affect in Deleuze and Guattari". In: Ian Buchanan and Gregg Lambert (Eds.): *Deleuze and Space*, pp. 189–206. Edinburgh: Edinburgh University Press.
Deleuze, Gilles (1988): *Foucault*. Edited and translated by Seán Hand. Minneapolis: University of Minnesota Press.
Deleuze, Gilles (1990): *The Logic of Sense*. Edited by Constantin Boundas and translated by Mark Lester and Charles Stivale. London: The Athlone Press.
Deleuze, Gilles (1994): *Difference and Repetition*. Translated by Paul Patton. New York: Columbia University Press.
Deleuze, Gilles (2006a): *Nietzsche and Philosophy*. Translated by Hugh Tomlinson. New York: Columbia University Press.
Deleuze, Gilles (2006b): *The Fold: Leibniz and the Baroque*. Translated by Tom Conley. Minneapolis: University of Minnesota Press.
Deleuze, Gilles, and Félix Guattari (1987): *A Thousand Plateaus: Capitalism and Schizophrenia*. Translated by Brian Massumi. Minneapolis: University of Minnesota Press.
Deleuze, Gilles, and Félix Guattari (1994): *What is Philosophy?* Translated by Graham Burchell and Hugh Tomlinson. New York: Columbia University Press.
Deleuze, Gilles, and Michel Foucault (2004): *Intellectuals and Power*. In: Gilles Deleuze: *Desert Islands and Other Texts*, pp. 206–213. Edited by David Lapoujade and translated by Michael Taormina. New York: Semiotext(e).
Derrida, Jacques (1976): *Of Grammatology*. Translated by Gayatri Chakravorty Spivak. Baltimore, London: The Johns Hopkins University Press.
Foucault, Michel (1986): "Of Other Spaces". *Diacritics* 1. No. 16, pp. 22–27.

Foucault, Michel (1998): *The Essential Works of Foucault, Vol. 2: Aesthetics, Method, and Epistemology*. Edited by James D. Faubion and translated by Robert Hurley et al. London: Penguin.
Frémont, Christiane (1996): "Komplikation und Singularität". In: Friedrich Balke and Joseph Vogl (Eds.): *Gilles Deleuze: Fluchtlinien der Philosophie*, pp. 61–79. München: Wilhelm Fink Verlag.
Frichot, Hélène (2013): "Deleuze and the Story of the Superfold". In: Hélène Frichot and Stephen Loo (Eds.): *Deleuze and Architecture*, pp. 79–95. Edinburgh: Edinburgh University Press.
Härle, Clemens-Carl (1996): "Über das Verhältnis von Philosophie und Politik bei Deleuze". In: Friedrich Balke and Joseph Vogl (Eds.): *Gilles Deleuze: Fluchtlinien der Philosophie*, pp. 150–178. München: Wilhelm Fink Verlag.
Lawlor, Leonard, and Janae Sholz (2017): "Speaking Out for Others: Philosophy's Activity in Deleuze and Foucault (and Heidegger)". In: Nicolae Morar, Thomas Nail and Daniel W. Smith (Eds.): *Between Deleuze and Foucault*, pp. 139–159. Edinburgh: Edinburgh University Press.
Naicker, Veeran (2019): "*Ressentiment* in the Postcolony: A Nietzschean Analysis of Self and Otherness". In: *Angelaki* 24. No. 2, pp. 61–77.
Nietzsche, Friedrich (1967): *On the Genealogy of Morals*. Edited by Walter Kaufmann and translated by Walter Kaufmann and R. J. Hollingdale. New York: Random House.
Nietzsche, Friedrich (1986): *Human, All too Human: A Book for Free Spirits*. Translated by R. J. Hollingdale. Cambridge: Cambridge University Press.
Nietzsche, Friedrich (2006): *Thus Spoke Zarathustra: A Book for All and None*. Edited by Adrian del Caro and Robert Pippin and translated by Adrian del Caro. Cambridge: Cambridge University Press.
Nietzsche, Friedrich (2007): *Ecce Homo: How to Become What You Are*. Translated by Duncan Large. Oxford: Oxford University Press.
Ott, Michaela (2018): *Welches Außen des Denkens? Französische Theorie in (post)kolonialer Kritik*. Wien: Turia + Kant.
Patton, Paul (2000): *Deleuze and the Political*. London: Routledge.
Quadflieg, Dirk (2011): "'Zum Öffnen zweimal drehen': Der *spatial turn* und die doppelte Wendung des Raumbegriffs". In: Suzana Alpsancar, Petra Gehring and Marc Rölli (Eds.): *Raumprobleme: philosophische Perspektiven*, pp. 21–38. München: Wilhelm Fink Verlag.
Robinson, Keith (2010): "Towards a Political Ontology of the Fold: Deleuze, Heidegger, Whitehead and the 'Fourfold' Event". In: Sjoerd Van Tuinen and Niamh McDonnell (Eds.): *Deleuze and the Fold. A Critical Reader*, pp. 184–202. Basingstoke: Palgrave Macmillan.
Saldanha, Arun (2017): *Space After Deleuze*. London: Bloomsbury Academic.
Smith, Daniel W. (2017): "Two Concepts of Resistance: Foucault and Deleuze". In: Nicolae Morar, Thomas Nail and Daniel W. Smith (Eds.): *Between Deleuze and Foucault*, pp. 174–199. Edinburgh: Edinburgh University Press.
Spivak, Gayatri Chakravorty (1976): "Translator's Preface". In: Jacques Derrida, *Of Grammatology*, pp. ix–lxxxvii. Translated by Gayatri Chakravorty Spivak. Baltimore, London: The Johns Hopkins University Press.
Spivak, Gayatri Chakravorty (1983): "Displacement and the Discourse of Woman". In: Mark Krupnick (Ed.): *Displacement: Derrida and After*, pp. 169–195. Bloomington: Indiana University Press.

Spivak, Gayatri Chakravorty (1988): "Can The Subaltern Speak?". In: Cary Nelson and Lawrence Grossberg (Eds.): *Marxism and the Interpretation of Culture*, pp. 271–313. Urbana-Champaign: University of Illinois Press.

Spivak, Gayatri Chakravorty, Donna Landry, and Gerald M. MacLean (1996): *The Spivak Reader: Selected Works of Gayatri Chakravorty Spivak*. New York: Routledge.

Spivak, Gayatri Chakravorty (1999): *A Critique of Postcolonial Reason. Toward a History of the Vanishing Present*. Cambridge, London: Harvard University Press.

Weizman, Eyal (2006): "The Art of War: Deleuze, Guattari, Debord and the Israeli Defence Force". *Mute*. http://www.metamute.org/editorial/articles/art-war-deleuze-guattari-debord-and-israeli-defence-force, visited on August 20, 2019.

Widder, Nathan (2012): *Political Theory After Deleuze*. London: Continuum.

Gabriel Valladão Silva
Fake or Just Stupid? – Post-Truth Politics, Nihilism and the Politics of Difference in Light of Deleuze's *Nietzsche and Philosophy*

> And ye shall know the truth, and the truth shall make you free.
> John 8:32 – Jair Bolsonaro's personal motto

Abstract: In the tumultuous debate about the "post-truth" deflation of the value of facts in political reasoning, so-called "postmodern" thinkers (and Nietzsche as their forerunner) are frequently blamed for having laid the foundations for the crisis at hand. The main intention of this chapter is to question this simplistic diagnosis. To this end, it argues that, by substituting the will to power as the 'differential' and 'genetic' element of interpretation and evaluation for the notion of essence as identity and of truth as correspondence, Deleuze allows us to conceive of a Nietzschean "politics of difference", from whose standpoint it is possible to criticise so-called "post-truth politics" not for having abandoned truth, but rather for clinging to the hollowed-out scheme of identity after truth has already abandoned us.

1 Introduction

The last few years have been marked by a concern with the rise of a new style of political discourse, which has ultimately become known as 'post-truth politics'. It is my aim in this chapter to draw upon Gilles Deleuze's reading of Nietzsche in his *Nietzsche and Philosophy* in order to suggest an alternative label for this new kind of rhetoric, namely, that of the 'politics of reactive nihilism'. I will contend that the characterisation of certain phenomena, previously identified in terms of post-truth, as forms of nihilism allows for a different critical assessment of them from the standpoint of what can be called a 'politics of difference'. The main standard of this is not the opposition between truth and falsity, but rather the different ways in which affirmation is pursued: either as a direct affirmation of the Self as difference, or as an indirect affirmation of the Self as identity through the negation of the Other as 'that which differs'.

To this end, I will begin with a detailed analysis of an example – the globally reported mid-2019 fires in the Brazilian Amazon region and the Bolsonaro administration's handling of them – in order to question the notion, implied by the term 'post-truth', that the argumentative strategies of political discourses associated with this label are altogether divorced from truth. I will argue that the term post-truth is not only too vague and inaccurate, but downright inadequate for establishing an effective critical standpoint on the object it has been coined for. The reason for this is that so-called post-truth politics, far from being indifferent to the value of truth, does in fact maintain a strict, albeit inverted, relation to it.

Turning to Deleuze's interpretation of Nietzsche, I will suggest that the rise of what is being called post-truth politics is analogous to what Deleuze describes as the passage from the 'negative nihilism' of higher values, oriented by the idea of a 'true world' of being opposed to life, to what he calls 'reactive nihilism'. The latter consists in the degradation of the notion of a true world while maintaining the oppositional schema through which the actual world is rejected as a false world of mere appearance. From the perspective of reactive nihilism, the value of truth, having been voided of its positive content, becomes a subversive power of corrosion of that which differs. Accordingly, the politics of reactive nihilism would be the opportunistic weaponisation of the opposition between truth and falsity in a strategy of separating active forces from what they can do, without offering any kind of positive project in return. This instrumentalisation of truth and falsity alike in the service of a base and petty will is what Deleuze calls stupidity. The last two sections of this chapter will be dedicated to the analysis of Deleuze's Nietzschean critique of stupidity and the possibility of overcoming nihilism through a 'transvaluation of values', that is, by adopting the affirmation of difference as a new standard for the production and evaluation of discourses and actions.

2 If a Tree Falls in a Forest ...

On August 7, 2019, the physicist and engineer Ricardo Galvão was officially discharged from his post as the director of the Brazilian Institute of Space Research (*Inpe*). The dismissal was commanded directly by President Jair Bolsonaro himself, who even stated in an interview: 'I don't ask. Certain things I command. That's why I'm the president'.[1] This was only the latest of many purges that

---

[1] Luciana Amaral, '"Não peço. Certas coisas, eu mando', diz Bolsonaro sobre demissão no

the Bolsonaro administration carried out since the President took office at the beginning of 2019, which so far included the dismissal of three ministers and of dozens of high-ranking officials. Like in other cases, the dismissal of Ricardo Galvão was surrounded by repeated public accusations and intense media exposure.

The reason behind this particular discharge was the publication, in July 2019, of preliminary data that suggested alarming rates of increase of deforestation in the Amazon region, compared to the same period in the previous year. This data had been collected by *Inpe* through a satellite monitoring system called *Deter* (Real-Time Detection System for Deforestation in the Legal Amazon Region), and was made available online for the public on the institute's website, as part of its regular procedure. In spite of there being nothing out of the ordinary in the way the data was collected and made available (except, of course, for the alarming message they conveyed), President Bolsonaro publicly questioned the veracity of the numbers and the integrity of those who published them. At an event on July 19, he said that he was 'convinced that the data are false', and that he had 'a feeling that this doesn't correspond to reality'. He also suggested that Ricardo Galvão might be 'working for an NGO', insinuating that the publication of the numbers had been motivated by a will to sabotage the government.[2] Later the same day, Bolsonaro expressed his concern about the fact that the publication of such data may damage the image of Brazil on an international level.[3] Brazil is a beneficiary of international programmes aimed at preserving the Amazon rainforest, of which the largest, the Amazon Fund, maintained mainly by Norway and partly by Germany, has received donations of almost eight hundred million Euros so far. Heads of State like Angela Merkel and Emmanuel Macron have been pressuring the Brazilian government to keep a responsible environmental policy, threatening to discontinue aid programmes and to block trade deals if commitments like those of the Paris Agree-

---

Inpe", *UOL*, August 4, 2019, para. 2, https://noticias.uol.com.br/meio-ambiente/ultimas-noticias/redacao/2019/08/04/nao-tinha-clima-para-continuar-diz-bolsonaro-sobre-presidente-do-inpe.htm, visited on August 12, 2019. My translation.

2 Giovana Girardi, "Bolsonaro acusa Inpe de divulgar dados mentirosos sobre desmatamento", *O Estado de S. Paulo*, July 19, 2019, para. 7, https://sustentabilidade.estadao.com.br/noticias/geral,bolsonaro-acusa-inpe-de-divulgar-dados-mentirosos-sobre-desmatamento,70002929326, visited on August 12, 2019. My translation.

3 Danielle Brant, "Bolsonaro critica diretor do Inpe por dados sobre desmatamento que 'prejudicam' nome do Brasil", *Folha de S. Paulo*, July 19, 2019, https://folha.com/o1mhwxgd, visited on August 12, 2019. My translation.

ment are not kept. So far, Bolsonaro's policies have been exceptionally unreceptive to environmental issues.

Brazil's scientific community reacted immediately to Bolsonaro's attacks on Galvão and *Inpe*, publicly defending the integrity and scientific value of the institute and its researchers. Galvão himself responded in an interview the next day, accusing the President of making 'improper comments' and 'unacceptable attacks' on him and other scientists 'without any grounds'. He also stressed that *Deter* is only an 'alert system' which provides real-time data for *Ibama* (the Brazilian Institute for the Environment and Renewable Natural Resources), of the Ministry of the Environment, to act on.[4]

In the following weeks, Bolsonaro kept reiterating his attacks on Galvão and *Inpe*, constantly oscillating between the accusation of improper publication of sensitive data on the deforestation of the Amazon ('terrible publicity against Brazil', a 'campaign against [the] fatherland') and the suspicion that the data themselves were wrong or even manipulated.[5] In his contradictory statements, he even repeated, in the form of an accusation, the very words Ricardo Galvão had used in his response days before: 'There is something fishy there', said Bolsonaro on the issue, 'something happened. And our suspicion is that the data are alerts about deforestation. And an alert is not [actual] deforestation'. According to him, to make public 'important data such as these', the director of *Inpe* should 'be sure about what he is saying'. The President then promised to immediately deliver the 'real data', which, at the time of writing, still has not been done.[6] Instead, on the same day, the Minister for the Environment, Ricardo Salles, stated after a meeting with the Minister for Science and Technology and the staff of *Inpe* and *Ibama* that, although there has in fact been an increase in the deforestation of the Amazon, 'it was recognised by all those present that the numbers do not reflect reality'. At the same time, he admitted that there is indeed a 'correlation' between the data provided by *Deter* and those provided by *Prodes* (*Inpe*'s programme which provides a definitive annual report on defores-

---

4 Giovana Girardi, "Bolsonaro tomou 'atitude pusilânime e covarde', diz diretor do Inpe". *O Estado de S. Paulo*, July 7, 2019, para. 9–13, https://sustentabilidade.estadao.com.br/blogs/ambiente-se/bolsonaro-tomou-atitude-pusilanime-e-covarde-diz-diretor-do-inpe/, visited on August 12, 2019. My translation.
5 Diego Garcia, "Questão ambiental é para veganos que só comem vegetais, diz Bolsonaro", *Folha de S. Paulo*, July 27, 2019, para. 5, https://folha.com/kf0lgv9h, visited on August 13, 2019. My translation.
6 Gustavo Uribe, "Após críticas a Inpe, Bolsonaro diz que instituto terá novos dados sobre desmatamento". *Folha de S. Paulo*, July 31, 2019, para. 6–11, https://folha.com/wyko75ij, visited on August 13, 2019. My translation.

tation), and said that 'the problem is that the percentages made public have been used to produce polemics in the media'.[7]

Even after the dismissal of Roberto Galvão, Bolsonaro and his Minister for the Environment kept their contradictory lines of attack. On August 5, the President stated that 'bad Brazilians dare to make campaigns with false numbers against our Amazon'. He insisted that the publication of the numbers was precipitate and that one should 'check the veracity of the numbers, because numbers don't lie'. Responding to accusations that the government was trying to censor the publication of inconvenient data, Bolsonaro said that 'the suspicion, the alert about deforestation ... might not be true.... We are not afraid of the truth, but I can't tolerate irresponsibility of employees in making public certain data'.[8] In a joint television interview with Galvão on August 11, Salles started out by saying that he had not affirmed 'that the numbers are [being] manipulated. What is manipulating [sic] is the way in which the numbers are presented, the sensationalism created around this way [sic]'. Galvão responded by saying that the data 'wasn't presented differently' from before, and agreed, as he had already done, that the data cannot be used to compare deforestation areas with previous years, repeating that *Inpe* 'never said this'. However, later in the interview, Salles said again that the government had proven that 'the numbers were wrong'.[9]

During the whole process, amidst his repeated public attacks on Galvão and the researchers at *Inpe*, Bolsonaro kept reiterating his concern about the damage which the exposure of such alarming data could do to Brazil's image, although it was mainly he who kept stoking the debate. Moreover, during the same period, he kept feeding the media with preposterous and even scatological statements about environmental issues. On one occasion, he told a journalist that the solution for preserving the environment was 'to poop every other day';[10] on another, that the discovery of 'a little petrified Indian poop' on a site could interfere with

---

7 Angela Boldrini, "Salles diz que dados de desmate não são corretos mas confirma que há aumento". *Folha de S. Paulo*, July 31, 2019, para. 2, 16, https://folha.com/q2a6prbg, visited on August 13, 2019. My translation.
8 João Pedro Pitombo, "Maus brasileiros divulgam números mentirosos sobre Amazônia, diz Bolsonaro". *Folha de S. Paulo*, August 5, 2019, para. 2, 6, 11, https://folha.com/7h1k3wi8, visited on August 12, 2019. My translation.
9 GloboNews Painel (Producer), *Ministro do Meio Ambiente debate desmatamento com ex-Inpe*, video file. August 11, 2019, https://globosatplay.globo.com/globonews/v/7834949/, visited on August 12, 2019. My translation.
10 Talita Fernandes, "Bolsonaro sugere fazer cocô dia sim, dia não para preservar o ambiente", *Folha de S. Paulo*, August 9, 2019, para. 2, https://www1.folha.uol.com.br/ambiente/2019/08/bolsonaro-sugere-fazer-coco-dia-sim-dia-nao-para-preservar-o-ambiente.shtml, visited on August 13, 2019. My translation.

the obtention of building permits for important projects.¹¹ On the same day as one of his remarks about the bad faith of people like Ricardo Galvão 'campaigning against Brazil', Bolsonaro stated that environmental issues matter 'only to vegans, who only eat vegetables', that worrying about the environment is a 'psychosis', and that Brazil cannot 'live off the environment'.¹²

It is not too much to say that Bolsonaro's hysterical rants against environmentalism, and the big noise made around the numbers made public by *Inpe*, played an important role in inducing major newspapers such as *The New York Times*, *The Economist* and *The Guardian* to publish, between the end of July and the beginning of August 2019, feature articles and even whole series on the dangers menacing the Amazon forest under the Bolsonaro administration. When Svenja Schulze, the German Minister for the Environment, announced that in the face of Bolsonaro's policies in the Amazon region Germany would be suspending an aid package of thirty-five million Euros,¹³ the President said that Germany wanted to 'buy the Amazon', and that Brazil 'doesn't need' the funds. Questioned about the impact of Germany's action on Brazil's image worldwide, Bolsonaro answered: 'Do you think that big countries are interested in the image of Brazil, or in taking possession of Brazil?', again clearly contradicting the concern he had shown previously for that same image.¹⁴

---

11 Paula Sperb, "Cocozinho petrificado de índio barra licenciamento de obras, diz Bolsonaro", *Folha de S. Paulo*, August 12, 2019, para. 3, https://folha.com/yfap3lx1, visited on August 13, 2019. My translation.

12 Diego Garcia, "Questão ambiental é para veganos que só comem vegetais, diz Bolsonaro", *Folha de S. Paulo*, July 27, 2019, para. 3, 10, https://folha.com/kf0lgv9h, visited on August 13, 2019. My translation.

13 Georg Ismar, "Bundesregierung legt Brasilien-Projekt auf Eis", *Der Tagesspiegel*, August 9, 2019, para. 1, https://www.tagesspiegel.de/politik/regenwald-rodung-bundesregierung-legt-brasilien-projekt-auf-eis/24889568.html, visited on August 13, 2019. My translation.

14 Bernardo Caram, "'Brasil não precisa disso', diz Bolsonaro sobre repasse cortado pela Alemanha", *Folha de S. Paulo*, August 11, 2019, para. 4, 9, https://www1.folha.uol.com.br/ambiente/2019/08/brasil-nao-precisa-disso-diz-bolsonaro-sobre-repasse-cortado-pela-alemanha.shtml, visited on August 13, 2019. My translation. On the following day, Schulze responded to Bolsonaro's provocation, saying that 'this shows that we are doing exactly the right thing' (No author, "Governo alemão rebate Bolsonaro sobre verba para a Amazônia", *Deutsche Welle*, August 12, 2019, para. 1, https://www.dw.com/pt-br/governo-alem%C3%A3o-rebate-bolsonaro-sobre-verba-para-a-amaz%C3%B4nia/a-49994397, visited on August 13, 2019. My translation). A few days later, Norway, the biggest contributor to the Amazon Fund, announced that it would be suspending its contribution of three hundred million NK (about thirty million Euros) for 2019. See Renata Grandelle, Cristina Fibe and André de Souza, "Noruega paralisa repasses para o Fundo Amazônia", *O Globo*, August 15, 2019, https://oglobo.globo.com/sociedade/noruega-paralisa-repasses-para-fundo-amazonia-23879397, visited on August 16, 2019.

On August 19, 2019, as I was finishing this chapter, the skies over São Paulo, Brazil's largest city, over 3,000 km south of the Amazon region, darkened as a consequence of an unusually high number of forest fires in territories of Brazil and of some of its neighbouring countries. Although data from *Deter* and even from other international monitoring systems, including images from NASA satellites, showed that a great number of these fires were set on private properties and illegal deforestation areas, the President said that his main suspicion was that NGOs could be causing them as a form of retaliation against the cutting of public funds that financed their activity.[15] Indeed, the Bolsonaro administration drastically reduced not only the support for environmental NGOs active in the Amazon region, but also the budget and the autonomy of public agencies such as *Ibama*, responsible for monitoring and combatting fires and illegal deforestation. The international funding terminated due to the government's negligence of environmental issues was also used for equipment such as helicopters to combat forest fires. After very negative repercussions from his statement, Bolsonaro once again confessed that he was only raising random suspicions: 'I never … accused the NGOs. [I spoke of] suspicion', he said to journalists, and complemented, with an ironic tone: 'Is it the Indians? Do you want me to blame the Indians? Are you going to write the Indians tomorrow? Do you want me to blame the Martians? To my understanding, there is a very strong indication that these NGO people lost their teat. It's simple'.[16] So far, no concrete plan to contain the fires and the deforestation in general has been presented by the Brazilian government.

---

15 'We took away money from NGOs, allocations from abroad, of which 40% went to NGOs', said Bolsonaro on 2 August, 'We also terminated this issue of allocating money to NGOs from public institutions here, so that these people are sensing this lack of money. So, there may be – I am not affirming that there is – criminal activity of these NGOers to raise attention directly against me, against the government of Brazil' (Jornal Nacional [Producer], "Declaração de Bolsonaro sobre queimadas provoca protestos", video file, August 22, 2019, https://globoplay.globo.com/v/7861425/, visited on August 22, 2019. My translation).
16 Jornal da Record (Producer), "'A maior suspeita vem das ONGs', diz Bolsonaro sobre queimadas", video file, August 22, 2019, https://recordtv.r7.com/jornal-da-record/videos/a-maior-suspeita-vem-das-ongs-diz-bolsonaro-sobre-queimadas-22082019, visited on August 26, 2019. My translation.

3 Is Post-Truth Politics really Beyond Truth? Or is it just Fake News?

It was in the wake of the rise of this grotesque and puzzling new style of political discourse – at the time of the election of Donald Trump and of the Brexit referendum – that the *Oxford Dictionaries* elected the adjective post-truth as the 'Word of the Year 2016'.[17] Considering the example given above, one could be tempted to say that, in fact, Bolsonaro has, in a certain way, left behind the criteria of truth altogether, as the term post-truth suggests. It is clear, at least, that the discourse of post-truth politics is neither a truth-telling discourse, nor the mere opposite of "telling the truth". It goes beyond truth, but also beyond "untruth" in the sense of a false account or a misinterpretation of facts that is passed off as true. Telling a lie in this sense still depends on a positive evaluation of truth; it implies the intent of making untruth participate in the "power" of truth. It is this positive relation to the value of truth still contained in the more current conception of lying that does not seem to apply to the obscure and contradictory lines of argument adopted by Bolsonaro and other representatives of the so-called post-truth paradigm. When Bolsonaro insists on questioning the precision of numbers that were never supposed to be precise, when he makes improbable accusations against political opponents, when he raises abstruse conspiratorial hypotheses about issues that have very simple, but inconvenient causes, and, in doing all this, constantly contradicts himself, it seems like the construction of a coherent lie that could pass for truth is the least of his concerns. He is past that, he is post-truth.

But what does that really mean, to be post-truth? As soon as one starts trying to grasp the specificity of the kind of discourse, characterised as post-truth, it becomes clear that the concept of post-truth is itself – not unlike other concepts qualified by the prefix 'post-' – underdetermined as such: it tells us nothing about what, exactly, comes after truth, or about the specific way in which what is being called post-truth politics goes beyond truth. Despite suggesting that the object it designates cannot be determined exclusively with reference to the notion of truth, the concept of post-truth nonetheless preserves this very same reference as its only determination, and, thus, does not offer sufficient analytical means to apprehend the specificity of its object.

---

[17] Neil Midgley, "Word of the Year 2016 is …", *Oxford Dictionaries*, 2016, https://en.oxforddictionaries.com/word-of-the-year/word-of-the-year-2016, visited on July 13, 2018.

Moreover, the ways in which Bolsonaro reacted to the environmental crisis in the Amazon region – by accusing his staff of dishonesty (Galvão had to 'be sure about what he is saying'), by questioning the accuracy of the numbers produced by the *Deter* system ('check the veracity of the numbers, because numbers don't lie'), by raising doubts and counter-hypotheses about what is going on and about who is responsible for it ('there may be, I am not affirming that there is ...') – suggest that, in fact, he is still very much occupied with truth-related issues, although in a very peculiar manner. The relation of post-truth politics to truth may no longer be the positive one implied by the traditional truth-untruth opposition, but it has not disappeared altogether either. Bolsonaro might not be afraid of the truth, as he said, but he and his colleagues are certainly more inept than most of us when it comes to getting a grip on it.[18]

Before turning to Deleuze's reading of Nietzsche, in search of a more adequate concept to describe so-called post-truth politics, I would like to approach another term frequently associated with it, in an attempt to clarify a little further the peculiar relationship of this kind of political discourse with truth, namely, the notion of 'fake news'. In an article for the *Harvard Political Review*, Samarth Desai exposes the danger of associating the concept of fake news with traditional methods of government propaganda. 'So far', he writes:

> most efforts to place fake news within a historical context have focused on the history of misinformation and propaganda in politics, but this is a misguided approach to understanding the concept in its current use.... Trump's weapon isn't propaganda; instead, it is the idea of a biased, duplicitous media that will stop at nothing to take him down. (Desai 2017, para. 8)

The same article cites a study commissioned by Stanford University which allows one to conclude that the role of actual misinformation through social media in the election of Donald Trump was smaller than one might suspect. What this means is that so-called post-truth politics is not so much about producing fake news and getting people to believe in them – which would still imply a positive relation to the value of truth – as it is about discrediting inconvenient narratives by labelling them as fake news. One should not forget that it is none other than Donald Trump himself who popularised the term fake news, using it in ref-

---

18 In this sense, too, they are still part of the 'dogmatic' tradition with its 'clumsy advances' on truth (see BGE 3).

erence to the mainstream media and its liberal agenda – a strategy that is being employed liberally by Bolsonaro and other opportunists worldwide.[19]

This allows us to conclude that the power of truth-oriented discourse is, in fact, still elemental to post-truth politics; it is merely turned into a *subversive* power. In this sense, the relation of post-truth discourse to truth can be said to be a purely negative one; it is a negationist discourse, in the broadest sense of the word: it negates whatever stands in the way of power without affirming anything in turn, and it is this same negative orientation that allows it to be so utterly inconsistent. Unlike the lies of traditional propaganda, it does not have to offer anything in exchange for the established truth it questions. Ideological propaganda – be it in the case of the Catholic Church of the seventeenth century or of the totalitarian regimes of the twentieth century – implies a strong control, a homogenisation, and, thus, a reduction of information flows (through censorship, surveillance, monopoly of the media and so forth) in order to pass off a false narrative as true. By contrast, the core strategy of post-truth politics lies in promoting confusion and distrust over narratives inconvenient to its political agents by calling out fake news and disseminating volatile "alternative facts". The very incoherence of Bolsonaro's objections to the data produced by the *Deter* system already lays bare that, ultimately, he does not defend any position at all: his promise of "real data" does not refer to anything beyond the supposed unreality of the data at hand; his frivolous accusations against "NGOers" are backed by nothing. There is, in fact, no 'real data', no alternative account of what is happening in the Amazon region, but just 'a feeling' that the data at hand 'don't correspond to reality', a 'suspicion' against NGOs that, in the president's own words, could be just as well directed against 'Indians' or even 'Martians'.

In this sense, the effectiveness of this so-called post-truth politics is in fact still highly dependent on the formal schema that supports a rigorous separation between truth and falsity within discourse. The dualistic structure that, for Nietzsche, lies at the basis of the belief in truth is not done away with, but just dissociated from any specific content in order to become an instrument of

---

19 Cf. Chris Massie, "WH Official: We'll say 'fake news' until media realizes attitude of attacking the President is wrong", *CNN*, February 7, 2017, https://edition.cnn.com/2017/02/07/politics/kfile-gorka-on-fake-news/index.html, visited on August 15, 2018. Trump even organised Fake-News Awards at the beginning of 2018, with a list of the major alleged misreports of the so-called "mainstream media" on him and his administration in the year before (Jen Kirby and Libby Nelson, "The 'winners' of Trump's fake news awards, annotated", *Vox*, January 17, 2018, https://www.vox.com/2018/1/17/16871430/trumps-fake-news-awards-annotated, visited on September 18, 2018).

political opportunism.[20] There is no actual ideology behind Trump's or Bolsonaro's discourse, but there is nonetheless an oppositional schema that remains unchanged, although void of all specific content. It is precisely from this second feature – the cynical appropriation of the dualistic structure of truth-based discourse while having dispensed with its positive referential content – that Bolsonaro's post-truth rhetoric draws its efficacy, as well as its immunity to objections based on the value of truth – and it is precisely this feature that the term post-truth fails to grasp.

4 The Politics of Reactive Nihilism

Having thus established not only the inaccuracy, but the conceptual inadequacy of the term post-truth for designating the specific kind of discourse disseminated by figures such as Trump and Bolsonaro, I would now like to turn to the concepts of 'nihilism' and 'reactivity' as developed by Deleuze in his *Nietzsche and Philosophy*,[21] in order to suggest that so-called post-truth politics might be better understood if considered as a late political manifestation of what Deleuze calls reactive nihilism. We have seen that, ultimately, the most pernicious element of this kind of politics lies not so much in the fact that it parts with the positive reference to truth, but that it does so while still preserving certain formal elements of truth-centred discourse. It is precisely this hollowing-out of the schema of truth-based discourse that Deleuze describes as the passage from the negative nihilism of higher values to another, purely reactive kind of nihilism.

According to Deleuze, negative nihilism, on the one hand, presupposes a 'fiction', the idea of 'another world' 'opposed to life', by means of which one 'falsifies and depreciates' life, and expresses a 'will to nothingness' in the sense of a will to 'deny' and to 'annihilate' life (Deleuze 1983, p. 147). This is the nihilism of higher values that poses a true world in opposition to the actual, lived world, which, in turn, is devalued in contrast with the former. Reactive nihilism, on the other hand, goes one step further. It is no longer the devaluation of life through the fiction of higher values, but the devaluation of higher values them-

---

20 Cf. BGE 6: 'This way of judging typifies the prejudices by which metaphysicians of all ages can be recognized: this type of valuation lies behind all their procedures. From these "beliefs" they try to acquire their "knowledge", to acquire something that will end up being solemnly christened as "the truth". The fundamental belief of metaphysicians is *the belief in oppositions of values*'.
21 Unless otherwise specified, I will be quoting from the English translation by Hugh Tomlinson, first published in 1983.

selves, of those very same values that had been used for the implicit devaluation of life: 'Thus the nihilist denies God, the good and even truth – all the forms of the suprasensible. Nothing is true, nothing is good, God is dead' (Deleuze 1983, p. 148).[22] But even though the positive content of the true world disappears, the oppositional structure that supported it remains. Deleuze describes the transition from negative nihilism to reactive nihilism as follows: 'Previously essence was opposed to appearance, life was turned into an appearance. Now essence is negated [*Maintenant on nie l'essence*] but appearance is retained: everything is merely appearance, this life [*cette vie*] which is left to us remains for itself an appearance' (Deleuze 1983, p. 148, translation modified). The ideal sphere, the criterion of evaluation, disappears, but the life we are left with is still a 'depreciated life', 'stripped of meaning and purpose'(Deleuze 1983, p. 148).

According to Deleuze, Nietzsche's important insight into the history of nihilism is precisely to have pointed out that nihilism in this second, more current sense derives from an earlier form of nihilism, that is, from the negative nihilism of higher values: it is not so much a negation of higher values (an anti-intellectualism, an immoralism, an atheism), but a consequence of the nihilism already contained in the ascetic ideal that these same values expressed. The continuity between these two stages of nihilism, which would allow Nietzsche to state that the latter is a mere development of the former, derives from the fact that the values of negative nihilism which served as standards of (d)evaluation were themselves already produced by means of an inversion, whose story is told in the first essay of the *Genealogy of Morals*. According to Deleuze, for Nietzsche, 'In the beginning, at the origin, there is the difference between active and reactive forces' (Deleuze 1983, p. 55). There are, however, two ways of conceiving of this distinction, and, consequently, two different ways of evaluating it. The first, from the active, affirmative, noble point of view, begins by valuing one's own distinctiveness as distinction. From this perspective, one's own difference in relation to everything else is taken as something valuable in itself, and the "Other" is considered "bad" (*schlecht*) only secondarily, relative to the primary valuing of one's own distinctiveness. The Other is merely imbued with a lesser degree of affirmation than that primary distinctiveness, but in no way opposed to it. On the contrary, being 'that which differs', the Other must be affirmed as a sine qua non of the distinction being affirmed (Deleuze 1983, p. 78). The reactive image of the origin, in contrast, is inverted: '"yes" from the point of view of active forces becomes "no" from the point of view of reactive forces and affirmation of the

---

[22] For Nietzsche's appreciation of the will to truth as an instance of the ascetic ideal, cf. GM III, 24.

self becomes negation of the other' (Deleuze 1983, p. 56). In other words, that which from the active perspective was merely perceived as difference, as a not-self in relation to the self-affirmed distinction, is now seen negatively, as an anti-self, so to speak, which will serve as a basis for constructing an image of the self, not through direct 'affirmation' of this self as distinction, but through 'contradiction' of that primary Other perceived negatively as 'evil' (*böse*) (Deleuze 1983, p. 56).[23]

It is important to note that the wills mobilised by both of these schemas will themselves, but whereas the noble will affirms itself directly as difference, the base will affirms itself indirectly as the opposite of that which differs from it, and, thus, as identity.[24] Consequently, there is a reactive process at the root of the ideals of negative nihilism, including truth itself in the sense of a true world, opposed to life. It is the application of this same reactive schema to the false positivity of those ideals that produces the passage from negative nihilism to reactive nihilism, so that the latter is not so much a negation, but rather a potentiation of the former. As mentioned, in reactive nihilism higher values are devalued, but the hollowed-out oppositional schema itself remains, along with the depreciation of life it entails.

The nihilistic form of politics I have been analysing so far, having no positive point of anchorage, follows the same reactive schema that gives rise to the inverted image of difference at the basis of the negative nihilism of higher values. As in the latter, the primary move of this kind of discourse is to construct an oppositional schema in which the positive pole is obtained through the negation of that which differs as a negative pole. All that disagrees with one's perspective is relegated indiscriminately to the negative domain of the Other and automatically devalued. However, unlike in the case of negative nihilism, where the positive pole crystallises into a world of higher values, the values supporting the oppositional structure are utterly irrelevant for the strategy of the politics of reactive nihilism. Instead, identity is sustained solely through the constant negation of an Other which has become merely formal, a diffuse mass of all that differs. As a consequence, the very identity of the positive pole becomes equally formal, too; hence the characterisation of what is being called post-truth politics as a purely reactive form of nihilism, unable to establish values in the stronger sense of the word. It is an eminently *cynical* and *opportunistic* power-strategy, much less sta-

---

23 For the definition of the essence of force as difference, see Deleuze (1983, 42–45).
24 Cf. Deleuze (1983, p. 78): 'What a will wants is not an object, an objective or an end. Ends and objects, even motives, are still symptoms. What a will wants, depending on its quality, is to affirm its difference or to deny what differs.... What a will wants is always its own quality and the quality of the corresponding forces'.

ble and much more flexible than traditional forms of ideology. It faces the self with an abyss of complete senselessness in order to produce an image of a menacing Other that threatens an identity which, in turn, is left as a pure blank space to be filled by each individual in each particular case – a mere point of view, an empty, displaceable space labelled 'us', the dimensionless centre of a skeleton of a traditional dualistic moral world view, oppressed from all sides by a formless matter of all that differs.

It is this corroding, not only of the established senses, values and ideals, but of all possible affirmation, whilst maintaining the hollowed-out schema of opposition, that makes the politics of reactive nihilism the pinnacle of the reactive type: it reacts to all and, consequently, has no activity of its own. As the duplicitous motto 'liberal in economics, conservative in customs' indicates, figures like Trump and Bolsonaro in fact have no distinct project. Instead, empty slogans like 'America first' and 'Make America great again' and 'Brazil above everything, God above all' deliver a hollow shell of identity, constructed in opposition to all possible forms of a constantly shape-shifting Other: immigrants, Muslims, Blacks and Hispanics, liberals, terrorists, globalists, gays, feminists, the liberal media, the Left, etc. The volatility of these labels becomes all the more evident when one observes their tendency to shift their sense and even to merge with one another into bizarre hybrids (the notion of a 'feminist-gayist-communist conspiracy' in Brazil, for example), being at times constructed through a simple inversion of elements of political discourse considered to be mainstream (christophobia, heterophobia, reversed racism, etc.).[25]

Just as in Deleuze's description of the triumph of reactive forces, the current rise of the politics of reactive nihilism is not due to a persuasive and inspiring

---

25 The Twitter account of Carlos Bolsonaro, the President's son in charge of his social media communication, delivers an extreme example that lays bare the pure and empty formalism of the politics of reactive nihilism. On June 8, 2019, Carlos posted the following tweet: 'The big cheeky exempt guy [*isentão safado*] is as we alerted from the beginning. The IDEA comes from A, but they attribute it to B. They place all their bets on the prostitution peculiar to them for 2022 [next Brazilian elections]. The same gang that hijacked Brazil bets on cleaning itself off on those who fight to help to save Brazil pretending that B never existed' (Carlos Bolsonaro (@CarlosBolsonaro), "O isentão safado é como alertamos desde o início", Twitter, June 8, 2019, 7:57 p.m., https://twitter.com/carlosbolsonaro/status/1137418406842572801). On July 19, 'Let us never forget that diameter and depth is a criterion of competence only for a few. We are all equal and competence and character isn't measured by that which this hysterical minority tries in the service of a domination plan of useful idiots. Good evening to all! [thumbs up]' (Carlos Bolsonaro (@CarlosBolsonaro), "Nunca esqueçamos que diâmetro e profundidade só é critério de competência para alguns", Twitter, July 19, 2019, 5:19 a.m., https://twitter.com/carlosbolsonaro/status/1152055406442766337).

project, but, on the contrary, to a degradation and devaluation of all political forces that may differ from the standpoint of its actors at any given moment. According to Deleuze, in order to prevail over active forces, reactive forces do not unite to form a greater force, but proceed through the means of a division or subtraction, which 'separates active force from what it can do and negates its difference [*qui en nie la différence*] in order to make it a reactive force' (Deleuze 1983, p. 57, translation modified). The same goes for the politics of reactive nihilism, whose unity is based solely on the negation of all that differs and whose power comes from the degradation of the political sphere to a reactive back and forth of pointless negation. It drags down the political debate to such a level of baseness that all the forces that differ from it are led to deplete themselves in a futile effort to negate it, thus becoming reactive themselves.

5 Passive Nihilism and the Umwertung

According to Deleuze, there is still a third phase in the history of nihilism, which, in turn, is 'the final outcome [*extrême aboutissement*] of reactive nihilism', namely, 'passive nihilism'. It is the nihilism of the 'last man' described in Nietzsche's *Thus Spoke Zarathustra*, and its maxim is: 'fading away passively rather than being led from outside' (Deleuze 1983, p. 149). But this ultimate consequence of nihilism – the final triumph of reactivity and the complete expiration of the will – is only something foretold to Zarathustra by the diviner: 'There are many avatars, many variations on the nihilist theme, before we reach this point' (Deleuze 1983, p. 151).

There are, indeed, signs suggesting that the politics of reactive nihilism of our day, being the purest avatar of reactive nihilism so far, might also be one of the last, its rise perhaps being due more to the passive apathy of a majority that is tired of life than to the frantic fanaticism of the few actually enthralled by its morbid spell. Indeed, its corroding strategy of devaluation is not one of persuasion and enthusiasm – it does not really offer anything to be enthusiastic about – but rather, it is one of exhausting the will through a pointless game of mirrors that, in the end, reflect nothing specific. It is the politics of the lesser evil par excellence that draws its political capital mainly from the erosion of other political projects. Perhaps even the rabid behaviour of the desperate few carried away by the inconsistent rants of the discourse of the politics of reactive nihilism is but a last convulsion before politics as we know it slips into a passive slumber, before democracy suffers a natural death, from within, from the extenuation of the political will of the masses (and not from without, by assassination, as many had feared). As a matter of fact, in Deleuze's reading of Nietzsche, there is indeed a kind of passive positivity, a 'false affirmation', that still belongs to the reign of nihilism. It is the affirmation of the ass ('I-A') or of the camel, which say 'yes to everything which is no', that is, to the burden of nihilism and to the weight of the negative, as if they were affirming the 'real' (Deleuze 1983, p. 184). It is a "yes" of conformism, of passive acceptance, of *indifference*, and not of active affirmation.

But, having arrived at this "final outcome" of nihilism, the question of what comes next arises again. Is there such a thing as 'post-nihilism'? Since, according to Deleuze, Nietzsche identifies nihilism as the very motor of history (Deleuze 1983, p. 152), and the 'becoming reactive of all forces' as the destiny of humanity as such (Deleuze 1983, p. 167), for which activity, in the sense of Deleuze's active forces, is ultimately nothing but the prerequisite – 'a health which only exists as the presupposition of a becoming-sick' (Deleuze 1983, p. 167) – the question of how to overcome nihilism seems to become rather hopeless. Nonetheless, according to Deleuze, there still is something beyond nihilism, to which nihilism itself, in all its forms, is but a presupposition. The moment in which this transition occurs is the so-called *Umwertung*, 'transmutation' or 'transvaluation' (Deleuze 1983, p. 170), that is, no longer a mere 'change of values, but a change in the element from which the value of values derives' (Deleuze 1983, p. 171). 'As long as we remain in the element [o]f the negative', Deleuze writes, 'it is no use changing values or even suppressing them, it is no use killing God: the place and the predicate remain, the holy and the divine are preserved, even if the place is left empty and the predicate unattributed' (Deleuze 1983, p. 171). The present-day politics of reactive nihilism, as analysed so far, proves that the empty structure of reactivity at the heart of nihilism can remain even after the highest values – including truth – have been devalued and dispossessed. But then how can nihilism be overcome? Deleuze's answer is simple: 'In fact nihilism is defeated, but defeated by itself' (Deleuze 1983, p. 172). The *Umwertung* which defeats nihilism is itself the 'complete and finished form of nihilism' (Deleuze 1983, p. 172).

Just as there is a kind of passive and indifferent positivity, the false positivity of the ass or of the camel, which confounds affirmation with the acceptance of the weight of the real; just as there is a kind of petty joy particular to the last men; there is also, according to Deleuze, an active kind of negativity, an 'active destruction', which is 'the point, the moment of transmutation in the will to nothingness', where this will 'crosses over to the side of *affirmation*' (Deleuze 1983, p. 174). This transmutation, the moment of the *Umwertung*, is a reversal of the relation between reality and affirmation, in which reality ceases to be something positive, an object of affirmation, a being to which the will must passively acquiesce in order to be affirmative. On the contrary, it is affirmation which is, in fact, being, or, to put it even more radically, from the point of view of the *Umwertung*, being and nothingness are both '*merely the abstract expression of af-*

firmation and negation as qualities (qualia) of the will to power' (Deleuze 1983, p. 186). What the 'transmutation' does is relate the negative 'to affirmation in the will to power' as its true '*ratio essendi*', turning it into 'a simple mode of being of the powers of affirming' (Deleuze 1983, p. 191).²⁶ Consequently, from this new point of view, there is no true opposition between affirmation and negation, the relation between these qualia of the will to power is not a univocal one: opposition is just the way in which difference is apprehended from a negative perspective, as we have already seen in the case of the two images of the origin. From the positive point of view, affirmation and negation merely differ from each other as modes of affirmation of the will to power.²⁷ Negation, being of that which differs, is also a kind of affirmation, albeit an indirect and sickly one. Conversely, the new image of affirmation, far from being the mere acceptance of what is given, is still a form of evaluation, which implies hierarchisation, and, consequently, a kind of negation (the 'no' of the lion as opposed to the 'yes' of the camel); but it is an evaluation 'from the perspective of a will which enjoys its own difference' (Deleuze 1983, p. 185). To this will, what is considered bad is only secondary and relative to the primary position of the affirmation of its own 'distinction' (Deleuze 1983, p. 185).

6 Conclusion: Critique of Stupidity, Saying "No" to all that is "No"

This conception might seem far removed from the issue of the discourse of so-called post-truth politics I had proposed to discuss in this chapter, and even further from the very concrete case of the current environmental crisis in Brazil and the Bolsonaro administration's response to it, which I have used to illustrate it. As a matter of fact, Deleuze himself was criticised for the abstractness of the con-

---

26 On the affirmation as the *ratio essendi* of the will to power, see Deleuze (1983, pp. 173–175). According to Deleuze (1983, p. 50), the will to power is 'the genealogical element of force, both differential and genetic', 'the principle of the synthesis of forces'.
27 Cf. Deleuze (1983, p. 188): 'If we understand affirmation and negation as qualities of the will to power we see that they do not have a univocal relation. Negation is *opposed* to affirmation but affirmation *differs* from negation. We cannot think of affirmation as "being opposed" to negation: this would be to place the negative within it. Opposition is not only the relation of negation with affirmation but the essence of the negative as such. [And difference is the essence of the affirmative as such]'. The sentence in brackets is missing in the English translation. I have translated it based on the original French text (Deleuze 2014, p. 295).

ception he developed in *Nietzsche and Philosophy*.[28] Indeed, his main targets in this work are purely philosophical positions such as the conception of negativity in dialectics and the Heideggerian notion of Being. But there is nonetheless a deep political sense to the view he proposes. Deleuze's Nietzschean answer to nihilism, of which, as we have seen, the politics of reactive nihilism known as post-truth can be considered an important avatar, is in no way a return to the highest values, including truth. In fact, for Deleuze, the very concepts of being, reality and truth are themselves 'avatars of nihilism', namely, of the negative nihilism of 'superior values' (Deleuze 1983, p. 184). Instead of rehabilitating these values, Deleuze proposes a complete shift of the frame in which evaluation is made. From this shift follows a politics of difference, whose main criterion is not truth or being, but affirmation itself, in the sense of a primary affirmation of the will as that which produces distinction – a criterion which alone suffices to reject the schemas of the politics of reactive nihilism as hostile to life. This rejection itself is in no way reactive, but *aggressive* in the sense that it is a negation derived from a primary positive stance.[29]

According to Deleuze, this aggressivity, as 'the active expression of an active mode of existence' (and no longer as the 're-action of *re-sentiment*'), is in fact the only form of negation that deserves to be called 'critique' (Deleuze 1983, p. 3). It is the only position able to deliver the means for a 'decision' in the face of the 'crisis' as the "critical" and "decisive" moment of nihilism that will pave the way for a '*great politics*' (EH Destiny, 1). From this eminently critical point of view, the essence of an event, that which is decisive about it, lies not so much in its being true or not, but in the *interpretation* within which it appears, and the *evaluation* of life that is being enacted through that interpretation. As Deleuze says:

> there is no truth that, before being a truth, is not the bringing into effect of a sense or the realisation of a value. Truth, as a concept, is entirely undetermined. Everything depends on the value and sense of what we think. We always have the truths we deserve as a function of the sense of what we conceive, of the value of what we believe. (Deleuze 1983, p. 104)

---

28 See, for example, Wahl (1963, pp. 378–379).
29 Cf. Deleuze (1983, p. 179): 'It is only under the sway of affirmation that the negative is raised to its higher degree at the same time as it defeats itself: it subsists no longer as a power and a quality but as the mode of being of the one who is powerful [*il subsiste non plus comme puissance et qualité, mais comme manière d'être de celui qui est puissant*]. Then, and only then, the negative is aggression, negation becomes active, and destruction becomes joyful [*la négation devient active, la destruction joyeuse*]' (translation modified).

This means that, from the standpoint of the *Umwertung*, the categories of thought that are actually critical are not truth and falsity, but 'the *noble* and the *base*, the *high* and the *low*, depending on the nature of the forces that take hold of thought itself' (Deleuze 1983, p. 104). It is by questioning the nature of these forces and of the type of will that they are aligned with that one achieves a critical standpoint.[30] From this perspective, truth and falsity are only relatively differentiated elements contained in a certain discourse which is not decisively determined by their relative preponderance. 'Stupidity', writes Deleuze:

> is not error or a tissue of errors. There are imbecile thoughts, imbecile discourses, that are made up entirely of truths; but these truths are base, they are those of a base, heavy and leaden soul. The state of mind dominated by reactive forces, *by right*, expresses *stupidity and, more profoundly, that which it is a symptom of: a base way of thinking*. In truth, as in error, stupid thought only discovers the most base – base errors and base truths that translate the triumph of the slave, the reign of petty values or the power of an established order. (Deleuze 1983, p. 105)

This means that, from the point of view of Deleuzian critique, the preposterousness of the politics of reactive nihilism is measured not so much by the amount of falsity contained in its discourse, as by the utter baseness of the will presiding over it, the reactivity of the forces it mobilises, and the intentional and unintentional stupidity with which it constructs interpretations in order to support the pettiness of a life form that draws its power from the decomposition of other forces, through the negative valuation of all that differs. Similarly, turning this critical point of view to the case with which I began this chapter, what is outrageous about the way in which Bolsonaro and his administration are dealing with Brazil's current environmental crisis is not so much the fact that they are lying, but that they are wilfully playing dumb – by constantly confusing the inaccuracy of data with their invalidity, by falsely attributing responsibilities, by failing to estimate correctly the probability of hypotheses, and so forth. The discourse of the politics of reactive nihilism pretends not to know what it knows and does not truly care to know what it does not know. In the hands of reactive nihilism, the value of truth, far from disappearing, becomes a corrosive substance of depreciation in the service of a base form of life. It serves to shroud a contempt for differing life forms in a mist of uncertainty and crippling suspicion. It tires the will with its resistance to grasping the simplest things, thus separating forces from what they can do. The source of the stupidity of Bolsonaro's politics of re-

---

30 On this method based on the who?-question, instead of the truth-oriented what?-question, see especially the section "The Form of the Question in Nietzsche" (Deleuze 1983, pp. 75–78).

active nihilism lies not so much in a defective intellect as in the baseness of its will, a will that can only triumph by degrading the powers of affirmation against which it is pitted. It deserves nothing less than the destructive aggressivity of a critique rooted in affirmation, with which it will be met sooner or later, when the passive and complacent I-A of the Brazilian people turns into a disdainful "no" against the negativity keeping it separated from what it can do.

Bibliography

Deleuze, Gilles (1983): *Nietzsche and Philosophy.* Translated by Hugh Tomlinson. London, New York: Continuum.
Deleuze, Gilles (2014): *Nietzsche et la philosophie.* Paris: Presses Universitaires de France.
Desai, Samarth (2017): "Linguist-In-Chief: Trump and the Meaning of Fake News". In: *Harvard Political Review*, April 1, 2017, http://harvardpolitics.com/united-states/linguist-chief-trump-meaning-fake-news/, visited on July 15, 2018.
Nietzsche, Friedrich (1989a): *Ecce Homo.* Edited and translated by Walter Kaufmann. New York: Vintage Books.
Nietzsche, Friedrich (1989b): *On the Genealogy of Morals.* Edited by Walter Kaufmann and translated by Walter Kaufmann and R. J. Hollingdale. New York: Random House.
Nietzsche, Friedrich (2002): *Beyond Good and Evil.* Edited by Rolf-Peter Horstmann and Judith Norman and translated by Judith Norman. Cambridge: Cambridge University Press.
Nietzsche, Friedrich (2006): *Thus Spoke Zarathustra.* Edited by Adrian del Caro and Robert Pippin and translated by Adrian del Caro. Cambridge: Cambridge University Press.
Wahl, Jean (1963): "Nietzsche et la philosophie". In: *Revue de Métaphysique et de Morale* 68. No. 3, pp. 352–379.

Julie Van der Wielen
The Idiot: Deleuze's Nietzsche for a Politics of Difference

Abstract: Following Philippe Mengue, this chapter explains the importance of the figure of the idiot in Deleuze's philosophy. The idiot allows for a conception of resistance relevant in the context of micropolitics. It implies a peculiar notion of political action: it is not the action of a consciously engaged individual, but rather the excretion of indetermination by someone or something inane, which creates an openness and thereby allows for something different to emerge, to go its course and be affirmed. This chapter relates this Deleuzean perspective to Nietzsche's "anti-politics" and his interpretation of Christ. It argues that Deleuze mobilises Nietzschean ideas in a transcendental way, in order to conceive of a persona that would allow for political change, which explains and justifies an "anti-political" stance.

1 Introduction

We call politicians idiots when we think they are incompetent, useless or harmful. It thus appears very provocative to argue that idiots should play a role in politics. Yet this is what Philippe Mengue seems to maintain in his book *Faire l'idiot: la politique de Deleuze* (2013).[1] According to Mengue, the figure of the idiot, which is a very significant Nietzsche-inspired notion in Deleuze's thought, would be a significant protagonist of politics, especially in the context of our current surveillance capitalism. I propose to examine the political significance of this Nietzschean notion against the backdrop of Deleuze's ontology of difference, which is also Nietzsche-inspired. Deleuze's reading of Nietzsche will allow me to advance an understanding of the political that does not rely on substance metaphysics, or on teleological or conscious agency, and which could be called a-political or anti-political in a very particular sense. This understanding of the political will simultaneously explain in what sense Nietzsche can be called a political or apolitical thinker, which in turn will shed light on why it is so difficult to understand Nietzsche's thoughts on politics in a coherent way, as a determinate political position or theory.

---

[1] To translate it literally: *To Play the Idiot* or, rendering the French expression: *To Act the Fool: Deleuze's Politics* – not translated to my knowledge.

In the second section, I will introduce Deleuze and Guattari's notion of the conceptual persona, which they consider one of the necessary conditions of philosophy, and argue with Mengue that the figure of the idiot plays a privileged role in Deleuze's thought: it is Deleuze's main conceptual persona, of which all other conceptual personae are variants. In the third section, I will explain Deleuze's notion of micropolitics, which will allow me, in the subsequent section, to illustrate the significance the idiot has for politics, according to Mengue. More precisely, I will illustrate how Melville's idiot, Bartleby, epitomises resistance or political action in the context of micropolitics, as described by Deleuze. In the fifth section, I will show how the notion of the idiot that runs through Deleuze's works is profoundly inspired by Nietzsche's interpretation of Christ in *The Anti-Christ*. Following from all this, in the last section, I will describe how Deleuze takes up the Nietzschean will to power in order to establish a transcendental – or, rather, genealogical – principle for his ontology of difference, which will allow me to give a specific Deleuzian interpretation of the Nietzschean politics of difference.

2 The Idiot: Deleuze's Conceptual Persona

The assiduous reader of Deleuze will have noticed that the idiot is a recurrent theme in his thought. Indeed, Deleuze writes about different "idiots" throughout his works. In *Difference and Repetition*, he mentions Eudoxus from Descartes' dialogue "The Search for Truth by Means of the Natural Light", as well as Shestov, the Russian philosopher. Deleuze calls Eudoxus an idiot because he does not have the knowledge an educated person of his time should have (Deleuze 1994, p. 130). Shestov is portrayed as an even more tenacious idiot, as he 'recognises himself no more in the subjective presuppositions of a natural capacity for thought than in the objective presuppositions of a culture of the times, and lacks the compass with which to make a circle' (Deleuze 1994, p. 130). This means that he not only lacks the knowledge he should have, but, unlike Eudoxus, does not even recognise the value of rational thought. In *Cinema 2*, Deleuze refers to the 'Dostoevskian condition' of the protagonist of Kurosawa's *Idiot* (based on the character of Prince Myshkin in Dostoevsky's homonymous novel), which consists in a refusal to see what is considered important or relevant in a given situation because he always feels that something else is more pressing (Deleuze 1997, p. 128). This makes the character become a seer who cannot or will not react to the given situation.

The very same idiots reappear in Deleuze and Guattari's *What is Philosophy?* (1994), where they acquire an important status, namely, as 'conceptual personae', which are necessary conditions for philosophical thought (Deleuze and Guattari 1994, pp. 61–83). Indeed, for Deleuze and Guattari, the conceptual persona personifies the more or less implicit pre-philosophical conditions, in the form of presuppositions and inclinations, through which the author is able to construct philosophical problems and to create philosophical concepts. More precisely, the conceptual persona embodies the author's presuppositions about what it means to think. Deleuze and Guattari find Nietzsche very unusual in this respect: they remark that 'few philosophers have worked so much with both sympathetic (Dionysus, Zarathustra) and antipathetic (Christ, the Priest, the Higher Men; Socrates himself become antipathetic) conceptual personae', and that, unlike in other authors, 'in Nietzsche, the conceptual personae involved never remain implicit' (Deleuze and Guattari 1994, p. 65). According to them, this would explain why some mistake Nietzsche for a poet. However, even if one may recognise literary, mythological, historical, social-psychological or other types in the conceptual personae, they should not be confused with such types, as they acquire their significance as conceptual personae exactly when they cease to be reducible to them and become conditions for a certain philosophical thought. Nevertheless, these personae then 'do not lose their concrete existence but, on the contrary, take on a new one as thought's internal conditions for its real exercise with this or that conceptual persona' (Deleuze and Guattari 1994, p. 69).

To illustrate their notion of conceptual persona, Deleuze and Guattari explain that Descartes' *cogito* is not entirely free from presuppositions, but that Descartes creates this concept through the Idiot as a conceptual persona. According to Deleuze, Descartes' Eudoxus is an idiot because he is not a schoolman. He is a private thinker who believes only in his own innate rational capacities to find indubitable truths, and who will not trust anything else. As they put it, 'a very strange type of persona who wants to think, and who thinks for himself, by the "natural light"' (Deleuze and Guattari 1994, p. 62). Then Deleuze and Guattari describe how they see in Shestov a Russian version of Descartes' idiot. Shestov's writings also show a private thinker, but one who has undergone some important transformations, influenced by Dostoevsky's idiot. As mentioned earlier, the idiot Shestov does not even believe in reason; he has no desire for indubitable truths and does not accept their value. Deleuze and Guattari note that this allows Shestov to affirm absurdity, and to give it a creative power for thought:

> The old idiot wanted, by himself, to account for what was or was not comprehensible, what was or was not rational, what was lost or saved; but the new idiot wants the lost, the incomprehensible, and the absurd to be restored to him. This is most certainly not the same persona; a mutation has taken place. And yet a slender thread links the two idiots,

as if the first had to lose reason so that the second rediscovers what the other, in winning it, had lost in advance: Descartes goes mad in Russia? (Deleuze and Guattari 1994, p. 63)

This example illustrates how, according to Deleuze and Guattari, conceptual personae animate authors and enliven the history of philosophy. It also shows that conceptual personae can have precursors, a history, and that they can undergo transformations and variations. The seed of the notion of conceptual persona, it should be noted, is already present in *Difference and Repetition*, where Deleuze affirms that 'Cowardice, cruelty, baseness and stupidity are not simply corporeal capacities or traits of character or society; they are structures of thought as such. The transcendental landscape comes to life: places for the tyrant, the slave and the imbecile must be found within it' (Deleuze 1994, p. 151). This explains why the same idiots that appear in *Difference and Repetition* serve as examples in *What is Philosophy?*

According to Mengue, in Deleuze's own thought it is also the idiot that figures as the main conceptual persona (Mengue 2003, pp. 10–11). He cites two lectures in which Deleuze says that doing philosophy is always playing at being an idiot, and that acting as an idiot has always been a function of philosophy (Mengue 2003, p. 61).[2] Deleuze there alludes to Descartes again, but this time he also mentions Socrates, whom Deleuze and Guattari refer to as Plato's main conceptual persona and who is known for saying that the only true wisdom is in knowing that you know nothing, and that he could not teach anyone anything, but only make them think (Deleuze and Guattari 1994, p. 63).

One can also show in Deleuze's written works that the conceptual persona through which he thinks is the idiot. In *Nietzsche and Philosophy*, Deleuze says that philosophy 'is always against its time, critique of the present world' (Deleuze 2002, p. 107), and in the central chapter of *Difference and Repetition*, "The Image of Thought", he affirms that real thought (and not mere recognition or representation) always goes against the current opinions and the accepted ways of thinking, that is, against doxa and common sense, and that the true thinker does not possess, or does not want to accept, the knowledge and beliefs everyone adheres to (Deleuze 1994, pp. 129–167). As a result, 'the thinker is necessarily solitary and solipsistic' (Deleuze 1994, p. 282), a private thinker, this is to say, an idiot. Furthermore, when Deleuze portrays those who do not feel represented in how and what one should think according to the spirit of the time,

---

2 Cf. Deleuze, Vincennes-Paris VIII: La voix de Gilles Deleuze en ligne, http://www2.univ-paris8.fr/deleuze/, 02/12/80 and 07/06/83.

and establishes this lack of representation as a condition for real thought, his description can stand for a description of the figure of the idiot:

> How could they not be isolated when they deny what 'everybody knows ...'? And passionate, since they deny that which, it is said, nobody can deny? Such protest does not take place in the name of aristocratic prejudices: it is not a question of saying what few think and knowing what it means to think. On the contrary, it is a question of someone – if only one – with the necessary modesty not managing to know what everybody knows, and modestly denying what everybody is supposed to recognise. Someone who neither allows himself to be represented nor wishes to represent anything.... Such a one is the Untimely, neither temporal nor eternal. (Deleuze 1994, p. 130)

We can thus say that the idiot is Deleuze's main conceptual persona and that personifying an idiot is a condition for thought. In other words, all conceptual personae are variations of the Idiot, which allow the authors who embody them to think against the established ways.

The attentive reader will have noticed that in the cited passage Deleuze uses the term 'the Untimely', which suggests that he is thinking of Nietzsche, or at least of the conceptual persona of the *Untimely Meditations*. This assumption becomes even more plausible when one considers that this text is one of Nietzsche's most neglected but most personal works, in which he writes about specific events, cultural movements and authors of his time (UM Introduction, vii). If this assumption is correct, then Deleuze seems to write against the common interpretation of Nietzsche's thought as aristocratic (he says that 'such protest does not take place in the name of aristocratic prejudices' [Deleuze 1994, p. 130]). It also implies that he is strongly influenced by Nietzsche for his idea of what it means to think and for his conceptual persona of the Idiot.

3 Deleuze's Micropolitics: A Politics of the Event

According to Mengue, examining the role the idiot plays in Deleuze's thought would reveal the sense and relevance of Deleuze's notion of 'micropolitics', by indicating the shift this notion performs for political thought (Mengue 2013, pp. 10–12). Mengue lists the main characteristics that distinguish Deleuze's micropolitics from 'macropolitics', that is, from what we usually understand by politics: a politics that involves a sovereign state (even if it is considered as something that should be abolished in favour of another type of rule) and the individuals subjected to it (Mengue 2013, pp. 15–18).

Deleuze's micropolitics begin with the matter-of-fact realisation that any type of societal organisation necessarily implies a particular codification of rights, permissions and prohibitions, and that this unavoidably entails that some rights, desires or individuals remain unrepresented, oppressed or repressed. This does not condemn Deleuze to political pessimism, however, because it goes together with another very fundamental realisation, namely, that codification is never fully successful, and that there are always leakages, so to speak, that there are always certain things that escape organisation (Deleuze and Guattari 2005, p. 216). Despite this, Mengue rightly remarks, Deleuze is not an anarchist: he believes that there will always be a state, in one form or another (Deleuze and Guattari 2000, pp. 217–221), and that only primitive societies can ward it off (Deleuze and Guattari 2000, pp. 145–153). His micropolitics rather represent a kind of counter-politics, a politics of minorities, or more precisely a 'minor politics', which is not reducible to the macropolitical 'political minorities' and which aims to liberate or to give a voice to that which remained unrepresented or to that which could not be expressed in a certain established order (just like philosophical thought and literature for Deleuze should give a voice to that which has not yet been thought; see, for example, *Kafka: For a Minor Literature* and *Essays Critical and Clinical*).

It is in this sense that Deleuze's politics would be a politics of the event. As Deleuze establishes in *Difference and Repetition* and *The Logic of Sense*, the event is not to be confused with its empirical manifestation: it constitutes the sense of a material happening, and as such it is irreducible to the material conditions that express it and never exhausted by these latter, given that it can continue generating effects (See Deleuze 1994, notably pp. 54–57, 155–158, and 188–191 and Deleuze 1990: 4–11). This is why Deleuze affirms that the event insists rather than existing: 'an ideal event ... is an objective entity, but one of which we cannot say that it exists in itself: it insists or subsists, possessing a quasi-being or an extra-being, that minimum of being common to real, possible and even impossible objects' (Deleuze 1994, p. 156). Sense is of a different nature to the material conditions that cause it, and it has a certain autonomy. Since its effects do not follow material causality, Deleuze ascribes to sense or the event 'quasi-causality': 'the event is subject to a double causality, referring on the one hand to mixtures of bodies that are its cause and, on the other, to other events which are its quasi-cause' (Deleuze 1990, p. 94). This means that, in a politics of the event, the emphasis is not on historicity but on unsuspected becomings. These are a-historical or extra-historical in the sense that their advent and their meaning cannot be made sense of from the point of view of the existing, as they exceed the individuals through whom they are expressed as much as the determinations of the established order.

In *Difference and Repetition*, Deleuze associates his notion of the event with the distinction between being in power and being powerful that he draws from

Nietzsche, according to which 'masters are certainly powerful men, but not men of power, since power is in the gift of the values of the day' and 'A slave does not cease to be a slave by taking power' (Deleuze 1994, p. 54). For Deleuze, the difference, on the one hand, between the powerful and the ones who are in power, and, on the other hand, between the established values (which may have been new in their day) and the values that will be eternally new, is the same difference as the one between the event and its empirical manifestation – it is a difference in kind: 'the difference is one of kind, like the difference between the conservative order of representation and a creative disorder or inspired chaos which can only ever coincide with a historical moment but never be confused with it' (Deleuze 1994, p. 54). Deleuze also links this to Nietzsche's notion of the eternal return, which operates a selection in a way that goes beyond the established values and possibilities: 'Nietzsche reproaches all those selection procedures based upon opposition or conflict with working to the advantage of the average forms and operating to the benefit of the "large number". Eternal return alone effects the true selection' (Deleuze 1994, p. 54). In *The Logic of Sense*, Deleuze parenthetically mentions transmutation in the context of the strange nature and causality of incorporeal events:

> All the old paradoxes of becoming must again take shape in a new youthfulness – transmutation ... between future and past, active and passive, cause and effect, more and less, too much and not enough, already and not yet. The infinitely divisible event is always *both at once*. It is eternally that which has just happened and that which is about to happen, but never that which is happening (to cut too deeply and not enough). The event, being itself impassive, allows the active and the passive to be interchanged more easily, since it is *neither the one nor the other*, but rather their common result (to cut – to be cut). Concerning the cause and the effect, events, *being always only effects*, are better able to form among themselves functions of quasi-causes or relations of quasi-causality which are always reversible (the wound and the scar). (Deleuze 1990, p. 8)

The micropolitical perspective, with its politics of the event, is especially relevant in the context of our current western society, which forms what Deleuze and Foucault call a 'control society' and which is, it should be noted, experiencing a considerable political crisis, to such an extent that democracy is losing its credibility (Deleuze 1995, p. 177). Even if different regimes of power are always present simultaneously in a society, there is, according to Deleuze, always one form of power that dominates, and we are shifting towards a new dominant regime of power, a new organisation of power. Indeed, following Foucault's intuition with the notion of biopolitics and biopower, Deleuze affirms that we are currently transitioning from disciplinary societies to societies of control. This transition is concomitant with the transition from industrial capitalism to a capitalism of dispersion and overproduction, in which the factory is replaced by the business (Deleuze 1995, pp. 180–181). Regimes of discipline govern by organising society in closed spaces of confinement with their own laws, in order to compose a segmented society that relies on discipline and organisation: 'Individuals are always going from one closed site to another, each with its own laws: first of all the family, then school ("you're not at home, you know"), then the barracks ("you're not at school, you know"), then the factory, hospital from time to time, maybe prison, the model site of confinement (Deleuze 1995, p. 177). By contrast, the new type of regime, the control society, relies on information and communication technologies (Deleuze 1995, p. 180), which allows for more mobility, flexibility and openness, which tolerates more liberties and requires fewer restrictions, but at the price of constant control and modulation. Indeed, while the disciplinary society functions as a mould, ruling through confinement and coercion, the control society operates through modulation; that is, it manages a fluctuating, metastable state of affairs through constant evaluation and adjustment. The way in which businesses manage their employees, through the creation of rivalry and competition, which divides individuals, as well as the introduction of continuous assessment instead of exams, illustrate this method of control through modulation (Deleuze 1995, p. 179). The object of control is here no longer the person and its body. Rather, the individual is divided into a collection of pieces of information, of fluxes of data that can be tapped, controlled, and modulated. Consequently, in control societies 'Individuals become "*dividuals*", and masses become samples, data, markets, or "*banks*"' (Deleuze 1995, p. 180). This is what the term micropolitics indicates: it is a politics that goes beyond, or rather beneath, the level of the individual. When Deleuze and Foucault introduced this idea they were strongly inspired by Nietzsche, who had already explored what is situated beyond or beneath the individual and its purported substance.

Mengue remarks that political action or resistance cannot mean the same in societies of control as in disciplinary societies (Mengue 2013, pp. 27–28). This is because, contrary to disciplinary societies, which exert power through subjugation and restriction and thus through the oppression of possibilities of life, control societies exert their power by enhancing, protecting, and even creating such possibilities. The classic example of this is the electronic bracelet of prisoners or mentally ill persons, which allows them to move around freely instead of being confined, but which traces them at every moment. But there are even more far-reaching examples, which, moreover, concern everyone. For example, the welfare state offers its citizens support, but in doing so it also acquires information about them, which it subsequently uses in decisions or for awareness campaigns in schools, on television or in public spaces. The Internet, together with computers and cell phones, allows for great mobility, it allows one to find one's way nearly everywhere, as well as to buy train or plane tickets at any moment to go nearly anywhere, but at the same time it makes it possible for information to be collected, which is then used, for instance, for advertising.

In these examples, freedom and possibilities of life are not directly opposed to control: the same instances that grant possibilities exercise control and modulation. As a consequence, political resistance can no longer take the shape of confrontation or sabotage, as it does in disciplinary societies. Indeed, even if these are adequate reactions against repression, they are misplaced in the context of control societies, since any direct, violent confrontation or sabotage means either renouncing one's possibilities, or affirming and reinforcing the legitimacy of that which it confronts, as disorder suggests that there needs to be more control and security. The shift towards control societies thus calls for an alternative idea and method of political resistance and political action. Deleuze remarks that, for the control society, 'the passive danger is noise and the active, piracy and viral contamination' (Deleuze 1995, p. 180). In other words, instead of sabotage or confrontation, the effective way of resisting in a control society is by interfering, that is, by blurring the determinations so that instances of control do not get a grip, as well as by using the different channels that usually exert control in order to disseminate something that would normally not circulate.

4 Bartleby: The Idiot as a Principle of Resistance

This is where the idiot comes in, according to Mengue. For him, the political significance of the idiot appears most clearly in "Bartleby; or, The Formula" on Melville's "Bartleby, the Scrivener: A Story of Wall Street" (Deleuze 1998, pp. 68–90). Even though Deleuze does not explicitly affirm it, Mengue claims that Bartleby would be a variation of the Idiot, he would even be the Deleuzian Idiot par excellence (Mengue 2013, p. 61). This is why he concentrates mostly on Bartleby in his book. To summarise Bartleby's story: the pitiful but very neat-looking Bartleby gets hired as a scrivener in a law office. Unlike the other two scriveners, who have their own room, he is stationed in the attorney's office, in such an arrangement that he can hear everything without being seen. He works very well (though extremely silently and mechanically) at the beginning, but then, when the attorney asks Bartleby to compare one of his copies to the original, all starts going wrong: Bartleby responds, 'I would prefer not to' (Melville 1995, p. 20), and from then on, this phrase becomes his answer to absolutely everything. Bartleby's formula makes the attorney go mad at times, it brings chaos into the office, and it puts Bartleby in all kinds of bizarre positions: despite the disapproval of his colleagues, he is exempted from some of the usual assignments, his relation with the attorney becomes very unusual, when the attorney relocates his office and Bartleby does not want to leave the office he ends up on the street, and when he does not accept the attorney's kind offer to go home with him, since he 'would prefer not to make any change at all' (Melville 1995, p. 41), he ends up in prison, where he starves to death, as he 'prefers not to dine' (Melville 1995, p. 44).

In this tragi-comical story, Bartleby's behaviour seems idiotic because he keeps on repeating the same strange phrase and has a very inappropriate attitude that goes against common procedures and common sense. As Deleuze remarks, Bartleby's formula is grammatically and syntactically correct, but uncommon: it is unusual to use the verb 'prefer' in that way (instead of saying 'I would rather not'), and the phrase has an abrupt ending, which leaves what is rejected undetermined. For Deleuze, because of this, the phrase forms 'an inarticulate block' and 'has the same role, the same force, as an *agrammatical* formula' (Deleuze 1998, p. 68). The formula, as Bartleby keeps repeating it, has an effect of contamination: the attorney and the other people at the office start using the verb prefer, which they normally do not use, and while at first Bartleby declines to carry out certain activities in order to continue copying, after a while he even stops this activity. According to Deleuze, this is because 'the formula that successively refuses every other act has already engulfed the act of copying, which it no longer even needs to refuse' (Deleuze 1998, p. 71). The formula ends up contaminating the act of copying because, as it leaves what it prefers not to do indeterminate, it also does not advance an alternative preference, and so 'it hollows out an ever expanding zone of indiscernibility or indetermination between some nonpreferred activities and a preferable activity' (Deleuze 1998, p. 71).

Furthermore, Deleuze notes, Bartleby's phrase even does violence to language as a whole, as it destroys the double reference one normally finds in speech acts, namely, to a designated object, state of affairs or act on the one hand, and to an interlocutor on the other (Deleuze 1998, p. 73–74). Indeed, the phrase is disconnected from the action that 'it prefers not to' do, and which is left in suspense, as well as from the action in reference to which the non-preferred is rejected. It is also disconnected from the interlocutor, who did not expect this phrase and does not know how to react to it, and from whom Bartleby usually walks away upon uttering the formula. The formula also isolates Bartleby from the whole of society: if he would simply refuse to do what he is asked, he could be considered and treated as a rebel, but he keeps on enunciating something of the order of preferences in contexts where preferences are not deemed relevant, which makes him a lunatic or an outsider at best, with whom no one knows how to deal or what to do. Just as his formula, Bartleby is without references: no one knows anything about him, and it is almost impossible to ascribe any particular quality to him. As Deleuze puts it, 'Bartleby is the man without references, without possessions, without properties, without qualities, without particularities: he is too smooth for anyone to hang any particularity on him' (Deleuze 1998, p. 74).

It should be clear now why, for Mengue, Bartleby epitomises Deleuze's micropolitics and its concomitant notion of resistance: despite the fact that he works in the constant presence of the attorney, Bartleby manages to escape his authority completely by introducing confusion and indetermination. His formula contaminates the whole office, where disorder increases with each expression, and it even makes the attorney question his assumptions about good practice and about language. Bartleby gets the attorney to make exceptions for him, to give him a preferential treatment. Additionally, Bartleby wins the affection of the attorney, who even invites him into his home. But most importantly, none of this is actually intended or willed by Bartleby. How could it be? The pallid scrivener just 'prefers not to ...'. As Deleuze notes, all the formula expresses is 'the growth of a nothingness of the will' (Deleuze 1998, p. 71). This is in line with Mengue's description of micropolitics as a politics of the event, in which to resist means to introduce indetermination in such a way that the existing order does not get a grip, in order to make room for the unexpected and even hitherto unfeasible, that is, for the Deleuzian event, which exceeds and goes against the established order, and which is not really produced or brought about by anyone, but which expresses singular, impersonal forces (Mengue 2013, p. 30).

It may seem odd to speak so positively about Bartleby, whose story is actually that of a creeping depression, which ends in total catatonia and death – it is the story of nihilism, of the will to nothingness. However, one can understand the revaluation of values as an overcoming of nihilism by itself, and thus as requiring the self-destruction of that which manifests will to nothingness, in favour of the expression of forces that could not come to expression. This is indeed how Deleuze understands transvaluation:

> For Nietzsche, all the previously analysed forms of nihilism, even the extreme or passive form, constitute an *unfinished, incomplete* nihilism ... the transmutation which defeats nihilism is itself the only complete and finished form of nihilism ... nihilism is defeated, but defeated by itself. (Deleuze 2002, p. 172)

Deleuze refers to the Prologue to *Thus Spoke Zarathustra*, where Zarathustra upholds that 'Human being is something that must be overcome' (Z Prologue, 3) and that he loves those who want their own downgoing (Z Prologue, 4), and he reads *The Will to Power* in the French translation of the Würzbach edition in four volumes, of which the third volume is entitled *Nihilism Overcome by Itself*.

In this perspective, Bartleby is the perfect illustration of transmutation. Indeed, even if Bartleby succumbs to it, his formula, by introducing indetermination, makes the established order dissolve, in favour of all kinds of forces that would otherwise not be visible or that would be cancelled out by this order. The forces of order that act upon one become visible, but they miss their usual effect and become as questionable as everything else, and other forces which would usually not find expression become visible (the attorney's fathering tendencies, his possible homophilic feelings, people's weakness for politeness and their compliance, etc.).

As Deleuze points out, Bartleby's story tells of the advent of American society, and thus literally expresses an event which is of far-reaching social and political significance. Indeed, before Bartleby makes his appearance, everything in Melville's story is very English, and could come from a novel by Dickens set in London. For instance, in the two comical scriveners, who are mirrors of each other (the one, calm and tidy in the morning when sober, and agitated and disorderly in the afternoon, after some beer; and the other one, the reverse) work for an attorney who fathers them. But when Bartleby enters the picture:

> something strange happens, something that blurs the image, marks it with an essential uncertainty, keeps the form from 'taking,' but also undoes the subject, sets it adrift and abolishes the paternal function ... everything begins à l'anglaise but continues à l'américaine, following an irresistible line of flight…. The paternal function is dropped in favor of even more obscure and ambiguous forces. The subject loses its texture in favor of an infinitely proliferating patchwork: the American patchwork becomes the law of Melville's oeuvre. (Deleuze 1998, p. 77)

Deleuze calls Bartleby 'the new Christ' (Deleuze 1998, p. 90). As Mengue notes, this not only indicates his huge appreciation for the character, it also points to the fact that 'the conceptual persona of the idiot implicitly relies upon not only the literary and philosophical character of Prince Myshkin from Dostoevsky's *Idiot*, but also, and just like the latter, upon the Christ of the Gospels' (Mengue 2013, p. 66, my translation). This again would point to the strong Nietzschean influence of Deleuze's Idiot. Indeed, the Christ that shapes the figure of the Idiot is not the Christ of Christendom, it is the Nietzschean Christ, as Mengue observes:

> Underlying the figure of the Idiot there is a Christ, a Christ that runs obliquely from Spinoza ('Thus Spinoza is the Christ of philosophers') to Bartleby ('the new Christ'). There is a Deleuzian Christianism, but one that is so Nietzschean that it merges with the plane of immanence, the plane of life. (Mengue 2013, p. 66, citing Deleuze and Guattari 1994, p. 60 and Deleuze 1998, p. 90, my translation)

5 Nietzsche's Christ: An Affirmation of Life

The Nietzschean Christianism Mengue refers to is to be found in Nietzsche's *Anti-Christ*. In this book, Nietzsche again tells how Judeo-Christian morality became base and vile, this time through concrete, historical explanations, in order to show, by contrast, what type of morality does have value and should be aspired to. A large part of the book is devoted to a description of the psychological type of Jesus as he appears in the Gospels. Nietzsche claims that the significance of this figure was distorted, even turned on its head, by Saint Paul and the Christians, and that even Jesus' own disciples misunderstood him, as they were soiled by the decadent times in which they lived and by their worship of him.

For example, Jesus has often been seen as a hero or a genius, which is profoundly unevangelical, according to Nietzsche, given that 'Everyone is a child of God – Jesus did not claim any special privileges.... And to make Jesus into a *hero!* – Even this word "genius": what a misunderstanding it is!' (A 29). Nietzsche also remarks that: 'The polar opposite of struggle, of any feeling of doing-battle, has become instinct here: an incapacity for resistance has become morality here ("resist not evil", the most profound saying of the Gospels, the key to their meaning in a certain sense), blessedness in peace, in gentleness, in an *inability* to be an enemy' (A 29). Nietzsche writes that it would be more accurate to call Jesus an 'idiot' (A 29) and he affirms that 'It is a pity that there was no Dostoevsky living near this most interesting decadent, I mean someone with an eye for the distinctive charm that this sort of mixture of sublimity, sickness, and childishness has to offer' (A 31). This indicates that his interpretation of Jesus strongly relies on Dostoevsky's, who took his inspiration from the figure of Jesus when creating the protagonist of *The Idiot*.

According to Nietzsche, the figure of Jesus has been distorted mainly through a thorough misunderstanding of his message. The glad tidings are usually understood as the good news that Jesus, the son of God, forgives all sins and that there will be salvation for everyone, that everyone can earn their blissful afterlife, on the simple condition of leading a life of repentance. Supposedly, Christ suffered and died on the cross for all the guilt in the world, to save all sinners. According to Nietzsche's interpretation, the meaning of Jesus' message is very different: 'What are the "glad tidings"? That the true life, the eternal life has been found – it is not just a promise, it exists, it is *in each of you:* as a life of love, as a love without exceptions or rejections, without distance' (A 29). The glad tidings are thus not a promise that separates us from God and from blissfulness and condemns us to a worldly life of suffering. On the contrary, it is the good news that the kingdom of God is here, that life is love, that it is everywhere and in all equally, and hence that this life does not require repentance, the asking of forgiveness, justification or judgment. It also does not need scripture or dogma, and is not even capable of being translated into such terms: it is merely life as bliss; blessedness as the one and only reality, which just needs to be lived.

Nietzsche claims that the Christian interpretation of the glad tidings is exactly opposed to their original meaning and that it is appallingly harmful and disgraceful because it is hostile to life (A 37). Indeed, Nietzsche remarks: 'Christianity has taken the side of everything weak, base, failed, it has made an ideal out of whatever *contradicts* the preservation instincts of a strong life; it has corrupted the reason of even the most spiritual natures by teaching people to see the highest spiritual values as sinful, as deceptive, as *temptations*' (A 5). To be sure, according to the Christians, in this earthly life we should resist temptations, have pity, and be remorseful (since, even if we do resist temptations, we are still all sinners) – we should lead a very sober life and support the weak, which necessarily leads to the conservation and diffusion of weakness (A 7). This evidently does not correspond to a strong life. Furthermore, through the figure of the priest, who is supposed to sanctify all meaningful occasions, this Christian morality diminishes the intrinsic value of significant life events (such as birth, marriage, illness and death), as the priest is considered to be the one who bestows value upon them (A 26).

For Nietzsche, Jesus' original message is exactly the reverse, and it announces a blissful and uncomplicated life, not at all one of suffering: 'the "glad tidings" are just that the contradiction is gone; the kingdom of heaven belongs to the *children*; the faith expressed here is not a hard-won faith, – it is here, it has been from the start, it is, as it were, an infantilism receded into spirituality' (A 32). So, rather than a redeemer (A24), a fanatic or a militant (A 32) who died for other people's guilt (A 32 and 27), Nietzsche sees in Jesus an innocent and childlike character, for whom life is bliss, who does not ask anything of anyone, who does not judge and does not ask for reasons, but who only feels and who does not demand anything, neither belief nor repentance, and who does not know the concepts of reward, punishment and sin (A 33).

Nietzsche's Christ is thus simple, without dogma and without pretensions. Just like Bartleby, he is stripped of everything, which makes him untimely in the sense that he does not belong to his time; he could be of any time, as he does not think like the people of his time and does not seem to have any knowledge or culture:

> He does not know anything about culture, even in passing, he does not need to struggle against it, – he does not negate it.... The same is true about the state, about the whole civic order and society, about work, about war – he never had any reason to negate 'the

world', the ecclesiastical concept of 'world' never occurred to him.... Negation is out of the question for him. – Dialectic is missing as well, there is no conception that a belief, a 'truth', could be grounded in reasons (– his proofs are inner 'lights', inner feelings of pleasure and self-affirmations, pure 'proofs of strength' –). A doctrine like this cannot contradict, it has no idea that there are, that there could be any other doctrines, it has no idea how even to form the thought of an opposing judgment.... If it comes across an opposing judgment, it will feel deeply sympathetic and grieve over this 'blindness' – since it sees the 'light' – but it would not offer any objections. (A 32)

Since he does not understand the concept of reasons and of justification, Nietzsche's Christ cannot know and does not need objection, negation or contradiction. He never makes distinctions and never offers any resistance, not even to the ones who are evil to him (A 33).

This implies that, in contrast to what the Church has made of him, there is no room for transcendence or idealism in Jesus' mind and practice, according to Nietzsche. Transcendence always devalues and judges life in favour of fictions, such as God, the soul, and sin (A 15), or of an imaginary world beyond this one, such as the afterlife (A 43 and 58). But Jesus represents a practice of life, a simple and unconditioned affirmation of life, of what is here (A 33) – it is a life of pure immanence, as Deleuze would say.[3] It also implies pure belief in, or affirmation of, the earth, to use another Deleuzian term (which appears notably in *What is Philosophy?*, but which is also present throughout Nietzsche's *Thus Spoke Zarathustra*). In their chapter on conceptual personae, Deleuze and Guattari write that the most pressing problem today is probably that we have lost faith in the world (Deleuze and Guattari 1994, p. 75), and they maintain that thinking always happens between the earth and the territory, that is, between the earth as it is and how it is interpreted and serves as a basis for thought (Deleuze and Guattari 1994, p. 85). This points to the importance that the notion of the earth, as well as of the capacity to affirm it, beyond all transcendent mediations, has for thought. As a matter of fact, for Deleuze and Guattari, 'there is Philosophy whenever there is immanence' (Deleuze and Guattari 1994, p. 43). As a result, it seems that Deleuze relies on Nietzsche's interpretation of Christ for his notion of the Idiot, in order to establish a connection between the concepts of immanence, life forces, the earth and thought.

This conception of thought is inherently political, certainly in the sense of micropolitics as sketched above. Indeed, according to this view, thought consists in the affirmation and expression of forces of life that are suppressed by the es-

---

[3] For an explanation of this term see "Immanence: A Life", which Deleuze wrote just before his death in 1995 (Deleuze, 2007).

tablished order, which corresponds to what political action or resistance is in the context of Deleuze's micropolitics of the event. In this view, political action could be seen as a kind of thought: such action also consists in affirming and liberating that which does not find expression, that which is suppressed. For Deleuze and Guattari, conceptual thought is not the only type of thought – art and science are both forms of thought, expressed through affects and percepts in the case of art and through prospects in the case of science (Deleuze and Guattari 1994, p. 24). Thus, political action too could be seen as thought, namely, as a practice that generates something new. In any case, for Deleuze and Guattari, creating concepts seems equivalent to creating a possible, different future, to starting a political movement:

> The creation of concepts in itself calls for a future form, for a new earth and people that do not yet exist.... Art and philosophy converge at this point: the constitution of an earth and a people that are lacking as the correlate of creation. It is not populist writers but the most aristocratic who lay claim to this future. This people and earth will not be found in our democracies. Democracies are majorities, but a becoming is by its nature that which always eludes the majority. (Deleuze and Guattari 1994, p. 108)

This description of thought as aristocratic is not inconsistent with what we have seen before, namely that the Idiot does not think out of aristocratic prejudices: real thought is aristocratic in the sense that it will, by definition, never happen in those who feel represented by the majority and who agree with the current opinions and ways of thinking. It also needs a strong nature, one which is able to affirm life and to think for itself. But this thought does not think out of aristocratic prejudices, it thinks simply because it is not represented in the established order and affirms other expressions of life.

6 Deleuze's Nietzschean Ontology of Difference

When we consider the idiot in relation to the ontology of difference that Deleuze develops through his reading of Nietzsche in *Nietzsche and Philosophy*, it allows us to deepen the notions of micropolitics and of the politics of the event, to qualify them as constituting a politics of difference. This reading of Nietzsche simultaneously offers an interesting interpretation of his political thought, which connects the terms of will to power, transmutation or transvaluation, and great politics in a coherent, systematic conceptual framework.

Deleuze interprets Nietzsche as completing Kant's critical project. Indeed, Kant did not manage to perform a real critique, because he did not question the main objects of this critique – the value of the true, the good and the beautiful – but only the way in which we can achieve them. The conceptual persona through which Kant thinks is certainly not the Idiot; it is rather the Judge or the Legislator who creates rules to maintain order: his *Critiques* assign each faculty particular roles and rights, in delimited domains. As Deleuze puts it, 'the only object of Kant's critique is justification, it begins by believing in what it criticises' (Deleuze 2002, p. 90). What is more, Deleuze notes, Kant's idea of the values that should be pursued, as well as the path that leads to them, 'mysteriously coincides with these established values' (Deleuze 2002, p. 93). For Deleuze, Nietzsche provides the means to perform a true, radical critique, which does not leave values untouched, but which offers principles for their evaluation and creation. Deleuze associates this critical project with Nietzsche's notion of great politics: it would be the announcement of great politics (Deleuze 2002, p. 90), in a similar way that the 'I will' of the lion announces the 'yes' of the value-creating child in Zarathustra's discourse on the metamorphoses of the spirit (Z Metamorphoses).

According to Deleuze, what Kant would need in order to complete his critique is a genealogical method, instead of a transcendental one (Deleuze 2002, p. 91). His transcendental principles merely determine abstract conditions of possibility and not concrete conditions of genesis, of production (for example, the a priori forms of space and time, even if they may indeed be considered necessary conditions for experience, do not explain the real, concrete genesis of experience in a subject). As a consequence, these principles remain external to the conditioned, and they leave it untouched and unquestioned. A genealogical method, by contrast, would be able to account for the emergence or production of actions, concepts and values and simultaneously allow one to evaluate them, as it would enable one to trace their origin and to ask what interest they serve. As Deleuze explains:

> From this form of question [which one is it?] there derives a method. Any given concept, feeling or belief will be treated as symptoms of a will that wills something. What does *the one that* says this, that thinks or feels that, will? It is a matter of showing that he could not say, think or feel this particular thing if he did not have a particular will, particular forces, a particular way of being. What does he will the one who speaks, loves or creates? And conversely what does the one who profits from an action that he does not do, the one who appeals to 'disinterestedness', what does he will? (Deleuze 2002, p. 78)

Nietzsche's genealogical method finds its reason in the will to power as a differential, genetic principle: 'Nietzsche calls the genealogical element of force the will to power. Genealogical means differential and genetic' (Deleuze 2002, p. 52). This is to say that the will to power indicates the relation between different forces in a genetic, productive synthesis which makes things come about. This principle is always double, according to Deleuze: 'Forces in relation reflect a simultaneous double genesis [of quantity and quality]: the reciprocal genesis of their difference in quantity [obeying or commanding] and the absolute genesis of their respective qualities [active or reactive]' (Deleuze 2002, p. 51). In other words, for a given relation of forces, the will to power always determines, on the one hand, according to the quantity of the force, which force dominates and which one is dominated, and on the other hand, on the basis of the qualities of the forces it is composed of, active or reactive, it produces an affirming or denying will to power. As a result, a will to power can be said to be affirmative or negative, depending on the quantity (obeying or commanding) and quality (active or reactive) of the forces it expresses. Deleuze notes: 'active and reactive designate the original qualities of force but affirmative and negative designate the primordial qualities of the will to power. Affirming and denying, appreciating and depreciating, express the will to power just as acting and reacting express force' (Deleuze 2002, p. 53).

Since this principle concerns particular forces that are in a productive relation to each other, it is not a transcendental principle in the Kantian sense, for it does not concern abstract conditions of possibility but concrete and plastic conditions of production and of becoming. It even implies chance as the element that determines what forces are given in the relation (Deleuze 2002, p. 53). It constitutes an ontology of difference, since the difference between the forces is the most fundamental fact. Indeed, for Deleuze 'Hierarchy is the originary fact, the identity of difference and origin' (Deleuze 2002, p. 8), and 'In the beginning, at the origin, there is the difference between active and reactive forces' (Deleuze 2002, p. 55). Reactive forces define what is good and bad in opposition to what they are not, and they call what is bad for them 'evil', just as the weak do, according to Nietzsche's description in *On the Genealogy of Morality* (GM I, 10). They are forces of adaptation or conservation, which are expressed in *ressentiment* or the spirit of revenge and in bad conscience. In order to prevail, they separate active forces from what they can do, and prevent the strong, active forces from exercising their strength, under the pretext that this would be evil. Reactive forces also limit themselves; they do not go to the limit of what they can. Active forces, on the contrary, do go to their limits; and they do not separate forces from what they can do. They are plastic, dominant and subjugating forces, which affirm their difference, that is, their relation to other forces, and make it an object of enjoyment and affirmation (Deleuze 2002, p. 61), just like the masters do, according to Nietzsche (GM I, 10).

It follows from this that the genetic principle of the will to power allows one to evaluate a given type, or a given value, as affirmative or depreciative of life. Nietzsche devotes several books to the exposition and description of reactive types. Even though active forces are the stronger ones, Nietzsche observes that the weak, reactive forces can prevail and that, surprisingly, they even tend to do so. Deleuze finds one of the finest remarks in Nietzsche's *The Will to Power* to be: 'The strong always have to be defended against the weak' (Deleuze 2002, p. 58). He concludes in his reading of Nietzsche that our psychology – human psychology – is a reactive one and that our history is a becoming-reactive; it is the history of *ressentiment* and of nihilism. Indeed, he affirms that 'the instinct of revenge is the force which constitutes the essence of what we call psychology, history, metaphysics and morality. The spirit of revenge is the genealogical element of *our* thought, the transcendental principle of *our* way of thinking' (Deleuze 2002, p. 35). This is because being reactive is contagious, it tends to spread like an infectious disease, as reactive forces separate active forces from what they can do, and as reactive feelings such as pity and modesty allow the weak to thrive. For this reason, Deleuze notes a generalised becoming-reactive of forces. 'History thus appears as the act by which reactive forces take possession of culture or divert its course in their favour. The triumph of reactive forces is not an accident in history but the principle and meaning of "universal history"' (Deleuze 2002, p. 139).

In this perspective, Deleuze considers that Nietzsche's objective – to which we should all aspire – is a reversal of this tendency, of this becoming-reactive of forces. This would be what Nietzsche means by transmutation and transvaluation (Deleuze 2002, p. 35). As Deleuze explains, transmutation or transvaluation means '[c]hange of quality in the will to power. Values and their value no longer derive from the negative, but from affirmation as such. In place of a depreciated life we have life which is affirmed' (Deleuze 2002, p. 175). Transvaluation does not primarily concern the existing, established values, which should be rejected, abolished or struggled against. It only has a bearing on these values as a result of the reversal in the will to power that is at the origin of values, and not because it is in opposition to them. As such, transmutation is primarily a becoming-active through affirmation, and 'Affirmation is not action but the power of becoming active, *becoming active* personified. Negation is not simple reaction but a *becoming reactive*' (Deleuze 2002, p. 54). Deleuze relates this to what he calls (evidently alluding to Nietzsche's Christ) Nietzsche's 'glad tidings' (Deleuze 2002, p. 35). This means that, in order to resist nihilism and the becoming reactive of forces, we do not have to struggle, but simply to affirm chance and to embody an affirmative will to power, just as the Idiot does. This is tragic at the same time as it is joyful: it is tragic because it requires the affirmation of the necessity of chance, but it is joyful and positive because it is not oppositional, it is not a struggle or a fight, but an innocent and creative play of forces that are to be affirmed.

Deleuze relates this becoming-active to Nietzsche's notion of the overhuman: 'we do not really know what a man denuded of *ressentiment* would be like. A man who would not accuse or depreciate existence – would he still be a man, would he think like a man? Would he not already be something other than a man, almost the Overman?' (Deleuze 2002, p. 35). Since Deleuze relates evaluation and transvaluation to the notion of critique, transvaluation would also be linked to Nietzsche's notion of 'great politics' announced by such a critique. The notion of transvaluation itself seems to have a political connotation, just like the notion of will to power, but certainly not in the usual sense. As Deleuze remarks, one should not see the will to power as a will that wants power, 'as if power were the ultimate aim of the will and also its essential motive. As if power were what the will wanted' (Deleuze 2002, p. 80). This conception of the will to power would imply that the object of the will is an object of representation, the object of a struggle or a competition, which would be a reactive understanding of the will and one that is subjected to the established order. As Deleuze says:

> When we make power an object of representation we necessarily make it dependent upon the factor according to which a thing is represented or not, recognised or not. Now, only values which are already current, only accepted values, give criteria of recognition in this way. The will to power, understood as the will to get oneself recognised, is necessarily the will to have the values current in a given society attributed to oneself (power, money, honours, reputation). (Deleuze 2002, p. 81)

This means that transvaluation or becoming-active can only happen outside of what we take to be the political realm and, one can even say, against all the forms of politics currently known. This, though, should not be understood as a reaction or a struggle against existing politics or determinate political views, but as something that, through its power of affirmation, dissolves and discredits the status quo: something of the order of the event. Nietzsche's thought, as directed towards the project of transvaluation, is thus distinctly political in a sense, as it wants to affirm and to liberate suppressed life forces; but it is certainly not a politics, but rather an anti-politics. It is a thought that affirms difference, and that puts the emphasis on becoming and on creation.

7 Conclusion

Deleuze is strongly inspired by his reading of Nietzsche when he suggests that the figure of the idiot plays the role of a principle for thought as well as for political change. In Deleuze's philosophy, the idiot, the private thinker, dissolves the structures of the established order, because he does not know what he should know or how he should think or act. Since he does not know or believe in anything transcendent, he does not judge or devaluate, he only believes and affirms without reasons, simply articulating the forces of life that affect him without offering any resistance. In this way, the idiot articulates or expresses things that remained unarticulated, and he dissolves or at least puts into question the established order. As there are many kinds of idiot, this is a plastic principle, but one which always articulates a belief in the earth, in immanence, and thus it liberates the active forces from the reactive ones: it is a principle of transvaluation, a becoming-active.

The role and significance of this figure reveals a thought which is both very political and anti-political. To put it in Mengue's terms, it points to a micropolitics of the idiot as a non-politics that politics needs in order not to be reduced to a function of management and police (Mengue 2013, p. 49). One can also call this a politics of the event, as it is concerned, not just with the current, empirical state of affairs, but with its sense and its potentialities, which do not follow the causality of material bodies. This would explain Nietzsche's difficult relation to politics and political thought. As we saw, Deleuze offers an interpretation of Nietzsche as an ontological thinker, one who elaborates an ontology of difference, in which the relation between different types of forces and the resulting will forms the main, genetic and genealogical principle. Deleuze also interprets Nietzsche's thought as directed to transvaluation or transmutation, that is, to the becoming-active of the will, which must necessarily happen outside the established order, and as such can only be understood from a new perspective, and which must thus necessarily be an anti-politics.

Bibliography

Deleuze, Gilles (1990): *The Logic of Sense*. Edited by Constantin V. Boundas and translated by Mark Lester and Charles Stivale. London: The Athlone Press.
Deleuze, Gilles (1994): *Difference and Repetition*. Translated by Paul Patton. New York: Columbia University Press.
Deleuze, Gilles (1995): "Postscript on Control Societies". In: Gilles Deleuze: *Negotiations, 1972–1990*, pp. 177–182. Translated by Martin Joughin. New York: Columbia University Press.
Deleuze, Gilles (1997): *Cinema 2: The Time-Image*. Translated by Robert Galeta and Hugh Tomlinson. Minneapolis: University of Minnesota Press.
Deleuze, Gilles (1998): "Bartleby; or, the Formula". In: Gilles Deleuze: *Essays Critical and Clinical*, pp. 68–90. Translated by Michal A. Greco and Daniel Smith. London: Verso.
Deleuze, Gilles (2002): *Nietzsche and Philosophy*. Translated by Hugh Tomlinson. London: Continuum.
Deleuze, Gilles (2007): "Immanence: A life". In: *Two Regimes of Madness. Texts and Interviews 1975–1995*, pp. 384–389. Edited by David Lapoujade and translated by Ames Hodges and Mike Taormina. New York: Semiotext(e).

Deleuze, Gilles, and Félix Guattari (1994): *What is Philosophy?* Translated by Graham Burchell and Hugh Tomlison. New York: Columbia University Press.

Deleuze, Gilles, and Félix Guattari (2000): *Capitalism and Schizophrenia, vol. 1: Anti-Oedipus.* Translated by Robert Hurley, Helen R. Lane and Mark Seem. Minneapolis: University of Minnesota Press.

Deleuze, Gilles, and Félix Guattari (2005): *Capitalism and Schizophrenia, vol. 2: A Thousand Plateaus.* Translated by Brian Massumi. Minneapolis: University of Minnesota Press.

Melville, Herman (1995): "Bartleby, The Scrivener." In: Herman Melville: *The Writings of Herman Melville, vol. 9: The Piazza Tales and Other Prose Pieces 1839–1860*, pp. 13–45. Edited by Harrison Hayford, Alma A. MacDougall and Herschel Parker. Evanston: Northwestern University Press.

Mengue, Philippe (2013): *Faire l'idiot: la politique de Deleuze.* Paris: Éditions Germina.

Nietzsche, Friedrich (2002): *Beyond Good and Evil: Prelude to a Philosophy of the Future.* Edited by Rolf-Peter Horstmann and Judith Norman and translated by Judith Norman. Cambridge: Cambridge University Press.

Nietzsche, Friedrich (2006): *Thus Spoke Zarathustra.* Edited by Adrian Del Caro and Robert Pippin and translated by Adrian Del Caro. Cambridge: Cambridge University Press.

Nietzsche, Friedrich (2007a): *The Anti-Christ.* In: *The Anti-Christ, Ecce Homo, Twilight of the Idols and Other Writings*, pp. 1–68. Edited by Aaron Ridley and Judith Norman and translated by Judith Norman. Cambridge: Cambridge University Press.

Nietzsche, Friedrich (2007b): *On the Genealogy of Morality.* Edited by Keith Ansell-Pearson and translated by Carol Diethe. Cambridge: Cambridge University Press.

Nietzsche, Friedrich (2007c): *Untimely Meditations.* Edited by Daniel Breazeale and translated by R. J. Hollingdale. Cambridge: Cambridge University Press.

Part 4 **The Politics of the Agon**

Pia Morar
Disparate Conceptions of the Agon: Nietzsche and Agonistic Democracy

Abstract: Nietzsche has been regarded as both an 'aristocratic radical' and an 'agonistic democrat'. In this chapter I aim to shed light on this discrepancy by closely examining the agon as a political concept throughout Nietzsche's earlier and later thought. As a measured and productive competition, the agon forms part of Nietzsche's life-long philosophical engagement with conflict and struggle within the individual as well as society. I begin by outlining the etymological and historical significance of the term and Nietzsche's initial understanding of it. I then trace the development of the agon in Nietzsche's later works in relation to the order of rank and the pathos of distance. In light of this, I contend that Nietzsche's conception of the agon is incompatible with the democratic application of the concept, since for him the agonal principle was exercised only among individuals of equal rank.

1 Introduction

The philosophy of Friedrich Nietzsche has had a wide-ranging influence on liberal and illiberal thinkers alike, including Deleuze, Derrida, Foucault, Heidegger and Schmidt. More recently, Nietzsche's philosophy has come to be associated less with liberalism and democracy per se, but rather with a novel form of radical democracy known as 'agonistic democracy'. Agonistic democrats such as William Connolly, Lawrence Hatab, David Owen and Alan Schrift emphasise the competitive aspect of political confrontation, in contrast to the mainstream deliberative models of liberal democracy.[1] They rely on Nietzsche's concept of the agon, primarily in relation to his later works, in an attempt to reconceive liberal democracy along agonal lines. However, there are other Nietzsche scholars, including Frederick Appel, Don Dombowsky and Bruce Detwiler, who deny that Nietzsche's thought is compatible with agonistic democracy. They contend that Nietzsche's philosophy cannot be squared with democracy, due to his extensive criticism and rejection of democracy, liberalism and egalitarianism.[2] In response, the agonists concede that Nietzsche himself was not a democrat, and

---

[1] See Connolly 2002; Hatab 2002; and Schrift 2000.
[2] see Appel 1999, pp. 146–161; Dombowsky 2004; Detwiler 1990; and Berkowitz 1995

that his 'own political judgements may be seriously flawed' (Schrift 2000, p. 222).[3] Nonetheless, they argue, his thought offers useful and important insights or 'conceptual resources' for agonistic democracy (Schrift 2000, p. 222). They do so by appealing to the agon and other concepts they believe could be useful for their agonistic conception of democracy, such as Nietzsche's perspectivism, his concept of will to power or his critique of the subject (Schrift 2000, p. 223; cf. Hatab 2002, p. 137).

A shortcoming on both sides of this debate, it seems to me, is that scholars frequently provide only a brief gloss of Nietzsche's concept of the agon before delving into a closer examination of his later works and the related concepts he introduces in them. Relatively little attention is given to Nietzsche's early works, where he first introduces the agon and explicitly discusses it.[4] And while Nietzsche's later works no doubt refer to some form of agonistic competition and struggle, he ceases to employ 'agon' as a central term of art. Indeed, only in "Homer's Contest" and "The Greek State" does Nietzsche explicitly examine the agon as the principle underlying Greek society. Given that the agonistic democrats draw on Nietzsche's concept of the agon to support their theory of agonistic democracy, his earlier works are in fact vital for understanding the way in which he conceived of the agon and its role in society. Accordingly, in this chapter, I shall examine Nietzsche's earlier writings exclusively in order to outline the agon as he understood it there. I shall then consider the extent to which the agon is compatible with, or conducive to, agonistic democracy theory. Here a further difficulty arises, namely, that Nietzsche does not himself provide a detailed historical account of the agon. Rather, in characteristic manner, he is already two steps ahead, analysing the effects and benefits of the agon on Greek culture. For this reason, I believe that particular attention should be paid to the work of Jacob Burckhardt, Nietzsche's colleague and close associate at Basel. In contrast to Nietzsche, Burckhardt offers a highly detailed treatment of the Greek

---

[3] In this chapter, I refer to the proponents of agonistic democracy as 'agonistic democrats' or 'agonists'.

[4] There are of course scholars who have examined Nietzsche's agon in great depth, both in his earlier as well as in his later works, such as Christa Davis Acampora's *Contesting Nietzsche* (2013), or Yunus Tuncel's *Agon in Nietzsche* (2013). However, in the agonistic democracy literature, Nietzsche's earlier works, including "Homer's Contest", tend to receive a rather brief treatment. David Owen (2018), for instance, only briefly defines the agon as it is outlined in "Homer's Contest" before likening it to Nietzsche's will to power (pp. 289–300); this pattern can likewise be found in the works of Schrift (2000, p. 228) and Appel (1999, pp. 33 and 140). Exceptions to this include Herman Siemens' "Nietzsche's Agon" (2013), as well as Frank Cameron and Don Dombowsky (2008, pp. 1–23 and 31–71).

agon in his lectures on "Greek Cultural History" (*Griechische Kulturgeschichte*).⁵ Moreover, Burckhardt's thoughts about the Greek aristocracy, and his rather elitist account of the agon, made a strong impact on Nietzsche's understanding of that phenomenon. His work therefore provides essential background and context for understanding Nietzsche's conception of the agon.

Focusing on Nietzsche's earlier works ("Homer's Contest" and "The Greek State" in particular) in relation to Burckhardt's thought, I argue that Nietzsche's notion of the agon is in fact quite distinct from the one endorsed by the agonistic democrats. In his earlier writings, Nietzsche was largely concerned with the cultural and artistic achievements of the Greeks, which for him were the result of agonal competition among great and noble men. His agon is thus limited to an elite group of people, and not open to society at large, as the agonists would have it. In this chapter, I shall first provide a brief overview of the agon as Burckhardt understood it and consider how this shaped Nietzsche's thinking on the subject, before proceeding to examine Nietzsche's own conception of the agon. I will then examine the central characteristics of the agonal competition envisaged by the agonistic democrats, arguing that their conception differs from Nietzsche's to the extent that it brings their reliance on his agon into question.

2 Jacob Burckhardt's Conception of the Agon

The Greek term *agôn* (from *agein*) initially referred to a 'gathering' or a 'place for gathering', from which it acquired its second meaning of 'contest', 'competition' or 'combative game', as it was common for the Greeks to hold various contests at social gatherings or meetings (Weiler 1974, p. 25). After the fifth century BCE, the latter meaning increasingly replaced the former, such that agon came primarily to refer to diverse forms of competition between individuals, as well as larger social groups in the areas of athletics, music, art, poetry and rhetoric (Siemens 2018, p. 315). The agon thus characteristically refers to a complex, broad spectrum of competitive social interactions ranging from musical and athletic contests to violent confrontations between warring peoples (Weiler 1974, p. 35). Burckhardt is perhaps the most notable defender of the view that agonal contestation permeated the entirety of Greek life. The neo-Latin term 'agonal' was in fact

---

5 Burckhardt's extensive lecture notes on Greek cultural history were posthumously edited and published by his nephew Max Oeri in 1898–1902 (Burckhardt 2014, p. i). The English translation appeared in 1963 under the title *History of Greek Culture*, and in 1999 as *The Greeks and Greek Civilization* (Sigurdson 2004, p. 10).

coined by Burckhardt in order to convey the ubiquity of the agon throughout what he refers to as the 'agonal age', that is, the period following the Doric migrations from 1050 BCE until the end of the sixth century BCE (Burckhardt 2014, p. 431). During this period, agonal competition occurred more or less automatically 'whenever many Greeks came together', and were in fact considered integral to any social gathering (Burckhardt 2014, p. 439).[6] This is highlighted by the fact that agonal competitions were even held at burial ceremonies of the nobility to ensure that a large number of guests would attend (Burckhardt 2014, p. 439). Burckhardt emphasises that agonal contestation spanned a wide range of human activities: they included athletic contests (gymnastics, fist fighting, chariot races, wrestling, discus and javelin throwing, etc.), yet, crucially, they also entailed artistic competitions (Burckhardt 2014, pp. 440 and 445). This feature is, according to Burckhardt, unique to the Greeks, who competed for greatness in the artistic and intellectual realm: in poetry, drama, music, the fine arts and philosophy.[7] The prize for agonal competition usually consisted of a wreath and, of course, lasting glory among the Greeks (Burckhardt 2014, p. 442).

Burkhardt comprehensively examined Greek culture and the agon in his lectures "On the Study of History" (*Über das Studium der Geschichte*) and "Greek Cultural History", which Nietzsche found both enjoyable and intellectually stimulating.[8] Moreover, the agon was a topic of intense, prolonged discussion be-

---

[6] 'Wenn überhaupt viele Griechen zusammenkamen, [ergaben] sich Agone ganz von Selbst [Whenever many Greeks came together, agons occurred of themselves]'.

[7] Burckhardt names Hesiod as an example, who sailed to Chalkis for the burial of Amphidamas and received a tripod as a prize for delivering the best hymn at the (agonal) funeral festivities (Burkhardt 2014, pp. 440 and 446).

[8] Nietzsche attended "On the Study of History" in 1870. His enthusiasm for these lectures is recorded in his letter to Carl von Gersdorff on November 7, 1870: 'Every week I attend one of his lectures on the Study of History, and I believe I am the only one of his sixty listeners who grasps the profundity of his line of thought with its curious breaks and twists at any point where the subject threatens to become dangerous. For the first time in my life I have enjoyed a lecture, but then it was the sort of one I myself might give when I am older' (KGB II/1, Bf. 107, my translation). About the latter he said (May 1, 1872), 'Burckhardt's summer seminar will be something singular: you are missing out on a lot, given that you can't sample it' (KGB II/1, Bf. 214, my translation). It is frequently claimed that Nietzsche did not attend Burckhardt's lectures on "Greek Cultural History", which were held six times from 1872 to 1885/1886 (see Ottmann 1987, p. 19; also Siemens 2018, p. 330). However, given Nietzsche's explicit reference to Burckhardt's lectures in the above-mentioned letters, as well as his implicit discussion of Burckhardt's lectures in his *Nachlass* from 1872–1873, it seems likely that he attended Burckhardt's class in 1872, albeit perhaps irregularly (see Labhart 2000, pp. 146–148. In any case, Nietzsche did receive detailed notes on these lectures from his former students Adolf Baumgartner (in 1874) and Louis Kelterborn (in 1875) (Labhart 2000, p. 148). Nietzsche studied and annotated these notes with great

tween them (Pletsch 1991, pp. 114–116; see also Jensen 2016, p. 7).⁹ In line with Burckhardt's thinking, Nietzsche considers sustained agonal power struggles within and between different peoples to be a tremendous catalyst for artistic and cultural flourishing. Nietzsche describes this relation in "The Greek State", where he explains that a 'mysterious connection ... between state and art, political greed and artistic creation, battlefield and work of art' formed the basis of Greek society (GSt 42; KSA 1, 772). He further conceives of the Greek agon as the 'the bloody jealousy of one town for another, one party for another, this murderous greed of those petty wars, the tiger-like triumph over the corpse of the slain enemy' (GSt 41; KSA 1, 771). Burckhardt had already outlined this relation in *The Civilization of the Renaissance in Italy* (Burckhardt 1988, pp. 23–28; cf. Ruehl 2004, p. 91), a book he published ten years prior to Nietzsche's "The Greek State". In this work, which Nietzsche studied intensely in early 1871, Burckhardt traces the cultural developments of the Renaissance to violent power struggles of the Northern Italian aristocracies (Burckhardt 1988, pp. 24–59) – a connection he later detected among the Greek nobility and its cultural productivity, and which Nietzsche likewise adopted (GSt 40; KSA 1, 771; cf. Ruehl 2004, p. 91).

According to Burckhardt, agonal contestation had no strictly utilitarian motive, that is to say, it did not have a particular aim, the way, for example, warfare does. Rather, its purpose lay in competition for competition's sake, or in 'the victory itself' (*der Sieg an sich* [Burckhardt 2014, pp. 439 and 442]). Burckhardt maintains that the ability to engage in this 'cheerful diversion' (*heiterer Zeitvertreib*) was unique to the Greek aristocracy (Burckhardt 2014, p. 439).¹⁰ In contrast to the Romans, for example, who were averse to anything 'goalless' ('nichts Zweckloses'), the Greeks relished their seemingly goalless agonal competitions (Burckhardt 2014, p. 439). Yet, for Burckhardt (and for Nietzsche, as we shall see), it was this aristocratic mentality which was directly responsible for the greatness of the Greeks. Given that the Greek aristocracy valued leisure, freedom, and the seemingly goalless contests these enabled, they were able to fulfil their potential by constantly measuring themselves against others. Burckhardt ex-

---

care. Moreover, Nietzsche and Burckhardt had already discussed the agon and many topics that were covered in "Greek Cultural History" before Burckhardt held the lectures, and they continued to do so while he held them (see Ruehl 2004, p. 91).
9 For a detailed account of Burckhardt and Nietzsche's discussions about the Greeks, see Felix Stähelin's Introduction to *Griechische Kulturgeschichte*, (1930, pp. xxiii–xxix).
10 Burckhardt distinguishes the Greek aristocracy from the majority of the population, mainly farmers who were dependent on wealthy, land-owning aristocratic families, and of course an ample slave population, who worked for the aristocracy, but also performed bureaucratic functions for the state (Burckhardt 2014, pp. 52–53).

plains that 'if at all possible, the Greek desires to be a holistic individual, he can do so by devoting himself wholly to public life, gymnastics and noble culture' (Burckhardt 2014, p. 447). In this regard, Burckhardt compares the Greeks to the aristocracy of the Italian Renaissance, insofar as both were fully developed human beings, many-sided and multi-talented (Burckhardt 2014, p. 438; cf. Sigurdson 2014, p. 118).

Moreover, as an historian of art and culture, Burckhardt is especially interested in the cultural and artistic legacy of the Greeks, and he attributes their achievements to their aristocratic social order, their widespread agonal competitions and the well-rounded education they received (Burckhardt 2014, p. 440; cf. Hinde 2000, p. 272). He therefore endorses a hierarchical ordering of society in which a small class of elite people, such as scholars and artists, can fully devote themselves to their artistic and intellectual endeavours. The cultural productivity of such great individuals depends on their privileged status in contrast to common people, who must work (Burckhardt 1982, p. 297; cf. Ruehl 2004, p. 109).[11] In this sense, the agon is, for Burckhardt, linked to the Greek aristocracy, which did not have to concern itself with labour, and therefore had the luxury to engage in their goalless competitions (Burckhardt 2014, pp. 439 and 447). These, in turn, are responsible for the vast cultural and artistic achievements of the Greeks.

So, we see that Burckhardt's notion of the agon is dependent on the Greek nobility, insofar as the agonal age was fundamentally characterised by the rule of the aristocracy. Throughout this period, aristocratic rule was widespread, and Greek society was marked by the 'unity of the aristocracy, prosperity, and excellence' (Burckhardt 2014, p. 438). The right to rule was predicated on noble birth, land ownership, skill in weaponry, as well as knowledge of the law and sacrificial rituals (things the lower classes did not possess [Burckhardt 2014, p. 438]). According to Burckhardt, it was this aristocratic class that engaged in the agon and was in turn held together by its agonal culture. He does not discuss the role of the lower classes or the slaves in relation to the agon, as they engaged in common labour, such as crafts, trade and agriculture, which was not agonal in nature and was frowned upon by the nobility (Burckhardt 2014, pp. 438 and 449). Rather, Burckhardt emphasizes that it was the aristocratic class which created the 'tradition' of the agon, for it introduced the 'actual noble agon' of chariot races, which soon attracted numerous visitors and led

---

[11] Burckhardt considers artists, poets and philosophers to be 'great individuals', but also noble spirits like Julius Caesar, or Alexander the Great. For a detailed account of Burckhardt's notion of the great individual, see Sigurdson (2014, pp. 155–160).

to the establishment of regular agonal contests, such as the games at Olympia (Burckhardt 2014, p. 441). In addition, Burckhardt maintains that other systems of governance, such as a tyranny or a democracy, hinder the Greek agon: the former by stunting the goallessness of the agon in favour of the enhancement of power, the latter by weakening the Greek aristocracy and its tradition of combat and victory (Burckhardt 2014, pp. 438 and 441). Evidently, the agon as Burckhardt understands it is contingent on the rule of the Greek aristocracy. Having broadly outlined Burckhardt's conception of the agon, I shall now examine Nietzsche's conception of it, which remains decidedly close to Burckhardt's understanding of the agon and of Greek society more generally.

3 Nietzsche's Conception of the Agon

Nietzsche discusses the agon most extensively in an unpublished essay titled "Homer's Contest", which he gave to Cosima Wagner in 1873 (Siemens 2018, p. 314).[12] Here, Nietzsche traces the excellence and artistic achievements of the ancient Greeks to their agonal culture, which is, according to him, a direct result of the envy incited by the 'good Eris' (HC 3).[13] In pre-Homeric times, Nietzsche maintains, there was only one Eris goddess. This goddess was considered evil, for she instilled the 'vein of cruelty' in man, a tiger-like desire for destruction (*Vernichtungslust* [KSA 1, 783]).[14] The desire to annihilate and engage in destructive conflict (*Vernichtungskampf* [KSA 1, 787]) is what moved the Greek world to rejoice in the fighting scenes of *The Iliad*, and compelled Achilles to mutilate grotesquely Hector's corpse (KSA 1, 784 and 789). However, alongside this evil Eris, a "good" Eris goddess, representing jealousy, resentment and envy, eventually emerged. Nietzsche explains that this Eris was perceived as good insofar as 'She drives even the unskilled man to work, and if someone who lacks possessions looks upon another who is rich, the first will hurry himself to sow and plant in the same way as the other and to order his house well' (HC 3). In

---

12 This is likewise evident in the very title of the work: "Homer's Wettkampf" (i.e., *contest*) and is further underscored in his *Nachlass*, where Nietzsche considers an alternative title for the work: 'Homer and Hesiod in competition [*Homer und Hesiod im Wettkampf*]' (KSA 7, 396).
13 Burckhardt, too, distinguishes between the good and bad Eris, tying agonal competition to the envy the good Eris provokes. However, for him, the good Eris came before the evil Eris. Moreover, in contrast to Nietzsche, the two Eris goddesses are less central to his account of the agon (Burkhardt 2014, p. 440).
14 In this chapter, I refer to both Christa Davis Acampora's translation of "Homer's Contest" (with some alterations) and to the KSA for the original text of "Homer's Wettkampf".

short, this Eris spurred people to compete with their neighbours. Here the underlying drive was not utterly to destroy one's opponent, as it was with the evil Eris, but rather to challenge one another through competition and contest (*Wettkampf* [KSA 1, 787]). Thinking of one's competitor not as someone to be destroyed – as the evil Eris would have it – but as someone against whom one struggles, and by whom one is challenged, is what led to the unparalleled greatness of the Greeks, according to Nietzsche (KSA 1, 787). Thus, agonal competition – incited by the envy of the good Eris – provided the conditions for the flourishing of Greek culture, insofar as envy and ambition were regarded as healthy motivations. This attitude drove the Greeks to compete in almost every area of their lives: education, poetry, art, etc. (KSA 1, 788–790). Like Burckhardt, Nietzsche thus highlights the pervasiveness of the agon within Greek culture.

The artistic and cultural character of the agon is also of particular importance to Nietzsche.[15] In his earlier works, Nietzsche is largely concerned with the role of art and culture in the enhancement of human existence, famously claiming that life is 'justified' only as an 'aesthetic phenomenon' (BT 5; KSA 1, 47). Regarding art and culture as primary motivations and means of redemption for existence, he repeatedly emphasises that the aim of education, the state, and society lies in the cultivation of art, culture and human greatness.[16] In "Schopenhauer as Educator", Nietzsche argues that education should primarily serve to produce rare individuals, that is, the geniuses on whom true culture depends (SE 3). He further contends that 'the goal of all culture' is the promotion of 'the procreation of genius' (SE 3). Likewise, in "Homer's Contest" he focuses on the institutions and practices of the Greeks, which led to their remarkable cultural achievements. He pays particular attention to the agonistic competition among artists and poets, arguing that even Pindar and Simonides suspiciously and jealously competed with each other: 'drama was given to the people only in the form of a marvellous wrestling of musical and dramatic artists. How wonderful! "Even the artist resents the artist!"', Nietzsche muses (HC 6).

The significance of this agonal rivalry among artists lies in the fact that 'All talent must develop by means of a struggle' (KSA 1, 789), meaning that talent is

---

15 That is not to say that Nietzsche's concern for art and culture can be traced back to Burckhardt's influence. Rather, their prioritisation of the aesthetic realm was in part due to their shared admiration for Schopenhauer's philosophy, along with his concern for art and culture. See Müller (2005, p. 58); see also Jensen (2013, p. 111).

16 Nietzsche's interest in the cultivation of great art and literature was of course a life-long project. But it was especially central to his earlier works, in contrast to his later works, where his notion of greatness includes great political men, such as Napoleon, Caesar, etc. (see BGE 256; and GM 16).

heightened through continual contestation among the best competitors. Nietzsche further explains that:

> What, for example, in Plato is of special artistic significance in his dialogues is mainly the result of a rivalry with the art of the orators, sophists and dramatists of his time, invented for the purpose of enabling him to say at last: 'Look, I too can do what my great rivals can; indeed, I can do it better than they. No Protagoras has written myths so beautiful as I, no dramatists created such an animated and fascinating whole as the *Symposium*, no orator has composed such a speech as I put down in the *Gorgias* – and now I reject it altogether and condemn all imitative art! Only the contest made me into a poet, into a sophist, into an orator!' (HC 6)

Hence, according to Nietzsche, it was the perpetual agonistic struggle which led to Plato's literary and artistic achievements: his dialogues, his myths, and his beautiful speeches were the direct result of his agonal rivalry with Protagoras, Gorgias and others. So, too, Homer's and Hesiod's hymns and lyric are for Nietzsche the outcome of agonistic competition.[17] Artistic competition was, however, by no means restricted to contemporaries. Citing Xenophanes' rivalry with Homer, Nietzsche claims that 'even a dead man can still excite a living one to burning jealousy' (HC 4). The agon could thus transcend temporal boundaries, whereby even long-deceased individuals could still incite competition. The artistic and cultural accomplishments of the Greeks were thus the result of their ubiquitous agonal competitions, which motivated the rivals to rise above one another.

Here it is important to note that, for Nietzsche, the agon is not solely an artistic endeavour. In "Homer's Contest", he outlines the political, athletic and bellicose nature of the agon as well (HC 5). So, too, in "The Greek State" he discusses the character of Greek agonal politics. The agon thus pervades all aspects of society. Nonetheless, in his view, the highest expression of the agon is the cultural and artistic one: it is *this* agon which Nietzsche repeatedly praises (KSA 7, 16 [14], 396; KSA 7, 396–398; and HC 5), as it is this form of competition which led to the cultural achievements of the Greeks (HC 5).

4 Agonal Competition among the Great

Nietzsche, like Burckhardt, is primarily concerned with agonal competition among great and noble men. He believes that the agonal contests of the Greeks

---

17 'The hymns of Homer as the *result* of *competitive singing*. As well as those of Hesiod. A singer of the Iliad, as of the Odyssey. The names Homer and Hesiod are prizes of victory' (KSA 7, 16 [5], 396, my translation).

occurred between rivals worthy of each other – that is, between Greek men comparable in their ability and greatness (HC 4–6). For Nietzsche, it is the '*great* Hellene' who 'passes on the torch of contest', such that 'every great virtue sets afire new greatness' (HC 4). Accordingly, one of the central reasons why the Greeks were able to attain such immeasurable cultural success was because they had no shortage of exceptional men, who, through continual contest, motivated each other to greatness: Plato competed with the sophists, Homer with Hesiod, and Pindar with Simonides (HC 6). In contrast, agonal competition between great artists, and consequently great art, has become rare in modern society, Nietzsche laments, due to the fact that artistic geniuses themselves have become rare: 'Artists in competition. (This is rare for us, due to a lack of greatness: Schiller and Goethe)'.[18]

In addition to fostering competition among great individuals, the Greeks ensured that the contest would remain stimulating and productive through the institution of ostracism (*ostrakismos*), that is, exiling competitors who interfered with the continual contestation due to their pre-eminence. Ostracism regulated and restricted agonal competition by preventing a single individual from achieving uncontested victory. The Greeks maintained that 'Among us no one should be the best; but if anyone is, then let him be elsewhere and among others' (HC 5). The reason for this was that perpetual contest would wither away if there was a single victor with whom no one could compete. Thus, the Greeks protected their competitions from the hegemony of a single genius by means of 'a second genius' (HC 5). The function of ostracism was to remove individuals who significantly towered over others so that the 'play of forces' could be kept alive, thereby allowing for a continual contest (KSA 1, 789).[19]

Significantly, Nietzsche holds that it was the great individuals of noble birth who were able to achieve cultural and artistic success in competition with one another. For this reason, Greek greatness and genius are intimately tied to the aristocracy. This is suggested in Nietzsche's notes of the time, in which he praises 'Contest! And that which is aristocratic, of high birth, and noble among the Greeks! [*Der Wettkampf! Und das Aristokratische, Geburtsmäßige, Edle bei den*

---

18 'Künstler im Wettkampfe. (Bei uns aus Mangel an Größen selten: Schiller und Goethe)' (KSA 7, 16 [4], 396, my translation).
19 It may seem paradoxical that the Greeks banished certain exceptional individuals, in order to continue the cultivation of great men. Yet ostracism functioned first and foremost as a stimulant, rather than a 'safety valve', for the Greeks believed that it was only natural that there should be several geniuses who incite each other to great deeds (HC 5). As soon as the great deed of a single Greek raised him beyond competition, he would become corrupt and would thus be unable to bear his fame without struggle.

Griechen!]' (KSA 7, 16 [9], 396, my translation).[20] In this respect, his account resembles Burckhardt's, who, as indicated, attributes the greatness of the Greeks in large part to their aristocratic mentality and social order. Nietzsche was intimately familiar with Burckhardt's account and in fact took it a step further, most notably in "The Greek State".[21] There he insists that the majority of society has to toil and labour 'in order to make the production of the world of art possible to a small number of Olympian men' (GSt 34; KSA 1, 767). The Olympian men of whom Nietzsche speaks are the Greek creative geniuses, men of tremendous talent who feel compelled to produce art and to create. These geniuses are themselves a sub-section of the noble class: that is to say, they are members of the Greek aristocracy who submit themselves to the hardship of creative work – in contrast to most aristocrats, who feel a disdain for work of any sort.[22] In this regard, Nietzsche's account differs slightly from Burckhardt's, in that he distinguishes between the laborious artistic work of the genius and the somewhat lighter agonal competitions in which the nobility at large engaged. Nonetheless, their accounts resemble each other, insofar as they both regard the Greek genius as the outgrowth of a strong aristocratic class, which, in contrast to the common man, need not engage in daily work and can thus pursue creative endeavours

---

[20] Nietzsche's concern with great geniuses who promote culture, and the sacrifices the majority of society must make for their sake, is likewise central to "Schopenhauer as Educator" and "The Greek State". For a longer discussion of this topic, see Frank Cameron and Don Dombowsky (2008, pp. 1–23 and 31–71).

[21] Nietzsche's familiarity with Burckhardt's work and the influence Burckhardt had on him, becomes clear in his writings of the time. For instance, Burckhardt maintains that in a sense a tyranny is preferable to a democracy, as it is able to ensure the privileged status of the intellectual and artistic elite, arguing that 'under an enduring tyranny, the arts and sciences thrive as well as or even better than in a republic; Greek culture would hardly have reached its full height without such … institutions; even Athens needed its Peisistratean age' (Burckhardt 1982, p. 297; cf. Ruehl 2004, p. 91). Burckhardt's account of Athens' debt to Peisistratus occurs almost verbatim in Nietzsche's fifth (incomplete and unpublished) essay of the *Untimely Meditations*, "We Philologists", where Nietzsche argues that 'Without the tyrant Peisistratos the Athenians would have never had tragedies', thus closely mirroring Burckhardt's claim (KSA 8, 6 [29], 109). In addition, the relation between artistic flourishing and political domination is central in "The Greek State". See also Ruehl (2004, pp. 88–92).

[22] He says: 'And even upon this height of "work" the Greek at times is overcome by a feeling that resembles shame. Plutarch, with ancient Greek instinct, once said that no youth of noble birth, on beholding the Zeus in Pisa, would have the desire to become himself a Phidias, or on Seeing the Hera in Argos, to become himself a Polyklet; and just as little would he wish to be Anacreon, Philetas or Archilochus, however much he might revel in their poetry. To the Greek artistic creativity falls just as much under the undignified conception of work as any ignoble craft. But if the compelling force of the artistic impulse operates within him, then he must create and submit himself to that hardship of work' (GSt 39; KSA 1, 766).

and engage in artistic competition (GSt 39–40; KSA 1, 766). Thus, Nietzsche's agon, like Burckhardt's, is elitist, insofar as it is tied to aristocratic men of noble birth, who, unlike the common man, can fully devote themselves to agonal competition.

It is worth noting that Nietzsche does not explicitly limit the agon to the nobility, insofar as agonal competition ran through every facet of society. The good Eris spurred every Greek to action: the carpenter envied the carpenter and even the beggar envied the beggar (HC 5). Yet this does not mean that Nietzsche cared about the agon of the common people, rather, his point is that agonal competition among all Greeks gave rise to their agonal culture, which in turn allowed for the agonal competition among the great Greeks of the aristocracy. For the agon Nietzsche praises, and the agon in which he is ultimately interested, is the one which occurred among great and noble individuals of equal ability: between Homer and Hesiod, for example (KSA 7, 16 [9], 396) – individuals who had the talent to produce great works, and it was their agon which led to the cultural success of the Greeks (HC 4). It was also these individuals who, in contrast to the lower classes, had the time, means and drive to devote themselves to artistic production and agonal competition (GSt 39–41; KSA 1, 766–769). Thus, the agon, as Nietzsche principally envisages it, occurred between creative geniuses, whom he, like Burckhardt, believed were most likely to emerge from within the Greek aristocracy, and who had the desire and ability to engage in agonistic competitions.

In sum, Nietzsche's agon entails certain key features: in line with his aesthetic and cultural concerns at the time, agonal competition has a deeply artistic nature, insofar as the rivalry among creative geniuses led to the aesthetic and literary achievements of the Greeks. For Nietzsche, this rivalry occurs between competitors of comparable greatness whose rivalry led to the impressive cultural accomplishments of the Greeks. I shall now examine the extent to which, if at all, this concept of the agon is compatible with agonistic democracy.

5 The Theory of Agonistic Democracy

Agonistic democracy relies on the concept of the agon to introduce a novel form of democracy. In contrast to Habermasian and Rawlsian theories of democracy, which are oriented towards deliberation, rational discourse and consensus as ultimate goals of a democracy, the agonists contend that absolute consensus represents an unattainable ideal and that politics will always entail 'winners' and 'losers' (Mouffe 2000, p. 15).[23] They conceive of agonistic democracy as an ongoing process of contestation in which both the political identities and the political order constitute the subject matter of political contest (Wenman 2015, p. 34; cf. Mouffe 1999, pp. 751–756). Here, agonistic political contestation can take various forms: public debate, verbal disputes, peaceful decision-making and protests, and so on – as long as the contestants refrain from violence or violations of the established democratic rule of law (Wenman 2015, p. 45 and 202–205; and Mouffe 2000, p. 34).[24] Consequently, non-violent conflict, competition and dissent function as fundamental political values. Consistent with Nietzsche's agon and the institution of ostracism, the agonists maintain that political contestants do not seek to destroy one another – as the evil Eris goddess would encourage them to do. Rather, they engage in a non-violent, 'productive' and 'stimulating' contestation (Honig 2008, pp. 209 and 229), for the agonists contend that certain political virtues are cultivated through political contestation: for example, respect for one's opponents, character and identity formation through political involvement, and so on. William Connolly, for instance, conceives of democracy as an ennobling process of individual identity-formation in relation with, and in opposition to, various different identities (Connolly 1988, p. 64; and Connolly 2002, p. xiv). This process is only possible in a pluralistic society comprised of diverse, at times oppositional, but nonetheless open-minded citizens (Connolly 2004, p. 36; and Connolly 2005, p. 123). David Owen likewise values agonistic politics as a means to cultivate nobility, albeit from a more perfectionist angle (Owen 2002, pp. 121 and 128–130). For him, the aim of agonistic politics is to cultivate 'exemplary democratic citizens' who create standards of excellence in competition with diverse individuals in a pluralistic society (Owen 2002, pp. 120 and 128). Thus, in line with Nietzsche's thought, agonistic democrats regard widespread contestation as a productive activity, which, for them, captures various viewpoints reflective of numerous positions, which in turn contribute to a politics of 'agonistic pluralism' (Mouffe 2000, p. 101).

At first glance, it would seem that Nietzsche's conception of the agon is similar to, and compatible with, agonistic democracy, in that both emphasise the

---

23 'Agonists' such as Chantal Mouffe, Bonnie Honig, and William Connolly, among others, are contemporary political theorists whose work endorses some form of agonistic democracy. Nietzsche scholars Lawrence Hatab, Alan Schrift and Hermann Siemens rely primarily on Nietzsche's thought to support the theory of agonistic democracy.

24 There is of course some debate concerning the nature and scope of what constitutes legitimate agonal contestation and the extent to which this occurs under the established democratic rule of law. Not all agonists hold that the political agon ought to occur within this framework. For an overview of this debate, see Wenman (2015, pp. 15–18 and 201–216).

productive and stimulating nature of non-destructive agonal contestation. But upon closer examination, it becomes apparent that Nietzsche's agon is dissimilar to, and in fact incompatible with, the aim and structure of agonistic democracy. For the agonists promote values, and a general framework, which starkly contradict Nietzsche's artistic and elitist conception of the agon.

6 Two Distinct Conceptions of the Agon

Firstly, agonistic democracy is incompatible with Nietzsche's elitist agon because it entails an inclusive agon, in which every political member is equally entitled to participate. The agonistic democrats replace the traditional liberal-democratic notion of equal rights with the principle of 'agonistic respect', which, according to Hatab, "'captures all the practical features of egalitarianism' without having to solve the theoretical puzzle concerning the complex ways in which human beings are equal (Hatab 2002, p. 140). Nonetheless, the principle of agonistic respect entails equal and inclusive competition between every member of society, which is not compatible with Nietzsche's exclusive agon (Hatab 2002, pp. 140–142; Connolly 1988, p. 190; and Owen 2002, p. 124). For instance, Hatab maintains that agonistic respect is based on 'political inclusiveness', whereby every position is 'given a hearing', while the participation of others is respected and heeded (Hatab 2008, p. 257). His notion of agonistic respect is predicated on inclusivity, insofar as every member of the political community shows an awareness of and respect for the fact that one's viewpoint is 'agonistically implicated with opposing viewpoints' (Hatab 2008, pp. 257 and 269). This allows the contestants to respect their counterparts on the basis of their participation in the contest (Hatab 1995, pp. 69–70). Similarly, for Connolly, agonistic respect is a civic virtue that introduces 'forbearance into the inevitable element of public conflict between alternative identities' (Connolly 1988, p. 190), whereby individual citizens strive for greater 'responsiveness to difference' (Connolly 1995, p. 69). It is practised by individuals of different faiths, identities, or creeds by virtue of their becoming aware of the 'comparative contestability' of their beliefs (Connolly 2007, p. 140). Here, different viewpoints and beliefs are not only respected, but esteemed. Accordingly, for Connolly, an equal and inclusive agon is central to a well-functioning agonistic democracy. Similarly, Alan Schrift agrees with Connolly that an 'ethos of agonistic respect amidst a world of dissonant interdependencies is crucial to the fabric of democratic politics' (Schrift 2000, p. 230; cf. Connolly 1988, p. 195). Lastly, according to David Owen, the notion of respect amounts to a 'political-recognition respect' within the framework of an 'agonistic deliberation', which refers to a 'deliberative contestation' within and over 'the terms of democratic citizenship' (Owen 2002, p. 128). Agonistic democrats therefore promote a form of agonistic competition which is committed to inclusivity and equality, insofar as every member of the political arena is respected and has a positive role to play in the agonistic political contest.

The notion of agonistic respect is incompatible with Nietzsche's elitist agon, where not everybody is given a hearing, since this is not the aim of society. Rather, as I have shown, for Nietzsche 'The proper aim of the state [is] the Olympian existence and ever-renewed procreation and preparation of genius' (GSt 45; KSA 1, 776). To this end, Nietzsche further contends that 'all other things are only tools, expedients, and factors towards realization' (GSt 45; KSA 1, 776). This is because, in contrast to the agonistic democrats, who are concerned with the intricacies of a healthy, vibrant, and egalitarian political society, Nietzsche's primary interest lies in the cultivation of cultural and artistic greatness. In his earlier works in particular, Nietzsche repeatedly emphasises that the main goal of society is to promote art and culture (SE 3; GSt 40 and 45; and HC 6), and for Nietzsche, as for Burckhardt, cultural achievements come about through continual agonistic competitions between the creative geniuses who are a sub-set of the aristocracy. The remainder of society does not participate in this agon, as these people are not competitive in terms of their ability, nor does their position within society allow them to become so. Rather, Nietzsche's agon in fact demands that the common people be excluded from the truly great, artistic agon, as their labour provides the conditions for this agon to occur in the first place. Nietzsche's notion of the agon and agonal competition is therefore distinct from that of the agonists insofar as he has an entirely different aim – the enhancement of cultural and artistic achievements within an elite group of society – in contrast to the inclusive political competition promoted by the agonistic democrats.

7 Conceptual Resources for Agonistic Democracy in Nietzsche's Thought

This incompatibility notwithstanding, the agonists rarely argue that Nietzsche's agon (and his thought in general) is itself democratic in nature, but rather that his thought 'provides conceptual resources' (Schrift 2000, p. 222) or 'offers significant advantages' (Hatab 2002, p. 137) for democracy, and is congenial to democracy in some form or other. Connolly, for instance, argues for a 'reinvigorated democracy' along the lines of Nietzsche's agonal competition (Connolly 1988, p. 105), while Hatab insists that democracy can be 'redescribed in a Nietzschean manner' (Hatab 1995, p. 2). And indeed, just because Nietzsche's agon, as he envisages it in "Homer's Contest" and "The Greek State", is not democratic, this need not imply that certain aspects of his agon and his thought in general could not be useful for agonistic democracy. For instance, Nietzsche's notion that struggle and competition are vital for human flourishing seems to capture a fundamental aspect of human interaction, which underlies any form of political order, whether democratic or not. This line of reasoning is pursued by Hermann Siemens, among others, who is not strictly speaking an agonist, but who has written extensively on Nietzsche's agon and its contested status in relation to agonistic democracy.[25] Siemens focuses on Nietzsche's agon – which he understands as involving a kind of 'agonal hatred', rather than respect (Siemens 2013, pp. 92–94) – and the will to power, which for him underlies the agon, to argue that Nietzsche's thought can be conducive to a democratic equality (Siemens 2013, pp. 95–97). Siemens argues that the agonal power struggle 'issues in affirmative ideals that exclude domination' in favour of 'an equilibrium of powers' that is 'compatible with a democratic politics of identity' (Siemens 2013, p. 95). Thus, for Siemens, agonal hatred is conducive to democracy, insofar as agonal enemies do not seek to dominate or subjugate one another, but rather to develop and flourish through their productive agonal struggle (Siemens 2013, p. 94).

In like manner, Schrift maintains that Nietzsche's thought offers helpful conceptual resources for agonistic democracy (Schrift 2000, p. 222), and argues that Nietzsche 'could have been' a democrat (Schrift 2000, p. 230). Citing *Beyond Good and Evil*, *Twilight of the Idols* and other later works (Schrift 2000, pp. 229–231),[26] Schrift points out that Nietzsche's notions of conflict and struggle can help one understand democracy in agonistic terms, whereby one *struggles* for 'freedom' and 'independence' (Schrift 2000, p. 232). He maintains that Nietzsche's thought 'here *fits nicely* with the idea of democracy as always "to come"' (Schrift 2000, p. 232), that is, as something for which one struggles by means of the agon. Thus, according to Schrift, Nietzsche's conception of the agon is useful for democracy insofar as it shows how democracy can be con-

---

25 Siemens himself criticises the agonistic democrats for ignoring 'Nietzsche's hostility to modern democracy', and their notion of agonistic respect, which he regards as a softened 'appropriation' of Nietzsche's agon (Siemens 2013, p. 83). Nonetheless Siemens, like the agonistic democrats, essentially focuses on those agonistic principles in Nietzsche's thought which are useful for democracy or a politics of equality. It is for this reason that I group him with the agonists here.

26 Schrift refers primarily to Nietzsche's later writings, including BGE 200, 208, and 257; TI Skirmish, 39; and GS 293, etc.

ceived as an ongoing, yet productive struggle against our worthy enemy', our democratic competitor (Schrift 2000, p. 233). Yet this struggle is not something we must regrettably endure; instead, it is 'the only means by which we will be able to engage in democratic political practices' (Schrift 2000, p. 232). Thus, like Siemens, Schrift contends that Nietzsche's notions of struggle and productive conflict serve to ground and enrich our understanding of agonistic political competition. In this sense, then, it seems that Nietzsche's thought can be conducive to democracy if we refer to his notion of stimulating, productive competition, or the agonal principle of the good Eris, according to which one refrains from destroying one's competitor.

Nonetheless, as I have shown, if we focus on the way in which Nietzsche himself understood and discussed the agon in his earlier works, it seems quite clear that his agon is incompatible with the one endorsed by the agonistic democrats.[27] Indeed, both Schrift and Siemens rely on Nietzsche's later works, construing the agon along the lines of Nietzsche's will to power (Siemens 2013, p. 95) and the pathos of distance (Schrift 2000, p. 228), whereby two opposing, struggling forces compete with one another – a principle they then expand to struggle between different democratic factions. However, a discussion of the relations between Nietzsche's will to power and the agon lie beyond the scope of this chapter.[28] For our purposes, it is relevant that Nietzsche's agon, as he explicitly discusses it, is unambiguously tied to the Greek aristocracy. Against this background, I return to the question posed at the beginning of this chapter, namely, the extent to which Nietzsche's agon is compatible with, or conducive to, agonistic democracy. I have shown that Nietzsche conceives of the agon as an elitist institution, whose function was to bring about cultural greatness, a task to which only a small number of artistic geniuses, who were themselves the product of the Greek aristocracy, were capable of rising. Nietzsche was not interested in the agon of the common people, and therefore did not think of the agon within a democratic framework. That being said, it is possible to maintain that Nietzsche's thought is conducive to agonistic democracy, insofar as certain principles he introduces (such as his notion of stimulating conflict and forbearance from destruction among competitors) may function as useful and insightful concepts that underlie agonistic democracy. One can, therefore, as Schrift, Siemens and other agonistic democrats do, examine certain aspects of Nietzsche's agon and discern the elements which are fruitful for democracy.

---

27 The same can be said of the agonal principle present in Nietzsche's later works, it seems to me. This, however, is a topic for another paper.
28 For a thorough treatment of Nietzsche's notion of competition, struggle and the agon in relation to his later thought see Siemens (2018, pp. 314–332) and Owen (2018, 299–313).

However, this stance is far less tenable in relation to Nietzsche's own concept of the agon, as it actually appears in his early writings, and in relation to Burckhardt's work. Consequently, the question arises to what extent agonistic democracy is still grounded in Nietzsche's concept of the agon. This, then, raises a further question: why rely on Nietzsche to uphold notions of democratic agonism when there are other thinkers, such as Foucault, Arendt, and Deleuze and Guattari, for instance, whose notion of the agon in fact presupposes democracy,[29] and whose thought would thus be likely to provide much stronger grounds for agonistic democracy? Given that Nietzsche's concept of the agon is not compatible with agonistic democracy, it would be more useful to seek conceptual resources in the agon of other thinkers.

Bibliography

Acampora, Christa Davis (2013): *Contesting Nietzsche*. Chicago: The University of Chicago Press.
Appel, Fredrick (1999): *Nietzsche Contra Democracy*. Ithaca: Cornell University Press.
Arendt, Hannah (1981): *Vita activa oder vom tätigen Leben*. München: Piper.
Berkowitz, Peter (1995): *Nietzsche: The Ethics of an Immoralist*. Cambridge: Harvard University Press.
Burckhardt, Jacob (1964): *History of Greek Culture*. Edited and translated by Palmer Hilty. London: Constable Publishers.
Burckhardt, Jacob (1982): *Über das Studium der Geschichte*. Edited by Peter Ganz. München: Beck.
Burckhardt, Jacob (1988): *Die Kultur der Renaissance in Italien: Ein Versuch*. Edited by Konrad Hoffmann. Stuttgart: A. Kröner.
Burckhardt, Jacob (1999): *The Greeks and Greek Civilization*. Edited by Oswyn Murray and translated by Sheila Stern. New York: St. Martins Press.
Burckhardt, Jacob (2014): *Griechische Kulturgeschichte: Alle Vier Bände in einem Buch*. Berlin: Michael Holzinger.
Cameron, Frank, and Don Dombowsky (Eds.) (2008): *Political Writings of Friedrich Nietzsche: An Edited Anthology*. Basingstoke: Palgrave Macmillan.
Connolly, William E. (1988): *Political Theory and Modernity*. Ithaca: Cornell University Press.

---

[29] In his essay "The Subject and Power", Foucault speaks of a mutual 'agonal' power struggle in politics (Foucault 2000, p. 344). Arendt speaks of the 'fiercely agonal spirit' of the Greek *polis* and the drive to distinction as a political ideal (Arendt 1981, p. 187, my translation). As a matter of fact, Arendt's view of the agon was likewise shaped by her study of Burckhardt, however, her agon is not elitist as Nietzsche's (Nullmeier 2000, p. 172; see also Wenman 2015, p. 48). Meanwhile, Deleuze and Guattari conceive of the agon as rivalry among free men, 'as the rule of a society of friends' (Deleuze and Guattari 1994, p. 9).

Connolly, William E. (1995): *The Ethos of Pluralization*. Minneapolis: Minnesota University Press.
Connolly, William E. (2004): *The Ethos of Pluralization*. Minneapolis: Minnesota University Press.
Connolly, William E. (2002): *Identity/Difference: Democratic Negotiations of Political Paradox*. Minneapolis: University of Minnesota Press.
Connolly, William E. (2007): *Democracy, Pluralism and Political Theory*. Edited by Samuel Allen Chambers and Terrell Carver. London: Routledge.
Deleuze, Gilles, and Félix Guattari (1994): *What is Philosophy?* Translated by Graham Burchell and Hugh Tomlinson. London: Verso.
Detwiler, Bruce (1990): *Nietzsche and the Politics of Aristocratic Radicalism*. Chicago: University of Chicago Press.
Dombowsky, Don (2004): *Nietzsche's Machiavellian Politics*. Basingstoke: Palgrave Macmillan.
Foucault, Michel (2000): "The Subject and Power". In: Michel Foucault: *Power: The Essential Works of Michel Foucault 1954–1984*, vol. 3, pp. 326–349. Edited by James D. Faubion and translated by Robert Hurley. New York: New Press.
Hatab, Lawrence J. (2008): *Nietzsche's On the Genealogy of Morality: An Introduction*. Cambridge: Cambridge University Press.
Hinde, John Roderick (2000): *Jacob Burckhardt and the Crisis of Modernity*. Montreal: McGill-Queens University Press.
Honig, Bonnie (2008): *Political Theory and the Displacement of Politics*. Ithaca: Cornell University Press.
Jensen, Anthony K. (2013): *Nietzsche's Philosophy of History*. Cambridge: Cambridge University Press.
Jensen, Anthony K. (2016): *An Interpretation of Nietzsche's "On the Uses and Disadvantage of History for Life"*. London, New York: Routledge.
Labhart, Lukas (2000): "*pro ommaton poiein:* Nietzsches Teilübersetzung von Aristoteles' *Rhetorik*, Zur Lehre vom Stil, und *Also sprach Zarathustra*". In: Renate Reschke (Ed.): *Nietzscheforschung*, Band 7, pp. 141–157. Berlin: Walter de Gruyter.
Mouffe, Chantal (1999): "Deliberative Democracy or Agonistic Pluralism?" In: *Social Research* 66 No. 3, pp. 745–758.
Mouffe, Chantal (2000): *The Democratic Paradox*. London: Verso Books.
Müller, Enrico (2005): *Die Griechen im Denken Nietzsches*. Berlin: Walter de Gruyter.
Nietzsche, Friedrich (1980): *Sämtliche Werke, Kritische Studienausgabe in 15 Bänden*. Edited by Giorgio Colli and Mazzino Montinari. München: Deutscher Taschenbuch Verlag.
Nietzsche, Friedrich (1986): *Sämtliche Briefe, Kritische Studienausgabe in 8 Bänden*. Edited by Giorgio Colli and Mazzino Montinari. München: Deutscher Taschenbuch Verlag.
Nietzsche, Friedrich (1996): "Homer's Contest". In: *Nietzscheana*, vol. 5, pp. 1–8. Translated by Christa Davis Acampora. Urbana: North American Nietzsche Society.
Nietzsche, Friedrich (1997): "Schopenhauer as Educator". In: *Untimely Meditations*, pp. 125–194. Edited by Daniel Breazeale and translated by R. J. Hollingdale. Cambridge: Cambridge University Press.
Nietzsche, Friedrich (1999): *The Birth of Tragedy and Other Writings*. Edited by Raymond Geuss and Ronald Spiers and translated by Ronald Spiers. Cambridge: Cambridge University Press.

Nietzsche, Friedrich (2008): "The Greek State". In: Frank Cameron and Don Dombowsky (Eds.): *Political Writings of Friedrich Nietzsche: An Edited Anthology*, pp. 38–46. Basingstoke: Palgrave Macmillan.
Nullmeier, Frank (2000): *Politische Theorie des Sozialstaats*. Campus: Frankfurt.
Ottmann, Henning (1987): *Philosophie und Politik bei Nietzsche*. Berlin, New York: Walter de Gruyter.
Owen, David (2002): "Equality, Democracy, and Self-Respect: Reflections on Nietzsche's Agonal Perfectionism". In: *The Journal of Nietzsche Studies* 24. No. 1, pp. 113–131.
Owen, David (2018): "Constructing the Agon". In: Paul Katsafanas (Ed.): *The Nietzschean Mind*, pp. 298–313. New York: Routledge.
Pletsch, Carl (1991): *Young Nietzsche: Becoming a Genius*. New York: Simon and Schuster.
Ruehl, Martin A. (2004): "Politeia 1871: Young Nietzsche on the Greek State". In: Paul Bishop (Ed.): *Nietzsche and Antiquity: His Reaction and Response to the Classical Tradition*, pp. 79–97. Rochester: Camden House.
Schrift, Alan D. (2000): "Nietzsche for Democracy". In: *Nietzsche Studien* 29. No. 1, pp. 220–230.
Siemens, Hermann (2018): "Nietzsche's Agon". In: Paul Katsafanas (Ed.): *The Nietzschean Mind*, pp. 314–333. New York: Routledge.
Siemens, Hermann (2013): "Reassessing Radical Democratic Theory in the Light of Nietzsche's Ontology of Conflict". In: Keith Ansell Pearson (Ed.): *Nietzsche and Political Thought*, pp. 83–106. London: Bloomsbury.
Sigurdson, Richard (2014): *Jacob Burckhardt's Social and Political Thought*. Toronto: University of Toronto Press.
Stähelin, Felix (1930): "Einleitung des Herausgebers". In: Jacob Burckhardt: *Griechische Kulturgeschichte*, pp. xxiii–ix. Stuttgart: Deutsche Verlags-Anstalt.
Tuncel, Yunus (2013): *Agon in Nietzsche*. Milwaukee: Marquette University Press.
Weiler, Ingomar (1974): *Der Agon im Mythos: Zur Einstellung der Griechen zum Wettkampf*. Darmstadt: Wissenschaftliche Buchgesellschaft.
Wenman, Mark (2015): *Agonistic Democracy: Constituent Power in the Era of Globalisation*. Cambridge: Cambridge University Press.

Sven Gellens
Agonal Human Rights: A Re-evaluation of Democracy Through Nietzsche's Physio-Psychology of Will to Power

Abstract: This chapter addresses how the ontology of will to power, by means of its agonal understanding of society, can transform Human Rights into a physio-psychological framework for human thriving, allowing great individuals to come into being through maximising diversity and safeguarding democracy from the dangers of uniformisation. It argues that through his ontology of will to power, Nietzsche is able to present an integrated idea of humankind, characterised by a recursive interaction between the environment, the intellect and the body and delivers a philosophical ontology to ground Human Rights on a different basis than within a universal, rationalistic or liberal framework. If Human Rights could be backed by scientific findings on basic human needs, this would allow us to remodel Human Rights as preconditions for actualising the (maximum) range of human possibilities.

1 Introduction

The meaning Nietzsche allocates to 'democracy' goes through different developmental stages in his oeuvre. The early Nietzsche infuses *The Birth of Tragedy* (1872) with 'a profoundly anti-democratic message' (Ruehl 2004, p. 88), a message also found in his unfinished and only posthumously published essay "The Greek State" (1871) (Ansell-Pearson 1994, pp. 73–74). By the time of the publication of *Human, All Too Human* (1878), Nietzsche has abandoned Plato's hierarchical template of societal organisation (Brobjer 2004, p. 252), a key inspiration for his anti-democratic political views, and exchanged this political inspiration for that of the emancipatory promises of democracy, albeit focusing more on its prospective possibilities, rather than its actuality (Siemens 2009, pp. 22–25). The later Nietzsche, especially after 1886 (the year *Beyond Good and Evil* was published) returns to his initial critique of democracy as negating diversity and differences and promoting uniformisation (van Tongeren 2000, p. 141 and Siemens 2009, p. 29).

Research on whether Nietzsche is a political thinker or not has gone through different stages as well. First, Nietzsche was seen as a weak constructive political thinker, later on, the idea that his views do contribute to modern political theory won ground (Siemens 2000, p. 59 and Siemens and Roodt 2008, p. 1). Contemporary commentators explicitly focus on the constructive parts of Nietzsche's political philosophy in order to (re)construct a conception of democratic organisation and place his critiques of democracy within this constructive framework (see, e.g., Mouffe 1993, pp. 127–128; Owen 2002, p. 128; Patton 2014; and Ikuta 2017). Despite all this, there is still no detailed exploration of human rights in Nietzsche's constructive philosophy. In this chapter, I attempt to show that by transposing human rights into the ontological framework of the will to power they can function as preconditions for human flourishing, thus contributing to the deliberate formation (*Bildung*) of great individuals and counteracting the intrinsic tendency of cultural development to level out differences. As such, I will demonstrate why human rights deserve a place in contemporary Nietzsche research and determine which conceptual innovations his philosophy holds for democratic political theory.

In section 2, I will provide a brief overview of the will to power as a productive ontology to describe our current super-diverse societies. In section 3, I argue from a Nietzschean perspective that an agonal structure of conflicting powers can be a more sustainable approach to democracy than traditional rationalistic-liberal theories. In the fourth section, I make use of the agonal framework to reframe human rights from a universal presupposition of moral innateness into physio-psychological needs that maximise diversity and safeguard against the danger of cultural levelling. Finally, in section 5, I briefly outline how agonal human rights can realise a politics of difference, preserving a pathos of distance in citizens that functions inclusively rather than exclusively, and, as such, allows for individuals to thrive.

2 The Will to Power and the Agon

In *The Birth of Tragedy*, Nietzsche understands nature as 'chaos'. The gradual specification of this view will lead up to the theory of will to power, which finds its first crystallised form in 1884.[1] Jean Granier describes the identification of the world-view of the will to power with a form of chaos, as follows:

---

[1] 'Will to power, … was clearly formulated for the first time in *Z[arathustra]* in 1884' (van Tongeren et al. 2004, p. 643, my translation). Before 1884, Nietzsche wrote many texts in which he describes the world as chaos, e.g., GS 109: 'The astral order in which we live is an exception; this order and the considerable duration that is conditioned by it have again made possible the exception of exceptions: the development of the organic. The total character of the world, by contrast, is for all eternity chaos, not in the sense of a lack of necessity but of a lack of order, or-

> This primitive text of nature has absolutely nothing in common with a 'thing in itself', with an intelligible 'being', or with a 'cosmos'. It is not a book written by a superior intelligence, it is what Nietzsche calls *chaos*. The primitive text of nature is thus *the chaotic being that manifests itself as a significant process.* (Granier 1977, p. 137)

As Nietzsche had already mentioned in 1882, there is one particular constraint on our understanding of the world or nature as chaos. We have to be cautious when claiming death to be the opposite of life: 'The living is only a form of what is dead, and a very rare form' (GS 109 and 110). The organic is a special form of the inorganic as a higher level of complexity, which evolved out of the less complex inorganic. As Rüdiger Grimm notes, 'By pointing out similarities in what we have heretofore called "inorganic" or dead matter and living beings, [Nietzsche] has shown them to be fundamentally similar, differing only in degree of complexity and quantity of power' (Grimm 1977, p. 15).

The will to power is a (speculative) proposition advanced to resolve the question what the nature of the individual or the organism actually is.[2] Therefore, it does not concern an inner source of (teleological) development. It refers to quanta of power, the primary drive of which is appropriation – or assimilation. Nietzsche's references to exploitation as the primary function of everything living (BGE 259) should be understood, contrary to what Keith Ansell-Pearson claims (1997, 105), not as an expression of aristocratic radicalism, but as a different way of saying that the primary drive of life is appropriation.[3] In other words, when viewed in terms of the will to power, all living beings can be seen as (maximally) manipulating their inner and outer environment:

> life itself is essentially a process of appropriating, injuring, overpowering the alien and the weaker, oppressing, being harsh, imposing your own form, incorporating, and at least, the very least, exploiting, – but what is the point of always using words that have been stamped with slanderous intentions from time immemorial? Even a body within which (as we pre-

---

ganization, form, beauty, wisdom, and whatever else our aesthetic anthropomorphisms are called' (GS 109).

2 Cultural evolution has brought this issue once again to the fore by reinvigorating the concept of group selection. See Robert Wilson, who investigates the notion of 'organism' in his *Genes and the Agents of Life* and proposes an alternative way of conceiving organisms in the sense of contemporary philosophy of biology, where 'Species are not simply comprised of individuals but are themselves individuals, not natural kinds' (Wilson 2005, p. 11).

3 '"Exploitation" does not belong to a corrupted or imperfect, primitive society: it belongs to the *essence* of being alive as a fundamental organic function; it is a result of genuine will to power, which is just the will of life – Although this is an innovation at the level of theory, – at the level of reality, it is the *primal fact* of all history. Let us be honest with ourselves to this extent at least!' (BGE 259).

supposed earlier) particular individuals treat each other as equal (which happens in every healthy aristocracy): if this body is living and not dying, it will have to treat other bodies in just those ways that the individuals it contains refrain from treating each other. It will have to be the embodiment of will to power, it will want to grow, spread, grab, win dominance, – not out of any morality or immorality, but because it is alive, and because life is precisely will to power. (BGE 259)

This ontology of will to power enables Nietzsche to present an integrated idea of humankind, characterised by a recursive interaction between the environment, the intellect and the body. An individual is not isolated, but always embedded in an immediate biological and socio-cultural environment. Herman Siemens explains the *agon* as the communal setting in which individuals function (Siemens 2000, pp. 59 and 70). Lawrence Hatab describes it in the following way:

The *agōn* can be seen as a ritualized expression of a world-view expressed in so much of Greek myth, poetry, and philosophy: the world as an arena for the struggle of opposing (but related) forces.... Nietzsche argues that the *agōn* emerged as a *cultivation* of more brutal natural drives in not striving for the annihilation of the Other, but arranging contests that would test skill and performance in a competition. Accordingly, agonistic strife produced excellence, not obliteration, since talent unfolded in a struggle with competitors.... The Greek *agōn* is a historical source of what Nietzsche later generalized into the dynamic, reciprocal structure of will to power. And it is important to recognize that such a structure undermines the idea that power could or should run unchecked, either in the sense of sheer domination or chaotic indeterminacy. (Hatab 2014, p. 115)

The idea of the agon presents communal life as the social instantiation of the pluralistic ontology of the will to power. With this idea, we can see the benefits of the will to power for political theory. An agonal structuration of society embeds individuals in the communal in order to stimulate or even boost plurality and diversity, not to sacrifice the individual completely to universal and uniform modes of conduct. As such, it generates the conditions for individuals to be free: in an agonal society, individuals demarcate the public space of freedom in their interaction with others and are not subjugated to external laws that determine freedom, as is the case in a Kantian framework, in which freedom and justice are generated by laws and hence do not emerge from the autonomous individual (Siemens 2000, 71, 75).[4] This constructive, pluralistic view makes the will to

---

[4] With this remark on the necessity of laws to establish freedom, I limit myself to commenting on Kant's account of outer freedom and not inner willing. Arthur Ripstein reminds us that we should not confuse independence and autonomy in Kant's writings. Kant establishes an idea of equal freedom of all people based on their universal inherent right of freedom. Violation of this independence from the constraint of others is wrongdoing and requires a right or enforce-

power a more productive ontology with which to describe our current super-diverse societies than traditional rationalistic-liberal approaches (Geldof, Schrooten and Withaeckx 2017). In what follows, I will discuss briefly how the description of super-diverse societies can help us develop a form of democracy that better concords with contemporary societal needs.

3 Agonal Democracy

Siemens makes it very clear that when Nietzsche is talking about democracy he rarely does so in the context of a discussion of governmental forms. Rather, democracy is about a general disposition or set of values or ideals. As a form of state, it is instrumental to Nietzsche's main focus, namely, culture, for this is the vehicle for 'enhancing and extending human possibilities' (Siemens 2009, p. 21). A first contribution of the will to power to democracy as an organisational form of social interactions and structures is most clearly the understanding of individuals as bundles of complex power relations. The ontology of the will to power asserts that nothing else exists than powers that constantly manipulate their environment. The concept of diversity – in evolutionary terms we would call this 'variation' – is an adequate reflection of reality, both in the individual and in the social domain. The plural nature of diversity is not an abnormality that has not yet been integrated in an identity. Identities are 'appearance[s] that things are the same' (LNB 26; KSA 11, 36 [23], 26). The specific advantage provided by this agonal world-view is that the identities of others, or their differences that cannot immediately be ascribed to fixed identities, are not problematic in themselves, but are a reflection of the plural nature of being. The will to power also ontologically collapses the individual and the social environment when it comes to diversity. Having constructive contact with others requires similar competences as dealing with one's own (inner) diversity. Classical political

---

able obligation to remove or prevent hindrances to freedom, exactly in an attempt to safeguard the reciprocal limits on freedom: 'The universal Principle of Right is not a principle for self-legislation' (Ripstein 2009, p. 359). Hannes Unberath explains this as follows: 'The state's worth exclusively stems from fulfilling the basic function, assuring the citizens of a maximum degree of external freedom, of independence from constraint by others, under universal laws. This prerogative of freedom places Kant at the very heart of classical liberalism' (Unberath 2008, p. 367). Autonomy is *the idea* of the imposition of the supersensible moral law present in all humans on to the sensible world and concerns, contrary to independence, a positive idea of freedom, situated in the noumenal world and applicable to the sensible through moral action (Kant 1996, 5:43)

theories, which understand individuals as rational actors, have a tendency to focus on the identity of actors in society, making it more difficult truly to accept the otherness of other actors, or of the self. Both kinds of otherness can often only be endured when they can be integrated to a certain degree into the identity of the majority. For example, deliberative democrats consider rational deliberation aimed at reaching a consensus to be the requirement for an attitude of reciprocity and mutual respect between parties (Farrelly 2004, p. 141). Parties who do not follow this striving for consensus and mutual respect position themselves outside the scope of democratic functioning. This rationalistic approach to participation fails to acknowledge that it is itself an expression of a particular configuration of power relations. The sought-after objectivity of logical argumentation and decision-making does not lie outside the practices of the deliberation itself. Other modes of participation, for example, by children, illiterates, people with different cultural frameworks, etc., can thus only be understood as marginal or problematic. By contrast, an agonal view will always have a constructive outlook on the participation of marginalised or minority groups, as they are merely forces among others.

This brings us to the second advantage of the agonal framework for democracy, namely, that differences and conflicts are the key characteristics of nature. Conflicts contain unique generative powers, which are left untouched in a rationalistic framework focused on consensus or harmony. An agonal framework by contrast suggests that conflicts in themselves are not problematic, for example, as loci of the absence of democracy. Rather, the lack of coping strategies in the citizens of a society is problematic. Forces that are possibly destructive need to be transformed into constructive agonal powers that stimulate cultural production (Siemens 2000, p. 72). Citizens should therefore be empowered to demonstrate differential activities and to cope with conflicts. This is not gratuitous. A society needs to achieve this or it will succumb to the inherent danger in the development of culture in societies, namely, mediocrity as a social force, reinforced by the fragile nature of humans and their urge to communicate (see also GS 354), stabilising the community's cultural landscape and levelling out group members. In *Beyond Good and Evil* 268, Nietzsche further writes:

> assuming that needs have only ever brought people together when they could somehow indicate similar requirements and similar experiences with similar signs, then it follows, on the whole, that the easy *communicability* of needs (which ultimately means having only average and *base* experiences) must have been the most forceful of the forces that have controlled people so far. People who are more alike and ordinary have always been at an advantage; while people who are more exceptional, refined, rare, and difficult to understand will easily remain alone, prone to accidents in their isolation and rarely propagating. Immense countervailing forces will have to be called upon in order to cross this natural, all-

too-natural progressus in simile, people becoming increasingly similar, ordinary, average, herd-like, – increasingly *base!* (BGE 268)

This intrinsic tendency of societies to make the members of a cultural group more similar, base and herd-like finds its expression in the democratic tendencies of nineteenth-century European States. When, in *Beyond Good and Evil* 202, Nietzsche calls 'the democratic movement ... the heir to Christianity' (BGE 90), it is precisely to denote the process of levelling that lies at the heart of the socialist and Christian calls for equality for all, and should not be ascribed exclusively to his political disparagement of any mass-movement; for instance, when he says, in *Beyond Good and Evil* 203:

> We who have a different faith –, we who consider the democratic movement to be not merely an abased form of political organization, but rather an abased (more specifically a diminished) form of humanity, a mediocritization and depreciation of humanity in value: where do *we* need to reach with our hopes? (BGE, 91)

This threat to cultural development is addressed as a case study in section 262 of *Beyond Good and Evil*, where Nietzsche discusses the question of breeding an aristocratic community. He draws the reader's attention to a cultural evolutionary process parallel to what is now known as 'adaptive radiation',[5] claiming that the emergence of a culture depends on the successful survival of groups in unfavourable ecological niches. Curtailing cultural variation among group members stabilises the group and thus engenders a 'sturdy' type of human. Referring to a cultural group or community as a 'species', Nietzsche reiterates the incorporation of cultural change into a model of biological evolution:

> A *species* originates, a type grows sturdy and strong, in the long struggle with essentially constant *unfavorable* conditions. Conversely, people know from the experience of breeders that species with overabundant diets and, in general, more than their share of protection and care, will immediately show a striking tendency towards variations of the type, and will be rich in wonders and monstrosities (including monstrous vices). You only need to see an aristocratic community (such as Venice or an ancient Greek polis) as an organization that has been established, whether voluntarily or involuntarily, for the sake of *breeding:* the

---

5 The importance of adaptive radiation has become widely accepted by now in evolutionary theory and refers to evolutionary specialisations, displaying great ecological and morphological diversity, arising from a common ancestor. Michael Alfaro explain it as follows: 'An ecological adaptive radiation is the rapid evolution of morphological differences and species richness in a closely related group .... Adaptive radiations are spurred when a lineage gains access to ecological opportunity – the potential to diversify into new niches along a similar ecological axis' (Alfaro 2014, p. 594).

> people living there together are self-reliant and want to see their species succeed, mainly because if they *do not* succeed they run a horrible risk of being eradicated. Here there are none of the advantages, excesses, and protections that are favorable to variation. The species needs itself to be a species, to be something that, by virtue of its very hardness, uniformity, and simplicity of form, can succeed and make itself persevere in constant struggle with its neighbours or with the oppressed who are or threaten to become rebellious. (BGE 262)

Reducing variation to one specific, successful type promotes qualities that will be passed on to the later generations as virtues. This accumulative – 'voluntarily or involuntarily' – breeding of younger generations gradually adapts individuals or groups to their environment.[6] Educating a 'sturdy' type is hence no longer experienced as necessary for survival, but it becomes 'a form of *luxury*, ... an archaic *taste*' (BGE 262). When the community no longer needs to struggle continuously with unfavourable conditions, the pace of cultural change turns 'tropical' and cultural variation becomes abundant. This brings forth a completely new set of moralities and individuals:

> Variation, whether as deviation (into something higher, finer, rarer) or as degeneration and monstrosity, suddenly comes onto the scene in the greatest abundance and splendor; the individual dares to be individual and different. At these turning points of history, a magnificent, diverse, jungle-like growth and upward striving, a kind of *tropical* tempo in the competition to grow will appear alongside (and often mixed up and tangled together with) an immense destruction and self-destruction. This is due to the wild egoisms that are turned explosively against each other, that wrestle each other 'for sun and light', and can no longer derive any limitation, restraint, or refuge from morality as it has existed so far. It was this very morality that accumulated the tremendous amount of force to put such a threatening tension into the bow: – and now it is, now it is being 'outlived'. (BGE 262)

The old morality provided an appropriate answer to unfavourable conditions in the past; 'being outlived', it failed to provide successful answers to the changing conditions newer generations face. These generations, characterised by more cultural variation, were urged to provide new answers, new moralities. At such moments of transition in the development of a community, cultural accumulation engenders an expenditure of cultural variants, which Nietzsche designates as 'the genius of the race' (*das Genie der Rasse*):

---

[6] Cf. *Beyond Good and Evil* 188, which explains morality as a form of long-term compulsion. See also Gerd Schank's claim that 'Nietzsche uses Darwinian terms, such as "selection", ... with a new metaphorical meaning ... the word "*Züchtung*" in Nietzsche's usage means "education", not biological breeding' (Schank 2003, p. 243).

> The 'individual' is left standing there, forced to give himself laws, forced to rely on his own arts and wiles of self-preservation, self-enhancement, self-redemption. There is nothing but new whys and hows; there are no longer any shared formulas; misunderstanding is allied with disregard; decay, ruin, and the highest desires are horribly entwined; the genius of the race overflows from every cornucopia of good and bad; there is a disastrous simultaneity of spring and autumn, filled with new charms and veils that are well suited to the young, still unexhausted, still indefatigable corruption. (BGE 262)

This genius of the race, which expresses itself as an abundant eruption of creativity, threatens – but thereby also rejuvenates – the stability of the community. To control this threat, a conservative reflex sees to it that it is not the exceptional individuals, those steering the future development of the community, who thrive and multiply in these chaotic times, but rather the 'mediocre'. As Nietzsche goes on to explain:

> Danger has returned, the mother of morals, great danger, displaced onto the individual this time, onto the neighbor or friend, onto the street, onto your own child, onto your own heart, onto all of your own-most, secret-most wishes and wills: and the moral philosophers emerging at this time – what will they have to preach? These sharp observers and layabouts discover that everything is rapidly coming to an end, that everything around them is ruined and creates ruin, that nothing lasts as long as the day after tomorrow except one species of person, the hopelessly *mediocre*. (BGE 262)

The sustainability, to use contemporary terminology, of a society is therefore concerned with finding a continuously shifting balance between rejuvenating and stabilising forces.[7] According to Siemens (2000) and Hatab (2014), Nietzsche believes that the agonal structure of conflicting powers can itself generate an immanent concept of non-violent justice[8] – but where do human rights fit in? Human rights can maximise diversity,[9] become a safeguard against the danger of cultural levelling resulting in the uniformisation of citizens, and hence a strong model for a self-sustaining society. Let us take a closer look at this.

---

7 Also see Gellens and Biebuyck (2012) for an extensive account of this interplay between conservative and innovative forces in *Human, All-Too-Human*.
8 With this claim, Siemens and Hatab overlook the rhetoric of violence and annihilation in Nietzsche's later works; hence I do not share their position. This issue, however, goes far beyond the scope of this chapter. For the most recent *status quaestionis*, see Pearson (2018).
9 See, e.g., the *Universal Declaration of Human Rights*, article 2 with its focus on entitlement to all rights and freedoms for everyone, without distinction of any kind; article 3 as right to life, liberty and security of a person; and article 19 on freedom of opinion and expression.

4 Human Rights

The *Universal Declaration of Human Rights* (1948) has been criticised predominantly for its claim to be *universal* (see, e.g., Ignatieff 2001, p. 78 and Rorty 1993, p. 255). I will illustrate various points of criticism of it from three perspectives. The first one is a historical perspective: when western societies reacted with astonishment to the killing of hundreds of pro-democracy demonstrators in Tiananmen Square in 1989, the Chinese government claimed that the western culture of human rights was 'imperialism in disguise'; and this was followed up in one way or another by other Asian and African countries (Goodale 2018, p. 598). The second perspective is a conceptual one: Amartya Sen, in his book *The Idea of Justice* (2009), demonstrates that the position of human rights in contemporary discourse is paradoxical. On the one hand, Sen sees what he calls a revolution of rights across the world, that is, opposing injustices such as torture, discrimination, etc., stimulated by the very concept of human rights. Yet, on the other hand, the endorsement of human rights cannot be grounded rationally since they concern a particular expression of a western (individualistic) culture. The third perspective is a psychological one: some researchers have tried to demonstrate that humans have an innate psychological capacity to 'identify and respond to rights' (Bradley Kar 2013, p. 147). To describe this view from the perspective of human rights would be to say that these rights are descriptions of the basic needs with which everyone can identify.[10] Charles Helwig, Martin Ruck and Michele Peterson-Badali claim that most convincing findings of the last twenty-five years of psychological research on morality show that children already possess 'a conceptualisation of civil liberties as universal rights', and they believe this to be 'independent of social convention or law':

> Several aspects of reasoning about civil liberties and rights were identified that appear to be continuous across development in childhood and adolescence. These include the conceptualization of civil liberties as universal rights believed to be independent of social convention of law, and their association with rationales that historically have been invoked to justify and support these rights in philosophical and political theorizing. (Helwig, Ruck and Peterson-Badali 2014, p. 50)

Abraham Maslow's (1954) famous pyramidal hierarchy of needs, although heavily contested and invalidated with regard to its hierarchical claims, seems to hold with reference to basic human needs. In other words, everyone has a series of

---

[10] For a brief overview of the line of argumentation behind the 'basic needs' argument for human rights, see Griffin (2008, pp. 87–90).

simultaneous needs: physiological needs, such as food, shelter and sleep; safety needs, such as health, personal and emotional safety; social belonging, such as friendship, intimacy and family; esteem, such as self-confidence and freedom; and self-actualisation, as in reaching one's highest potential. Building on the scientific corpus of psychology, one can detect a trend aimed at validating the existence of *universal* human rights as a judiciary translation of basic human needs (Brown 2013 and McFarland, Webb and Brown 2012).

This last, briefly summarised perspective demonstrates an interesting trend, especially in light of Nietzsche's plea for a transformation of psychology into depth-psychology. Nietzsche's genealogy not only aims at understanding the mental by mapping the information-processing devices of the brain responsible for conscious and unconscious activities, it also purports to understand higher complex processes as synergetic offshoots of lower complex levels. Consequently, he calls this version of psychology 'physio-psychology' (*Physio-Psychologie*), whose goal is to grasp psychology 'as morphology and the *doctrine of the development of the will to power*' (BGE 23). If human rights could be backed with scientific findings on basic human needs, this would allow a remodelling of human rights as preconditions for actualising the (maximum) range of human possibilities. In this manner, I agree with Paul Patton when he claims that:

> Nietzsche thus provides a framework for the manner in which a consistent naturalism might approach the question of justification for particular rights, namely by way of the historical and contingent character of the bases of those rights. The particularity of moral rules and the rights to which they give rise does not, however, mean that they lack normative force. Rather, it implies that this should be understood in terms of the feelings, beliefs and values that effectively motivate actions on the part of the agents concerned. (Patton 2008, pp. 486–487)

The issue at stake is that of a new paradigm in which human rights are to be given a foundation in basic human needs by an empirical approach, rather than a philosophical or theological one. John Mikhail argues that this foundation can be found in 'the cognitive and brain sciences, broadly construed' (Mikhail 2012, p. 164). I would argue, from a Nietzschean perspective, that these empirical endeavours, although very interesting as representing a paradigm shift, are still constrained, often implicitly, by a philosophical understanding of human beings as primarily rational agents.[11] As James Griffin shows, the (philosophical) frame-

---

11 See John Mikhail's and Herbert Gintis' contributions to Goodman, Jinks and Woods (2012). Mikhail provides an overview of the *status quaestionis* (Mikhail 2012, pp. 160–202); and Gintis claims that human rights are a direct, culturally evolved exponent of human nature: 'Human

work constituting human rights has not changed substantially since the eighteenth century:

> The eighteenth century came to an end with comprehensive lists of what were meant to be the most basic or important natural or human rights.... The notion of human rights that emerged by the end of the Enlightenment – what can reasonably be called the Enlightenment notion – is the notion we have today. There has been no theoretical development of the idea itself since then.... The idea is still that of a right we have simply in virtue of being human, with no further explanation of what 'human' means here. (Griffin 2008, p. 13)

Nietzsche's philosophy, as I will show, holds the promise of a paradigm shift in this debate. The will to power, as a framework that maximises plurality and diversity, can reframe human rights and align them with scientific findings on the conditions for human thriving. We can find this naturalistic or scientific reasoning in Nietzsche's writings, epitomised in the figure of the physicist. In section 335 of *The Gay Science*, entitled "Long live physics!",[12] Nietzsche clarifies that 'intellectual conscience' (*intellectuelle[s] Gewissen* or *Redlichkeit*) impels us to accept the pedigree of a judgement. Individuals should therefore refrain from making universalist claims from within the position of their 'opinions and value judgements'. Just like the physicist, who studies what is 'necessary and lawful in the world', the individual must become a 'learner' and 'discoverer' so as to become a creator of judgements that are deliberate self-expressions of their own individuality, but that could parallel findings that can be scientifically validated (GS 335).[13] Nietzsche's philosophy, especially from *Daybreak* onwards, understands science as an instrument that will not yield knowledge of a true external

---

rights, in this conception, are powers that individuals inherently demand and that intrinsically serve their personal needs for dignity, autonomy, and personal authority' (Gintis 2012, p. 136).

12 'Your judgement, "that is right" has a prehistory in your drives, inclinations, aversions, experiences, and what you have failed to experience; you have to ask, "how did it emerge there?" and then also, "what is really impelling me to listen to it?" ... We, however, want to *become who we are* – human beings who are new, unique, incomparable, who give themselves laws, who create themselves! To that end we must become the best students and discoverers of everything lawful and necessary in the world: we must become *physicists* in order to be creators in this sense – while hitherto all valuations and ideals have been built on *ignorance* of physics or in *contradiction* to it' (GS 335).

13 Pierre Hadot claims that ancient philosophers practiced physics as a spiritual exercise in order to achieve serenity and peace of mind (Hadot 2008, p. 131). Nietzsche's use of physics may be seen as an implicit reference to these ancient philosophical traditions. This does not mean that Nietzsche merely relocates an ancient *topos* to the nineteenth century but infuses it with the meaning of empirical verification. Instead, it suggests that modern science can become a gay science, contributing to the self-realisation of individuals.

reality, but a taxonomy of how our organs or senses perceive and construct the world.[14] Nietzsche's biologism thus creates an opportunity to insert human rights into a constructive political philosophy. Let me illustrate this with an example.

There is a connection between article 25 of the *Universal Declaration of Human Rights*, on the one hand, namely, the 'right to a qualitative living standard, including food, clothing, shelter and medical care for all people', and, on the other, the theory of attachment which demonstrates that a healthy attachment between a child and (a small number of) primary care-givers is crucial for long-term mental and physical health. This shows that article 25 does not need to be grounded on a universal presupposition of human nature or moral innateness. The empirically well-established presence of this critical period – approximately the first three years of infancy – can function as a formal criterion beneficial to the development of the self-actualisation of individuals.[15] This physio-psychological need, as we can describe it in Nietzschean terminology, subtends the human right in question and any possible laws based on it. Claims about moral innateness or preferred values cannot be deduced from the formal criterion that grounds the human right, because the physio-psychological need describes the possibility of content, rather than the actuality of content. The need allows for a plurality of actualisations of specific contents in the form of laws (in different societies) or values (as expressed by multiple individuals or preferred by various communities) and can therefore not be made synonymous to them but must precede them.

I will finish this point with a brief discussion of Nietzsche's analysis of the criminal as subject to an excluding form of socialisation, in *Twilight of the Idols*,

---

14 As stated in *The Gay Science* 112, science is 'an attempt to humanize things as faithfully as possible; we learn to describe ourselves more and more precisely as we describe things and their succession' (GS 113). See also *Daybreak* 48, where he identifies science with the dictum 'know yourself'. These references anticipate a possible critique of grounding human rights on a scientific basis, by arguing that Nietzsche contests the idea that science is value-free. I do not argue that science needs to be value-free, but rather that it can contribute to human thriving to a greater degree than other more intuitive approaches. The scientific method is the most robust method of gathering and establishing knowledge humankind has utilised so far. Such a description of science, and more particularly, such an application of science, is not opposed to Nietzsche's views on science.

15 Attachment theory has also been criticised for privileging only a western middle-class perspective and ignoring how child care is practiced in much of the rest of the world. Although a valid critique, I do not propose attachment theory as a moral or normative principle, but rather as a formal criterion for personal development, and refrain from commenting on the various modalities wherein a healthy attachment can be actualised.

Skirmishes, 45. He describes this process as one in which 'society' (*die Gesellschaft*) ostracises the virtues, as expressions of the strongest drives, of an individual, producing a contradictory inner condition, in which the feelings of individuals turn against their own instincts, which have a negative social connotation. Nietzsche clarifies that, for instance, the criminal's character is the result of a situation of inner contradiction between his or her most foundational forces, prohibiting growth into a higher – or more constructive – version of him or herself. This section illustrates that it is crucial for individuals to be in an environment that allows for constructive contact with their own plural instinctual constitution. Nietzsche does not ground this on a set of moral standards or values, but describes it as a formal criterion that aims at maximising personal development, for the criminal him or herself is only discussed insofar as his or her case can be generalised to all 'people [*Naturen*] who, for some reason, lack public approval, who know that they are not seen as beneficial or useful, – that Chandala feeling that you are not seen as equal but as excluded, unworthy, polluted' (TI Skirmishes, 45). This approach to human rights would allow their transformation into basic principles for the maximal actualisation of different individuals and, as such, would work as preventative measures for the inherent danger of cultural development, namely, the uniformisation of individuals.

Before we delve deeper into what agonal human rights might look like, I would like to briefly address a possible criticism of the tension between human rights and suffering. Nietzsche clearly states in *Beyond Good and Evil* 225, that 'The breeding of suffering, of *great* suffering – don't you know that only *this* breeding created every enhancement in humanity so far?' (BGE 225). This is why Nietzsche mostly argues against 'democratic taste and its modern ideas' (BGE 44), namely, because this modernity considers suffering as something that needs to be abolished. From an agonal point of view, by contrast, a world without suffering seems absurd and is therefore not something a position based on agonal human rights would take up. Besides this ontological reading, section 225 of *Beyond Good and Evil* also allows for a historical interpretation. When Nietzsche claims that suffering has been the sole cause of elevation, this does not entail that it should continue – there could be more effective ways of transforming people, and not all types of suffering are conducive to human greatness. This short digression shows, then, that, when it comes to human thriving, Nietzsche's position on suffering is complex and multi-facetted. In *Beyond Good and Evil* 62, for example, he argues against 'religions *of the suffering*', as they 'have preserved too much of *what should be destroyed*' (BGE 62), but mainly this digression demonstrates that an agonal framework can be a valid human rights approach.

5 Agonal Human Rights

An agonal perspective, rooted in the will to power, can transform the conceptual framework of human rights, reconceiving their claim to universality, and transforming their indivisibility and interdependence into structuring principles of power-relations and organisations whose aim is to allow individuals to thrive. From this perspective, human rights would not promote equality for all, but equal opportunities for becoming who you are, that is, true equity. Siemens (2009, pp. 25–28 and 30) and Vladimir Jelkić (2006, p. 400) point out that Nietzsche is not concerned with obtaining an anti-democratic aristocracy or a pyramidal society, as the laws of Manu advocate (cf. A 57). He wants to implant into human society a natural order that provides room for the pathos of distance (BGE 257), a feeling of rank (*Rangordnung*), epitomised by great individuals who are the experimenters, and not the sole beneficiaries – a natural order that can bring forth greatness.

As we read in section 62 of *Beyond Good and Evil*, the problem with the 'European of today' is that they are a 'herd animal, something well-meaning, sickly, and mediocre', who live by the moral principle of equality, in the section referred to by the Christian motto of 'equality before God', which 'has prevailed over the fate of Europe so far' (BGE 57). In its propagation of the morality of 'herd animals', as Nietzsche describes it in section 202 of *Beyond Good and Evil*, 'the *democratic* movement is the heir to Christianity' (BGE 202). The apex of this uniformisation of individuals is, according to Nietzsche, reached in the figure of the socialist:

> in fact, [socialists] are one and all united in thorough and instinctive hostility towards all forms of society besides that of the *autonomous* herd (even to the point of rejecting the concepts of 'master' and 'slave' – ni dieu ni maître reads a socialist formula –); they are united in their dogged opposition to any special claims, special rights, or privileges (which means, in the last analysis, that they are opposed to *any* rights: since when everyone is equal, no one will need 'rights' anymore –). (BGE 202)

This opposition to socialism goes back to section 473 of *Human, All-Too-Human*, published eight years before *Beyond Good and Evil*, for the main reason that socialism 'aspires to the annihilation of the individual' (HH 473). The cultural levelling of diversity and the promotion of the becoming-similar of individuals prompts Nietzsche to consider socialism along similar lines as despotism. This striving for equality is responsible for the disappearance of the 'different orders of rank and chasms in rank between different people' as a guiding principle for living together in European society (BGE 62), whereas this principle – the pathos of distance – is the motor of development for a higher people or great individuals. Nietzsche understands the pathos of distance as an elementary natural law: 'Caste-order, the most supreme, domineering law, is just the sanction of a natural order, natural lawfulness par excellence – chance and "modern ideas" have no sway over it' (A 57). To emphasise the ineluctable necessity of diversity for life as well as for individual development, Nietzsche presents it as a biological law. In doing so, he also underlines that the pathos of distance is biologically grounded and thus he counters the "democratic" tendencies towards equality with the argument that diversity and plurality are conditions of life.

Importantly, human rights, placed within an agonal framework as demonstrated here, would realise a politics of difference by maximising diversity, thus preserving a pathos of distance in citizens that functions inclusively rather than exclusively (see also van Tongeren 2000, p. 149). Moreover, agonal human rights would safeguard democracy against the tyranny of the masses or, as it is called in *Beyond Good and Evil* 202, the '*autonomous* herd' (BGE 90). I hope to have shown (albeit not for all human rights – to do so would go beyond the scope of this chapter), that Nietzsche's philosophy holds constructive conceptual potential for innovations that can contribute to democratic political theory. I also hope to have shown that insofar as Nietzsche can be considered a positive democratic thinker, this requires those involved in research on his work to take a closer look at how his account relates to research on human rights. The secular institution of human rights makes them essential to the infrastructure of democracy, although intellectual support for their abstract universality no longer has any momentum, as Claude Lefort has clarified in *Democracy and Political Theory* (1988, pp. 37–41). Nietzsche's ontology of will to power as an agonal physio-psychology can be an impetus for this paradigmatic shift in thinking about human rights, and conversely human rights themselves can open up a new – and perhaps unsuspected – area of Nietzsche-research, thus enabling their mutual enhancement.

Bibliography

Alfaro, Michael (2014): "Key Evolutionary Innovations". In: Jonathan Losos (Ed.): *The Princeton Guide to Evolution*, pp. 592–598. Princeton, Oxford: Princeton University Press.

Ansell-Pearson, Keith (1994): *An Introduction to Nietzsche as Political Thinker*. Cambridge: Cambridge University Press.

Ansell-Pearson, Keith (1997): *Viroid Life: Perspectives on Nietzsche and the Transhuman Condition*. London, New York: Routledge.

Bradley Kar, Robin (2013): "The Psychological Foundations of Human Rights". In: Dinah Shelton (Ed.): *The Oxford Handbook of International Human Rights*, pp. 104–155. Oxford: Oxford University Press.
Brobjer, Thomas (2004): "Nietzsche's Wrestling with Plato and Platonism". In: Paul Bishop (Ed.): *Nietzsche and Antiquity*, pp. 241–259. Rochester: Camden House.
Brown, Chris (2013): "Human Rights and Human Nature". In: Cindy Holder and David Reidy (Eds.): *Human Rights: The Hard Questions*, pp. 23–38. Cambridge: Cambridge University Press.
Farrelly, Colin (2004): *Introduction to Contemporary Political Theory*. London: SAGE Publications.
Geldof, Dirk, Mieke Schrooten and Sophie Withaeckx (2017): "Transmigration: The Rise of Flexible Migration Strategies as Part of Superdiversity". In: *Policy and Politics* 45. No. 4, pp. 567–584.
Gellens, Sven, and Benjamin Biebuyck (2012): "The Mechanism of Cultural Evolution in Nietzsche's Genealogical Writings". In: *Philosophy Today* 56. No. 3, pp. 309–326.
Gintis, Herbert (2012): "Human Rights: An Evolutionary and Behavioral Perspective". In: Ryan Goodman, Derek Jinks and Andrew Woods (Eds.): *Understanding Social Action, Promoting Human Rights*, pp. 135–159. Oxford: Oxford University Press.
Goodale, Mark (2018): "The Myth of Universality: The UNESCO 'Philosophers' Committee' and the Making of Human Rights". In: *Law and Social Inquiry* 43. No. 3, pp. 596–617.
Goodman, Ryan, Derek Jinks and Andrew Woods (Eds.)(2012): *Understanding Social Action, Promoting Human Rights*. Oxford: Oxford University Press
Granier, Jean (1977): "Nietzsche's Conception of Chaos". In: David Allison (Ed.): *The New Nietzsche: Contemporary Styles of Interpretation*, pp. 135–141. Cambridge: MIT Press.
Griffin, James (2008): *On Human Rights*. Oxford: Oxford University Press.
Grimm, Rüdiger (1977): *Nietzsche's Theory of Knowledge*. Berlin, New York: de Gruyter.
Hadot, Pierre (2008): *N'oublie pas de vivre: Goethe et la tradition des exercices spirituels*. Paris: Albin Michel.
Hatab, Lawrence (2014): "Nietzsche's Will to Power and Politics". In: Manuel Knoll and Barry Stocker (Eds.): *Nietzsche as Political Philosopher*, pp. 113–134. Berlin, New York: de Gruyter.
Helwig, Charles, Martin Ruck and Michele Peterson-Badali (2014): "Rights, Civil Liberties, and Democracy". In: Melanie Killen and Judith Smetana (Eds.): *Handbook of Moral Development*, pp. 46–70. New York, London: Psychology Press.
Ignatieff, Michael (2001): *Human Rights as Politics and Idolatry*. Princeton: Princeton University Press.
Ikuta, Jennie (2017): "'Nothing is really equal': On the compatibility of Nietzsche's egalitarian ethics and anti-democratic politics". In: *Constellations* 24. No. 3, pp. 339–355.
Jelkić, Vladimir (2006): "Nietzsche on Justice and Democracy". In: *Synthesis Philosophica* 42. No. 2, pp. 395–403.
Kant, Immanuel (1996): *Critique of Practical Reason*. In: *Practical Philosophy*, pp. 133–272. Edited and translated by Mary J. Gregor. Cambridge: Cambridge University Press.
Killen, Melanie, and Judith Smetana (Eds.) (2014): *Handbook of Moral Development*. 2nd ed. New York, London: Psychology Press.
Lefort, Claude (1988): *Democracy and Political Theory*. Translated by David Macey. Minneapolis: University of Minnesota Press.

Maslow, Abraham (1954): *Motivation and Personality*. New York: HarperCollins.
McFarland, Sam, Matthew Webb and Derek Brown (2012): "All Humanity is my Ingroup: A Measure and Studies of Identification with all Humanity". In: *Journal of Personality and Social Psychology* 103. No. 5, pp. 830–853.
Mikhail, John (2012): "Moral Grammar and Human Rights: Some Reflections on Cognitive Science and Enlightenment Rationalism". In: Ryan Goodman, Derek Jinks and Andrew Woods (Eds.): *Understanding Social Action, Promoting Human Rights*, pp. 160–202. Oxford: Oxford University Press.
Mouffe, Chantal (1993): *The Return of the Political*. London: Verso.
Nietzsche, Friedrich (2001): *The Gay Science*. Edited by Bernard Williams and translated by Josephine Nauckhoff. Cambridge: Cambridge University Press.
Nietzsche, Friedrich (2002): *Beyond Good and Evil: Prelude to a Philosophy of the Future*. Edited by Rolf-Peter Horstmann and Judith Norman and translated by Judith Norman. Cambridge: Cambridge University Press.
Nietzsche, Friedrich (2003): *Writings from the Late Notebooks*. Edited by Rüdiger Bittner and translated by Kate Sturge. Cambridge: Cambridge University Press.
Nietzsche, Friedrich (2007a): *The Anti-Christ*. In: *The Anti-Christ, Ecce Homo, Twilight of the Idols and Other Writings*, pp. 1–68. Edited by Aaron Ridley and Judith Norman and translated by Judith Norman. Cambridge: Cambridge University Press.
Nietzsche, Friedrich (2007b): *Twilight of the Idols*. In: *The Anti-Christ, Ecce Homo, Twilight of the Idols and Other Writings*, pp. 153–230. Edited by Aaron Ridley and Judith Norman and translated by Judith Norman. Cambridge: Cambridge University Press.
Nietzsche, Friedrich (2007c): *Daybreak: Thoughts on the Prejudices of Morality*. Edited by Maudemarie Clark and Brian Leiter and translated by Reginald John Hollingdale. Cambridge: Cambridge University Press.
Nietzsche, Friedrich (2008): *Human, All Too Human: A Book for Free Spirits*. Translated by Reginald John Hollingdale. Cambridge: Cambridge University Press.
Owen, David (2002): "Equality, Democracy, and Self-Respect: Reflections on Nietzsche's Agonal Perfectionism". In: *Journal of Nietzsche Studies* 24. No. 1, pp. 113–131.
Patton, Paul (2008): "Nietzsche on Rights, Power and the Feeling of Power". In: Herman Siemens and Vlasti Roodt (Eds.): *Nietzsche, Power and Politics*, pp. 471–488. Berlin, New York: de Gruyter.
Patton, Paul (2014): "Nietzsche on Power and Democracy circa 1876–1881". In: Manuel Knoll and Barry Stocker (Eds.): *Nietzsche as Political Philosopher*, pp. 93–112. Berlin, New York: de Gruyter.
Pearson, James S. (2018): "Nietzsche's Philosophy of Conflict and the Logic of Organisational Struggle". PhD diss., Universiteit Leiden. Available at https://openaccess.leidenuniv.nl/bitstream/handle/1887/60927/James%20Pearson.%20Nietzsche%27s%20Philosophy%20of%20ConflictAmended.pdf?sequence=3.
Ripstein, Arthur (2009): *Force and Freedom: Kant's Legal and Political Philosophy*. Cambridge: Harvard University Press.
Rorty, Richard (1993): "The Priority of Democracy to Philosophy". In: Gene Outka and John Reeder (Eds.): *Prospects for a Common Morality*, pp. 254–278. Princeton: Princeton University Press.
Ruehl, Martin (2004): "'Politeia' 1871: Young Nietzsche on the Greek State". In: Paul Bishop (Ed.): *Nietzsche and Antiquity*, pp. 79–97. Rochester: Camden House.

Schank, Gerd (2003): "Race and Breeding in Nietzsche's Philosophy". In: Nicholas Martin (Ed.): *Nietzsche and the German Tradition*, pp. 237–244. Berlin: Peter Lang.
Sen, Amartya (2009): *The Idea of Justice*. London: Allen Lane.
Siemens, Herman (2000): "Agonale Gemeenschappen van Smaak". In: Marc van den Bossche and Maurice Weyembergh (Eds.): *Links Nietzscheanisme*, pp. 59–80. Eindhoven: Damon.
Siemens, Herman (2009): "Nietzsche's Critique of Democracy (1870–1886)". In: *Journal of Nietzsche Studies* 38. No. 1, pp. 20–37.
Siemens, Herman, and Vlasti Roodt (2008): "Introduction". In: Herman Siemens and Vlasti Roodt (Eds.): *Nietzsche, Power and Politics*, pp. 1–36. Berlin, New York: de Gruyter.
Unberath, Hannes (2008): "Freedom in the Kantian State". In: *Annual Review of Law and Ethics* 16, pp. 321–367.
Van Tongeren, Paul (2000): "Vriendschap en Politiek". In: Marc van den Bossche and Maurice Weyembergh (Eds.): *Links Nietzscheanisme*, pp. 135–150. Eindhoven: Damon.
Van Tongeren, Paul, Gerd Schank and Herman Siemens (2004): *Nietzsche-Wörterbuch*, vol. 1. Berlin, New York: de Gruyter.
Wilson, Robert (2005): *Genes and the Agents of Life*. Cambridge: Cambridge University Press.

Part 5 **Plurality, Affirmation, Immanence**

Marinete Araujo da Silva Fobister
Nietzsche and a Politics of Difference: Realising the Forces in the Margins

Abstract: Recent political events in the West have resulted in increased polarisation. Nietzsche warned about nihilism, the 'uncanniest of guests'. Vattimo argues that nihilism brings disorientation, therefore we should cultivate complexity to live affirmatively with difference. This chapter aims to explore whether Nietzsche's view of the will to power can support the recognition of the value of the forces present in migrants. As an example, it discusses the experience of children of ethnic minorities in the 'London Effect'. It argues that through exposure, bodies may produce what can be called an 'excess of force', and by suffering difference we may recognise the reorganisation of forces being produced in our time. Moreover, the chapter considers earthy aspects embedded in the production of forces that are often overlooked, hence revealing a reality that escapes the current dualistic, metaphysical approach.

1 Introduction

The world has been experiencing significant socio-political and cultural changes in the last few years, particularly due to issues relating to immigration, and this has raised concerns about the future and how society can respond to these changes. The return to nationalism and the anti-immigration discourse associated with it are some of the symptoms generated by the current polarisation, as well as a nostalgia for an idealised view of the past. Hence, part of society is seeking a return to the past, to old, devalued values, in an attempt to project them into the future.

Nietzsche diagnosed nihilism as an event affecting the West ever since modernity and explained that this would involve the devaluation of the highest values of western society. He forecast 200 years of nihilism until the West would overcome this event. However, nihilism can take on very different forms (e.g., passive, active, complete [cf., e.g., WP 3, 22 and 23]).[1] Nietzsche also warned that the acknowledgement and the experience of nihilism would bring uncertainty and have corrosive effects on western culture.

---

1 See also Vattimo (2006, ch. 9).

Nietzsche invites us to overcome the limitations of the framework provided by a metaphysical interpretation of the world. This framework is still present in the West and reinforces a kind of binary view which may prevent aspects of a greater complexity beyond binary oppositions from being taken into account. It is necessary to move away from ideas of us/not-us (the morality of the slave, inclusion/exclusion) towards a valuing of differences in their micro-realisations, in order to embody the complexity of the world in a general economy of the whole. We must not forget that, according to Nietzsche's analysis, this dualistic interpretation of the world is gradually weakening, although it still pertains in culture but in a lesser form. Its presence can still be detected in the wave of nostalgia that seems to be present in the socio-political scenario in the West and in the language that brings such events into presence.

Due to its ambiguous nature, if nihilism involves – as Nietzsche understands it– on the one hand, the devaluation of the highest values which the West used to rely upon, it may also bring with it opportunities to overcome the limitations of the old metaphysical schemas. As he states, 'the horizon lies open again' (GS 343). Therefore, from a Nietzschean perspective on current events, and considering his diagnosis of nihilism, some questions should be raised. It is important to question the complexity of the events of our time, paying particular attention to the kind of language we still use to discuss them, in order to bring to light their multiple contexts and forces. According to Nietzsche, the world is a complex plurality of forces in constant struggle (see, e.g., WP 1067), consequently, in order to discuss some of the salient events of our time, it is crucial to investigate the forces generating them.

This chapter aims to explore how Nietzsche's ideas can provide fresh perspectives on the growth of nationalism the consequent perceived crisis brought about by migration in Europe. We may remember that during the nineteenth and twentieth centuries, Europe experienced a movement of net emigration. However, this scenario has changed since the end of World War II, in the 1950's, when it started experiencing net immigration.[2] In addition, migration is now part of in-

---

[2] According to information released by the European Commission, the nature of migration in Europe has changed, particularly after the World War II. From the middle of the twentieth century, Europe has steadily become a place for net immigration, including intra-regional movements of refugees and displaced people due to World War II; flows of workers from Southern Europe and Ireland to Industrial hubs in Central and Western Europe; immigration and reverse migration in relation to colonies and ex-colonies; immigration from Turkey and North Africa due to working agreements signed by Switzerland, Germany and Austria and the settlement of their families; from the 1970s onward, immigration of low-skilled workers from North Africa, Asia and Turkey due to a demand for services and domestic sector work; migrants from Eastern Europe

ternational policy and one of the aspects recognised by the UN initiative "Transforming Our World: The 2030 Agenda for Sustainable Development".³ Hence, because of the challenges that migration brings, it is now recognised internationally as a major event of our time, and we must seek answers to the question of how to live affirmatively in this complex scenario. I intend to look at possible ways of acknowledging the values and the complexity present in the current wave of immigration – which bring different groups and ways of life together – from the perspective of the will to power. The focus will be on the educational attainments of the children of recent migrants. In this chapter, I am trying to gesture towards forms of difference beyond the dualisms with which the global event of migration is usually conceived. I suggest that the forces involved may have been misrecognised or excluded when a binary metaphysical interpretation of the world is used in the attempt to make sense of current events. I will discuss how Nietzsche's ideas can inspire the cultivation of new evaluations, and the recognition and reorganisation of marginal forces that often escape attention, by discussing how the will to power can be understood as a kind of "engine" that can be found in all forms of life, and thus how a politics of difference can always already be taking place.

I will concentrate on the so-called 'London Effect'. This concept was examined in a research project conducted by Simon Burgess (2014), which indicated that pupils of minority ethnic backgrounds, specifically recent migrants, in London had a better attainment at secondary school than students in other parts of the country. Although the London Effect focuses chiefly on the school attainment of children in London and compares it with other parts of England, I believe that my analysis of these results can also be relevant to understanding similar aspects of migration in other big European cities. I will discuss these results in light of Nietzsche's perspective of the will to power and discuss some aspects

---

seeking asylum in Western Europe; from the 1990s consolidation and expansion of the EU freedom of movement; new waves of immigration from North and Central Africa, Latin America and Asia to Southern Europe; geopolitical unrest in the Middle East and North Africa increasing the number of asylum seekers to Southern Europe trying to reach Northern European countries. The refugee crisis which began in 2015 has seen a surge in the number of refugees and migrant workers trying to reach Europe. For more detailed information, see https://migrationdataportal.org/regional-data-overview/europe.

3 This Agenda is a global initiative that aims to eradicate poverty, to strengthen gender equality, to build peaceful and inclusive societies, to protect human rights and to protect the planet and its natural resources. Specific recognition for migrants can be found in its item 29 where it mentions their positive contribution to inclusive growth and sustainable development. Further information can be found at https://sustainabledevelopment.un.org/post2015/transformingourworld.

of it by way of my interpretation of geophilosophy.[4] I argue that human beings, when continuously exposed to a new language and a new geographical and physical space, may produce what may be termed an 'excess of forces'. By 'force' I mean something like an energy that arises in the struggle that bodies are going through in the current movement of migration into and within Europe. In discussing bodies, I follow Deleuze's Nietzsche-inspired point that 'every relationship of forces constitutes a body – whether it is chemical, biological, social or political' (Deleuze 1983, p. 40). By excess of forces, I here mean the surplus energies that bodies are actively producing in the current scenario of migration, and that are expanding beyond what reactive perspectives can grasp. There is thus a circular movement between all kinds of forces constituting bodies and bodies producing (excess) forces, and both processes should be borne in mind.

This excess, arising in the process of relocating, is not usually taken into account in discussions of migration or of its implications for education. I will suggest that the acknowledgement of these forces and of the struggles accompanying their production could offer a different way of looking beyond the categories by which migrants are often framed, and this could shed some light both on different ways of life. Nietzsche's ideas of forces and will to power are appropriate here because they allow a reframing of the way migrants are often categorised, opening up possibilities for revealing other complexities pertaining to them. I will conclude by arguing that experiencing difference can offer a new way of understanding the struggles and excess of forces currently being produced by them, when these forces are often being systematically concealed by the reactive views embedded in the *ressentiment* still frequently used to make sense of the world.

2 Migration and Nihilism: Different Kinds of Homelessness

Nietzsche understands transcendent values as those values of western society, established since Socrates and Plato, that are based on a metaphysical understanding of the world, which privileges what is eternal, fixed and beyond the world of experience. However, Nietzsche understands the death of God as the historical moment in which these values entered into decline during modernity, such that values have lost their basis but still persist in western society, albeit in

---

[4] I started this discussion in the paper "The Moderate Man and the Weak God: Nietzsche, Vattimo, and Nihilism Today", delivered at the 23rd International Conference of the Friedrich Nietzsche Society, in Bath, 2017.

devalued forms. Hence, in nihilism, the West is experiencing the dissolution of its foundations. As a result, there is a feeling of homelessness and nostalgia, a sense of being in exile or not being at home in one's own home. According to Jeffrey Metzger, 'The fact that nihilism is "the uncanniest of all guests" ... suggests that [it] makes our home itself foreign and alien. [Its] chill figure is not simply unwelcome; it renders us homeless' (Metzger 2009, p. 1). This feeling of homelessness brought about by nihilism may affect people in different ways and may impact our emotions in engaging with others and with the world.

Instances of this can be seen in education, too, as the educational system is increasingly embedded in the nihilism of our time, not least because of the focus on a teleological view of education. As one expert puts it, 'School effectiveness and school improvement have become mini-industries in educational research with their preoccupations with the management of teaching and learning and of an increasingly technical conception of education' (Blake et al. 2000, p. 3). This outcomes-based orientation of education may give rise to certain emotions, such as fear, hopelessness, anxiety and anger, among others, due to the lack of certainty and of foundation that nihilism brings with it. Whereas this unfolding of nihilism alone cannot explain the current rise of these emotions, it provides another potentially revealing angle. Such focus on attainment in education detaches people from the plurality and complexity of the world which they inhabit,[5] hence perpetuating the feeling of homelessness. This insight into how schools reinforce the nihilistic characteristics of our time will inform part of my analysis of the struggles migrant children are facing today.

It seems that nihilism, as discussed by Nietzsche, has brought to the West a common feeling of not being at home, not only through the feeling of nostalgia, but also through the fact that it has dissolved the deceptive feeling of certainty that a metaphysical interpretation of the world had hitherto offered. These devalued foundations still persist in the culture, particularly in language, which is still imbued with metaphysical, dualistic and binary interpretations. Language enforces policies and practices in dealing with people, particularly disadvantaged ones, for instance, migrant children. Nietzsche criticised this way of seeing the world:

---

5 Vasco d'Agnese explains this through neoliberal forces in education. He states that 'priceless educational aims are put at risk. Reducing persons to their economic value and features tames students' critical agency, imaginative vision, ability to concretely recognize plurality and differences, and talent to imagine the world other than it is by channelling these dispositions toward predefined ends; thus these qualities lose their potential to open new paths' (d'Agnese 2019, p. 699).

> The general imprecise way of observing sees everywhere in nature opposites (as, e.g., 'warm and cold') where there are, not opposites, but differences of degree. This bad habit has led us into wanting to comprehend and analyse the inner world, too, the spiritual-moral world, in terms of such opposites. An unspeakable amount of painfulness, arrogance, harshness, estrangement, frigidity has entered into human feelings because we think we see opposites instead of transitions. (WS 67)

The kind of language based on a binary, oppositional way of interpreting difference reinforces perceptions that perpetuate the us/not-us dichotomy, and it thus prevents more equitable interactions from taking place. Due to this, different scenarios appear and some of these will be explored in the following. Migrants, as I conceive the term, are all people who have left their home, be they Europeans moving around the continent due to the Freedom of Movement endorsed by the EU Treaty, be they refugees, asylum seekers, migrant workers – documented or undocumented – from any country in the world, or any other person who has moved from their country of origin to a European country. There are also those who have migrated and have the same feeling of homelessness as those who never left. It is a complex and multidimensional picture.[6] However, for the purposes of this chapter, I will be focusing more on migrant children and their families from different backgrounds moving to or within the West. Hence, it might be that westerners, western migrants, and non-western migrants could be sharing a sense, a feeling of homelessness, but from different perspectives. It might thus be that this feeling of nostalgia, and the struggles that emerge as a result, can acquaint us, to a certain extent, with a kind of shared feeling.

If this analysis succeeds, then we might have a common ground for a recognition that could temporarily suspend the language that reinforces opposition, that is, the language of slave morality, of the us/not-us. The acknowledgement of this mutual struggle can help to promote a politics of difference in which the recognition of difference does not come by way of fixed views of the other that reduce that difference to a pervasive separation. It may instead give some space for the suspension of the language that reinforces stereotypes and allow space for the temporary immersion in the experience of difference. This experience of difference would first come in the acknowledgement of the shared feeling of homelessness. In this context, this shared feeling of homelessness does not come from a single group/class nor from a single perspective or by a sup-

---

[6] There may also be people who did not leave their physical home, did not migrate, but who still have the feelings of homelessness or nostalgia indicated by Metzger, and perhaps also feelings of anger, anxiety and fear. Such feelings may have been instigated by a mourning for the lack of foundations the West is now experiencing, and the confusion and complexity this brings with it.

posed sense of identity. Instead, this sense of homelessness may come either from the nihilism that affects the West, as explained by Nietzsche, in which values are perceived as external to us, or from the feeling of displacement when a person migrates. Another reason could be the educational system that focuses mainly on raising standards and passing exams without addressing questions about the broader meaning of human existence. This is a complex scenario that may arise from a combination of the above factors, with or without other aspects not discussed here. However, this experience could reach another stage if we try to analyse it from the perspective of the will to power.

3 The Will to Power and Migration

Before discussing how the will to power relates to what I call an excess of forces being produced in our time of mass migration, it is important to explain how the perspective of the will to power will underpin the discussion. Nietzsche understands the will to power as something common to all forms of life and even to all beings. This drive is not restricted by class, geographical space, or levels of education, and not even limited to certain species. The will to power, for Nietzsche, is the way in which bodies express power. Nietzsche famously writes, 'where I found a living creature, there I found will to power' (Z II, Self-Overcoming). He argues that the will to power is the cardinal force in all organic beings: 'a living thing wants above all to *discharge* its force' (WP 650), and 'life as such is will to power' (BGE 13). For him, the will to power is thus not related to the instinct for self-preservation, as other theories may suggest, but solely to the purpose of self-overcoming. Paul Patton explains that, although Nietzsche was not the first thinker to propose an interpretation of actions in terms of power, his views differ from other thinkers:

> For Nietzsche, will to power is not a matter of individual bodies striving to maintain their power or persevere in their being, in the manner of Hobbes or Spinoza ..., but simply the expenditure of energy itself. The power of a body is expressed when it acts with all of the force or energy with which it is endowed. (Patton 2000, p. 50)

The will to power has a completely non-dualistic character as Nietzsche has a monistic view of the world which integrates all living beings, and which he explains thus: 'And do you know what "the world" is to me? ... *This world is the will to power – and nothing besides!* And you yourselves are also this will to power – and nothing besides! (WP 1067) and "Granted that one succeeded in explaining our entire instinctual life as the development and ramification of *one* basic form of will ... one would have acquired the right to define all efficient force unequivocally as: *will to power*. The world seen from within" (BGE 36). Patton illustrates this view by explaining that the will to power is 'the immanent principle in terms of which all human drives are to be understood' (Patton 2000,p. 51). Nietzsche thus differentiates the will to power from dualistic conceptions of power by placing it as an inner principle manifested in plurality and in all living beings. We should also remember that, related to the concept of the will to power in Nietzsche, there is the idea of forces. In this context, Andrea Rehberg explains that the will to power helps to attune thinking to a 'world of flux and becoming, to a microcosm of impersonal forces that is incessantly at play in the world' (Rehberg 2002, p. 39), and that 'Nietzsche pits a quasi-monistic (yet by no means unitary) conception of productivity against dualistic divisions of the world ..., even though the "monism" of will to power is offset by its profoundly agonistic character' (Rehberg 2002, p. 44). According to Patton, Nietzsche sees physical bodies as constituted by relations of conflict or collaboration between forces. In explaining the relation between the will to power and forces, Patton references Deleuze's interpretation by stating that:

> forces are essentially related to other forces and the will to power must be understood as the inner principle of the relation between forces. Chance brings particular forces into relation with one another, but the will to power determines the character and the outcome of the relations between forces: whether a particular force is primarily active or reactive. (Patton 2000, p. 52)

From this perspective, forces are related to other forces and their quality can be of obeying or commanding. As Patton further clarifies, 'the inner principle of relations between forces, the will to power is manifest both as a capacity to affect and a capacity to be affected' (Patton 2000, p. 53). An important qualification is that a force that obeys does not stop being powerful. As Deleuze explains, 'Obeying is a quality of force as such and relates to power just as much as commanding does' (Deleuze 1983, p. 40). Hence, when being in a struggle forces may acquire different hierarchical positions which can be active or reactive. Deleuze further explains that these are original qualities which express the relation of force with force (Deleuze 1983, pp. 39–40). Nietzsche understands as 'active' a force 'reaching out for power' (WP 657), whereas 'reactive' force refers to the mechanical and utilitarian accommodations, the regulations which express all the power of inferior and dominated forces' (Deleuze 1983, p. 41).

It is, moreover, important to clarify that, for Nietzsche and Deleuze, the will to power and its forces are pre-subjective, as this allows a view of things which goes beyond the idea of identity which leads to the separation of people or groups according to pre-conceived identities. Nietzsche argues that there is no such a thing as a fixed identity; instead, each one of us is always already composed of a plurality of different forces. This then means that we have more complex ways of interacting than simply through the opposition between apparently fixed identities. As the will to power and forces are pre-subjective, Nietzsche's views of them provide a new perspective by exposing the body's struggles before reactive perspectives are applied.

But Nietzsche's perspective on the will to power also gives us another way to understand how relations of power can occur between beings, beyond some of the usual categories of power that may compartmentalise people and separate them under the influence of binary metaphysical language. The categories I am referring to here are gender, age, class, ethnicity and disability, among others. By proposing this approach, I am not denying or rejecting the value and importance of such categories, particularly for promoting social justice and fairness. What I am trying to do is to analyse the current event of migration in Europe from another perspective, namely that of the will to power (as well as, a little later, geophilosophy). I am trying to bring together different elements of power as they reveal themselves, elements which are not only restricted to human relations.

Rehberg points out the challenges associated with the will to power in attempting to overcome metaphysical schemas of thought (also embedded in language), namely, when the will to power is explained in terms of representation, given that the idea of representation is exactly what the will to power tries to undermine (Rehberg 2002, p. 39). Some of these assumptions about the will to power espouse an individualised and anthropomorphised view that portrays it as:

> the autonomous intentionality of a human being who seeks to extend his domination over others. But the chief importance of the will to power is precisely to steer thinking away from such macro-conceptions and to attune it to a more subtle world of flux and becoming, to a microcosm of impersonal forces that is incessantly at play. (Rehberg 2002, p. 39)

Based on this, I would suggest that migrants, when portrayed solely according to negative, binary or reductive labels, may be seen by the wider society as powerless, even though this is clearly based on subjective and anthropocentric assumptions. In fact, portraying migrants in this way may not grasp the complexity of the dynamic of forces in which they might be embedded, and may conceal vital and important aspects of their struggles, particularly those struggles that do not originate or develop solely in human relations. Moreover, the process of migrating per se might be providing some possibilities for the expansion of forces due to the nature of the migration itself, which can require reterritorialization, and the inevitable struggle that the body has to endure when inhabiting a new territory. Deleuze and Guattari explain that 'movements of deterritorialization are inseparable from territories that open onto an elsewhere; and the process of reterritorialization is inseparable from the earth' (Deleuze and Guattari 1991, pp. 85–86). In keeping with this, I would argue that this movement of Europeans around the continent and the presence of non-European migrants in the West in the second half of the twentieth century (now accentuated by new waves of other migrants) may be generating a certain quantum of as yet unidentified forces. Patton clarifies an important point regarding power and recognition. He states that, for Nietzsche, power is an effective capacity and not a representation that can be recognised (Patton 2000, p. 50). This suggests that the excess of forces discussed here entails struggles of humans both with other humans and with non-human sources, and that it may escape the reactive lens if it remains in non-representational form. If this analysis succeeds, it may create possibilities of new valuations to be done in a life-affirming way.

Migration may also bring with it challenges and a range of different emotions. People move for a broad variety of reasons, which can go from economic motivations and fleeing war to being affected by climate change. As a result of migration, a person may experience solitude, fear, homesickness or a new sense of belonging, depending on the reasons why they left their homeland. However, this process of leaving the familiar for the unfamiliar may also require the displacement of one's multiple selves, which may bring unique opportunities for challenging and overcoming one's limits: developing new and stronger ways of facing adversity, developing resilience and plasticity, or, in other words, cultivating new strengths and forces. In that sense, migrant children may experience a dual kind of struggle in being affected by the challenges that moving to another environment entails while also struggling at school to get the expected grades and to fit in. Therefore, this consistent multi-ethnic movement of migration that has been happening in Europe for much of the last century may indeed be generating an excess of forces. In order to explain how other elements may play an important part in the generation of this excess of forces, I will discuss some aspects of geophilosophy.

4 Geophilosophy and the Will to Power in Migration

Previously, I explained how the will to power, as inherent in all forms of life, and as an extensive, monistic field in which identities arise, can support the reframing of the recognition of the other beyond dualistic categories. I also suggested that identifying common struggles, such as the feelings of homelessness brought about both by nihilism and by migration, could shed some light on new ways to recognise difference beyond fixed and reductive criteria.

I will now look at this scenario not only through these ideas but also in conjunction with certain aspects of geophilosophy. Nietzsche reminds us of the ways in which the faith in metaphysics separates human beings from the immanent world, detaching their experiences from the world as it appears. In *Thus Spoke Zarathustra*, he reminds us of the risks that infidelity to the earth and to the body brings with it, when denying them in favour of a supposed transcendent world, and he exhorts us instead to remain faithful to the earth (Z I, Prologue, 3). The fiction of a metaphysical world arose in the denial of the suffering and the immanence of human beings, although the power of this fiction has been waning throughout modernity. Even so, the nihilism inherent in metaphysical world views still persists today, albeit in weakened form. It is this which still prevents the earthly aspects of human existence from being affirmed, even though it is clear that such affirmation would allow human beings to overcome reductive ways of life and would allow for more meaningful and complex relations with the immanent world being formed. Here I am especially interested in how human beings' relation to the earth may play an important part in the experience of migration. Moreover, I am attempting to show how these earthly aspects may shed more light on our previous discussion of the will to power as being inherent to all forms of life and how the displacement present in the mass migration of our time may reveal interesting aspects of immanent aspects that can support other ways of understanding this process.

The term 'geophilosophy' was first introduced by Gilles Deleuze and Félix Guattari in *What is Philosophy?*, although they credit Nietzsche with being the first geophilosopher (Deleuze and Guattari 1994, p. 102). Deleuze and Guattari saw geophilosophy in terms of a territory of thinking. As explained by Michael Peters, Deleuze and Guattari define philosophy as concept creation (Peters 2004, p. 217).[7] Stephan Günzel argues that Deleuze and Guattari question the status of a geographical paradigm in the positioning of philosophical problems (Günzel 2003, p. 78). The intention here is not merely to follow Deleuze and Guattari's interpretation of geophilosophy, but instead, inspired by their interpretation, to make a further attempt at interpreting Nietzsche's reminder of the necessity of fidelity to the earth. By returning to Nietzsche's valorisation of the earth, I

---

[7] Cf., e.g., Deleuze and Guattari, *What is Philosophy?* (1994, pp. 2 and 11) and Michael Peters, "Geophilosophy, Education and the Pedagogy of the Concept" (2004, p. 217).

intend to look at the ways in which immanent aspects of nature can contextualise human action and help to find new ways for humans to flourish. This attempt is also aligned with what Gary Shapiro states when he says that 'Nietzsche argues that geography takes precedence over history in contextualizing human action' (Shapiro 2008, p. 13). Shapiro shares Nietzsche's question about 'what it means for human life to flourish in a thoroughly immanent world' (Shapiro 2008, p. 9). I will also borrow Günzel's idea that 'the "meaning of the earth" [*Sinn der Erde*] literally signifies a radical this-worldly orientation that includes the air, the sea, the mountains, and all sorts of landscapes, as long as their conception is connected to the surface' (Günzel 2003, p. 81). In addition to the aspects mentioned by Shapiro and Günzel, in the urban areas to which many migrants typically move, there are a variety of features, such as council estates, parks, skate ramps, cycle paths, financial and cultural hubs, as well as air pollution, which are all connected to the surface of the earth, and these features are also relevant to the discussion of how the excess of forces in migration, as previous explained, is being created.

What is relevant here is the influence of geographical aspects when the body is reterritorialised, thereby creating an excess of forces. This includes the bodily struggle each person endures in relation to new climates, landscapes and other earthly aspects related to the surface when migrating to another territory. It also includes the different sights and sounds, the different food, fauna, flora, and the effort the whole body has to make when living in a new environment. In this sense, geophilosophy, understood in the context of the will to power, concerns how this immediate and constant exposure of the body, in its multiple and dynamic aspects, to unfamiliar geographical features may contribute to the production of an excess of forces. This production is related both to the process of moving to another geographical space (migration) and to the struggles that the exposed body suffers when inhabiting a new geographical space. Although many people may go through similar geophilosophical experiences, there is something unique in the way that each of them will deal with this struggle. However, these aspects may have a strong impact on them regardless of where they came from or the reasons why they migrated. It is by bringing together the impact of the geophilosophical aspects just mentioned and the aspects of the will to power as inherent in all forms of life, that it becomes possible to sustain the argument that the current multi-dimensional migration Europe is experiencing may be generating an excess of forces. I would suggest that this constant movement of people within and into the continent, and the presence of non-European migrants and refugees living in the West may be generating quanta of forces that have at least the potential to become active forces. This may be an important event when considering Nietzsche's diagnosis of nihilism and his prognosis for the flourishing of western culture.

Nietzsche himself described the effects of geographical aspects on his own creativity and strength, and how aspects of different countries had a positive effect on his work. In *Ecce Homo*, he writes how "Many concealed spots and heights in the landscape around [Nice] are hallowed for me by unforgettable moments ... the suppleness of my muscles has always been greatest when my creative energies were flowing most abundantly' (EH Books, Z, 4).

5 The London Effect

After the excess of forces, which I claim is related to geophilosophical aspects and to the will to power, has been discussed, I would now like to illustrate this claim with the results of the previously-mentioned research project "Understanding the Success of London Schools", conducted by Simon Burgess in 2009 and 2014, although the so-called London Effect was first highlighted by Chris Cook (2013).

According to their findings, whereas generally urban areas have been associated with poor pupil attainment, the progress of pupils in London, by contrast, is the highest in the country, possibly reflecting the fact that London also has many more recent migrants than the rest of the country. These basic points have been confirmed and reiterated in two reports on London, namely, by Centre for British Teachers[8] (Baars et al 2014) and Greaves et al. (2014). This highlights the role of a number of major policy interventions: London Challenge (see Department for Education and Skills 2003), TeachFirst and the rise of sponsored academies.

Burgess was interested in investigating the school attainment of minority ethnic groups in England, which he found was higher than the mainstream group. Burgess mentions the challenges of identifying the most important factor to be considered in his analysis of attainment, namely, whether it was ethnicity or the child's recent migrant status. He argues that 'ethnicity does not define immigration status, nor vice versa, but is quite highly correlated with it for some groups' (Burgess 2014, p. 9). Burgess found that there was no large-scale data on the immigration status of pupils, so he took two different approximations, immigrants of all ages, and the language spoken by pupils at home, to support his analysis.

---

8 The Centre for British Teachers is now called Education Development Trust.

Wilson, Burgess and Briggs then analysed data regarding the attainment gaps between ethnic groups in England. When investigating the reasons, one of their findings was that students from minority ethnic groups did not go to better schools, so the improvements happened despite this. Burgess wanted to understand what was behind the greatest attainment of migrant pupils in London. He mentioned other research showing that ethnic minority pupils make better progress through school than white British pupils (see Wilson et al. 2005 and 2011; Burgess et al. 2009).

The idea here is not to deny any of the attainments of minority ethnic groups, such as the praise for policies, family and community support, group aspirations etc., discussed by Burgess and other authors, but to look at these results in a different way. I would argue that Nietzsche's perspective of the will to power, when associated with aspects of geophilosophy, as previously discussed in this chapter, may help to explain the attainment of minority child migrants. It might be evidence that an excess of forces is being produced but is not yet being acknowledged. These children may be experiencing multiple struggles in relation to aspects of their reterritorialised bodies. There are children from the most diverse backgrounds in the world who have moved to London. They may bring with them ways of life in which their previous environment affected them that are unknown to the mainstream group of children. It is important to emphasise again that London is considered the most cosmopolitan city in the world and this multiplicity and plurality may be behind the London Effect. It is a city that receives migrants from all over the world, including non-European refugees and migrant children from both the EU and non-EU countries, and that in recent years has epitomised all these kinds of migration. It seems that a kind of power may be concentrated in this process of plural migration, but that it is not yet being acknowledged. This, I would claim, is a result of multiple aspects of interaction between and struggles of children from all over the world immersing themselves in a Europe experiencing nihilism. This struggle may happen when they are being exposed to new experiences in which the world reveals itself, when their bodies are being immersed in a different environment from their native country, and when they are entering the process of gradual reterritorialisation in their new environment.

I mentioned previously that a language that reinforces a separation between us and not-us is embedded in slave morality. This language may conceal the uniqueness of this growing excess of forces, particularly when aspects of the migrant children's authenticity and strength are being overlooked in favour of the focus on the kind of a perceived vulnerability that migrants may experience, in comparison with non-migrants. In fact, the language that is used to make sense of these dynamic individual or social situations keeps trapping people in a web of meanings projected on to them without considering the dynamic of their struggles, particularly when using a polarised or dualistic language that separates people into antagonistic groups.

This excess of forces might be building up in a constant struggle such as dealing with difficulties in human relationships (e.g., prejudices, social segregation, linguistic exclusion, bilingualism, etc.) both within and outside the home environment. If society keeps framing migrants from the kind of perspective that acknowledges only what they are perceived to lack in comparison to the general population, then migrants' successes may not be receiving sufficient recognition. In acknowledging the excess of forces that migrant children may be developing as a result of their geographical and social displacement, we may also acknowledge different groups as including people of comparable strengths.

By contrast, children from non-migrant groups may not face the same challenges but may nevertheless be experiencing a greater sense of detachment from traditional western values, and this detachment may extend to how they relate to their geographical space, and to their cultural environment, especially when we consider that they are being brought up in a society immersed in nihilism. This may then be an important factor to consider regarding how a shared feeling of homelessness (as previously discussed) can manifest itself.

After having established that 'there is no significant difference between the progress of white British pupils in London and in the rest of the country', Burgess argues that 'ethnic composition matters a great deal…. If London had the same ethnic composition as the rest of England, there would be no "London Effect"' (Burgess 2014, p. 3). Burgess later draws the following conclusion: 'the basis for the London performance is the ethnic composition of its school population' (Burgess 2014, p. 15). He also mentions that 'being a recent immigrant or being of non-White British ethnicity has a very substantial positive effect on progress through school' (Burgess 2014, p. 10). This could also be due to some children coming from ex-colonies who inherited some of the values and ways of life that were common in Europe at the time of their colonisation and that were imposed on their cultures, or again simply by encountering completely different ways of life. The last of Burgess' statements certainly seems to be in line with my claim that an excess of forces is arguably being produced by the daily struggles of migrant children and that this may be playing an important part in their educational attainment when directed towards school outcomes.

By exposing the narratives of migrant children and by acknowledging their strength and value, mainstream society may come to recognise those ways of life that they have either not experienced at all or that they are trying to ignore in their daily lives. Such an exposure could culminate in a reinterpretation of migrants' ways of life that could turn into new social practices or new values, and possibly change British society to a hybrid culture.

In this sense, Nietzsche foresaw the rise of a kind of human being whom he called the 'hybrid European'. He writes, 'The hybrid European ... definitely requires a costume: he needs history as his storeroom for costumes. He realizes ... that none of them fits him properly – he changes and changes' (BGE 223). This idea of the hybrid person has also been discussed by Shapiro, who explained the difference between the Last Man and the hybrid:

> Such hybrids, not the homogenized last men, are movements in the style of the good European: on the one hand homogenization, on the other hybridity.... Social, economic, and geographic mobility produces a multitude [*Menge*] adapted to globalized conditions as well as exceptional new combinations brought about by a variety of causes.... These hybrids are not themselves instances of a higher type but, rather, signs of the fertility of Europe's productive ferment. (Shapiro 2008, p. 24)

Whereas Shapiro has a more general view of this hybridity in Europeans and in European culture, in my view his analysis can be expanded to include the actual fertility occurring in Europe in the context of the multi-dimensional migration into and within Europe in our time. Hence, looking at the idea of an excess of forces being generated in our time in the context of the will to power and geophilosophy, we may be being exposed to the possibility of the hybridity explained by Nietzsche. If such forces are already at work, it may be that possibilities for drives and forces to grow and to expand could be created if properly acknowledged and cultivated. This, I will argue next, could be promoted by education.

6 Education and a Politics of Difference

Nietzsche invites us to understand difference beyond the traditional views of identity and entities. School is a kind of temporary home for many children as they spend a fair amount of time there. Due to international policies, such as "Education for All" and the "Education 2030 Agenda", it is a place which most children, regardless of their background, can attend. It is a place in which pupils from different backgrounds can meet in a way that may not be possible outside it. In that sense, the school receives both the migrant children, who are being continuously exposed to a new language, a new geographical and physical space and who are constantly producing an excess of forces, and the non-migrant children, who may be facing a constant struggle in dealing with the nihilism affecting the West, as previously discussed. Thus – albeit for very different reasons – both groups can feel displaced and exiled from the values that were once familiar, and which gave them a sense of rootedness in the past.

Education, then, could recognise the multiple struggles that migration brings with it, by acknowledging them and opening up a possibility for dialogue. This dialogue would account for the excess of forces that are being produced in migrant children by the process of migration. Such a dialogue may, in turn, be a way to shift dualistic, fixed views of migrants towards a greater recognition of other, more complex aspects. These complexities include the multiplicity of drives and forces that Nietzsche warns are dangerous to ignore.

Hence, instead of looking for foundations, for a fixed world-view, children from all backgrounds could embrace the continuous oscillations between processes of rootedness and uprootedness and perhaps find in each other a sense of shelter or a temporary home. It is in the challenge of finding what is similar and what is different by embodying the diversity and the plurality of the world that a politics of difference could emerge. This would account for the recognition of different struggles that would allow both migrants' and non-migrants' diversity to be embodied by the other. As previously discussed, the school seems to be one of the places in which such a politics could flourish. I have focused this work on children and on the general view of migrants, but this is not exhaustive. We must not forget that the picture is much more complex than I have been able to portray here. There is, moreover, a great complexity within the migrant group in terms of them being either of recent migration, first or second generations, as well as other levels of complexity in the composition of the mainstream group that could not be addressed in more detail here as it would be beyond the scope of the present chapter.

7 Conclusion

Nietzsche warned us that the world would experience two hundred years of nihilism (WP Preface, 2), and we are still going through it. Recent political developments in the West, such as the rise of nationalism, which seem to reflect a nostalgia for the old devalued (metaphysical) values, and the resulting sense of polarisation between migrants and non-migrants, have brought great risks not only for migrants and other people in situations of vulnerability, as addressed in this chapter, but also in the return of a framework that disregards or seeks to suppress difference and plurality. Such a framework, when embedded in a metaphysical basis, may produce a language that continues to endorse the slave morality that Nietzsche reminded us needs to be overcome.

It is necessary to look beyond the limiting use of a dualistic language and recognise the complexity of the world. In this chapter, when looking at the elements of the polarisation happening in the West, I discussed how Nietzsche's ideas can inspire a comprehensive reinterpretation of reality. I showed that by looking at current events in a way that is attuned to Nietzsche's diagnosis of nihilism and his prognosis for western culture, that incorporates aspects of Nietzsche's perspective of the will to power, and that includes earthly aspects and their impact on migrants, can lead to a broader understanding of migration in our time and its effects on society. Moreover, I also suggested that by examining aspects of migration through the aforementioned lenses can lead to a better understanding of the world in which we live and that this may – at least temporarily – suspend the kind of metaphysical, dualistic or binary language that reduces and negates complexity.

As previously mentioned, migrants may have a continual necessity to use different physical, emotional, sensory and cognitive resources in their struggle in their new environments, which requires the ability to endure a series of changes and challenges. These processes are usually ignored, yet these newly-created forces may expand and grow, and may do so even more so when they are acknowledged. The danger is, however, that if they are not met with conditions conducive to their expansion and growth, they may turn inwards and turn into resentment. Therefore, it is important to look closely at what kind of life opportunities these children have when leaving school. There are currently a significant number of young people neither in employment nor in education and there is a worry that they are being groomed by different kinds of extremist groups. If there is this excess of forces I have been discussing, it is important to think about what would happen to these forces if they did not find opportunities to expand and continue to grow, although an exploration of this is beyond the scope of the present chapter. My intention has been to show this excess of forces rather than discussing future directions they may take. It is necessary that schools acknowledge these forces and their complexity. In our time, students are taught to aim for better grades, which fosters individualism in a neoliberal economic context. However, students lack meaningful cultural practices that could hold their communities together – not least because, as argued by Nietzsche, nihilism has eroded the basis of contemporary culture.

It might be that in struggling and recognising the mutual suffering caused by different forms of the feeling of homelessness, young people could learn from each other and develop a sense of mutual responsibility. Perhaps this could shed light on a politics of difference embedded in life-affirming practices that could emerge in schools. As Nietzsche said, 'I do not exhort you to peace, but to victory. May your work be a battle, may your peace be a victory!' (Z I, War, 74).

Bibliography

Baars, Sam et al (2014): "Lessons from London schools: investigating the success". *CfBT Education Trust.* (https://www.educationdevelopmenttrust.com/EducationDevelopment Trust/files/60/60f327fd-cfbc-4d26-b914-0d0ccf84fd78.pdf, visited on August 10, 2019).

Blake, Nigel, Paul Smeyers, Richard Smith and Paul Standish (2000): *Education in an Age of Nihilism.* London: Routledge/Falmer

Burgess, Simon (2014): "Understanding the Success of London Schools". (unpublished manuscript, October, 2014, Portable Document Format. http://www.bristol.ac.uk/media-li brary/sites/cmpo/migrated/documents/wp333.pdf, visited on August 10, 2019).

Burgess, S., Wilson, D. and Worth, J. (2009): "Passing through school: the evolution of attainment of England's ethnic minorities". Report for the National Equality Panel. CMPO, University of Bristol. (http://www.bris.ac.uk/media-library/sites/cmpo/migrated/ documents/ethnicminorities.pdf, visited on August 10, 2019)

Cook, Chris (2013): "London School Children Perform the Best". *Financial Times*, Month Date, 2013, https://www.ft.com/content/8f65f1ce-5be7-11e2-bef7-00144feab49a, visited on August 13, 2019.

D'Agnese, Vasco (2019): "Dewey and Possibility: Challenging Neoliberalism in Education". *Educational Theory* 69. No. 6, pp. 693–717.

Deleuze, Gilles. (1983) *Nietzsche and Philosophy.* Translated by Hugh Tomlinson. London: Athlone Press.

Deleuze, Gilles, and Felix Guattari (1994): *What is Philosophy?* Translated by Graham Burchell and H. Tomlinson. New York: Columbia University Press.

DfES (Department for Education and Skills) (2003) *The London Challenge: transforming London secondary schools*, https://dera.ioe.ac.uk/10309/7/London%20Challenge% 20transforming%20london%20secondary%20schools_Redacted.pdfm, visited on August 13, 2019.

Greaves, Ellen, Lindsey Macmillan and Luke Sibieta (2014): "Lessons from London Schools for Attainment Gaps and Social Mobility". *Social Mobility and Child Poverty Commission Research Report SMCP-RR363.* https://www.ifs.org.uk/uploads/publications/docs/lon don_schools_june2014.pdf, visited on August 13, 2019.

Günzel, Stephan (2003): "Nietzsche's Geophilosophy" in Journal of Nietzsche Studies, vol. 25, pp.78–91.

Metzger, Jeffrey (Ed.) (2009): *Nietzsche, Nihilism and the Philosophy of the Future.* London: Bloomsbury.

Nietzsche, Friedrich (1968): *The Will to Power.* Edited by Walter Kaufmann and translated by Walter Kaufmann and R.J. Hollingdale. New York: Random House.

Nietzsche, Friedrich (1974): *The Gay Science.* Translated by Walter Kaufmann. New York: Random House.

Nietzsche, Friedrich (1986): *Human, All Too Human.* Translated by R. J. Hollingdale. Cambridge: Cambridge University Press.

Nietzsche, Friedrich (1990a): *Beyond Good and Evil.* Translated by R. J. Hollingdale. London: Penguin.

Nietzsche, Friedrich (1990b): *Twilight of the Idols and The Anti-Christ.* Translated by R. J. Hollingdale. London: Penguin.

Nietzsche, Friedrich (1992): *Ecce Homo.* Translated by R. J. Hollingdale. London: Penguin.

Nietzsche, Friedrich (1995): *Thus Spoke Zarathustra*. Edited and translated by Walter Kaufmann. New York: Modern Library.
Patton, Paul (2000): *Deleuze and the Political*. London: Routledge.
Peters, Michael (2004): "Geophilosophy, Education and the Pedagogy of the Concept". In: *Educational Philosophy and Theory* 36. No. 3, pp. 217–226.
Rehberg, Andrea (2002): "The Overcoming of Physiology". In: *Journal of Nietzsche Studies* 23. No. 1, pp. 39–50.
Shapiro, Gary (2008): "Beyond Peoples and Fatherlands: Nietzsche's Geophilosophy and the Direction of the Earth". In: *Journal of Nietzsche Studies* 35. No. 1, pp. 9–27.
Vattimo, Gianni (2006): *Dialogue with Nietzsche*. Translated by William McCuaig. New York: Columbia University Press.
Wilson, Deborah, Adam Briggs, and Simon Burgess (2005). *The Dynamics of School Attainment of England's Ethnic Minorities*. (unpublished manuscript, October, 2005, Portable Document Format. https://www.bristol.ac.uk/media-library/sites/cmpo/migrated/documents/wp130.pdf. Visited on August 13, 2019
Wilson, Deborah et al. (2011): "The Dynamics of School Attainment of England's Ethnic Minorities". In: *Journal of Population Economics* 24. No. 2, pp. 681–700.

George W. Shea, IV
Nietzsche, Foucault and the Politics of the Ascetic Ideal

Abstract: While traces of a post-metaphysical political theory are to be found throughout his *oeuvre*, Nietzsche himself never explicitly elaborates any such comprehensive theory. Yet, this chapter argues, it is possible to discern a politics beyond *ressentiment* and the ascetic ideal, which must be both experimental and pluralist. Inspired by Nietzsche, Foucault thinks the political as a play of force relations immanent to a concrete strategic field, and thus as a multiplicity of power relations existing in agonistic tension rather than as a duality in antagonistic opposition. This makes him one of the most significant inheritors of the Nietzschean challenge to overcome the politics of *ressentiment* and to think instead a politics of affirmation that makes difference constitutive of the political.

1 Introduction

Nietzsche's place within political theory is still a highly contested one. Scholars grappling with Nietzsche as a political thinker have developed a myriad of "Nietzsches": as apolitical (Brobjer 1998 and Kaufmann 2013), as sceptic (Shaw 2010), as perfectionist (Conway 1997), as aristocrat (Detwiler 1990; Appel 1999), as liberal (Connolly 1991), as agonist (Hatab 1995), etc. In this chapter, I will refrain from engaging in these debates or offering to name definitively Nietzsche's "political doctrine". Instead, I prefer to take seriously the question that motivates this collection of essays – namely, how might we understand Nietzsche as offering – or better yet, how might we mobilise Nietzsche to think – a "politics of difference"? I regard as central to this task an appreciation of Nietzsche's critique of metaphysics. As a post-metaphysical thinker, Nietzsche directly challenges the tenability of the metaphysical faith in the value of truth and all that it assumes. To sound out such idols is, as Nietzsche rightly recognises, to up-end the rational order that has governed western culture since at least Plato, though, we might ask, to what end? What are the ramifications of such a critique? There is, undoubtedly, more to Nietzsche's critique of metaphysics than could possibly be said about it in the span of a short chapter. Nevertheless, I want to focus here on what I regard to be the pluralistic dimensions of such a critique and their implications for developing a politics of difference. While clues and traces of a politics of difference can be found throughout Nietzsche's oeuvre, it is generally agreed that Nietzsche himself never elaborates an explicit political theory. Thus, I will suggest that if our aim is to distil a politics of difference from Nietzsche's thought, the work of Michel Foucault serves as one exemplary model for how we might go about conceiving such a politics. While there is much excellent scholarship already exploring significant connections between Nietzsche and Foucault[1] – for instance, focusing on the will to know, genealogy as a critical and transformative practice, freedom and self-fashioning, and the intersecting of truth, power, and the subject within history – I will advance a reading of Foucault's work in light of Nietzsche's critique of the ascetic ideal. By framing Foucault's work in light of Nietzsche's critique of the ascetic ideal, a connection which has gone underappreciated in the literature, I will specifically call attention to the import of Foucault's overt characterisation of genealogy as a "method" in contradistinction to metaphysical philosophy. On this basis, I will argue that Foucault's work can be read as a considered theorisation of the political implications of Nietzsche's critique of metaphysics, offering what might be regarded as a 'politics of affirmation' – in contrast to that of a 'politics of *ressentiment*' – one that makes possible a post-foundationalist political activism. In this light, I will further argue that Foucault's politics of affirmation brings into relief the contours of a politics of difference germinal in Nietzsche. In spelling out these implications, I will draw primarily on Nietzsche's *On the Genealogy of Morality* as well as on Foucault's later works.

2 Nietzsche: Diagnosing the Politics of the Ascetic Ideal

That Nietzsche's *Genealogy* is a nuanced and complicated text is, obviously, an understatement as it not only runs several different arguments simultaneously, but those different arguments additionally cut across and reinforce one another in often subterranean and significant ways. For this reason, the *Genealogy* is an extremely rich text and there is much to be made, and has been made, of its various themes. Nonetheless, despite the complicated staging of characters and motifs that Nietzsche sets out, the rhetorical tenor of the text crescendos in the third and final essay when Nietzsche introduces the ascetic ideal and begins to exam-

---

[1] See, e.g., Thiele (1990); Ansell-Pearson (1991); Mahon (1992); McWhorter (1992); Owen (1998); Shapiro (2003); Milchman and Rosenberg (2007); Lightbody (2010a and 2010b); Westfall and Rosenberg (2018); and Tuana and Scott (2020).

ine its meaning.[2] And yet, with this introduction, several questions immediately present themselves to us. Why the ascetic ideal at all? Why the hurried and frantic sense surrounding Nietzsche's inquiry? And, perhaps most significantly, why a sense of danger such that the ascetic ideal stands as the final and most dramatic of Nietzsche's motifs?

Near the close of the *Genealogy*, as Nietzsche begins to elaborate the stakes of philosophers having worn the mask of the ascetic priest for so long, he discloses to us what an inquiry into the meaning of the ascetic ideal entails for him. Here, he tells us, 'I do not want to bring to light what the ideal did; rather simply what it ... indicates, what lies hidden behind, beneath and within it' (GoM III, 23). More specifically, for Nietzsche, this involves bringing to light its aim, its purpose and its goal. We are told that this goal, the crowning jewel of the ascetic ideal, has been determined by the unconditional will to truth and the metaphysical faith in the value as such of truth (GoM III, 24).

For Nietzsche, this faith on the part of metaphysicians is tantamount to a deification of truth. Thus, whether in its priestly, philosophical, or even scientific garb, the ascetic ideal aims at the divine, and, in aiming at the divine, it ultimately aims at the transcendent. On this precise point, Nietzsche draws our attention in the *Genealogy* to a passage from *The Gay Science*, noting:

> The truthful man, in that daring and final sense which faith in science presupposes, *thus affirms another world* from the one of life, nature and history; and inasmuch as he affirms this 'other world', must he not therefore deny its opposite, this world, *our* world, in doing so? ... Our faith in science is still based on a *metaphysical faith*, – even we knowers of today, we godless anti-metaphysicians, still take *our* fire from the blaze set alight by a faith thousands of years old, that faith of the Christians, which was also Plato's faith, that God is truth, that truth is *divine*. (GoM III, 24)

On the one hand, this clearly represents the culmination of Nietzsche's critique of the ascetic ideal as life-denying; but, on the other hand, it also draws out the full implications of Nietzsche's critique of the logic of the metaphysicians' faith.

In the opening section of *Beyond Good and Evil*, "On the Prejudices of the Philosophers", Nietzsche states in no uncertain terms that 'The fundamental faith of the metaphysicians is *the faith in antithetical values*' (BGE 2). This is not, however, a banal faith in mere oppositions. Rather, Nietzsche wants to make clear to us that the unquestioned metaphysical faith in the value of

---

[2] Nietzsche's own account of the *Genealogy* in *Ecce Homo* remarks upon its distinctive tempo and drama: 'Gradually an increasing disquiet; isolated flashes of lightning; very unpleasant truths becoming audible as a dull rumbling in the distance – until at last a *tempo feroce* is attained in which everything surges forward with tremendous tension' (EH Books: GoM).

truth is the very impetus from which an entire metaphysico-ontological structure has emerged. As Nietzsche notes a few sections later, 'To explain how a philosopher's most remote metaphysical assertions have actually been arrived at, it is always well (and wise) to ask oneself first: what morality does this (does *he* –) aim at?' (BGE 6).

In the case of the *Genealogy*, Nietzsche is not merely critiquing Plato or the Stoics, or some other particular philosopher, but is instead bringing to light an assumed metaphysico-ontological structure that underpins the entire western philosophical tradition as a result of the value invested in a particular conception of truth. Thus, we find that because metaphysicians value truth, the intransient is therefore privileged over the transient; and, consequently, being over becoming, identity over difference, the one over the many, reason over the senses, the immaterial over the material, and the unhistorical over the historical. All of this culminates in the assumption of a metaphysical subject that can extricate itself from the contaminations of this world and attain the purity of another. This is further manifested even in the moralisation at the heart of substance ontologies that privilege unity, identity, duration, substance, cause, materiality and being as the true and the good in contrast to change, mutation and becoming, which are regarded as signs of 'appearance' that lead us astray (TI Reason. All of this is, for Nietzsche, symptomatic of an equation that has been assumed from the outset by the metaphysical faith in the value of truth: Being = Truth = Reason = Highest Value = God = The One and Only Rightful Authority (TI Reason; GoM III, 24).

It is, however, the moment when Nietzsche draws our attention to the dangers that lurk within the metaphysicians' faith that we begin to understand the hurried and frantic sense surrounding his analyses. Nietzsche's inquiry into the meaning of the ascetic ideal reveals the insidious way in which it functions both to arrest the circulation of other systems of interpretation and to mask itself as an interpretation. As Nietzsche notes:

> The ascetic ideal has a *goal*, – this being so general that all the interests of human existence appear petty and narrow when measured against it; it inexorably interprets epochs, races, and human beings, all with reference to this one goal, it permits of no other interpretation, no other goal, and rejects, denies, affirms, and confirms with reference only to *its* interpretation (– and was there ever a system of interpretation more fully thought through?); it does not subject itself to any power, in fact, it believes in its superiority over any power, in its unconditional *superiority of rank* over any other power, – it believes there is nothing on earth of any power that does not first have to receive its meaning, a right to exist, a value from it, as a tool to *its* work, as a way and means to *its* goal, to *one* goal. (GoM III, 23)

This follows directly from the very nature of metaphysical truth. As David Owen describes it in his own analysis of the *Genealogy*, the ascetic ideal:

> [Presents] itself as objectively valid, that is, as the only possible way of conceptualizing human existence. It is this in-built denial of its own perspectival character that, on Nietzsche's account, explains how we have come to be wholly captivated by the way of reflecting and evaluating human existence expressed in the ascetic ideal. (Owen 2007, p. 123)

Thus, within the order of metaphysics, it comes to be the case that since there is the one and only truth that stands above the fray of false claimants and imposters (appearance), since it itself stands in accord with itself for no other reason than already being itself (reality), the system of interpretation installed by the will to truth must of necessity deny all other interpretations, goals and orders other than itself – in other words, according to its own system of interpretation, it is the one and only order because it *is*, that is, Being = Truth.

What Nietzsche uncovers in all of this, and what is made manifest in the *Genealogy*, is that the unconditional will to truth is inherently political. Far from being the product of an innocent 'contemplation without interest' or 'the pure radiant gaze of the sage' (GoM III, 6; BGE 2), the will to truth at the heart of the ascetic ideal aims to enthrone itself as the highest authority and thus as the pinnacle of power with no other power or authority standing above it. It attempts to do this through its very structuring of the system of interpretations. According to the laws of a system of its own design, it presents itself as divorced from power – conceived of as corruption and bias – and thereby uncouples itself from power while simultaneously standing above power, yet functioning nonetheless as the pinnacle of power insofar as all other systems of interpretation are to conform to its law. Thus, it manages both to rule with an iron fist and to absolve itself entirely of ruling. In this way, its proclamations are not to be treated as mere edicts since they are purportedly expressions of Being itself – that is, its laws are not its laws, they are rather reality itself (though, in Nietzsche's estimation, a reality constructed on the basis of the metaphysicians' faith in the value of truth). Consequently, the system of interpretation inaugurated by the ascetic ideal is to be regarded as the one and only system and there are to be no other systems than it. Ultimately, as Nietzsche aims to show, the metaphysico-ontological structure installed by the metaphysical faith in the value of truth is a technique of power if not 'the ultimate sanction of power' (GoM III, 1).

Nietzsche's analysis further reveals that the system of interpretation established by the metaphysical conception of truth functions along the lines of a twofold operation of power. On the one hand, it divides by constructing an inside/outside of its domain – reality/appearance, true/untrue, legitimate/illegitimate, and thus proper power (justice) and abuse of power (corruption). On the other hand, it works to coalesce divergences and differences by governing the entirety of its domain as the one and only rightful domain into which everything is to be assimilated. Thus, through this twofold operation of division and coalescence, the will to truth sanctions the eradication of that which is untrue and other than itself while simultaneously bringing that which remains entirely under its control. In this way, nestled within the will to truth is the totalitarian, autocratic and homogenising will to the one. Everything is to succumb to its law with the intent that, ultimately, there will be no remainder, that nothing will remain "untamed" in a wilderness outside. Lawrence Hatab, in a slightly different context, similarly notes this homogenising tendency at work in the ascetic ideal:

> For Nietzsche, *any* development of culture out of natural conditions and any innovation will require a dynamic discomfort, resistance, and overcoming, that is, a contest with some Other. Nietzsche asks us not only to acknowledge this dynamic but also to be wary of its dangers, which are indicated in traditional constructs and their *polarization* of a conflicted field into the oppositions of good and evil, truth and error. The ascetic ideal in the end represents the desire to escape the difficulty of incorporating the Other (*as* other) into one's field of operation. Affirmation, for Nietzsche, is anything but comfortable and pleasant; it means taking on the difficulty of *contending [with] the Other without wanting to annul it*. (Hatab 2008, pp. 109–110)

In other words, the ascetic ideal cannot abide the existence of that which is other than it. Thus, it interprets *everything* in light of its *one* goal, excluding all others.

And yet, once again, we must ask: why the ascetic ideal? Why the unconditional will to truth that it harbours? How does a system of interpretation so hostile to anything outside of, and other than, itself emerge? Nietzsche provides an account of this emergence in the first essay of the *Genealogy* via his analysis of the slave revolt in morality. More specifically, in sections 13 and 14 of the first essay, Nietzsche sheds light on what he calls the 'fabrication of ideals' and tells the tale of the birds of prey and the little lambs. In this scenario, we have two separate systems of valuation – one in which the birds of prey enjoy eating the lambs and another in which the lambs resent being carried off and eaten by the birds of prey. According to Nietzsche's own estimation of this situation, there is nothing astonishing in the fact that there are these separate systems of valuation. This situation radically alters, however, when *ressentiment*, born from the resentment that the lambs hold against the birds of prey and in conjunction with a powerlessness and inability to do anything about their situation, grows creative. The lambs want revenge but cannot take it. And, in the very specific differential generated between these two systems, Nietzsche locates the transformation of the desire for revenge into the desire for justice. The distinctly interesting moment in this transformation, to which Nietzsche draws our attention, is the moment when the lambs move from demanding "lamb justice" to "true justice". They demand "justice as such" – a justice that is one and the same for all, a justice that transcends the two separate systems and binds them together. This is a justice, founded on a metaphysical conception of truth that not only aims to link the two previously distinct systems of valuation together in a permanent way, but also aims to cause the one to tilt and slide into the other, bringing it about that the former is subsumed into and reorganised by the latter. Ultimately, what Nietzsche's excavation of the ascetic ideal uncovers is that the will to truth, as a form of politics, functions as a technique of power that operates through division and coalescence to subsume that which is other than it into and under it. In this way, metaphysical truth, posited as univocal transcendence, functions strategically and tactically to capture a field of multiplicities in order to arrest the play of their differences; and it is precisely this technique of power, born from the will to truth – which is a will to the one – that embodies a politics of *ressentiment*.

Having elaborated the operations of this technique of power, Nietzsche raises the question of a counter-ideal, asking, 'Where is the counterpart to this *closed system* of will, goal, and interpretation?' (GoM III, 23, emphasis added). With Nietzsche having focused so intently on the priestly mask of the ascetic ideal, one might be tempted to hold up modern science and atheism as providing counter-ideals. However, Nietzsche dismisses science as the ascetic ideal's '*most recent and noble manifestation*' (GoM, III, 23). As for atheists, sceptics and nihilists, Nietzsche derisively retorts:

> These 'no'-sayers and outsiders of today, those who are absolute in one thing, their demand for intellectual rigour, these hard, strict, abstinent, heroic minds who make up the glory of our time, all these pale atheists, Antichrists, immoralists, nihilists, these sceptics, ephectics, *hectics* of the mind (they are one and all the latter in a certain sense), these last idealists of knowledge in whom, alone, intellectual conscience dwells and is embodied these days, – they believe they are all as liberated as possible from the ascetic ideal, these 'free, *very* free spirits': and yet, I will tell them what they themselves cannot see – because they are standing too close to themselves – this ideal is quite simply *their* ideal as well, they themselves represent it nowadays, and perhaps no-one else: they themselves are its most intellectual product, its most advanced front-line troops and scouts, its most insidious product, delicate and elusive form of seduction: – if I am able at all to solve riddles, I wish to claim to do so with this pronouncement! ... These are very far from being *free* spirits: *because they still believe in truth*. (GoM III, 24)

With these words, Nietzsche aims to place our thinking on an entirely different footing. Any particular ideal that aspires to displace the ascetic ideal via an appeal of the sort that it alone has finally arrived at the truth – in the same way that science claimed to have deposed religion and philosophy – is, simply, just another variant in the long line of successors operating in accord with the ascetic ideal. As Hatab again insightfully notes, 'It seems that the *anti*metaphysical posture here would sustain the binary thinking that constitutes a metaphysical faith (while *contending* with metaphysics would be a different story)' (Hatab 2008, p. 113). Of importance here is the realisation that any attempt to refute the ascetic ideal by means of an appeal to a metaphysical truth only replicates the ascetic ideal in the end – and this is most especially the case for those anti-metaphysical positions that take aim to refute metaphysics.[3] Thus, Nietzsche's question is all the more pressing. Where is the counter-ideal to the ascetic ideal? Who or what, in Hatab's words, can 'contend' with metaphysics?

Within the *Genealogy* itself, Nietzsche is far from forthcoming in terms of a clear and explicit answer. In section 25 of the third essay, Nietzsche briefly remarks that 'art' is 'much more opposed to the ascetic ideal than science is' (GoM III, 25), and in section 27, he quickly notes that the ascetic ideal has 'only one type of enemy and *injurer:* these are the comedians of this ideal – because they arouse mistrust' (GoM III, 27). However, in *Ecce Homo*, Nietzsche explicitly names Zarathustra as a counter-ideal, as the ascetic ideal's "competitor" (EH Books, GoM). This latter remark helps shed light on Nietzsche's allusions to Zarathustra at the end of the second essay and at the beginning of the third essay in the *Genealogy*. These cryptic allusions on Nietzsche's part open up an immense field of interpretative possibilities, and much has been made of them in Nietzsche scholarship.[4] However, exploring these possibilities is beyond the scope of this chapter since my aim here is not so much to elucidate specifically what the counter-ideal must mean within Nietzsche's own work, as it is to explore more generally what it might mean to take Nietzsche's critique of the ascetic ideal seriously and to understand its implications for mobilising a politics of difference. Thus, instead of exploring these overtly intra- and inter-textual questions within Nietzsche's oeuvre, I will examine what I regard to be the structural implications of rejecting the ascetic ideal that must be assumed by any conception of a counter-ideal.

First, it is quite obvious that whatever might stand as a counter-ideal to the ascetic ideal would have to be other than the ascetic ideal. Thus, if the ascetic

---

[3] Because of this very danger – the danger of remaining yoked to the ascetic ideal and the metaphysicians' faith – which Nietzsche so eloquently and precisely identifies, I elsewhere argue that we ought to read Nietzsche's own work as carefully and explicitly operating outside the bounds of metaphysics, and thus as 'post-metaphysical'. See Shea (2016).

[4] See Conway (1997); Conway (2008); Hatab (2008); Hicks and Rosenberg (2008); and Marsden (2009).

ideal tends towards one that excludes all others while also drawing everything into it, then a counter-ideal would have to be a multiplicity that could maintain itself in a dynamic tension without reintroducing the one.[5] Second, if the ascetic ideal tends towards identity, then a counter-ideal would tend towards difference. Both of these points entail that there is no one alternative to the ascetic ideal, but instead a plurality of alternatives. It is in the context of trying to render the contours of these alternatives explicit that I will argue that Foucault's work serves as one way to conceptualise a political ontology that affirms these multiplicities and differences.

3 Foucault: From a Politics of Ressentiment to a Politics of Affirmation

When read in the context of Nietzsche's critique of the ascetic ideal, Foucault's work on discourse, power, critique and resistance stands as an exemplary model of a post-metaphysical politics of difference committed to mobilising Nietzschean insights. The depth of this commitment is exemplified in the opening of his 1979 lectures at the Collège de France, *The Birth of Biopolitics*, where Foucault states explicitly one of the major methodological decisions that orients his historical inquiries:

> Historicism starts from the universal and, as it were, puts it through the grinder of history. My problem is exactly the opposite. I start from the theoretical and methodological decision that consists in saying: Let's suppose that universals do not exist.... So what I would like to deploy here is exactly the opposite of historicism: not, then, questioning universals by using history as a critical method, but starting from the decision that universals do not exist, asking what kind of history we can do. (Foucault 2010, p. 3)

I begin with this quote in order to highlight what I consider to be one of the most significant and often overlooked features of Foucault's work – namely, that the fundamental principles that guide and orient his investigations are not the result of an insight into the ultimate nature of things, that is, metaphysics, but are instead the result of careful and considered methodological decisions. The nature of these methodological decisions receives its most sustained treatment in Fou-

---

[5] I regard Luce Irigaray's account of female sexuality in distinction to a masculine phallogocentricism, in *This Sex Which Is Not One*, as providing an eloquent articulation of just such an alternative: 'within herself, she is already two – but not divisible into one(s) – that caress each other' (Irigaray 1985, p. 24).

cault's essay "Nietzsche, Genealogy, History" (Foucault 1997b), where he contrasts the methodological commitments of genealogy to those of metaphysical history. On Foucault's account, the metaphysical approach assumes the existence of self-identical and immobile structures that lie beneath history. These original identities, once unearthed, function as an origin, as the site of primordial truths that would provide a suprahistorical perspective from which to survey history as a singular and closed totality. In this way, the origin would provide a singular understanding of history as the result of either a cosmological cause – something like Platonism or monotheism – or as the progressive realisation of a teleological aim – something like Hegel or Marx.

Alternatively, according to Foucault, the genealogist has no *'faith* in metaphysics' and therefore 'refuses the certainty of absolutes (Foucault 1997b, pp. 371 and 379). For this reason, rather than start with the assumption that its objects of inquiry are self-identical and unified entities that remain the same through change, the genealogist instead approaches history as a network of fabricated assemblages, ruptures and multiple beginnings brought about through a play of forces and dominations. Thus, the genealogist neither feigns disinterested observation nor pursues ideal metaphysical absolutes, but rather affirms the very perspective from which she constructs historical formations from discontinuous and fragmented elements.[6] What this means, then, is that, methodologically, the genealogist divests herself of the task of washing away historical contingency so as to reveal a primordial truth that would in some way return us to the privileged position of a metaphysical origin – 'the homeland to which metaphysicians promise a return' (Foucault 1997b, p. 386). This also means that the genealogist is not engaged in the inverse task of disclosing the fundamentally contingent nature of history so as to "unmask" purported metaphysical absolutes as illusory since this would, in essence, be the very same task as metaphysical history – that is, contingency would stand as an inverted metaphysical origin that would eternally de-centre and fracture history rather than congeal and totalise it. For these reasons, the genealogist renounces any and all claims to origins – whether those are absolutes or contingencies, which is to say that from the outset, as a method, genealogy is avowedly post-metaphysical and post-foundational.

While Foucault makes no explicit statements in regard to the ascetic ideal, we can nonetheless see that his account of genealogy as a method departs

---

6 Thus, Foucault does not claim to engage in genealogy from "nowhere". Genealogy is precisely a method that is always already underway from somewhere, from a vested interpretative perspective or position. For this reason, at the end of the essay, Foucault describes the historical sense under the direction of genealogy as parodic, dissociative and sacrificial.

from the ascetic ideal's metaphysical commitments. First, by characterising genealogy as a method, Foucault evades the indictment Nietzsche brought against science and atheism – namely, that they still possess a metaphysical faith in truth. Thus, Foucault's use of contingency as a methodological starting point functions to 'contend' with metaphysics (in Hatab's words), rather than sustain it. Second, Foucault's understanding of his work as guided by method thereby explicitly situates it as one amongst many, and thus as affirming difference and multiplicity from the outset, which disables both the functioning and the effects of the technique of power named above. On Foucault's account, genealogy makes no claim to be the one and only true philosophical practice, denouncing all others as false or aberrant. Lastly, by affirming the positionality of the genealogical inquirer, Foucault additionally rejects the decontextualised and otherworldly epistemic subject of metaphysics. For these reasons, genealogy as a method is always underway as a hypothetical, provisional, experimental and dialogical form of inquiry – in contrast to metaphysics.

In May of 1978, several months before the 1979 lectures at the Collège de France, in a talk given to the French Society of Paris entitled "What is Critique?", Foucault similarly expands upon the specifically methodological dimension of his work. There, he claims that the theme with which his historical-philosophical work is concerned is the relationship between truth, power and the subject (Foucault 2007, p. 57). More specifically, Foucault tells us that his historical-philosophical inquiries are an examination of what he calls 'eventualization' (Foucault 2007, p. 59), which he defines as an investigation into 'the relationships between structures of rationality that articulate true discourse and the mechanisms of subjugation that are linked to it' (Foucault 2007, p. 56). According to Foucault:

> What we are trying to find out is what are the links, what are the connections that can be identified between mechanisms of coercion and elements of knowledge, what is the interplay of relay and support developed between them, such that a given element of knowledge takes on effects of power in a given system where it is allocated to a true, probable, uncertain or false element, such that a procedure of coercion acquires the very form and justifications of a rational, calculated, technically efficient element, etc. (Foucault 2007, p. 59)

In pursuit of these aims, Foucault is explicit about the methodological decisions that enable these inquiries, decisions that openly eschew the search for metaphysical origins in favour of constructing historical assemblages. First, inquiries into eventualizations suspend the traditional philosophical questions concerning both the validity of the systems of knowledge under consideration and the legitimacy of the practices in question. As Foucault notes, 'We are not attempting to find out what is true or false, founded or unfounded, real or illusory, scientific or ideological, or legitimate or abusive' (Foucault 2007, p. 59). Second, the very terms of the investigations, 'knowledge' and 'power', serve as an analytic grid for investigation: '[These] two terms have only a methodological function. It is not a matter of identifying general principles of reality through them, but of somehow pinpointing the analytical front, the type of element that must be pertinent for the analysis' (Foucault 2007, p. 60). Thus, as analytical terms, *savoir* and *pouvoir* refer, respectively, to the procedures and effects of *connaissance* at work in a given historical domain, and to the mechanisms that induce behaviours and discourses.[7]

Foucault calls this circular relation in which truth is linked with a system of power that produces and sustains it, and to effects of power that it induces and extends, a 'regime of truth' (Foucault 1997c, p. 132). Of particular importance for Foucault are the mechanisms of normalisation and subjectification at work in these regimes. Foucault famously surveys – via analyses of madness, medicine, knowledge, delinquency and sexuality – the ways in which regimes of truth fashion normal and abnormal subjects while simultaneously producing practices that not only divide and partition them, but also individuate, measure, compare and correct them.[8] For example, within the education system, "experts" – who are themselves constituted by acting in accordance with the correct methods for attaining knowledge – make claims about the nature of human beings and the ways they learn (knowledge); and, based on this knowledge, determine the appropriate methods of instruction (power). To determine the efficaciousness of the implemented methods of instruction, tests are administered to determine student comprehension (knowledge), whose results are then used to correct and adjust the methods of instruction (power). These pedagogical practices (power) legitimated in sources of correct knowledge (knowledge) have the further effect of sorting students (power) into the categories of proficient and deficient, or normal and abnormal, which are based on standardised tests that establish the statistical norm for comprehension of all students (knowledge) and identify deficient students for targeted means of correction – normalisation (power). According to Foucault:

> This form of power that applies itself to immediate everyday life categorizes the individual, marks him by his own individuality, attaches him to his own identity, imposes a law of truth on him that he must recognize and others have to recognize in him. It is a form of power that makes individuals subjects. There are two meanings of the word 'subject': sub-

---

[7] Colin Koopman and Tomas Matza (2013) highlight the significance of method and analytic in Foucault.
[8] This relation finds its most systematic treatment in Foucault's *Discipline and Punish*.

ject to someone else by control and dependence, and tied to his own identity by a conscience or self-knowledge. Both meanings suggest a form of power that subjugates and makes subject to. (Foucault 1997d, p. 331)

It is here, in his analyses of these regimes of truth – that is, in 'the ensemble of rules according to which the true and the false are separated and specific effects of power attached to the true' (Foucault 1997c, p. 132) – that we find Foucault identifying in specific historical discourses the very technique of power that Nietzsche identifies in the system of interpretation installed by the ascetic ideal, that is, the twofold operation of power: division and coalescence. Thus, for instance, the discourse of pedagogy lays claim to the instruction "proper" to all learning – constructing the inside/outside of legitimate/illegitimate instruction – while simultaneously organising all pedagogy internally according to its principles – that is, governing the entirety of its domain as the one and only rightful domain.[9] In this way, we can read Foucault as specifically carrying forward Nietzsche's analysis of the politics of truth.[10]

Central to these analyses is Foucault's conception of power, which receives its most elaborate treatment in *The History of Sexuality, vol. 1*. There, Foucault tells us:

> By power, I do not mean 'Power' as a group of institutions and mechanisms that ensure the subservience of the citizens of a given state. By power, I do not mean, either, a mode of subjugation which, in contrast to violence, has the form of the rule. Finally, I do not have in mind a general system of domination exerted by one group over another, a system whose effects, through successive derivations, pervade the entire social body. (Foucault 1978, p. 92)

Rather:

---

9 We might better see this in the way in which educators, students and administrators alike are all equally being made into "subjects of assessment" within the contemporary milieu of education.

10 In his inaugural lecture at the Collège de France, Foucault explicitly names Nietzsche as his precursor in analysing the manifestations of desire and power at work in true discourse: 'Thus, only one truth appears before our eyes: wealth, fertility and sweet strength in all its insidious universality. In contrast, we are unaware of the prodigious machinery of the will to truth, with its vocation of exclusion. All those who, at one moment or another in our history, have attempted to remould this will to truth and to turn it against truth at that very point where truth undertakes to justify the taboo, and to define madness; all those, from Nietzsche to Artaud and Bataille, must now stand as (probably haughty) signposts for all our future work' (Foucault 1972, p. 220).

> It seems to me that power must be understood in the first instance as the multiplicity of force relations immanent in the sphere in which they operate and which constitute their own organization; as the process which, through ceaseless struggles and confrontations, transforms, strengthens, or reverses them; as the support which these force relations find in one another, thus forming a chain or a system, or on the contrary, the disjunctions and contradictions which isolate them from one another; and lastly, as the strategies in which they take effect, whose general design or institutional crystallization is embodied in the state apparatus, in the formulation of the law, in the various social hegemonies. (Foucault 1978, pp. 92–93)

On this account, the power relations that serve as an analytic grid for Foucault's investigations are local, ubiquitous and unstable. This means that instead of locating the locus of power in the centralised point of a sovereign and its associated bureaucracies, Foucault will examine the networks of power relations formed between economies, doctors' offices, courtrooms, Child Protective Services, schools, workplaces and families, as well as the everyday practices between social groups and individuals. Thus, rather than confining his analyses of power relations to the great binary divide of rulers and ruled, which would form a pyramidal structure of the application of power from the top down, Foucault instead focuses on power relations as de-centred, multiple, multi-layered, mobile and reverberating networks of social interactions – that is, 'power comes from below' (Foucault 1978, p. 94). Foucault's description of power relations in his essay "The Subject and Power" attests to the complex and vast field of analysis that interests him:

> [Power] operates on the field of possibilities in which the behavior of active subjects is able to inscribe itself. It is a set of actions on possible actions; it incites, it induces, it seduces, it makes easier or more difficult; it releases or contrives, makes more probable or less; in the extreme, it constrains or forbids absolutely, but it is always a way of acting upon one or more acting subjects by virtue of their acting or being capable of action. A set of actions upon other actions. (Foucault 1997d, p. 341)

Such an analytic of power relations allows Foucault to examine and make intelligible the widest possible array of social interactions and practices without reducing them to a single grid or conception of intelligibility – and, by doing so, it allows him to evade the singular and totalising tendency of the ascetic ideal in the direction of a univocal and global system of interpretation.

Despite the ubiquitous presence of power relations, which might appear to reduce power to a homogeneous and undifferentiated medium, Foucault maintains that 'Where there is power, there is resistance' (Foucault 1978, p. 95). However, Foucault's conception of resistance is quite specific to his analytic of power relations. From the outset, as mentioned above, Foucault rejects a centralised locus of power that would exist in contrast to its 'other', an 'other' conceived of either in terms of an 'all-encompassing opposition between rulers and ruled' (Foucault 1978, p. 94), that is, those with power and those without, or in terms of a mutually exclusive and confrontational opposition between knowledge and power, that is, knowledge as positioned outside power but nonetheless serving as the foundation of its legitimate application.[11] In this way, for Foucault, power relations stand in an 'agonistic' relation to one another rather than in an 'antagonistic' relation (Foucault 1997d, p. 342). In other words, there is no "great war" of binary power relations arranged in a mutually exclusive and confrontational opposition to one another. Rather, for Foucault, the network of the social is composed of a multiplicity of power relations pursuing their own strategies and deploying their own tactics, and all without direction from a centre. For this reason, power relations, through interaction and play, can just as much reinforce, extend and strengthen one another as they can reverse, deplete and weaken one another. Thus, since there is neither a centre to power relations nor an outside of power relations, there is no privileged locus of refusal to power relations, but only the open play of multiple power relations and a multiplicity of resistances.

Moreover, since power relations are, on Foucault's account, both fluid and mobile, they can also be conceived of in terms of freedom and domination. As Foucault notes:

> When one defines the exercise of power as a mode of action upon the actions of others, when one characterizes these actions as the government of men by other men – in the broadest sense of the term – one includes an important element: freedom. Power is exercised only over free subjects, and only insofar as they are 'free'. By this we mean individual or collective subjects who are faced with a field of possibilities in which several kinds of conduct, several ways of reacting and modes of behavior are available. (Foucault 1997d, p. 342)

---

[11] Foucault is quite explicit on this point: 'Perhaps, too, we should abandon a whole tradition that allows us to imagine that knowledge can exist only where the power relations are suspended and that knowledge can develop only outside its injunctions, its demands and its interests. Perhaps we should abandon the belief that power makes mad and that, by the same token, the renunciation of power is one of the conditions of knowledge. We should admit rather that power produces knowledge (and not simply by encouraging it because it serves power or by applying it because it is useful); that power and knowledge directly imply one another; that there is no power relation without the correlative constitution of a field of knowledge, nor any knowledge that does not presuppose and constitute at the same time power relations' (Foucault 1995, p. 27).

For Foucault, freedom exists as an intrinsic feature of his analytic of power relations. Since power relations are inherently unstable, they are therefore capable of intensification and extension as well as de-escalation and reversal. Thus, freedom ultimately speaks to the element of modification in any relation of power. However, when the capacity for modification is absent, a state of domination exists:

> The analysis of power relations is an extremely complex area; one sometimes encounters what may be called situations or states of domination in which power relations, instead of being mobile, allowing the various participants to adopt strategies modifying them, remain blocked, frozen. When an individual or social group succeeds in blocking a field of power relations, immobilizing them and preventing any reversibility of movement by economic, political, or military means, one is faced with what may be called a state of domination. In such a state, it is certain that practices of freedom do not exist or exist only unilaterally or are extremely constrained and limited. (Foucault 1997a, p. 283)

On Foucault's account, then, freedom is not an arrangement or condition without power relations – as there is no "outside" of power relations – but is instead the inherently fluid dynamic of power relations themselves. Similarly, domination is not the unauthorised and illegitimate imposition of power on a just and innocent state of freedom, but rather is a particularly static ensemble of power relations. Thus, while the ascetic ideal installs a singular metaphysico-ontological interpretation of a mutually exclusive and antagonistic dichotomy between being either free from power relations or subject to them – a relation that is itself supposed to be arranged in light of a principle or truth that transcends them – Foucault alternatively constructs an analytic grid in which a multiplicity of power relations take form immanently to the dynamic that unfolds between them. In this way, through the construction of an analytic grid that understands power relations as operating immanently to a strategic field, Foucault manages to deploy a method that functions otherwise than that of the ascetic ideal, since his method puts out of play the metaphysicians' faith in antithetical values. It does this, first, by refusing the dichotomy of an inside/outside of power and, second, by refusing any appeal to an element that is simultaneously supposed to transcend and organise the system to which it is related.

Lastly, when it comes to conceptualising a resistance to, and reversal of, the effects of normalisation and subjectification in light of the aforementioned methodological commitments, Foucault further tells us:

> Thus you see that the question is no longer through what error, illusion, oversight, or illegitimacy has knowledge come to induce effects of domination…. The question instead would be: how can the indivisibility of knowledge and power in the context of interactions and multiple strategies induce both singularities, fixed according to their conditions of ac-

ceptability, and a field of possibilities, of openings, indecisions, reversals and possible dislocations which make them fragile, temporary, and which turn these effects into events, nothing more, nothing less than events? In what way can the effects of coercion characteristic of [these regimes of truth] not be dissipated by a return to the legitimate destination of knowledge and by a reflection on the transcendental or semi-transcendental that fixes knowledge, but how can they instead be reversed or released from within a concrete strategic field, this concrete strategic field that induced them, starting with the decision not to be governed? (Foucault 2007, p. 66)

Here, Foucault refuses the politics of *ressentiment* and thereby refuses its accompanying technique of power, which seeks both to escape and arrest the play of differences. According to the politics of *ressentiment*, only those in accord with metaphysical truth have the legitimate right to political speech as either advocacy or denunciation since all speech and action uncoupled from truth is, in the end, aberrant, corrupt and unjust, according to metaphysics. Alternatively, Foucault offers a conception of political resistance that operates immanently to, and affirms, differences. Thus, carrying the disavowal of the ascetic ideal and its politics of *ressentiment* to its logical conclusion, Foucault offers a conception of critique that empowers political actors to decry those arrangements they deem intolerable and to do so precisely without the certainty of truth on their side:

> I will say that critique is the movement by which the subject gives himself the right to question truth on its effects of power and question power on its discourses of truth. [Critique] will be *the art of voluntary insubordination*, that of reflected intractability. Critique would essentially insure the desubjugation of the subject in the context of what we would call, in a word, the politics of truth. (Foucault 2007, p. 47, emphasis added)

In evading the metaphysical impulse, Foucault locates critique in individuals' and groups' refusal to be governed. In this way, the impetus for political resistance is not the possession of truth – a strategy and tactic born from *ressentiment* – but rather the refusal to remain subject to social practices that one can no longer abide.

4 Conclusion

My account here of the ways in which we can read Foucault's work as operating outside the bounds of the ascetic ideal, and thus as either contending with metaphysics or as post-metaphysical, is by no means meant to be exhaustive. Rather, I hope merely to have shown some of the ways in which we can mobilise both Nietzsche and Foucault to sketch the contours of a politics of difference. More specifically, while Nietzsche arguably has no explicit politics of difference, his critique of the ascetic ideal and the politics of truth it inaugurates provide many of the necessary clues for how we might go about thinking their alternative. Furthermore, when we read Foucault's work in light of Nietzsche's critique, we find that Foucault offers what may be regarded as a politics of affirmation in contrast to a politics of *ressentiment*.

On this account, there are several distinguishing features that mark Foucault's work as offering a politics of affirmation, one that brings into relief a germinal politics of difference present in Nietzsche's work. First, in contrast to the ascetic ideal, which is driven by the metaphysicians' faith in the value of truth, Foucault is explicit that his work avoids appeals to origins and primordial truths. For this reason, the analytic grid and terms that constitute his work are not to be regarded as postulating theories of reality, but are instead to be understood as hypothetical, provisional and experimental principles for guiding inquiry. Thus, Foucault's own account of his work is as a method. Likewise, there are intimations in Nietzsche's own work that he understands the difference between the traditional metaphysical approach to philosophy and his own historical approach as methodological, as operating upon different ontological considerations, which is most apparent in *Human, All Too Human* (1, 12). Similarly, in the Preface to the *Genealogy*, Nietzsche even more clearly characterises his genealogical approach to history as a method (GoM Preface, 7–8). Fundamental to this notion of method on the part of both Nietzsche and Foucault is a self-reflexive awareness that their work is not to be regarded as advancing metaphysical absolutes but instead is to be regarded otherwise than as metaphysical philosophy. Nietzsche himself states unabashedly in the first chapter of *Beyond Good and Evil* that his reading of existence as will to power is 'only an interpretation' (BGE 22), which explicitly counters a metaphysical reading of his work and establishes an implicit move away from the politics of ressentiment and towards a politics of difference.

Second, Foucault's genealogical analyses of historically-specific discourses in the human sciences identify in concretised historical form the two-fold operations of power – division and coalescence – at work in the system of interpretation installed by the ascetic ideal and driven by the unconditional will to truth identified by Nietzsche. More precisely, like Nietzsche, Foucault's genealogical analyses draw attention to the normalising and subjectivating effects of a technique of power that aims to construct the inside/outside of its domain, and to absorb and reorganise that which is foreign to it according to its own laws. By drawing our attention to this technique of power and its concretised historical forms, both Nietzsche and Foucault draw our attention to the totalitarian, autocratic and homogenising mechanisms at work in the unconditional will to truth and the ascetic ideal, which is always a will to the one. Thus, to take leave of the politics of *ressentiment* is, of necessity, to affirm multiplicities and release the play of differences that the ascetic ideal precisely aims to arrest.

Third, and following from the previous point, Foucault employs a conception of power relations as a multiplicity of forces immanent to a strategic field that runs precisely counter to the opaque operations of power at work in the ascetic ideal and its technique of power. Reading Foucault backwards into Nietzsche, one might say that the ascetic ideal and its technique of power function precisely to produce a state of domination, one in which the play of multiplicities and difference is frozen by the ascetic ideal's move towards one, closed system of interpretation. Thus, Foucault's political ontology is, from the outset, constituted by an open, dynamic play of differences rather than by a closed, static singularity. In this vein, Nietzsche's call for a counter-ideal to the ascetic ideal, and not its destruction, is itself an affirmation of multiplicities and the play of differences.

Lastly, bringing all of the above features together, Foucault advances a conception of critique as voluntary insubordination that uniquely manages to affirm the play of these differences rather than arresting them. Whereas a politics of *ressentiment* aims to dissolve the tension between separate systems of interpretation and valuation by drawing the two together under a transcendent term that causes one system to be absorbed into and reorganised by the other, Foucault's politics of affirmation eschews a transcendent term that would permanently bind and fix them. Instead, his politics of affirmation empowers those subjects that find their position within a regime of truth untenable to call into question and resist that very structure, thereby affirming and even intensifying their difference. This is a politics that resists the impulse to subjugation and instead facilitates desubjugation. When read against the backdrop of Nietzsche's indictment of science and atheism as the latest manifestations of the ascetic ideal, since they still hold firm to the unconditional value of truth, Foucault's elaboration of a form of critique that renounces this very appeal to a foundational truth is all the more impressive. Thus, Foucault offers a conception of critique that operates otherwise than the technique of power at the heart of the politics of *ressentiment* and the ascetic ideal. In this case, we find that Foucault's conception of critique echoes Nietzsche's own delicate position in relation to the tyranny of metaphysical philosophy and the ascetic ideal, which is that of positioning oneself otherwise than metaphysics so as to contend with it rather than either remaining tethered to it, or worse, replicating it – the latter being quite possibly the greatest danger that any politics of difference faces, as Nietzsche indicated.[12]

Bibliography

Ansell-Pearson, Keith (1991): "The Significance of Michel Foucault's Reading of Nietzsche: Power, the Subject, and Political Theory". In: *Nietzsche-Studien* 20. No. 1, pp. 267–283.
Brobjer, Thomas (1998): "The Absence of Political Ideals in Nietzsche's Writing". In: *Nietzsche-Studien* 27. No. 1, pp. 300–318.
Connolly, William (1991): *Political Theory and Modernity*. Oxford: Blackwell.
Conway, Daniel (1997): *Nietzsche and the Political*. London: Routledge.
Conway, Daniel (2008): *Nietzsche's* On the Genealogy of Morals: *A Reader's Guide*. New York: Continuum.
Detwiler, Bruce: (1990): *Nietzsche and the Politics of Aristocratic Radicalism*. Chicago: University of Chicago Press.
Foucault, Michel (1972): "The Discourse on Language". In: *The Archaeology of Knowledge*, pp. 215–237. Translated by A. M. Sheridan Smith. New York: Pantheon.
Foucault, Michel (1978): *The History of Sexuality, vol. 1: An Introduction*. Translated by Robert Hurley. New York: Random House.
Foucault, Michel (1995): *Discipline and Punish: The Birth of the Prison*. Translated by Alan Sheridan. New York: Pantheon.
Foucault, Michel (1997a): "The Ethics of the Concern for the Self as a Practice of Freedom". In: *Essential Works of Michel Foucault 1954–1984, vol. I: Ethics: Subjectivity and Truth*, pp. 281–301 Edited by Paul Rabinow and translated by Robert Hurley et al. New York: The New Press.
Foucault, Michel (1997b): "Nietzsche, Genealogy, History". In: *Essential Works of Foucault, 1954–1984, vol. II: Aesthetics, Method, and Epistemology*, pp. 369–391. Edited by James D. Faubion and translated by Robert Hurley et al. New York: The New Press.
Foucault, Michel (1997c): "Truth and Power". In: *Essential Works of Michel Foucault 1954–1984, vol. III: Power*, pp. 111–133. Edited by James D. Faubion and translated by Robert Hurley et al. New York: The New Press.
Foucault, Michel (1997d): "The Subject and Power". In: *Essential Works of Michel Foucault 1954–1984, vol. III: Power*, pp. 326–348. Edited by James D. Faubion and translated by Robert Hurley et al. New York: The New Press.
Foucault, Michel (2007): "What is Critique?" In: *The Politics of Truth*, pp. 41–81. Translated by Lysa Hochroth and Catherine Porter. Los Angeles: Semiotext(e).
Foucault, Michel (2010): *The Birth of Biopolitics: Lectures at the Collège de France, 1978–1979*. Translated by Graham Burchell. London, New York: Palgrave.
Hatab, Lawrence J. (1995): *A Nietzschean Defense of Democracy: An Experiment in Postmodern Politics*. Chicago: Open Court.
Hatab, Lawrence J. (2008): "How Does the Ascetic Ideal Function in Nietzsche's Genealogy?" In: *Journal of Nietzsche Studies* 35/36, pp. 106–123.

---

12 I take this to be the thrust of Nietzsche's critique of science and atheism in GoM III, 24.

Hicks, Steven V., and Alan Rosenberg (Eds.) (2008): *Reading Nietzsche at the Margins*. West Lafayette: Purdue University Press.
Irigaray, Luce (1985): *This Sex Which Is Not One*. Translated by Catherine Porter. Ithaca: Cornell University Press.
Koopman, Colin, and Tomas Matza (2013): "Putting Foucault to Work: Analytic and Concept in Foucaultian Inquiry". In: *Critical Inquiry* 39. No. 4, pp. 817–840.
Lightbody, Brian (2010a): *Philosophical Genealogy – Vol. 1: An Epistemological Reconstruction of Nietzsche and Foucault's Genealogical Method*. New York: Peter Lang.
Lightbody, Brian (2010b): *Philosophical Genealogy – Vol. 2: An Epistemological Reconstruction of Nietzsche and Foucault's Genealogical Method*. New York: Peter Lang.
Mahon, Michael (1992): *Foucault's Nietzschean Genealogy: Truth, Power, and the Subject*. Albany: State University of New York Press.
Marsden, Jill (2009): "Nietzsche and the Art of the Aphorism". In: Keith Ansell-Pearson (Ed.): *A Companion to Nietzsche*, pp. 22–38 Malden: Blackwell.
McWhorter, Ladelle (1992): "Asceticism/Askēsis: Foucault's Thinking Historical Subjectivity". In: Arleen B. Dallery, Charles E. Scott and P. Holley Roberts (Eds.): *Ethics and Danger: Essays on Heidegger and Continental Thought*, pp. 243–254Albany: State University of New York Press.
Milchman, Alan, and Alan Rosenberg (2007): "The Aesthetic and Ascetic Dimensions of an Ethics of Self-Fashioning: Nietzsche and Foucault". In: *Parrhesia* 11. No. 2, pp. 44–65.
Nietzsche, Friedrich (2003a): *Beyond Good and Evil*. Translated by R. J. Hollingdale. New York: Random House.
Nietzsche, Friedrich (2003b): *Twilight of the Idols and the Anti-Christ*. Translated by R. J. Hollingdale. New York: Random House.
Nietzsche, Friedrich (2004): *Ecce Homo*. Translated by R. J. Hollingdale. New York: Random House.
Nietzsche, Friedrich (2017a): *On the Genealogy of Morality*. Edited by Keith Ansell-Pearson and translated by Carol Diethe. Cambridge: Cambridge University Press.
Nietzsche, Friedrich (2017b): *Human, All Too Human*. Translated by R. J. Hollingdale. Cambridge: Cambridge University Press.
Owen, David (1998): *Maturity and Modernity: Nietzsche, Weber, Foucault and the Ambivalence of Reason*. London: Routledge.
Owen, David (2007): *Nietzsche's Genealogy of Morality*. Montreal: McGill-Queen's University Press.
Shapiro, Gary (2003): *Archaeologies of Vision: Nietzsche and Foucault on Seeing and Saying*. Chicago: University of Chicago Press.
Shaw, Tamsin (2010): *Nietzsche's Political Skepticism*. Princeton: Princeton University Press.
Shea, IV, George W. (2016): "Nietzsche and Habermas on *Wille zur Macht*: From a Metaphysical to a Post-Metaphysical Interpretation of Life". In: *Nietzsche als Kritiker und Denker der Transformation*, pp. 134–144. Edited by Helmut Heit and Sigridur Thorgeirsdottir. Berlin: de Gruyter.
Tuana, Nancy, and Charles E. Scott (2020): *Beyond Philosophy: Nietzsche, Foucault, Anzaldúa*. Bloomington: Indiana University Press.
Westfall, Joseph, and Alan Rosenberg (Eds.) (2018): *Foucault and Nietzsche: A Critical Encounter*. London, New York: Bloomsbury.

Michael J. McNeal
The Quandary of Identity and the Prospective Appearance of Free Spirits in our Globalising Age

Abstract: Nietzsche's analyses of culture and identity permit an incisive assessment of the *décadence* characteristic of neoliberal globalisation, the hegemonic ideology of our age. Nietzsche's thinking about both the quandary of identity and the appearance of individuals was conditioned by his critique of *décadence*. He maintained that identity becomes problematic when degenerating values fail to affirm a society's cultural norms and enforce its rank order of difference. Developing Nietzsche's appraisal via the insights of Debord and Baudrillard, this chapter argues that a critical analysis of culture can illuminate how liberal modernity destabilises traditional values and subverts identities through alienating, media-driven spectacles of multiculturalism that banalise difference. However, a Nietzschean form of life-affirming, jovial ironism may sufficiently invigorate prospective free spirits to facilitate their self-overcoming.

1 Introduction

How may Nietzsche's analyses of culture and values be utilised to assess decadent characteristics of the West's neoliberal form of globalisation, as well as their implications for identity and the prospective appearance of free-spirited individuals? This chapter takes up these interrelated questions in an attempt to provide insights into Nietzsche's futural thought. It then advances corresponding practices through which the proposals entailed in that futural thought may be realised.

Evident during Nietzsche's lifetime, 'the totalising character of European decadence' and its resulting disruption of shared identic fictions (i.e., culture) occupied much of his attention (CW Epilogue). Indeed, the propagation of life-denying values in late-nineteenth-century Europe determined his understanding of the politics of difference. By applying his analysis to the present, we gain perspective on its continued imposition throughout the world via globalisation and the ideology of liberal democracy.[1] Undergirding the contemporary "internation-

---

1 The ideology of liberal democracy arose through post-Enlightenment discourses of rational-

al system", this globalisation complex originated in the Anglo-European "West"[2]. It universalises 'Europe's *democratic* movement', to transform our world according to a *novus ordo seclorum*, a dream rooted in values Nietzsche associated with slave morality (BGE 242).[3]

I utilise Nietzsche's critique of identity to assess globalisation's entrenchment of decadent values – the reigning liberal democratic ideology of our globalising age – and the quandary of identity it generates. I maintain that its putatively liberatory precepts corrupt cultures and impose the plebeianism exemplifying western decadence (see BGE 253). Specifically, the liberal democratic principles of equality and pity for all that suffers provide globalisation with apparent moral coherence. Emboldened by their sense of rectitude, its priestly exponents coerce conformity with their dogmatic beliefs,[4] strident dogmatists imagine that liberal values are, in some metaphysical sense, universal, rather than universally imposed. From this conceit they advocate "democratic

---

ism, universalism, secularism, humanism and progressivism (Ball et. al. 2011, pp. 192–193), and spawned the discourses of scientism, meliorism, and human rights, which further resignation to nihilism. Following many scholars, Chris Brown notes an oversimplified distinction 'between Anglo-American and Continental liberalism, between cosmopolitan and pluralist liberalism' (Brown 2007, p. 164). The aforementioned ideology entails significant elements of both conceptions of liberalism, each allowing for individual liberty and tolerating difference, despite different emphases.

2 The Anglo-European West refers to north-western Europe and the English-speaking European cultural realm outside of Europe (i.e., the US, Canada, Australia, New Zealand, etc.).

3 By 'globalisation' I refer to the western-led globalisation complex, which universally imposes neoliberal, laissez-faire economic policies (à la the Washington Consensus) and pushes liberal democracy in the political sphere. By decentring traditional subjectivities, it amalgamates autochthonous cultures and destroys indigenous forms of life. A totalising, anti-cultural project that infects societies and commandeers their values to replicate desires that virally propagate it, globalisation eliminates viewpoint diversity. This complex was formalised in the wake of World War II via globalising institutions (e.g., the IMF, WB, UN, WTO), forces (e.g., ever-increasing communication, mass travel, global entertainment), and processes (e.g., the "efficiency imperative", standardised accountancy, financial reporting, regulatory oversight). Stephen Gill anticipated this notion with his analysis of an ideologically conservative 'market civilisation', consisting of contradictory 'cultural, ideological, and mythic forms understood broadly as an ideology or myth of capitalist progress ... associated with the cumulative aspects of market integration ... configured by the power of transnational capital' (Gill 1995, p. 399). Some scholars contrast it with illiberal forms of globalisation advanced by China or Russia (e.g., the "Beijing Consensus"). However, thorough integration into the globalisation complex those nations significantly mitigate their challenges to it.

4 On Nietzsche's critique of liberalism and its exponents' tendency to 'mistake state-generated political agreement for real rational convergence' between political norms and the state's normative authority, see Shaw (2007, p. 139).

globalism", which aims to replace the existing nation-state system with the global governance of some "united states of the world" and eradicate all other politics of difference. Neoliberal practices reinforce the consumerist ethos and compel a gradual cultural homogenisation that is rationalised by the democratic institutions and emerging transnational civic ethos at the centre of the globalisation complex.[5]

According to Joseph Stiglitz, 'proponents of globalisation ... [consider it synonymous with] progress; developing countries must accept it, if they are to grow [economically] and fight poverty effectively' (Stiglitz 2003, p. 5). Globalisation's discursive or rhetorical promise of happiness through consumption – which resonates among those who 'experience suffering and displeasure as evil ... [and] a defect of existence' – introduces a spirit of revenge (GS 338), while the illusions of prosperity and contentment it circulates exacerbate *ressentiment*. Nietzsche's theory of decadence illuminates much about the form of nihilism that typifies our globalising age, particularly when supplemented by theories of twentieth-century philosophers whose thought Nietzsche influenced. When combined with Nietzsche's critique, their analyses of totalising spectacles, simulations of the real, and discipling governmentality (which are operative in globalisation) indicate some means by which healthy individuals may emerge through novel practices of self-creation rooted in the manipulation and subversion of those processes. Moreover, this affords insights into globalisation's decadence, its 'mediocritisation of man' (BGE 242) in our current 'age of the masses' (BGE 241), and the nihilism that results. By extension, such a syncretic Nietzschean analysis indicates possibilities for a praxis through which free spirits, for whom 'even life's mistakes have their own meaning and value', may discredit decadent values promulgated by globalisation (EH Clever, 9). By pursuing their *erōs*, Nietzsche expected prospective free spirits ('exceptional people who possess the most dangerous and attractive qualities') to exploit these 'conditions', make themselves 'stronger and richer' (BGE 242), and thereby hasten the appearance of philosophers of the future capable of 'teach[ing] humanity its future as its *will*' (BGE 203).

Nietzsche conceived of the free spirit – the exception 'who thinks differently from what, on the basis of his origin, environment, his class and profession, or on the basis of the dominant views of the age, would have been expected of him'

---

5 Wendy Brown observes that 'Governance is not identical with or exclusive to neoliberalism.... However, as it matured and converged with neoliberalism [throughout the second half of the twentieth century], governance has become neoliberalism's primary administrative form, the political modality through which it creates environments, structures constraints and incentives, and hence conducts subjects' (Brown 2015, p. 122).

(HH I, 225) – in response to Europe's crisis of decadence, which problematised identity. His exhortation to his readers (prospective free spirits) to 'become who you are' (GS 270), expressed the ethos it commended. He expected these 'last Europeans with a good conscience' to gain perspective necessary for recognising life-demeaning ideals (BGE 214). In our own age, this would entail recognition of the spectacles of contentedness and simulations of joy contrived to legitimate globalisation.[6] In opposition to them, such 'free, *very* free spirits' would undertake the task of 'translat[ing] humankind back into nature' (BGE 230). They would summon 'tremendous counter-forces [ungeheure Gegenkräfte] ... to cross [the] "*progressus in simile*"' that is moving 'human beings ... toward what is *base* [die Fortbildung des Menschen ... in's Gemeine]' (BGE 268, translation modified). In so doing they strive to 'arouse suspicion' of ascetic ideals (GM III, 27), to combat 'practice[s] of nihilism' and 'tendencies *hostile to life*' (A 7).

In light of the quandary of identity induced by globalisation, we must examine the extent to which the liberal democratic values globalisation propagates frustrate the prospective appearance of free-spirited individuals.[7] Could free spirits exploit that ideology to hasten the down-going of humanity towards its eventual overcoming?[8] A Nietzschean response to globalisation is needed to challenge its destruction of cultures that are formative of prospective free spirits.[9] Towards this, I examine Nietzschean tactics that may undermine and discredit the spectacularised meanings and simulated purposes characteristic of globalisation's nihilistic mode of existence.

Insofar as Nietzsche's moral psychology informs his mature thinking about identity and the appearance of individuals, his affirmation of difference advances a qualified cosmopolitanism that provides a heuristic for assessing globalisation's subversion of cultures according to post-Enlightenment rationality and purportedly "universal" values. This masks globalisation's discourses and their role in rationalising state-coerced economic liberalisation and democratisation.[10] Blending their qualified cosmopolitanism with an ironic stance towards

---

[6] Guy Debord asserts that 'the spectacle represents the dominant *model* of life.... In both form and content, the spectacle serves as a total justification of the conditions and goals of the existing system' (Debord 1983, p. 6).

[7] On Nietzsche's opposition to liberal notions of freedom, see Siemens (2005).

[8] For an explication of how they might, see Hatab (1999).

[9] Lawrence Hatab provides us with means of conceptualising how Nietzsche might be squared with the principles of agonic, meritocratic democracy in his innovative book *A Nietzschean Defense of Democracy*.

[10] Jean Baudrillard's understands our reigning liberal-democratic ideology as 'the process of reducing and abstracting symbolic material into a form. But this reductive abstraction is

the reigning ideals of the modern world, or *Weltironie*, free spirits would cultivate a Nietzschean disposition of globality.[11] Through it, these 'world-affirming individual[s]' could confront globalisation's ascetic practices and cast certain of liberal democracy's anti-natural principles in doubt (BGE 56).[12] In so doing, they would prepare the way for future philosophers strong enough to forge a new human consciousness and corresponding 'meaning of the earth' (Z Prologue, 3).

2 Nietzsche's Axiological-Historical Analysis of Decadence

In what sense does identity constitute a quandary in Nietzsche's view and how does his thinking address this? Eric Steinhart observes that 'Nietzsche strenuously denies that there is any identity anywhere ... [and that] the identity that does emerge from difference is merely apparent' (Steinhart 2005, p. 1). Nevertheless, Nietzsche recognised (and affirmed) that such appearances were essential to the formation and preservation of a people (*Volk*), from which individuals – his "higher types" – emerge. This response to the problem of identity, which runs through western philosophy – from the basic question "who am I?" to the exhortation" "know thyself" – indicates its importance to Nietzsche. He challenges its putative ontological necessity and exposes its psychological bases, namely, the desired unity and perceived persistence of the self.[13] He further notes its epistemological dubiousness and the metaphysical and grammatical conceits in its grounding of reality.[14]

---

given immediately as value (autonomous), as content (transcendent), and as a representation of consciousness (signified)' (Baudrillard 1988, p. 77).
11 Martin Shaw conceives globality as 'represent[ing] a new condition or age in which ... [there occurs] a sufficiently fundamental shift in the very principles on which modern social organisation is built for us to question the continuation of modernity' (Shaw 2000, p. 18).
12 These practices – including consumerism and over-consumption, over-population, pollution, global warming, environmental destruction – ramify anti-intellectualism and nihilism, and imperil life on our planet.
13 William Connolly observes that 'From a Nietzschean perspective, the self-constituted as a unified, self-responsible agent contains resentment within its very formulation' (Connolly 2002, p. 78).
14 Steinhart observes that 'identity, for Nietzsche, emerges from difference. Nietzsche challenges us to think of difference as logically prior to identity' (Steinhart 2005, p. 12).

Nietzsche's critique of decadence anticipated that our contemporary age would be more decadent than his own (late nineteenth-century Europe). Yet, despite the greater material comfort of many in the early twenty-first century (and perhaps because of it), would-be free spirits are more restricted in their becoming. Since the end of World War II, globalisation has homogenised bodies and mentalities across disparate cultures around the world. The signs of prosperity globalisation proffers as confirmation of its efficacy reproduce and propagate its ascetic ideals. Globalisation represents itself as 'a new culture [wherein] consumption is transformed into a means of individual and collective expression. Thus, a "new humanism" of consumption is opposed to the "nihilism" of consumption' (Baudrillard 1988, p. 12).

Nietzsche's thought lends itself to an appreciation of the non-Western world's plight, given its centuries-long subjugation by Anglo-European powers, for he is agnostic about what values conduce the vitality of a people so long as they affirm it and foster the flourishing of its noblest types. Healthy values sustain a culture and the forms of life it gives meaning. It is life-denying (decadent) values he opposes, but in this too he is neutral vis-à-vis culture: decadence results when the instincts a culture nurtures dissipate, causing its reigning values to lose credibility. Hence, he likens decadence to a socio-cultural illness. Nietzsche points to Judeo-Christian morality, which overthrew Rome's religious pantheon (A 58), and Socratic reason, which subverted classical Greece's noble values, as examples (TI, Socrates).

The antecedents of contemporary globalisation extend from the late Renaissance and Columbian exchange, circa 1500, to the Enlightenment and modernity. Globalisation first arose via Europe's exploration, imperialist conquests and colonisation of the world, producing mercantilism, the transatlantic slave trade and the genocidal annihilation of indigenous peoples that impeded resource extraction and territorial annexations. These developments proceeded through the industrial and scientific revolutions. They eroded confidence in traditional institutions and hastened the diminution of faith in Europe that Nietzsche associated with the death of God. Nineteenth-century Europe's anxiety over the absence of foundations and growing sense of existential meaninglessness was exploited by 'short-sighted ... politicians [with] ... no idea of the extent to which the politics of dissolution that they practice[d]' – ideological programmes including communism, anarchism, nationalism and anti-Semitism – could 'only be *entr'acte* politics' (BGE 256). Nietzsche took these programmes – all of which he opposed – to be misinterpretations of the many signs that '*Europe wants to be one*' (BGE 256).

Initially a 'process of increasing similarity between Europeans' (BGE 242), the *ressentiment* globalisation generated increased throughout the twentieth century. It contributed to the occurrence of both world wars, the first of which toppled Europe's decrepit monarchies, and the second being a battle-royal over the future ideological form globalisation would take, Nazism and Soviet communism being challengers to liberal democracy's global dominance. Following World War II, globalisation was formalised via the above-mentioned institutions, forces and processes.[15] Scientism – globalisation's secular faith – was then utilised to justify its imposition.[16] Foucault's insight into the deployment of science by ideology is illuminating in this context:

> the ideological functioning of the sciences ... structures certain of [science's] objects, systematises certain of its enunciations, [and] formalises certain of its concepts and strategies ... it is insofar as this development articulates knowledge ... [that it] functions or does not function in a whole field of discursive practices. (Foucault 1972, p. 185)

Throughout the Cold War era science was harnessed by the ideological proponents of globalisation in myriad ways (e. g., the "green", agricultural and digital "revolutions") to bolster the discursive practices and international order it imposes.

Globalisation's neoliberal character emerged in the mid-1970s with the outsourcing of labour and manufacturing from its post-industrialised centres. The liberalisation of capital flows, structural adjustment programmes to contend with debt crises throughout the global South and the steady reduction of social welfare spending in many developed countries furthered it.

At the same time, the material prosperity of the advanced economies (or "centres" of globalisation) began to decline.[17] Since the 2008 Great Recession, increasing economic precarity has given rise to intolerant dictatorships throughout the world.[18] These authoritarian regimes espouse convoluted mixtures of "traditionalist" ideology and/or reactionary nativism to incite and exploit conservative populism. They take succour from the discourses of globalisation, despite shirking – or rejecting – the norms of liberal democracy.

Faith in science and progress – and the fetish for technological innovation – have increased since Nietzsche's death. This has emboldened meliorists, whose quasi-religious belief that the world can be improved (a secularised form of Christian pity) is doctrine among the ideologues of liberal democracy. Nietzsche

---

15 See n. 1.
16 Scientism is the ideology that science provides the only epistemologically defensible and legitimate means of knowledge generation.
17 On declining economic prosperity throughout the developed world since the mid-1970s, see *Under Pressure: The Squeezed Middle Class*, at https://www.oecd.org/social/under-pressure-the-squeezed-middle-class-689afed1-en.htm, accessed 20 October 2019.
18 For example, Russia, Venezuela, Philippines, Hungary and Turkey.

identified the origins of this development, observing that despite succeeding faith in God, faith in science shared the same basis and served a similar function: 'Our faith in science is still based on a metaphysical faith, – even we knowers of today, we godless anti-metaphysicians, still take our fire from the blaze set alight by ... that faith of the Christians, which was also Plato's faith, that God is truth, that truth is divine' (GM III, 24).

Science has now demonstrated the physiological equivalence of all human beings and has discredited racist and ethno-national chauvinisms. However, this equivalence is also taken to validate the post-Enlightenment insistence on 'equality before the law' (BGE 22), a secularisation of the Christian notion of equality before God. This, in self-serving fashion, is seized upon by the herd – 'an aggregate of decadent forms from everywhere' in the world (A 51) – to advance the egalitarian view that all are *essentially* equal. As if to demonstrate that 'the instincts [driving globalisation] contradict' (TI Skirmishes, 41), this is at odds with the belief – naturalised through market capitalism – that money is the ultimate measure of individual dignity and social worth. The inconsistency between these notions seems resolved by the supposed ability of all to earn money and purchase status therewith. However, the conspicuous consumption extolled by globalisation undermines faith in the very ascetic ideals meant to validate it, because of the material prosperity it lauds.[19] Moreover, technology also augments the power of dictators, enhancing their ability to oppress those they misrule. A self-sabotaging regime that belies its own core "truths", globalisation raises anew the problem of the value of truth that Nietzsche broached in contemplating the death of God:

> Because the ascetic ideal has so far been master over all philosophy, because truth was set as being, as God, as the highest authority itself, because truth was not allowed to be a problem ... the very moment that faith in the God of the ascetic ideal is denied, there is a new problem as well: that of the value of truth. (GM III, 24)

This 'new problem ... of the value of truth' helps explain, in part, populist movements throughout the world. Thoroughly nihilistic, the globalised masses of the early twenty-first century are less equipped to deal with the want of truth than were the Europeans of Nietzsche's era, their resignation or passive nihilism notwithstanding. Contemporary ascetic priests of *ressentiment* – 'the apostles of "modern ideas"' – attempt to mollify these masses by substituting mindless con-

---

[19] Baudrillard calls consumption 'a characteristic mode of industrial civilisation ... [and] the virtual totality of all objects and messages presently constituted in a more or less coherent discourse' (Baudrillard 1988, pp. 21–22).

sumption and vacuous entertainment for traditional cultural practices that supplied them with existential meaning and ontological purpose (BGE 242). Their 'will to an end [is] the nihilistic will willing power' (A 9). What these 'levelers ... strive for ... is the universal, green pasture happiness of the herd' (BGE 44). The result has been a mass of 'exceedingly garrulous, impotent and eminently employable workers', irreverent in their cynicism towards all higher values and disdainful of authority (BGE 242).

How has globalisation conditioned prospects for overcoming its decadent values? Ever-increasing consumption throughout the globalised world – represented as material prosperity (even during recessions) – is likely to frustrate the development of prospective individuals because it occurs via the homogenisation of people's desires and ensuing convergence of values according to plebeian impulses. Nietzsche expected ascetic priests to 'be a fully shut window and bolted door with respect to these approaching *new* philosophers' (BGE 44), and the values they spread to accelerate 'the *total degeneration of human beings*' (BGE 203). The stultification of humankind – its entrapment in passive nihilism – is evinced by the form of governmentality that globalisation imposes and the spectacles of "flourishing" it enacts.

It is noteworthy that the etymology of the word 'person' stems from the Etruscan word *phersu*, meaning 'mask'. Nietzsche observed the significance of metaphorical masks in identity and noted that we employ such masks and encounter them in all of our dealings with others (GS 365). His analysis suggests that identity is unproblematic in healthy societies, whose cultures reinforce the reigning values formative of the persons and the range of types they authorise. Identity becomes problematic when decadent values fail to affirm a society's degenerating norms. At the individual level, this correlates with a person failing to meet the expectations of their community; their masks (the social roles they perform) prove inadequate, and fail to disguise the attributes or characteristics they should conceal, or to present the appearances that enable success. Perturbed by the erosion of the traditional meanings that formerly oriented them, declining communities experience contention over values, which results in divisive notions of selfhood. An anarchy of values ensues, beleaguering those masses whose decadent cultures thereafter afflict them. Part of a degenerating form of life, they suffer its dissipation, which further diminishes their vitality and puts them at odds with themselves.

Nietzsche identifies a historical example of this destabilisation of identity in ancient Rome, which he relates to decadent modern trends: 'As the imperial Romans became un-Roman in relation to the world which stood at his service, as he lost himself in the flood of foreigners which came streaming in and degenerated in the midst of the cosmopolitan carnival of gods, arts and customs, so the same must happen to modern man' (HL 5). This should not be mistaken as indicating xenophobia on Nietzsche's part, nor is he advocating intolerance, per se. Rather, he observes that an amalgamation of types and values banalises differences that formerly oriented them, just as globalisation is homogenising cultures throughout our world.[20] Under globalisation, such cultural integration is represented as facilitating the acceptance of difference, but it actually trivialises and eliminates it to accelerate assimilation. As mentioned before, this homogenising process destabilises every identity, and by extension every individual's self-conception. Such instability provokes reaction: in need of meaning, peoples often respond to their culture's degeneration by (re-)asserting "traditional" or "pure" identities, which foment conflicts that can escalate into wars.

Another problem intrinsic to conventional conceptions of identity relates to the illusion of free will and willing. Nietzsche reflected upon the unnoticed duality of willing, which 'we are in the habit of ignoring and deceiving ourselves about … by means of the synthetic concept of the "I"' (BGE 19). He suggests that the common-sense notion that we will our actions is integrally related to our illusion of subjecthood, which entails identity. This commonly unnoticed duality also deflects us from the role of the instincts in the construction of identity. The instincts are mediated by the socio-cultural milieu within which the range of identities a culture authorises are imagined, ergo the commonality in the evaluative stances between members of the same community. Yet, identity, like culture, continuously evolves. Nietzsche acknowledges this when he observes that 'we are unknown to ourselves'. Despite the identity we forge or acquiesce to, as socialisation constrains our becoming – from the dynamic flux we are, we nevertheless 'remain strange to ourselves … [and] do not understand ourselves' (GM Preface, 1). In striving to create meaning for ourselves and our world, what we take for our identity is an ever-changing kaleidoscope of new experiences and changing circumstances synthesised into a narrative that comes to be believed by its author, the "individual". As the artist of our 'self', always in a process of becoming, 'we *must* confusedly mistake who we are' (GM Preface, 1), both as artist and artwork. This is, in part, why Nietzsche considers the need 'to "give style" to one's character' so important among those capable of 'survey[ing] all the strengths and weaknesses that their nature has to offer and [of] then fit[ting] them into an artistic plan until each appears as art and reason and even [their] weaknesses delight the eye' (GS 290). Self-creation consists with

---

20 See the *World Values Survey*, which under "Findings and Insights" documents the broad 'cultural change that [via secular-rational values] is transforming industrialised societies with mass demands for increasingly democratic institutions' (http://www.worldvaluessurvey.org/WVSContents.jsp, accessed 24 October 2019).

his perfectionist stance: one ought to treat oneself as one's primary artistic project and embrace the 'discipline of great suffering' towards overcoming the foibles that impair one's desired selfhood (BGE 225).

Nietzsche's critique of decadence values stems from his assessment of the Judeo-Christian slave revolt in morality, which subverted and conquered Rome and its pantheon. He employs this to evaluate the Enlightenment and the modern period that followed it. Rather than liberating Europeans from Christian values that subjugated them for two millennia (a period he dubs 'the moral epoch of humanity' [BGE 55]), as the Enlightenment's exponents claimed, the diminution of Christian faith in Europe (i.e., the death of God) exacerbated the sickness that plagued the continent's peoples. In keeping with the 'great ladder of religious cruelty' and their 'sheer cruelty to themselves' the Enlightenment's champions 'sacrifice[d] God for nothingness' (BGE 55).

Enlightenment thinkers transmuted Christianity's life-denying values – and its will to truth – into secular ones, while preserving their pathos: 'the *democratic* movement is the heir to Christianity' (BGE 202). Rooted in the herd's "democratic bias", the Enlightenment's ascetic priests sought to sterilise and/or punish anything noble, ascending, or exhibiting rare excellence that contested its ideals. Similarly, their successors in our age of globalisation seek – out of a *hatred* of reality, from which they suffer – to exclude whatever refutes the 'good works' of liberal democracy (A 15). Nietzsche elaborated a related point in *Daybreak*: 'the residuum of Christian states of mind ... [appears] in "love of one's neighbour", in concern with the tremendous practical effect of ecclesiastical charity.... The more one liberated oneself from [Christian] dogmas, the more one sought as it were a justification of this liberation in a cult of philanthropy' (D 132). The Enlightenment, which Nietzsche understood, in part, as a secular slave revolt in morality, worsened Europe's ailment. This strikes many as counter-intuitive, as Enlightenment principles inspired the founding documents and institutions of the United States, motivated the French Revolution ('the last great slave revolt' [BGE 46]), toppled the *Ancien Régime* and most of Europe's monarchies, and produced the international human rights regime. Despite efforts to transmute Christianity's will to truth into a scientistic faith based upon reason, the existential void resulting from the insight that 'there are no eternal facts, just as there are no absolute truths' (HH Things, 2), left the masses bereft of greater significance and susceptible to suicidal nihilism. As globalisation's ascetic values of scientistic-consumerism have supplanted the autochthonous values of many non-western cultures throughout the world, overlapping and mutually reinforcing simulations of the real have come to mediate a world hostile to life affirming values, a *ressentiment* they also disguise. Likewise, globalisation's ascetic priests benefit from the ersatz culture of the 'last man' type (Z I, 5), a "globalised" form of culturally homogenised life sustained through the anti-agonic, anti-ironic will to truth. Propagated by those scientistic-consumerist values, it lulls the herd into a state of passive nihilism (GM I, 4–5).

3 The Reciprocal Ramification of Culture and the Drives

Nietzsche's moral psychology, which is integral to his analysis of the drives, informed his mature thinking about identity and its deterioration in decadent epochs. In his view, identity consists in multiple, determinative, socio-cultural practices and beliefs that comprise a shared imaginary. This conditions the instincts of a community's members and mediate them in turn. Herein he recognises the source of selfhood that a community's members experience. The phenomenological impression (feeling) of constituting a unified subject, which substantiates their sense of being, is ramified by psycho-physiological experiences compelled by their socio-cultural conditioning. These shared experiences affectively evoke the self and sustain the impression of continuity required for individuals to forget about the absence of ultimate foundations to this existence (KSA 12, 9 [91]). Salient to this is his observation that: 'The falseness of a judgement is for us not necessarily an objection to a judgement … the question is to what extent it is life-promoting, life-preserving, species-preserving, perhaps even species-cultivating. And we are fundamentally inclined to claim that the falsest judgements … are the most indispensable for us' (BGE 4). In a note from his late writings, he reflects upon the origins of the 'regulative fiction' of the notion of 'the I' (echoing points in his early, unpublished essay *On Truth and Lying in an Extra-Moral Sense*):

> What separates me most deeply from the metaphysicians is: I don't concede that the 'I' is what thinks. Instead, I take the I itself to be a construction of thinking, … in other words to be only a *regulative fiction* with the help of which a kind of constancy and thus 'knowability' is inserted into, *invented into*, a world of becoming. Up to now belief in grammar, in the linguistic subject, object, in verbs has subjugated the metaphysicians: I teach the renunciation of this belief. (KGW, 1885, 35 [35])

Values possess a similarly "fictional" origin. Their source is a will to truth from which values arise to function as a key mediator of our reality. Nietzsche notes that 'Only we have created the world that concerns human beings! But precisely this knowledge we lack, and when we catch it for a moment we have forgotten it the next' (GS 301).

The values reticulating a healthy society's politics of difference structure its members' shared reality and generate the meanings needed to secure and sustain them therein. An organising power, it subordinates and absorbs weaker value structures, disciplining social processes and subduing challenges by conducting the drives of its members, which are internalised to produce a shared conscience (GM III, 3). Nietzsche asserts that this excruciating process 'never happened without blood, torments and sacrifices' (GM II, 3). Its mnemonics of pain enable 'a calculable and constant ... scheme of behaviour' (KSA 13, 14 [122]), generating '"purposes", "aims", [and] "meaning" [that accord with] modes of expression and metamorphoses of ... the will to power' (KSA 13, 11 [96]).

Performative enactments of culture safeguard the identities it cultivates by re-enforcing the conceptions of selfhood that substantiate them, and thus preserving the culture. Our possibilities for becoming arise in accordance with the governing politics of difference – our shared conscience and the instinctual framework that condition our desires (KSA 12, 7 [60]). This compels a high degree of conformity with social norms and includes 'what others ... think they know ... about us' (GS 52). The operation of memory reinforces the presumed unity of the self, which leads us 'to speak about an I' (BGE 16).

The reigning moral values within a healthy society 'compel all other drives' and are themselves affirmed by the range of types and identities they permit (KSA 12, 7 [60]). By instructing the all-too-many 'to be a function of the herd and to ascribe value to [themselves] only as a function' (GS 116), morality makes communal life sensible. In this regard the autonomy – or sense of "freedom" – a person enjoys is determined by the politics of difference or rank order of types authorised by the socio-political structures in which they are imbricated. Underpinned by morality, the latter may also be understood, broadly, as serving 'The commanding element ... [that] wills simplicity out of multiplicity' (BGE 230), that is, a people from disparate persons.

The place one finds oneself, both geographically and in terms of one's status within one's community, is a feature of the shared notion of identity. Place both nurtures and is reflected in what one believes oneself to be capable of affecting or effecting vis-a-vis the prospective scope and extent of one's actions. Herein lies one reason for Nietzsche's agnostic stance towards the relative merit of differing systems of master morality, that is, the noble values of disparate cultures. As long as a people's values affirm its culture and facilitate the fullest flourishing of its exemplars, he is indifferent about the specific tenets of their morality. Note his respect for the 'Roman, Arabian, Germanic, Japanese nobility, Homeric heroes, Scandinavian Vikings', etc. The 'daring', 'unpredictability' and 'scorn for safety' that each exhibited in its own fashion roused his admiration (GM I, 11).

Regarding the aetiology of selfhood, Nietzsche maintained that although one's biological inheritance and inborn instincts may be mistaken as the original cause of oneself, one's (culturally generated) socialisation mediates them. Culture symptomatises the shared instincts of a community's members (GS 52), and reciprocally conditions the emergence of norms and traditions, which serve a sense-making function. However, as the liberal democratic ideology of globalisation disrupts autochthonous cultural norms and discredits traditions, identities are disturbed. The instinctual fundaments of identity that moderated one's experience of selfhood are thereby put at odds with customary identifications, sabotaging the self-conceptions of the afflicted community's members. As a people's culture declines, its shared identity is destabilised. This gives rise to nostalgic notions of selfhood, which come to serve as the bases for romantic and reactive assertions of bygone, allegedly more harmonious ages (BGE 223). Prospective free spirits resist efforts to recreate such longed-for, dreamed-of "authentic" pasts, as they amplify *ressentiment* and hinder chances for overcoming the present.

When a people's values no longer support a fortifying culture (form of life), identity becomes a predicament. This decadent state – the quandary of identity – generates the discombobulating awareness that identity is ultimately fictive, a determinative contrivance that provides constancy to existence. Among those 'higher', more spiritual 'men of knowledge' who are aware that they 'are not "knowers" when it comes to [them]selves', this is not harmful (GM Preface, 1). However, this insight is ruinous for the all-too-many who, having believed they knew themselves, come to see their existence as absurd, which compounds its intrinsic horror.[21] Moreover, globalisation's consumer spectacles and simulations of the real prove incapable of filling the vacuum left by their lost cultural groundings and traditional selfhood.

Nietzsche asserts that 'at the bottom of us, really "deep down", there is, of course, something unteachable, some granite of spiritual *fatum*, of predetermined decisions and answers to selected, predetermined questions' (BGE 231). This is not at odds with the formative function of the culture through which one becomes (according to one's culturally conditioned instincts) who one is (GS 270). However, the decadence of our age, its 'concept of "freedom" [serving as] one more proof of the degeneration of the instincts' ensures that the pruning needed to make individuals possible – where 'possible ... means complete' – is inhibited (TI Skirmishes, 41).

---

[21] On the ineliminable need for beliefs that falsify life by limiting one's perspective and horizons, see Acharya (2014, p. 75).

Prospective free spirits are aware of performatively enacting their settled-upon identities, believing in them only in a qualified sense. Among those with strength enough to endure the insight that selfhood is largely and collaboratively manufactured, an exceptional few possess the vitality and broad perspective needed to experiment upon themselves, nevertheless.[22] Conversely, as its received identities and sense of subjectivity are decentred, the herd is disoriented by a sense of the unreal; everything it held to be true about itself becomes suspect, plunging it further into anarchy (BGE 202).

Insofar as it co-extends with self-knowledge and character, identity is, again, related to the evaluations obliged by morality (GS 335). As cultures have been homogenised over the last century-and-a-half, the formative constraints upon becoming have weakened, eroding the efficacy of identity according to the worsening decadence of our age. The liberal democratic ideology imposed by globalisation ramifies a decadent development, in the form of the liberal subject, which is meant to preserve faith – albeit a secular, "rational" one – in metaphysically distinct entities. Regarding Nietzsche's critique of the liberal subject, Keith Ansell-Pearson observes that 'Nietzsche challenges what we might call the ontological assumptions that inform the positing of the liberal subject, [which] assumes individual identity and liberty to be a given, in which the individual exists independently of the mediations of culture and history and outside the medium of ethical contest and spiritual labour' (Ansell-Pearson 1994, p. xxvii). As an anti-cultural, ahistorical ideology originating in abstract reason, globalisation alienates the exemplars of the cultures its hijacks from them and their henceforth simulated cultures. It also, as previously mentioned, unmoors the vast majority from the meanings that formerly anchored them to their reality, casting them adrift in a fog of unedifying relativism and nihilism.

4 The Politics of "Individuality" in Decadent Societies and Epochs

In decadent epochs, identity becomes a source of psychic distress and social antagonism. Cleavages appear within the cultures of such afflicted peoples – be-

---

[22] Sheridan Hough links perspectivism to experience in ways that bear upon the extent to which self-experimentation is possible. Such individuals experiment within the parameters of the 'subjective sense [they have of themselves and their] world, [which] is only the *experience* of those environmental and historical elements that actually do constitute [their] perspective' (Hough 1997, p. 65).

tween their governing instincts and reigning morality, as decadent values fracture their formerly shared conscience. The governing drives (or "disciplinary regime") that naturalised society's conventions prove ineffective. This deprives the herd of a coherent sense of community, by which it was previously able to 'maintain itself and increase its power, [that is] its conception of reality' (WP 480). Consequently, chaos ensues. Nietzsche identified a proto-socialist impulse – an 'echo of Christianity' – in the secular morality of late-modern Europe that opposes the existence of individuals, that is, cultural exemplars healthy enough to create works that invigorate their respective societies: 'What is wanted – whether this is admitted or not – is nothing less than a fundamental remolding, indeed weakening and abolition of the individual.... Everything that in any way corresponds to this [uniform] body – and membership-building drive ... is felt to be good, this is the moral undercurrent of our age'. (D 132). Globalisation reduces the likelihood of greatness, abasing distinct peoples by merging them into ever larger and more alienating communities whose members are unified by an ersatz sense of belonging based upon the presentation of desires marketed to them and resulting in consumerism. Global society fosters and celebrates mediocrity, highlighting the need for free spirits, whose appearance it encumbers. This raises the dismal possibility that in attempting to differentiate themselves from the herd, they 'will always bring to consciousness precisely that in [them]selves which is "non-individual", that which is "average"; ... due to the nature of consciousness ... [their] thoughts themselves are continually as it were outvoted and translated back into the herd perspective' (GS 354). Subsequently, the would-be free spirit's struggle to become who it is they are is hampered by the self-deceptions of the all-too-many, whose sense of self-worth hinges upon being respected as equal *and* individual; genuine 'individuals ... [always] have herd instincts and conscience against them' (GS 149). As the all-too-many futilely endeavour to distinguish themselves as individuals, they may sentimentally identify with vestiges of their vanishing culture, clinging to what persists of it despite globalisation, but this primarily serves to increase their misapprehension of their world.

The incessant acclamations of the individual in contemporary globalised societies correspond with the self-deluding misinterpretations of existence circulated via spectacles of fulfilment and simulated happiness. The majority conform to the massified identities that globalisation authorises, which validate delusions of autonomy that sustain globalisation and enable liberal subjects to imagine that they know themselves. Despite furthering the deception of free will, knowledge of the culture they have lost, combined with desires generated by their frustrated instincts and alienation within massified societies, cast doubt on who they take themselves to be, sustaining the quandary of identity. Unable to determine who they are, they languish in what they take themselves to be. Sans a life-affirming culture to edify them, they are, in *identic* terms, powerless and lost. Nietzsche observed early signs of this malaise: '"I don't know where I am; I am everything that doesn't know where it is" – sighs the modern man…. *This* modernity made us ill – this indolent peace, this cowardly compromise, the whole virtuous filth of the modern yes and no' (A Preface, 1). The indifference that results is universalised by globalisation, which promotes tolerance of the diversity it banalises so that its arbiters – ersatz "cosmopolitans" – may "celebrate" and consume the multiplicity of a world they implicitly, unconsciously disdain.

The decadent values characteristic of globalised societies are *self*-subverting as well.²³ Their power of degeneration increases *Weltschmerz* ('world weariness' [GM III, 17]), which poisons the community their proponents mean to nurture (D 115). This is evident in the way they sow doubts about formerly accepted truths – 'the "morality of custom"' – that undercut belief in 'freedom of will' – an illusion without which 'humanity would never have come into existence' – yet continue to deny that 'All human beings are innocent of their existence' (GS 68). The discourses of liberal democracy insist upon the reality of free will as a means of maintaining the concept of the individual, a notion without which personal responsibility (*Verantwortlichkeit*) and legal accountability would be incoherent, and the desire to punish would be indefensible (GM II, 2 and 16). What is punished most are rare exceptions whose unassimilable differences threaten the status quo.

Having sabotaged the autochthonous values that previously anchored peoples to their worlds, globalisation discredits belief in any edifying truths and anything noble. Fredrick Appel observes that 'Encouraged by an ambient democratic culture … the herd develops distasteful character traits … [coming to] think of themselves as no worse than anyone else and capable of anything' (Appel 1999, p. 128). Deprived of any guiding order of rank, they hew to the coarse relativism of our globalising age, which paradoxically presumes its own universal legitimacy, vis-à-vis the "truth" it propagates. The *virtus dormitiva* of globalisation lies, counter-intuitively, in the over-stimulating effects of its profusion of images and consumer goods; its elimination of the 'judgements [that] must be *believed* true for the purpose of preserving beings of [any] type' (BGE 11).

With 'no power over themselves' these 'weak characters' come to resent any constraints as they succumb to globalisation's enticements to nihilism (GS 290).

---

23 The post-war international order that the increasingly sclerotic institutions of the globalisation complex were created to sustain are now perceived by some to be under threat from cultural transformations that globalisation itself generated. See Ikenberry (2011).

Aiming at 'The total degeneration of humanity ... into the perfect herd animal', globalisation spoils their reverence of anything higher (BGE 203). Yet as born 'Slaves [they] want the unconditional; they understand only tyranny, even in morality' (BGE 46). Misled about themselves by globalisation's egalitarian discourses, 'a standard that [falsely] makes them the equal of [those possessing] the qualities and privileges of spirit,' they reject all 'order of rank in the world' (BGE 219).

The bogus notions of individuality and self-determination promoted by globalisation rest upon the liberal democratic doctrine of free and equal persons. This legitimates the tyranny of the herd, while veiling their 'pessimistic suspicion of the whole condition of humanity' (BGE 260). The doctrine of equality abolishes any natural rank order of types, making the herd incredulous towards all authority and unleadable. Incapable of self-determination, the masses yearn to be led, nevertheless. Burdened by their unfree condition they pine for the certainty their discredited cultures and faiths provided. This intensifies their *ressentiment* of prospective free spirits capable of self-creation and of anything indicative of other possible worlds.

By dividing the shared conscience necessary for coherent community, globalisation reveals man to be the vanity of vanities. In a world it has denuded of illusory significance and persuasive, enduring meanings, this insight compounds the horror of the herd's existence.[24] Their 'new kind of enslavement' leaves them bereft of any *pathos* of distance and mechanism for achieving excellence (GS 377) and put at risk of devolving into blinking "last men" marooned in a nihilistic torpor. Not a condition likely to conduce the 'strengthening and enhancement of the human type', the possible appearance of free spirits in their midst may be rendered improbable (GM II, 2).

Globalisation banalises what is novel to diffuse any threat it may pose. What is innovative is reduced to trite signifiers for the herd, to whom it is marketed. This mediation of the politics of difference at both the mass and individual levels typifies globalisation's artificial form of cosmopolitanism. It was *against* this 'depersonification of spirit', the 'thoughtless goodwill, ... [and the] dangerous lack of concern for Yeses and Noes' characteristic of the 'objective man', that Nietzsche envisaged philosophers of the future capable of revaluing all values and transfiguring humankind (BGE 207).

---

[24] On the imperative of avoiding existentially deleterious truths, see Kain (2009, p. 19).

5 *Weltironie*, Globality, and Nietzschean Self-creation

Nietzsche presciently observed that 'the ascetic priest makes his appearance in almost any age; he does not belong to any race in particular; he thrives everywhere; he comes from every social class' (GM III, 11). In our own age, such a priestly caste of transnational bureaucrats and elected officials furthers the aims of globalisation. It subjects the cultures formative of individuals to a Procrustean bed that exacts conformity to the prerogatives of neoliberal capitalism and the discursive rationales of liberal democracy. They work to increase consumption, raise profit-yields, and monetise forms of creative activity. International, homeless, financial recluses, the arbiters of the globalisation complex refine their epistemic and psychological instruments of control via the systematic imposition of a phalanx of value- and expectation-transforming norms (GSt).²⁵ They encourage compulsive consumption, reduce all to the status of economic cogs, and extinguish the distinctive spirit of every culture that complex interpellates.

The life-affirming irony towards the world (*Weltironie*) informing the Nietzschean disposition of globality, which is 'typified by a maximal degree of the art and force of adaptation' (BGE 242), informs the practices prospective free spirits utilise in their attempts at self-overcoming. How may these practices conduce the ultimate defeat of globalisation? We might expect resistance to globalisation's ascetic values to be common, but they re-appropriate diverse expressions of alterity throughout the world and reward mimetic enactments of their ideals. Consequently, such rebellions do not rectify the culturally transformative a/effects of globalisation's liberal-democratic ideology or undo the changes it incites when they do occur. This is because the former alters the cultures it invades by replicating its decadent values within and through them, whilst the latter transforms them structurally.²⁶ As Debord notes, 'the social practice confronted by an

---

25 Nietzsche's use of this phrase may echo an anti-Semitic trope of his time. Nevertheless, the then emergent transnational "caste" he perceived evolved into today's multi-ethnic and sectarian professional elite who administer globalisation.

26 I agree with Edward Said that 'the grand narratives of emancipation and enlightenment mobilised people in the colonial world to rise up' against their subjugation by Anglo-European powers. However, while resistance succeeded in 'throw[ing] *off* imperial subjection', the informal mechanisms of control left in place continued to colonise the minds and attitudes of people, their subjugation having changed form (Said 1993, pp. xii–iii). James Scott's analysis illuminated

autonomous spectacle is at the same time the real totality which contains that spectacle' (Debord 1983, p. 7). Faith in liberal democracy, which is advocated by its ideologues (contemporary ascetic priests of *ressentiment*) raises the question: is an alternative to its politics and the consumer-capitalism it commends conceivable? The answer, increasingly, is no, as the totalising power of globalisation assimilates peoples and their mentalities while diffusing challenges to it. This is the case even in authoritarian regimes that have integrated with the global system, for example, the "People's Democratic Dictatorship" of China.

The changes globalisation triggers in the micro-political sphere – that is, at the level of rare exceptions (prospective individuals) – and at the level of the macro-political sphere (or community), could also be exploited by emerging free spirits (see Conway 1997, p. 49). Seen as misfits, they enhance opportunities for humankind's re-naturalisation, even when they fail to fulfil their aim, as the ramifications of their becomings cannot be anticipated (BGE 230). Their transmutation of the liberal democratic values rationalising globalisation disseminate their radically life-affirming disposition of globality. In Nietzsche's own language, the outlook of these 'argonauts of the ideal' (GS 382) and 'heirs of Europe's longest and most courageous self-overcoming' (GS 357) extols the 'task of assimilating knowledge and making it instinctive' (GS, sec. 11), to forge new 'material for a society' (GS 356). This Nietzschean globality – central to his quasi-cosmopolitan stance – increases recognition of 'the meaning of the earth' (Z Prologue, 3), and commends practices for re-dedicating humankind to it in 'anticipation of the overman' (Z I, Neighbour; see Shapiro 2016, pp. 6–9).

Nietzsche suggests that contending with decadence compels free spirits to differentiate between the type of pessimistic irony that ascetic priests deploy to foster self-deception and undermine confidence in life, and the *Weltironie* towards decadent values adopted by free spirits capable of '*golden* laughter' (BGE 294). The latter penetrates appearances and utilises disguises and artifice against the claimed wisdom of the priestly type. The former type fosters a 'dangerous mood of irony in regard to itself' that serves ascetic priests in estranging the masses from their inheritance (HL 5). The herd's separation from its instincts raises an 'even more dangerous mood of cynicism' that increases disrespect for higher values (HL 5). The resulting 'practical egoism through which the forces of life are paralyzed and at last destroyed' further diminishes their capacity to honour (BGE 212). Against this, Nietzsche urges 'irony with respect to [modern]

---

the transformative effects of "post-colonial" globalisation on cultures, vis-à-vis the green revolution in Malaysia (Scott 1985).

"selflessness"' (BGE 260), which in the context of his radical affirmation of life evokes the *Weltironie* of a Nietzschean globality.

A feature of modernity's 'physiological self-contradiction' is a form of *laissez-aller* that equates with the 'modern concept of "freedom"' (TI Skirmishes, 41). Popular ironism increases resignation and complacency, and disincentivises productive agonisms, contests originating in the envy of 'the good Eris' (HC). A Socratic form of irony, it foments 'plebeian *ressentiment*' and a 'new type of agon' that serves the self-preservation of decadents whose perverse notion of freedom is validated by the very social forces that expand a corrosive anarchy of the instincts (TI Socrates, 7; TI Socrates, 8).

Consequently, contemporary Europeans 'treat all great interests with irony, because ... [they have] no time to take them seriously' (D 162). An anti-cultural sclerosis, globalisation's relativistic ironism exacerbates indifference to higher values and discredits them. Within societies whose cultures and values are so paralysed, 'there are no longer any shared formulas; misunderstanding is allied with disregard' (BGE 262). Globalisation's reactive ironism encourages the passive resignation characteristic of '*the last man*' (Z I, 5). Its victims – those masses who live 'modestly and thoughtlessly, maybe even with indifference and irony' (GS 21) – become incapable of affirming anything.

Conversely, the globality of Nietzsche's free spirits entails an ironic stance towards the '"modern ideas" [of people who] believe ... in "progress"' (BGE 260), that exemplified late-nineteenth-century modernity and persists into our age of globalisation. A 'self-glorifying morality' emanates from their 'over-abundance of power' (BGE 260). This 'fundamental hostility and irony with respect to "selflessness" belong to a noble morality just as certainly as does a slight disdain and caution towards sympathetic feelings and "warm hearts"' (BGE 260). In addition to a sceptical stance towards the priestly philosopher's 'unconditional will to truth' (GS 344), free spirits embrace an agonic and subversive form of 'irony, even world-historical irony', which Nietzsche acknowledges 'loving' (EH Wagner, 4; cf. A 36). To inoculate against nihilism, free spirited ironists '[separate themselves] off from [those in whom] the opposite of such elevated, proud states is expressed' (BGE 260); *Weltironie* orients their opposition to values that diminish existence.

On recognising that identity conveys appearances (including internal psychological associations, social bonds, the sense of selfhood and belonging), Nietzsche exclaimed: 'how wonderful and new and yet how fearful and ironic my new insight makes me feel towards all of existence! ... What is "appearance" to me now! Certainly not the opposite of some essence – what could I say about any essence except name the predicates of its appearance!' (GS 54). Earlier he had observed that people 'reserve their reverence and feeling of happiness for works of imagination and dissembling ... in relinquishing reality and plunging into the depths of appearance' (D 550). Nietzsche's rejection of traditional Western metaphysics and faith in appearances, which presupposes an essence or thing-in-itself, has important implications for identity. Whereas faith in appearances serves to validate the spectacles of identity globalisation generates for the masses, Nietzsche's free spirits experiment with those spectacles to create values. They combat 'moral pessimism ... the whole attitude of "man against the world", of man as a "world-negating" principle, of man as the measure of the value of things, as judge of the world who finally places existence itself on his scales and finds it too light' (GS 346). For 'as knowers', Nietzsche expects that they shall '*want* to see differently ... *having in* [their] *power* the ability to engage and disengage [their] "pros" and "cons": [to] ... use the difference in perspectives and affective interpretations for knowledge' (GM III, 12).

6 Conclusion

What potential remains for the appearance of free-spirited individuals in our decadent age? Globalisation's elimination of difference erodes opposition to its disciplinary techniques, its regularisation of governance, and its homogenisation of cultures, to impose its disposition towards existence, one spread and enforced by globalisation's ascetic priests through manifold systems of control over life. Given it totalising effects, we must ask if most acts of resistance are always already vulnerable to interpellation and/or minimisation by its power configurations, which inhibit self-creation and overcoming. The short answer is no. As this assessment of globalisation via Nietzsche's critique of decadence suggests, the possibility of 'discover[ing] a realm of our invention here, a realm where we can still be original too, as parodists of world history', through which new meanings with regard to belonging and the politics of difference might be generated, remains (BGE 223). If the cognitive transformations enabled by a Nietzschean globality can subvert globalisation's values through derision, then its spectacularised meanings and simulations of purpose – along with the juggernaut of international human rights (which is advanced by 'vengeance-seekers disguised as judges, with the word justice continually in their mouth' [GM III, 14]) – may be utilised to facilitate the emergent, qualified cosmopolitanism it promises. Even the liberal democratic conception of justice could be employed to disrupt globalisation's imposition of "development" in favour of non-western, indigenous self-determination, and the protection of minority peoples and cultures, and their autochthonous values. Ultimately, the contests they inspire may conduce the appearance of philosophers of the future capable of revaluing its decadent values.

Free spirits *actively* pursue their own 'going under' and 'squander' themselves (Z I, 4). In the present, this need not entail reacting within the terms of the ideology of liberal democracy. The free spirit's challenges to decadent values take various expression, arousing other would-be free spirits to undertake tests of their own mettle as they too strive to become who they are. With the strength necessary for self-determination, which is to say the courage to suffer individuality, they may emerge in spite of pressures to make their desires conform to the spiritually sickening prerogatives of globalisation's 'religion of snug cosiness' (GS 338). They are therefore capable of legislating life-enhancing values predicated upon practices of radical yes-saying to existence, or Nietzschean globality.

Given humankind's enervating contemporary constitution as subjects imbricated within globalisation's power configurations it would seem reasonable to conclude, pessimistically, that the development of a socio-political regime conducive to communities based upon life-enhancing values will be frustrated so long as globalisation inhibits self-cultivation. Yet perhaps, counter-intuitively, this may not be the case, for while globalisation comprises a *Kulturstaat* that homogenises cultures and eradicates alterity, 'the spiritual leveling of one people [the democratic masses] is compensated for in the deepening of another [prospective free spirits]' (BGE 241). Prospective free spirits appreciate that 'society [even one dominated by the masses, serves] as the substructure and framework for raising an exceptional type of being up to its higher duty and ... state of being' (BGE 258). The herd's value lies in its usefulness as an instrument for the free spirit's creation of a new aristocracy.

Resisting resignation and 'wary of thinking disparagingly about this whole phenomenon because it is inherently ugly and painful' (GM II, 18), free spirits expose the life-denial of globalisation's ascetic ideals. This fortifies their disposition of globality, enabling them to 'gaze with many eyes and consciences from the heights into every distance' (BGE 211). The free spirits' radical yes-saying to life entails an implicit rejection of globalisation's myriad inducements to resignation. Their defiance of its nihilistic values comprise – and provoke – the constructive forms of contest that globalisation suppresses. Through their Nietzschean globality, or 'art and force of adaptation' (BGE 242), they attempt to create new values and corresponding identic fictions that confer a style to their characters and may resonate with other prospective free spirits. Furthermore, as 'comedians of ascetic ideals' (GM III, 27), these Nietzschean ironists lampoon the ascetic ideals of their day to discredit their proponents. Such destabilising mockery is also a piece of the critical praxis these subversive *farceurs* employ to re-naturalise humankind in ways consistent with Nietzsche's affirmative politics of difference.

Aware that 'All great things bring about their own demise through an act of self-sublimation: that is the law of life, the law of necessary "self-overcoming" in the essence of life' (GM III, 27), free spirits exercise their 'enormous diversity in practice, art, and masks' in attempting to overcome themselves (BGE 242). Self-sublimation facilitates the free spirit's attainment of 'the state in which man sees things most decidedly as they are not [der Mensch die Dinge am meisten so sieht, wie sie nicht sind], in which the 'power [Kraft] of illusion is at its peak [Höhe]... as is the power to sweeten and *transfigure*' (A 23, translation modified). That transforming power stimulates new feelings, mindsets, and ideals to strengthen and disseminate Nietzschean globality. Through 'individual successes in the most varied places [and cultures] on earth ... a *higher type*' may resists globalisation's multiple oppressions to condition the possibility for and hasten the appearance of those philosophers of the future capable of revaluing all values (A 4). Against globalisation's 'miserable type of well-being' (TI Skirmishes, 38) these '*true philosophers*' would establish a life-affirming politics of difference within their communities to enable the maximal flourishing of all (BGE 211).

The quandary of identity generated by our decadent modernity and propagated by the globalisation complex impels free spirits to consecrate themselves to a higher ideal. This includes the transfiguration of reactive conceptions of self and the individual to bring the 'democratic fragmentation of the will ... to an end', and realise the futural 'great politics' Nietzsche anticipated (BGE 208).[27] Against both the hegemonic, culture-annihilating neoliberal globalisation of our time, and the democratic globalism of similarly governed, normalised "world citizens" that its most ardent ideologues endeavour to create, their brave experiments may conduce new goals for humankind. In accordance with their Nietzschean globality free spirits strive to 'put an end to the gruesome rule of chance and nonsense that has passed for "history" so far' (BGE 203), and thereby engender previously unimagined and life-affirming worlds.

---

27 'What Nietzsche is proposing', Drochon argues, 'is the reformulation of *grosse Politik* on the basis of a master ... morality' (Drochon 2016, p. 160).

Bibliography

Acharya, Vinod (2014): *Nietzsche's Meta-Existentialism*. Berlin: De Gruyter.
Ansell-Pearson, Keith (1994): "Introduction". In: *On the Genealogy of Morality: A Polemic*, pp. ix–xxiii. Edited by Keith Ansell-Pearson and translated by Carol Diethe. Cambridge: Cambridge University Press.
Appel, Fredrick (1999): *Nietzsche Contra Democracy*. Ithaca: Cornell University Press.
Ball, Terence, Richard Dagger and Daniel O'Neill (2011): *Political Ideologies and the Democratic Ideal*. New York: Routledge.
Baudrillard, Jean (1988): *Selected Writings*. Edited by Mark Poster and translated by Jacques Mourrain. Stanford: Stanford University Press.
Brown, Chris (2007): "Liberalism and the Globalization of Ethics". In: William M. Sullivan and Will Kymlicka (Eds.): *The Globalization of Ethics: Religious and Secular Perspectives*, pp. 151–170. Cambridge: Cambridge University Press.
Brown, Wendy (2015): *Undoing the Demos: Neoliberalism's Stealth Revolution*. New York: Zone Books.
Connolly, William E. (2002): *Identity | Difference: Demographic Negotiations of Political Paradox*. Expanded ed. Minneapolis: University of Minnesota Press.
Conway, Daniel W. (1997): *Nietzsche and the Political*. London: Routledge.
Debord, Guy (1983): *Society of the Spectacle*. Translated by Fredy Perlman. Detroit: Black and Red Press.
Drochon, Hugo (2016): *Nietzsche's Great Politics*. Princeton: Princeton University Press.
Foucault, Michel (1972): *The Archaeology of Knowledge*. Translated by A. M. Sheridan Smith. New York: Pantheon Books.
Gill, Stephen (1995): "Globalization, Market Civilization, and Disciplinary Neoliberalism". In: *Millennium: Journal of International Studies* 24. No. 3, pp. 399–423.
Hatab, Lawrence (1999): *A Nietzschean Defense of Democracy: An Experiment in Postmodern Politics*. Chicago: Open Court.
Hough, Sheridan (1997): *Nietzsche's Noontide Friend: The Self as Metaphoric Double*. University Park: Pennsylvania State University Press.
Ikenberry, G. John (2011): *Liberal Leviathan: The Origins, Crisis, and Transformation of the American World Order*. Princeton: Princeton University Press.
Kain, Philip J. (2009): *Nietzsche and the Horror of Existence*. Lanham: Lexington Press.
Nietzsche, Friedrich (1968): *The Will to Power*. Edited by Walter Kaufmann and translated by Walter Kaufmann and R. J. Hollingdale. New York: Vintage Books.
Nietzsche, Friedrich (1980): *Sämtliche Werke, Kritische Studienausgabe in 15 Bänden*. Edited by Giorgio Colli and Mazzino Montinari. München: Deutscher Taschenbuch Verlag.
Nietzsche, Friedrich (1998): *On the Genealogy of Morality*. Edited and translated by Maudemarie Clark and Alan J. Swensen. Indianapolis: Hackett Publishing Co.
Nietzsche, Friedrich (2001): *The Gay Science*. Edited by Bernard Williams and translated by Josefine Nauckhoff and Adrian Del Caro. Cambridge: Cambridge University Press.
Nietzsche, Friedrich (2002): *Beyond Good and Evil*. Edited by Rolf-Peter Horstmann and Judith Norman and translated by Judith Norman. Cambridge: Cambridge University Press.
Nietzsche, Friedrich (2005a): *The Anti-Christ*. In: *The Anti-Christ, Ecce Homo, Twilight of the Idols and Other Writings*, pp. 1–67. Edited by Aaron Ridley and Judith Norman and translated by Judith Norman. Cambridge, New York: Cambridge University Press.

Nietzsche, Friedrich (2005b): *The Case of Wagner*. In: *The Anti-Christ, Ecce Homo, Twilight of the Idols and Other Writings*, pp. 231–262. Edited by Aaron Ridley and Judith Norman and translated by Judith Norman. Cambridge, New York: Cambridge University Press.

Nietzsche, Friedrich (2005c): *Ecce Homo*. In: *The Anti-Christ, Ecce Homo, Twilight of the Idols and Other Writings*, pp. 69–151. Edited by Aaron Ridley and Judith Norman and translated by Judith Norman. Cambridge, New York: Cambridge University Press.

Nietzsche, Friedrich (2005d): *Twilight of the Idols*. In: *The Anti-Christ, Ecce Homo, Twilight of the Idols and Other Writings*, pp. 153–229. Edited by Aaron Ridley and Judith Norman and translated by Judith Norman. Cambridge, New York: Cambridge University Press.

Nietzsche, Friedrich (2006a): "Homer's Contest". In: *On the Genealogy of Morality: A Polemic*, pp. 174–181. Edited by Keith Ansell-Pearson and translated by Carol Diethe. Cambridge: Cambridge University Press.

Nietzsche, Friedrich (2006b): *Thus Spoke Zarathustra: A Book for All and None*. Edited by Adrian Del Caro and Robert Pippin and translated by Adrian del Caro. Cambridge: Cambridge University Press.

Nietzsche, Friedrich (2007a): *Daybreak: Thoughts on the Prejudices of Morality*. Edited by Maudemarie Clark and Brian Leiter and translated by R. J. Hollingdale. Cambridge: Cambridge University Press.

Nietzsche, Friedrich (2007b): *Human, All Too Human*. Translated by R. J. Hollingdale. Cambridge: Cambridge University Press.

Nietzsche, Friedrich (2007c): *Untimely Meditations*. Edited by Daniel Breazeale and translated by R.J. Hollingdale. Cambridge: Cambridge University Press.

Nietzsche, Friedrich (2008): "The Greek State". In: Frank Cameron and Don Dombowsky (Eds.): *Political Writings of Friedrich Nietzsche: An Edited Anthology*, pp. 38–46. Basingstoke: Palgrave Macmillan.

Said, Edward W. (1993): *Culture and Imperialism*. New York: Vintage, Random House.

Scott, James C.,(1985): *Weapons of the Weak: Everyday Forms of Peasant Resistance*. New Haven: Yale University Press.

Shapiro, Gary (2016): *Nietzsche's Earth: Great Events, Great Politics*. Chicago: University of Chicago Press.

Shaw, Martin (2000): *Theory of the Global State: Globality as an Unfinished Revolution*. Cambridge: Cambridge University Press.

Shaw, Tasmin (2007): *Nietzsche's Political Skepticism*. Princeton: Princeton University Press.

Siemens, Herman (2005): "Nietzsche contra Liberalism on Freedom". In: Keith Ansell-Pearson (Ed.): *A Companion to Nietzsche*, pp. 437–455. Oxford and Malden: Basil Blackwell.

Steinhart, Eric (2005): "Nietzsche on Identity". In: *Revista di Estetica* 28. No. 1, pp. 241–256, http://www.ericsteinhart.com/articles/nidentity.pdf, accessed 18 October 2018.

Stiglitz, Joseph E. (2003): *Globalization and its Discontents*. New York: W. W. Norton.

Notes on Contributors

Marinete Araujo da Silva Fobister is a PhD candidate at the University College London Institute of Education, London. She has published on Nietzsche and has given papers at conferences organised by Kyoto University (Japan) and the University College London Institute of Education, some of which have been published. Her research involves examining the concept of nihilism as formulated by Nietzsche, Vattimo and Deleuze.

Glen Baier is Associate Professor of Philosophy in the department of philosophy at the University of the Fraser Valley in Abbotsford, British Columbia, Canada. His teaching and research interests are primarily in the history of nineteenth- and early twentieth-century Continental philosophy.

Tracy Colony is Professor of Philosophy at Bard College, Berlin. He is the translator of Heidegger's *Phenomenology of Intuition and Expression* (Continuum, 2010) and the author of many articles on Continental philosophy.

Niklas Corall is Research Associate at Paderborn University, Germany. He has given talks and published chapters on Nietzsche in German and English. His academic research interests lie in the field of contemporary social philosophy, especially concerning forms of modern power, normalisation, subjectivation and truth within social relations. His theoretical perspective is largely based on the framework established by Friedrich Nietzsche and Michel Foucault.

Sven Gellens is Associate Researcher at Ghent University (Belgium). He focuses on the philosophy of Nietzsche, Merleau-Ponty and themes in nineteenth-century and contemporary biological and cultural evolutionary theory. His main publications and research interests are concerned with 'transformation' in different domains, specifically the position of the body – how it incorporates information (*Einverleibung* in German), and with the emancipatory contribution of philosophising in active citizenship.

Lilian Valerie Kroth is currently working on her PhD project on Michel Serres at the French Department at the University of Cambridge. Prior to that she studied Philosophy (BA, MA) and worked as a research assistant in Philosophy at the University of Vienna. Her research interests are mainly the philosophy of space, aesthetics, Critical Theory and the philosophy of science.

Paulo Alexandre Lima is Research Assistant at Nova Institute of Philosophy. He teaches in the BA and MA programmes in the Philosophy Department of Nova University of Lisbon.

Michael J. McNeal is Visiting Assistant Professor of Political Science at Kenyon College and Adjunct Professor of International Relations at the University of Denver. He is the co-editor of *Joy and Laughter in Nietzsche's Philosophy: Alternative Liberatory Politics* (Bloomsbury, 2022), *European/Supra-European: Cultural Encounters in Nietzsche's Philosophy* (De Gruyter, 2020), and *U.S. Approaches to the Arab Spring: International Relations and Democracy Promotion* (I. B. Taurus, 2017). He is currently the secretary of the Friedrich Nietzsche Society.

Notes on Contributors

Pia Morar is a PhD student in ancient philosophy at the University of Toronto. She previously obtained an MA in philosophy from the Ludwig-Maximilians University of Munich, as well as an MSc in Comparative Politics from the London School of Economics. Her research interests lie in ancient philosophy and Nietzsche.

Jonas Oßwald is a DOC-Fellow of the Austrian Academy of Sciences, engaged in a PhD project on the philosophical relation between Gilles Deleuze and Michel Foucault, supervised by Arno Böhler (University of Vienna). Besides Deleuze and Foucault, his research interests include Nietzsche, Marx and William S. Burroughs.

William A. B. Parkhurst received his PhD from the University of South Florida in 2021. His research focuses on archival methodology with a focus on texts as material objects. His research has been accepted for publication in *Nietzsche-Studien*, *Nietzscheforschung*, *Studia Nietzscheana*, and *Schopenhauer-Jahrbuch*, among others.

Andrea Rehberg teaches Philosophy at Newcastle University. She co-edited *The Matter of Critique: Readings in Kant's Philosophy* (2000), edited *Nietzsche and Phenomenology* (2018), and she has published on Kant, Nietzsche, Heidegger, Lyotard and Nancy. She is on the editorial board of the *Journal of the British Society for Phenomenology*, as well as on the executives of several learned societies in continental philosophy, including the Friedrich Nietzsche Society. Her main research interests are Kant, Nietzsche, Heidegger and Deleuze.

George W. Shea is an Assistant Professor of Philosophy at Misericordia University. His research focuses on issues of normativity and critique in the context of post-metaphysical philosophies. He has published essays on the work of Nietzsche, Horkheimer and Foucault.

Gabriel Valladão Silva holds a BA and MA in Philosophy from the State University of Campinas (UNICAMP), Brazil. He is currently a PhD candidate in Philosophy at the Technische Universität Berlin. His research interests include modern German Philosophy (Kant, Schopenhauer, Nietzsche), French Philosophy and the history of philosophy in the twentieth century. He is the translator of philosophical works from German to Portuguese, including works by Schopenhauer, Nietzsche and Benjamin.

Julie Van der Wielen holds a BA, MA and MPhil from the Higher Institute of Philosophy of KU Leuven (Belgium) and is currently finishing her PhD with Diego Portales University (Santiago, Chile) and Radboud University (Nijmegen, The Netherlands).

Alan Watt is Lecturer at the Department of Environmental Sciences and Policy, Central European University. Alongside a focus on the intersection of environmental philosophy with the modern continental tradition he has written extensively on Nietzsche, including a study of Nietzsche and Bataille in the volume *Nietzsche's Gods*.

Ashley Woodward is Senior Lecturer in Philosophy at the University of Dundee. He is a member of the executive committee of the Friedrich Nietzsche Society. His publications on Nietzsche and his legacy include the books *Nihilism in Postmodernity* (Davies Group, 2009), *Understanding Nietzscheanism* (Acumen, 2011), the edited volume *Interpreting Nietzsche*

(Continuum, 2011) and articles in journals including *Nietzsche-Studien*, *Continental Philosophy Review* and *The Agonist*.

Index

active   4, 42, 45, 131f., 135, 137, 140, 164, 167, 184, 194f., 197f., 200, 209, 220–223, 269, 276, 280
agon   4, 8, 153, 227–235, 238–244, 248, 250, 331
agonism/agonal   3, 8, 100, 114, 152–155, 168, 227, 229–244, 247f., 250–252, 255, 260–262, 331
antagonism   153, 325
anthropocene   48–50
anti-politics   203, 222f.
aristocracy (Greek)   130, 229, 231–233, 236–238, 241, 243, 250, 261, 333
ascetic ideal   6, 10, 102, 121, 132–134, 140, 194, 289–299, 301f., 304–307, 314, 316, 318, 333
ascetic priest   129f., 132–134, 291, 318f., 321, 329f., 332

Bartleby   204, 211–214, 216
Brazil   185–189, 196, 199, 201
Burckhardt, Jacob   8, 228–235, 237f., 241, 244

Charim, Isolde   125, 127f., 137
Christ   203–205, 214–217, 221
competition   8, 22, 210, 222, 227–243, 250, 254
conceptual persona   7, 204–207, 214, 217, 219
contest   122, 153, 160, 228–231, 233–236, 239–242, 250, 259, 294, 325, 331–333
cosmopolitan   282, 312, 319, 327, 330
critique   7, 10, 30, 58, 64, 70, 75–77, 96, 98, 101–103, 108, 112, 128f., 132, 137f., 152–155, 163–165, 174–178, 180, 184, 199–202, 206, 218f., 222, 228, 247f., 259, 289–291, 296f., 299, 305–308, 311–313, 316, 321, 325, 332
Critique of Pure Reason   75f., 132

Deleuze, Gilles   1f., 4, 6–8, 33, 39f., 109–111, 117, 121, 132, 135, 138–140, 145–152, 154–160, 163–165, 167–179, 183f., 191, 193–201, 203–214, 217–223, 227, 244, 272, 276, 278f.
democracy   2, 4, 8, 17, 20f., 25, 122, 126, 197, 209, 227f., 233, 237–244, 247f., 251f., 256, 262, 311f., 314f., 317, 321, 327, 329f., 333
difference   1f., 4–10, 16, 33, 37, 40–46, 48–50, 55–57, 59, 61f., 65, 70, 96, 118, 141, 146, 152f., 160, 163–166, 168, 173, 177, 179, 183f., 194f., 197, 199f., 203f., 209, 218, 220, 222f., 240, 262, 269–272, 274, 279, 284–286, 289f., 292, 294–297, 299, 305–308, 311–315, 320, 323, 328, 332, 334
Dionysian   67f.
discourse   1, 6, 38, 95f., 98–110, 117, 124, 145–149, 151, 155–161, 163, 175f., 183f., 190–193, 195–197, 199, 201, 219, 238, 256, 269, 297, 299–301, 305f., 311f., 314, 317f., 327f.
dispute   15, 17f., 23, 27, 29f., 239
dissensus   5, 15, 20, 22, 24, 26, 29

equity   261
Eris   45, 233f., 238f., 243, 331
Euripides   64f., 67
event   2f., 24–26, 39, 48, 69, 106, 122, 132, 137, 169, 173f., 176, 185, 200, 207–209, 213f., 216, 218, 222f., 269–271, 277, 281, 286, 305
evolution   249, 253

fake news   1, 190–192
fold   86, 163f., 169, 171–175, 178f., 306
Foucault, Michel   1f., 4, 6f., 10, 75, 95f., 98, 103–111, 117, 145, 149, 153f., 163f., 167–172, 174–178, 209f., 227, 244, 289f., 297–307, 317

gaze   6, 57, 62f., 70f., 173, 293, 333
globalisation   10, 311–321, 324–334

human rights   1, 8 f., 247 f., 255–262, 271, 312, 321, 332

identity   1, 4, 6, 10, 28, 35, 41, 61, 75, 77 f., 86, 88, 95 f., 98, 103, 108, 111, 114–117, 128, 131, 135, 137 f., 174, 183, 195 f., 239, 242, 251 f., 275–277, 284, 292, 297, 300 f., 311 f., 314 f., 319 f., 322–326, 331 f., 334
immanence   6, 9, 121, 133, 138 f., 172 f., 214, 217, 223, 279
indetermination   44, 203, 212–214
individuality   95, 106, 108, 110 f., 113, 115–117, 258, 300, 325, 328, 333

Kant, Immanuel   42, 75 f., 87–89, 132, 154, 157, 218 f., 250 f.
Kulturstaat   333

metaphysics   4–6, 33, 35–41, 44, 47, 61, 75, 77, 101, 136, 139 f., 203, 221, 279, 289 f., 293, 296–299, 305, 307, 332
micropolitics   203 f., 207 f., 210, 213, 217 f., 223
Müller, Jan-Werner   125–129, 234

narrative   6, 95–97, 99, 101–103, 105–107, 109–118, 129, 163, 191 f., 283, 320, 329
nihilism   4 f., 7 f., 10, 33 f., 38, 41, 43, 45–50, 98, 133–135, 140, 153, 183 f., 193–198, 200–202, 213, 221, 269 f., 272 f., 275, 279, 281–286, 312–316, 318 f., 321 f., 325, 327, 331
nobility   4, 6, 121, 130 f., 136, 138, 230–232, 237–239, 323
noble   20, 40, 56, 105, 130, 136, 194 f., 201, 229, 232, 235–238, 295, 316, 321, 323, 327, 331
normalisation   95, 98, 109, 112, 300, 304

other   7, 39, 95, 103, 105, 128, 130 f., 135, 138 f., 164, 167, 172, 175–177, 183, 194–196, 236, 240, 250–252, 273 f., 277, 279, 285, 294, 300, 303, 319, 323
outside   128, 131, 149 f., 164, 166–174, 177–179, 197, 293 f., 301, 303 f., 306

parody   6, 75–77, 86 f., 90, 97
pathos of distance   9, 227, 243, 248, 261 f., 328
physiological   6, 9, 58, 121, 129–131, 133–138, 156, 166, 257, 318, 322, 331
physiology   136
physio-psychology   68, 257, 262
Plato   20 f., 33, 36, 38, 56, 58 f., 65, 67, 84, 101, 104 f., 206, 235 f., 247, 272, 289, 291 f., 318
police   15, 17 f., 21, 23, 25–29, 223
political philosophy   3, 8, 15–17, 20 f., 24, 248, 259
political, the   1–5, 7–10, 15–19, 21, 23–30, 47, 49, 55 f., 71, 87, 96, 105, 110 f., 115, 117, 121 f., 124–126, 128 f., 134–137, 145 f., 149, 151 f., 154 f., 159–161, 163 f., 168, 173 f., 176 f., 179, 183 f., 190–193, 196 f., 200, 203 f., 207–211, 214, 217 f., 222 f., 227 f., 231, 234 f., 237, 239–244, 247 f., 250 f., 253, 256, 262, 269 f., 272, 285, 289 f., 293, 297, 304 f., 307, 312 f., 323, 330, 333
politics   1–10, 15–30, 33, 49, 55–57, 70, 75 f., 87 f., 90, 95–97, 104, 107, 109, 117 f., 126, 141, 145 f., 149–151, 154, 156–160, 163–165, 173 f., 176, 179, 183 f., 190–193, 195–201, 203 f., 207–210, 213, 218 f., 222 f., 235, 238–240, 242, 244, 248, 262, 269, 271, 274, 284–286, 289 f., 295–297, 301, 305–308, 311, 313, 316, 323, 325, 328, 330, 332, 334
populism   1, 6 f., 121–127, 129 f., 134, 138, 317
postcolonialism   165
post-foundationalism   7, 145 f., 151, 153, 155 f., 160
post-truth   4, 7 f., 183 f., 190–193, 195, 199 f.
power   7, 9, 18, 20, 22–24, 39 f., 42, 95–97, 104–109, 125–127, 133 f., 137, 140, 146, 156–158, 160, 163, 167–172, 175, 177–179, 190, 192, 195, 197, 200 f., 208–210, 221 f., 231, 233, 242, 244, 248–252, 275–279, 282, 290, 292–

295, 297, 299–307, 318 f., 323, 326 f., 330–334

Rancière, Jacques   1, 4 f., 15–30, 151, 160
reactive   4 f., 7 f., 38, 41 f., 44 f., 129, 131 f., 134–137, 140, 164, 166 f., 183 f., 193–198, 200–202, 220–223, 272, 276–278, 324, 331, 334
ressentiment   9, 26, 38, 41, 43, 45, 47, 49 f., 75, 97, 129, 131, 164, 166–168, 170, 178, 220 f., 272, 289 f., 294 f., 297, 305–307, 313, 316, 318, 321, 324, 328, 330 f.
science   24, 56–58, 60, 62, 65, 83–86, 98 f., 101–103, 105, 109–111, 117, 152, 164, 186, 218, 237, 257–259, 291, 295 f., 299, 306–308, 317 f.
slave   4, 19, 22–24, 28 f., 75, 87, 90, 97, 121, 130, 134–137, 166, 201, 206, 209, 231 f., 261, 270, 274, 282, 285, 312, 316, 328
slave revolt   15 f., 19, 23, 87 f., 294, 321
slavishness   1, 6, 121, 129–132, 134–136, 138
Socrates   6, 20, 38, 55–71, 84, 205 f., 272, 316, 331
space   1, 7, 24, 28, 36, 122, 163–165, 168, 170, 172–179, 196, 210, 219, 250, 272, 275, 280, 283 f.
Spivak, Gayatri Chakravorty   7, 163–165, 172, 174–180
Stiegler, Bernard   1, 4 f., 33–51
stupidity   184, 199, 201, 206
subject   2, 27 f., 47, 75, 87–90, 98, 105, 109, 132, 139, 155, 163, 165 f., 169, 171, 173, 176–178, 214, 219, 228 f., 230, 290, 292, 299, 302, 305, 322, 325

technology   42, 186, 318
theoretical man   55 f., 60–63, 65, 67 f., 70
topology   7, 163–165, 167–175, 178–180
totalitarian   1, 10, 18, 192, 294, 306
tragedy   6, 33–35, 55–71, 78, 83, 86, 247 f.
transcendence   131, 139, 217, 295
transcendental   1, 75 f., 115, 148, 152–155, 160, 170, 203 f., 206, 219–221, 305
transvaluation   48–50, 133 f., 138, 140, 184, 198, 213, 218, 221–223
truth   6 f., 10, 22, 44, 60, 63, 70 f., 79, 95–110, 112 f., 115, 117 f., 172, 183 f., 187, 190–195, 198, 200 f., 204 f., 217, 289–296, 298–301, 304–307, 318, 321 f., 327 f.

universal   97, 221, 247 f., 250 f., 255–257, 259, 297, 312, 314, 319, 327

voyeur   6, 55, 57, 60, 62

Weltironie   315, 329–331
will   7, 39–42, 44, 46 f., 58, 115 f., 126 f., 130, 132, 140, 148, 155, 177, 193, 195, 197–202, 213, 219, 222 f., 249, 255, 276, 290, 295, 307, 313, 319 f., 326 f., 334
will to power   4, 8, 47, 68, 132 f., 136–140, 156, 166, 183, 199, 204, 213, 218–222, 228, 242 f., 247–251, 257 f., 261 f., 269, 271 f., 275–282, 284, 286, 306, 323
will to truth   6, 70, 96, 98, 102–104, 108 f., 117, 194, 291, 293–295, 301, 306, 321 f., 331

www.ingramcontent.com/pod-product-compliance
Lightning Source LLC
Chambersburg PA
CBHW020219170426
43201CB00007B/265